**Population and
Development in
Southeast Asia**

Fourteen of the fifteen papers in this volume were originally presented at three seminars on population growth and development in Southeast Asia organized by the Population Panel of the Southeast Asia Development Advisory Group (SEADAG) of The Asia Society, New York. The Panel was chaired by Dr. Irene B. Taeuber.

The Asia Society, a nonprofit educational institution, was founded in 1956 to enhance American understanding of Asia and Asians and to stimulate meaningful intellectual exchange across the Pacific. Within this framwork, SEADAG, which is funded by the United States Agency for International Development, seeks to promote and facilitate communication and collaboration among Asian and American scholars and policymakers concerned with development in Southeast Asia.

Population and and Development in Southeast Asia

Edited by

John F. Kantner
Lee McCaffrey
The Johns Hopkins University

Lexington Books
D.C. Heath and Company
Lexington, Massachusetts
Toronto   London

Library of Congress Cataloging in Publication Data

Main entry under title:

Population and development in Southeast Asia.

    "Fourteen of the fifteen papers . . . originally presented at three seminars on population growth and development in Southeast Asia organized by the Population Panel of the Southeast Asia Development Advisory Group."
    Bibliography: p.
    1. Asia, Southeastern—Population—Congresses. I. Kantner, John Frederick, 1920-   ed. II. McCaffrey, Lee, ed. III. Southeast Asia Development Advisory Group. Population Panel.

HB3635.P64	301.32'959	74-30885

ISBN 0-669-98145-1

Copyright © 1975 by D.C. Heath and Company

Published simultaneously in Canada

Printed in the United States of America

International Standard Book Number: 0-669-98145-1

Library of Congress Catalog Card Number: 74-30885

To Irene Barnes Taeuber

Contents

                H. Leedom Lefferts, Jr.   173

Chapter 10   Some Consequences of Population Growth in Java
                Masri Singarimbun   179

Chapter 11   Social Mobility and Fertility Control in a Squatter
                Barrio of Davao City, Philippines   *Beverly Heckart
                Hackenberg*   197

Chapter 12   Adaptive Processes and Development Policies in a
                Frontier Resettlement Community   *Carlos A.
                Fernandez II*   217

Chapter 13   Coping with Internal Migration in the Philippines:
                Problems and Solutions *Aprodicio A. Laquian*   235

Chapter 14   The Effect of Infant and Child Mortality and Preference
                for Sons Upon Fertility and Family Planning Behavior
                David M. Heer and *Hsin-ying Wu*   253

        Part V
        Directions for Research   281

Chapter 15   The Survey Method in Family Planning Research and
                Evaluation   *Ismail Sirageldin*   285

Chapter 16   Ancient and Emerging Questions   *Irene Taeuber*   317

        List of Contributors   325

        About the Editors   327

Introduction: Population Growth and Development in Southeast Asia

John F. Kantner

There is a vast outpouring of scholarly writing these days on conditions in Southeast Asia, most of it rather dispairing. And in recent years there have been many attempts to work toward improved human welfare for the peoples of Southeast Asia, but few efforts outside of the areas of Chinese culture have succeeded fully against the undertow of corruption, ineptness, social complexity, and flagging motivation.

But some progress has been made. The permeating importance of population in nearly all aspects of social and economic development is broadly recognized. Instead of treating it as an immutable condition as much a part of Asia as monsoons or dark hair, the view is now widely taken that population growth and population distribution are matters to be dealt with through positive action. Both rhetoric and resolve may soften in the face of strong ethnic differences;

The title of this introductory essay is taken from a paper by the late Irene B. Taeuber, who as chairman of the SEADAG population panel was the instigator of the three seminars from which the papers in this volume have been selected. In fact, more than the title has been borrowed from her essay. Many of the ideas are those which she incorporated in her report of the three seminars (Southeast Asia Development Advisory Group of the Asia Society, "Population and Development in Southeast Asia," Irene B. Taeuber, The Population Panel Seminar 1972). Where it could be done with only minor editorial fitting portions of her report have been lifted directly and appear in quotation marks without further reference or citation. It was never her intention that her report appear in its original form in the volume of collected papers which she helped to plan. The report, prepared for a different purpose, does not lend itself suitably as an introductory essay. But it does contain a great many trenchant observations on the situation in Southeast Asia and the role and responsibilities of scientists and administrators. The idea of a dialogue between academic social scientists and those from the realm of policy and programs was hers. It was she also who by verbal prods, clarifying summaries and coffee break conferences kept the seminars focused on the task set for them.

Irene Taeuber did not underestimate the complexities faced by those who attempt to stem the rushing currents of the real world. She had in fact an ill-concealed contempt for the simplifiers and the panaceasts and the Cartesians among her fellow social scientists who thought their two-dimensional formulations provided an approximation of reality. She thought in three dimensions at once and occasionally veered into a fourth. There were no disciplinary boundaries which confined her and for this reason, perhaps, she was free of cant about multidisciplinary or interdisciplinary roads to salvation.

The reach of her mind often exceeded her linguistic grasp. She had, in fact, a syntax all her own, the underlying principle of which was a strain toward inclusiveness. Sentences stretched unbroken into paragraphs so that no linkages would be broken and no juxtapositions missed. Collective nouns were rendered in the plural to extend their coverage. Like a bird caught in a room, her words beat incessantly against the lineal limitations of language. World citizen, scientific holist, and special friend of Asia, it is right and proper that wherever possible her words should break through this preface.

and all too frequently agreement on the importance of population does not carry into the planning and execution of specific development activities. Nonetheless, throughout the region population is recognized as a major problem about which something must be done—always, it is understood, within the limits of social tolerance, political stability, and collective competence.

The problem has been that given this mandate the formulators of policy and the designers of programs have not always known what to do—or more properly whether what they have decided to do is what they ought to be doing. Moreover it is exceedingly difficult to know whether a policy or a program that has not been a great success is a poor one inherently or merely one that has been poorly, sometimes disastrously, carried out. Both of course can be true.

There is no lack of example of failure in implementation. Indeed this is not surprising since the world over programs directed toward enhancement of the public welfare are frequently subject to abuse and misdirection.[a] Such would be expected a fortiori in countries where the watchword of bureaucracy is compliance rather than mission success. The inertia and risk avoidance of bureaucracy may call forth high level interventions but these have sometimes been based on nothing more than pure propulsion. Such administrative onslaughts in turn touch off protective reactions throughout the organization which tend to work against the achievement of program goals. In such circumstances, no one may think to ask whether the program itself is a good one, so pressing are the problems of implementation. Yet we know from endeavors in other areas that program strategy may be a crucial consideration. For example, in land reform, program failure, measured in terms of the distribution and security of land tenure, has been associated with centrally directed schemes; success, measured by the same criteria, with schemes in which responsibility devolves upon the local community. Population control programs in developing countries, with few exceptions, are centrally funded and centrally administered. Whether this is a significant consideration in connection with, say, fertility regulation or internal migration is not known. It is mentioned here to illustrate the kind of strategic question that is seldom raised.

The problem of knowing how to proceed, or even what questions to ask, is not made any easier by the lack of concert and mutual understanding among those who would help. On the one hand are the officials charged with program responsibilities, men of practical affairs for the most part, struggling in an uncharted area, often for dubious rewards. Their time horizons are short, determined both by the length of the segments into which government planning is broken and by their own career mobility, which for the most valuable among them leads to the expectation of transfer before the job is done. These

---

[a]There is no need to confine this generalization to efforts concerned with public weal. As the saying has it generally 'Man plans, God laughs'.

administrators see "research" as diversionary or, if they accept the term at all, may define it narrowly to entail little more than monitoring or troubleshooting.

At the other extreme are the academic social scientists who prefer the long view, who are suspicious of approaches that depend heavily on technological solutions and who, if they are not native to the areas in which they work, often are perceived as intellectual carpetbaggers.

In between these two groups are the funding agencies, both national and international. Their staffs are mixtures of practitioners, technicians, and quasi political generalists. Such social scientists as there may be in their employ rarely engage in penetrating research though they often do prepare useful compilations of scientific material or, using established methodology, may explore the implications of known facts and interrelationships. Operating with a strong mission orientation there is little scope or encouragement for basic scientific probing[b] although in certain areas of R & D the ability of these organizations to mobilize scientific manpower toward the achievement of specific tasks is considerable.

It is to be expected that such diverse problem orientations will produce stress and foster misunderstanding. The situation is not improved by the mutual dependence of these groups on each other, which requires them to share each others company. Academic social scientists are dependent on the funding agency since the day is long past when universities could field scientific groups unaided. Both the university group and the funding agency operate at the pleasure of the host government. Host governments for their part have grown increasingly independent in these matters, quite understandably perhaps but sometimes to their detriment. They too may depend on the funding agencies and may have to take into the bargain outside technical assistance in the form of program advisors, program elements for which they have little enthusiasm, and some future indebtedness.

The deus ex machina of our era being "communication," there has arisen a pandemic of conferences, seminars, and workshops; some narrowly technical, focused on how to achieve stated objectives; others with the broad objective of establishing or consolidating policy. As Irene Taeuber observed, academics approach these meetings as self-annointed "wise men" ready to minister to the intellectual needs of others, while administrators, be they governmental or funding agency, "view seminars as places where practical men meet verbalists."

But the suspicion of the "verbalist" goes deeper than any objection to his language habits. It rests on a belief that divergent goals are involved and that over time these will crop out in any agreement that might be made between the

---

[b]The administration of a funding operation puts great demands on the scientifically trained manpower of the funding organization, so that, in practice, intramural research tends to suffer. By retrenching on its external research program, a funding organization can devote itself more fully to its program of internal research. This seems to be the route taken recently by the Population Council, formerly one of the main stays of the academic community for research in population.

parties. The proposition was put most baldy by an official of one of the largest national funding agencies who said flatly, "We don't trust the universities"—a view that, in this instance, was fully reciprocated. Governments of countries with severe population problems and with policies and programs designed to cope with them have, in a few instances, rid themselves of international agencies and expatriate advisors and have sometimes shut out their own academic communities because of mistrust and perceived differences of objectives.

The seminars which gave rise to this volume were based on the proposition that each of these three parties, government administrator, academic scientist, and staff of supporting agencies have crucial contributions to make to population policy and programs. In organizing the seminars it was assumed (1) that scientific knowledge will enable the administrator to orient his plans and actions more effectively; (2) that at least some research scientists "can orient their activities to the expressed needs of administrators"; (3) that "multidisciplinary conversation yield multidisciplinary knowledge and approaches." Thus individuals concerned with population research were brought together in these seminars to see if through discussion it would be possible to achieve better "understanding of the role of population in development" and to "define and advance the frontiers of research" in ways that would be "significant for policy, planning and action." There was a further working assumption of some consequence, namely that "the most unexplored, the most controversial and possibly the most significant interrelations for policy consideration and planned transformation (are social)."

It was also the aim of the seminars to scan "the periphery of present concerns where research and dialogue might contribute to the formulation of wider policies and more effective (action)." Fundamentally, as Irene Taeuber recognized, social scientists have failed to consider the limits of their own knowledge, or to ask whether the questions which have claimed their attention are those which should be most urgently raised at this juncture in human affairs in Southeast Asia. "We know much and we are learning more year by year. But if by some miracle—or some mistake—we were given an unrestricted mandate with unlimited funds to design plans for the speediest possible demographic transition in Southeast Asia, we would have to dilute knowledge . . . with hunches and beliefs. Investment in . . . research . . . may be among the most practical of expenditures."

"Practicality" in the context of these seminars meant more than how to make family planning programs work better—a worthwhile goal to be sure, but a limited one however complex it might be. The view was taken that development and population are of a piece. In response to new relationships between technology, the environment, population, and social organization, a society may enter upon a course of sustained growth. In this process population increases, becomes redistributed, concentrated, set in motion, differentiated in function, organized into larger networks of interdependence, and integrated into new

dominions of common striving, emerging nations. There may be both expansion
and retraction in the area subject to common administration, the outcome being
determined by the degree to which the center can hold against the centrifugal
pull of ethnic and cultural diversity, inequity in regional terms of trade, and the
machinations of domestic and international politics. These are the forces which
give shape to national political struggles and which create their own antimatter
in the form of authoritarian regimes dedicated at least to order if not to the rule
of law. Development is seldom a "quiet revolution" although there may be
interludes of relatively tranquil transformation. Development proceeds by leaps
and lurches. It zigs as much as it zags and generates the energy for its gyrations
from the forces released in the collapse of social structures. Particularly in its
expanding mode, development involves the mixing of culturally diverse peoples,
the redistribution of power and privilege, and the erosion of the authority of
traditional agencies of social control. In societies undergoing growth and
expansion, struggle and strife are always near the surface and frequently break
through the weak political and institutional dikes that attempt to contain them.

This is the real world in which those concerned with population and its
role in human affairs have to contend. It is a world in which centers are set
against provinces, demographically dominant majorities against economically
potent minorities, urban-industrial sectors against rural-extractive areas. And
with it all a fundamental dilemma: weak, compromised governments are
unable to take strong measure to change underlying conditions and thus foster
development; strong authoritarian governments, on the other hand, may launch
ambitious programs but if they get underway at all, may run aground on the
shoals of established privilege and status.

In this setting the social scientist has not found it easy to get his bearing.
However, research activity has not been discouraged thereby. Factors have been
identified, tendencies discerned, relationships suggested with the boundaries of
terra incognito expanding as fast as those of terra cognito. Two general styles
of analysis have predominated—the heroic and the hackneyed. The heroic style,
behind a protective wall of ceteris paribus, proceeds by proxy and assumption
to analyse and plan for a world that does not exist. It is heroic in that it
assumes implicitly that the forces with which it explicitly deals are dominant
in the real world. For the besieged administrator the products of the heroic
approach are as useful as a copy of Euclid to a grenadier in the midst of a
cavalry charge. The hackneyed style, against a background of caution and reservation, picks away tentatively at selected facets of reality. It produces isolated
facts and relationships, which though they may be useful and in demand, e.g.,
population estimates or projections, leaves it to others to draw the implications
and fit the pieces together. "Whatever the simplicity or the sophistication of
the analytical approach, the individuals who respond and adapt, the milieu of
interrelations, the aspirations and the life styles are missing." With regard to
population research, "the questions are seldom asked, the research rarely

undertaken, as to why birth rates have *not* declined, why traditional patterns of fertility have persisted in the changing settings of modernizing . . . societies. Why is the demographic transition advancing so swiftly in West Malaysia while it is so delayed in the Philippines? What are the traditions, the values, the institutional bases and the reproductive mores that make people of Chinese and related cultures more responsive to . . . demographic modernization . . . than peoples of Hindu or Malay culture?"

To answer questions of this type, as Irene Taeuber recognized, requires "the statistically oriented analysts . . . anthropologists, geographers (and) other non-demographers." It is not an easy matter to get such diverse disciplines to work in an additive way. Each has its own "concepts, hypotheses and research designs (which) may be specific with reference to groups, cultures and subcultures." There is also the ever present concern that "the insights, hunches and speculations that are the rich by-products for demographers from anthropological or geographic field studies could be lost" if the uniform procedures and standardized modes of analysis which are characteristics of population studies were imposed on these fields. "The advance of hypotheses and the enrichment of the fields of knowledge require continuing contact and intellectual interplay rather than the subordination of one field to the methodological constraints of others. Population studies do not lose thereby." Nor do the larger efforts which, by utilizing the knowledge of demography and the social sciences, attempt to find solutions to social problems. The point to stress is that "the individual, institutional and community contexts of population growth and development are basic to realistic planning and to the selection of administrative organizations and operational approaches that will be effective and efficient in achieving specific goals." Research of this compass is rare.

Such was the thinking behind the seminars. If population experts are to speak usefully and convincingly to those who finance development activities, those who formulate policy or those who manage programs, they must first expand their own formulations through contact with other disciplines. In pursuit of this goal, demographers and social scientists from the East and the West were invited to present their research in the hope that scents leading to important new trials would be picked up.

"What then are the basic problems? What is essential in research? The critical problem is the rate of (population) growth; the critical component in growth is fertility.[c] The critical questions concern the conditions under which, and the rates at which, fertility declines. In European countries, there were long transitions of a century and a half or so. There was a transition of more than a century in Japan. Neither type of transition is assured automatically

---

[c]The major cause of high rates of population growth are of course the combination of low mortality and high fertility. In the present context "critical" signifies the variable that should be changed to achieve a diminution in the rate of growth.

in the countries of Southeast Asia, nor would either type be adequate if it occurred. . . . The economic, social and political outlook for the future is jeopardized seriously by the continuation of high rates of population growth. It is difficult to specify a limit to the time that is available for the reduction of rates of growth through declining fertility. It is possible to state that the prolongation of the time intensifies the difficulties of the transition in future years if it does not place smooth transition at hazard . . . in the context of decades and quarter-centuries the alternative 'solution' may come through increases in death rates rather than declines in birth rates."

Where does one start in all this? The answer surely is wherever one can. In the urgent conditions of Southeast Asia, action is its own excuse. But action guided by research is a more rational course. We have been critical of the research to date, finding much of it either too particularistic or too removed from reality. Thus in these seminars we sought to assemble researchers from different fields, all of whom in one way or another deal with the process of change and development and who, in their work, have attempted to come to grips with some aspect of population. For some, population is the focal topic; for others, the focus is some slice of social organization affected by or affecting population. If we are right that an expanded multidisciplinary framework is needed, then the convening of such a scientific assemblage should be a reasonable start toward this goal.

The organization in this volume has been imposed on the papers that were presented in the seminars and includes some additional material assembled or written by the editors. The chapters in Part I give a brief overview of the character and dynamics of population in Southeast Asia. Parts II, III, and IV contain chapters based largely on field studies of fertility and of the various modes of response, including rural-urban movement and alterations in community structure, whereby populations adjust to rapid population growth. The chapters in Part V, consider some of the issues in research, especially the problems of wringing more meaning from the survey method in such a way as to bridge the gap between conventional statistical analysis and the rich but weakly supported insights of field observors. Part V, and the volume, ends with a list of queries for research distilled from the proceedings by Irene Taeuber.

Part I

**Growth and Diversity
of Population in
Southeast Asia**

1

Population and Development
Irene Taeuber

Cultural Diversity

Southeast Asia is a laboratory area for the study of population change and transition. This would be true if there were only the differences in the structures and dynamics of the populations that are related to economic growth, occupational structure, education, migration, and distribution. But there is diversity within and between countries and similarity that extends beyond the boundaries of countries—in topography, climate, and resources as in all of those aspects of origin, culture, society, economy, and political form that are associated with man. There are monuments to man's creative genius and his enduring presence and there are areas where shifting cultivation has devastated the land. There are areas of rural density that approach or even exceed those in the deltas of the Yangtze, the Ganges, and the Nile, and there are sparsely settled areas. There is intensive utilization that yields marginal or submarginal living and there are underdeveloped resources.

Change is not new to Southeast Asia. Lying between or alongside East and South Asia, it has been influenced for millenia by the great cultures of the Han and the Hindu. Buddhism, Hinduism, the faith of Islam, and the ethics of Confucius are all ancient accretions. The cultures and economies of the indigenous peoples were changed with the migrations, the expansions and contractions, and the increases and declines of the successive intruders. There were southward-moving Chinese and peoples displaced by the Chinese. The migrants from the Indian subcontinent included peoples supplanted by invaders and southward-moving populations. Cultural expansions and expanding empires within Southeast Asia yielded diversities in languages and cultures and the intermingling of peoples in subregions and local areas.

The centuries of colonial and imperial suzerainty brought new further diversity and changed further what was already there. Spain and Portugal established enduring regimes in small areas. The Philippines, initially a Spanish area ruled through viceroys in the Americas, eventually became a colony of the

This chapter is an edited version of a portion of a paper by Irene Taeuber summarizing the Population Panel Seminars and published as a SEADAG report entitled, "Population Growth and Development in Southeast Asia." Tabular materials have been supplied by the editors.

3

United States. Indonesia was ruled by the Netherlands; Indochina by the French, Malaya and some island areas by the British. Thailand remained politically independent. Some Japanese have moved southward in ancient and in colonial times, but the rule of Imperial Japan reached Southeast Asia only briefly during World War II. Colonial rule introduced common attributes stemming from alien dominance in economic life and in the political and social structure. The impacts on population were so pervasive that there is a common colonial demography. Nevertheless in each area there were changes in law, administration, and economic organization that reflected the ruling country. Economic and cultural orientations in language, education, and contacts were predominantly toward the overseas colonial power rather than the countries of the region. Migrant and contract labor added further to ethnic diversities, the most notable in historic and current impact being the Chinese.

Although there were long-term migrating drifts and shifts of population, the major impacts were derivatives of political transformations: The end of the colonial regimes was swift and catastrophic rather than evolutionary. Wars, insurgencies, and insecurity altered the dynamics and the distribution of Southeast Asian populations. Today forms of government within the region cover the political spectrum; war, internal instability, and civil disorders alternate with sternly dictated regime of law and order.

Economic and social development and political stability are related to the diversities among people. The difficulties associated with rapid population growth, unequal pressures on living space, and life opportunities, and the frustrations of poverty accelerate the difficulties of diversity, thus threatening national unification which requires tolerance of differences and an acceptance of diversity.

Demographic Past and Future[a]

In 1920, Asia's 1.0 billion people were 55 percent of the earth's total population of 1.9 billion. Half a century later, in 1970, Asia's 2.1 billion people were 57 percent of the earth's total population of 3.6 billion. The Asian population in 1970 was larger than the total population of the earth in 1920. In relative terms, population had doubled. In numerical terms, there had been an addition of a billion people.

---

[a]This section is taken from a paper on *Demographic Transitions in Asian Regions*, Second Asian Population Conference, November 1-13, 1972. Tentative, Document POP/APC.2/IP/6. Major data sources: For 1920-1960: United Nations. Department of Economic and Social Affairs. *World Population Prospects as Assessed* in 1963. Population Studies No. 41. New York, 1966. 149 pp. Annex III, Table A3.1. For 1970: United Nations. Population Division. *World Population Prospects, 1965-1985, as Assessed in 1968*. Working Paper No. 30, December 1969. Sections separately paged. Total population estimates, medium variant, Table 1.

Table 1-1
Estimated and Projected World and Asian Population Growth

	Number (in millions)			Percentage Increase	
Area	1940	1970	2000	1940-1970	1970-2000
Earth	2,295	3,632	7,522	58.2	107.1
Asia	1,244	2,056	4,513	65.2	119.5
East	634	930	1,811	46.6	94.7
South	610	1,126	2,702	84.6	140.0

An extended time perspective may seem irrelevant, given the urgency of present problems of population and the magnitude of current growth. But if future population changes turn out to be simple replications of those of the recent past, the development problems of Asian countries will approach the insoluble. This fact is evident in a comparison of the estimated growth of the last three decades with the projected growth of the next three decades on assumptions of declining mortality and unchanging fertility.

In the 1940s, as in the preceding decades, Asia's population increased by about one-tenth. The modern decline in mortality began in the late 1940s and continued at variable but often accelerating rates through the 1960s. Expectancy of life at birth, fifty years or more today, may be close to seventy years by the end of the century. Fertility was high in the 1940s and remains high today. Decade growth increased from 11 percent in the 1940s to 24 percent in the 1960s. Without a transition to lower fertility, it will increase further to 26 percent in the 1970s, 30 percent in the 1980s, and 34 percent in the 1990s.

The enormity of the problems of growth is apparent in the numerical additions to the Asian population in the successive decades. The additions were 137 million in the 1940s and 396 million in the 1960s. If mortality declines but fertility does not, additions will be 533 million in the 1970s and 1.1 billion in the 1990s. Cumulative additions were 811 million between 1940 and 1970; they will be 2.5 billion between 1970 and 2000. If the demographic path of the recent past persists, the additions to Asia's population in the remaining decades of this century will be larger than the population of the earth in 1940.

The projection of continuity in growth is permissible for illustrative purposes, but persistent growth is not a tenable hypothesis as to future growth. The prediction of the Asian or the Southeast Asian future as of 1970 from the population structures and dynamics as of 1940 was not possible. These were not years of continuity in development, whether economic, social, or demographic. The prediction of the Asian or the Southeast Asian future as of 2000 from the population structures and dynamics as of 1970 is also impossible. Illustrations of future changes and the specifications of necessary paths to specific future goals of size or growth are quite possible. The range of future populations viewed as plausible is subject to numerical formulation and projection.

The future developments of population are not as fluid as the preceding remarks might seem to indicate, however. In normal periods, changes proceed through numbers of deaths and births that are both small in relation to the great central mass of the population. Changes in fertility affect only the entering cohort of births. Immediate and drastic changes in populations can come only through migration or mortality. Migration cannot be a major factor in the future of the great Asian populations and no country would plan for a removal of its population growth by death. The curtailment of growth or the reduction of numbers through natural cataclysm, disease, famine, or war would involve economic and social retrogression and thus an intensification rather than a resolution to the population problems of development.

The current projections of future populations by the United Nations are based on assessment as of 1968 and a terminal date as of 1985. If the focus is change between 1970 and 1985, the major uncertainties concern those below age fifteen in the latter year. Infants and children in preschool and early school ages in 1985 will be the survivors of the births that occur between 1970 and 1985. All those who will be aged fifteen and over in 1985 are now born; the major element of uncertainty as to future numbers in these ages is the level of mortality. It is these adult age groups whose decisions and actions will determine the levels of the fertility and the state and type of development between 1970 and 1985 and thus influence the growth in the years beyond 1985.

The general assumption in the United Nations projections is continuing transition, with the onset of the decline in fertility related to the state of development and the presence and type of population policy. The birth rate of the Southeast Asian population is projected as declining from 44.2 per 1,000 total population in 1965-1970 to 36.9 in 1980-1985, the death rate as declining from 16.1 in 1965-1970 to 10.3 in 1980-1985. If these declines occur, the rate of natural increase declines only slightly. The rate of population growth was 2.8 percent a year in 1965-1970. It would become 2.7 percent a year in 1980-1985. In the fifteen years from 1970 to 1985, the population thus would increase from 287 million to 434 million. The amount of the increase is 147 million. The relative increase is 51.4 percent.

The most urgent problem of the 1970s and the 1980s is employment. In Southeast Asia, men aged fifteen to sixty-four will be almost three-fifths again as numerous in 1985 as they were in 1970. This is a relatively firm figure, since all men who will be the adult ages in 1985 are now born. The difficulties of providing work for the increasing millions of men in the face of pervasive poverty, illiteracy, pressure on the land, and industrial backwardness are formidable. A resolution of the problems of labor and employment is essential not only for economic development and political stability but as a precondition of demographic transition itself. The employment of men at minimum levels of income influences the formation and the functioning of families whose present living and future aspirations are conducive to planned and limited parenthood.

Increases in the numbers of women aged fifteen to forty-four are comparable to those in the numbers of men in the productive years—almost three-fifths in the fifteen years from 1970 to 1985. If these increasing numbers of women marry at the same ages as their mothers and have children at the same rates, the number of births will increase along with the number of women. A reduction of almost 60 percent in age-specific fertility would be essential to hold the number of births relatively unchanging. Whether or not such a decline can or will occur is questionable.

The family planning programs which have been established throughout the region are receiving increasing priority. Advancing ages at marriage and declining fertility among the married are associated with education, labor force participation, particularly of women, and rising aspirations for the welfare of the family and children. These factors are operating even in the absence of government programs to induce positive motivation toward the use of birth control and to deliver family planning services. These various social and psychological changes are conducive to a natural transition apart from family planning programs but are also conducive to the adoption, the extension and the achievements of programs.

There are integral relations between economic and social development and demographic modernization. Increasing populations slow, if they do not preclude, economic and social developments. But economic and social developments are essential to creating the milieu and the motivations that lead to planned and smaller families. Movements to the solution of the life problems of adults in the present generation seem to be essential to solving the problems of population growth in the next generation.

The United Nations projections that provide the basis for the assessment of population growth in the years from 1970 to 1985 assume operating family planning programs and hypothesize declining fertility. The projected declines in fertility are sufficient to lessen but not to resolve the problems of increasing numbers in the adult ages in the years from 1985 to 2000. In Southeast Asia, youths below age fifteen in 1985 will be almost half again as numerous as youths below age fifteen in 1970. Since the youth of 1985 are the entrants to adult ages between 1985 and 2000, the increase in their numbers suggests the magnitude of the increases in manpower in the final fifteen years of the century.

Hypothetical Pathways

The analysis of the population prospects for the years between 1970 and

1985 has substantial reality. The problems of accommodating increasingly growing numbers and utilizing labor in rural areas, towns, and cities are inescapable.
There is a longer run also which is being shaped by the dynamics of the period
now in process. Some perspective on the dimensions of future populations
under hypothetical assumptions as to the speed of future declines in fertility
may contribute toward specification of the demographic changes that are
essential if economic and social development are to continue.

The projections are those of Tomas Frejka.[1] The assumptions are, briefly,
a continuing decline in mortality along with linear declines in fertility to a level
that yields a net reproduction rate of 1.0 at specified future dates. Populations
are projected from 1970 to 2150 so that numbers, vital rates, and age structures
can be traced from the present to the time when the maximum population
inherent in the stable structure will be reached. The paths to population stabilization are conjectural, but the nature of the processes of change and the
immensity of the growth inherent in declining mortality along with delayed
and slowly declining fertility are incontrovertible. The major imperatives for
present population and development policies if future problems of population
and development are to be resolved are outlined in sharp focus.

The population of the Southeast Asian region was estimated at 288 million
in 1970—14 percent of the total population of Asia. The average birthrate for
the years from 1965 to 1970 was 43.1, while the death rate was 14.2 yielding
on annual rate of growth of 2.9 percent. If the transition in fertility that yields
a net reproduction rate of 1.0 at very low levels of mortality occurs over the
thirty-five years between 1965-1970 and 2000-2005, the population will reach
a maximum of 842 million at the end of the twenty-first century. If the transition occurs over the fifty-five years between 1965-1970 and 2020-2025, growth
will continue through the first quarter of the twenty-second century and the
maximum population will be 1.3 billion. The *difference* in these two estimates
is more than twice the present combined population of Indonesia, the Philippines, Malaysia, and Thailand. Whether the transition to a net reproduction rate
of 1.0 takes thirty-five or fifty-five years, the time between the beginning of substantial decline in fertility and the stabilization of numbers will be almost a
century and a half. If transition is completed in thirty-five years, the maximum
population will be three times the initial one. If the completion of transition
occurs in fifty-five years, the maximum population will be four times the initial
one. In terms of past rates of decline, achieving a net reproduction rate of 1.0
in thirty-five years would be an outstanding accomplishment.

Tracing transition pathways and estimating the maximum future populations
implicit in these transitions is not prediction. No populations will maintain regular changes in vital rates over the next century. The changes that will occur are
related not only to present demographic facts but to policies, plans, and actions
of governments and to transformations in the characteristics, opportunities, and
motivations of people. Hypotheses of continuing declines in mortality to low

levels imply economic and social advance, nutritional sufficiency, health, shelter, and other amenities. The developments that are associated with declining mortality underlie changes in ways of living, opportunities, and aspirations that are conducive with increasing ages at marriage and smaller families. Thus population policies and family planning programs that contribute to declining fertility and to slower growth are essential to economic and social development. However, these same policies and programs, if successful, will contribute also to improved health and lower mortality and thus act as a secondary stimulus to population growth.

Data and Measurement

Official statistics of censuses and vital records are usually aspects of development, sometimes initiated as an aspect of the intrusion into less developed areas by colonial or imperial powers. The British heritage in Malaysia and Singapore includes enumerative censuses and an operative system of vital registration that has yielded usable data on fertility and mortality. Elsewhere there were ancient estimates and rough attempts at counts, sometimes involving inadequate civil or ecclesiastical registration systems. There were three enumerative censuses under American auspices in the Philippines, the last and most comprehensive one in 1939. Three modern censuses were planned or projected in Indonesia under the Netherlands, the last completed and completely published being the Census of 1930. There is a virtual hiatus of overall demographic data for the countries of of Indochinese Peninsula when they were colonies of France. Directives for censuses were issued but implementation was restricted, except occasionally in Cochin China. Published tabulations were largely estimates. The statistical organization of Thailand remained pre-modern until recent decades.

Registration systems in traditional and colonial times did exist in some areas of Southeast Asia. Here, as elsewhere in Asia, the population registers were used primarily for police control, local administration, or health surveillance. Vital registration and statistical data were incidental products and, as such, incomplete and inaccurate. Vital registration was notably deficient in the Philippines, still deficient but more usable in the Malay States. The Buddhist records of Thailand were not amenable to demographic analysis. On the other hand, the ecclesiastical records of the Catholic church in the Philippines are a notable and still insufficiently utilized resource.

The Japanese introduced variants of their system of *koseki* records and registrations along with quinquennial population censuses in their colonial and imperial areas in East Asia. There were plans, administrative organizations, and some limited attempts to introduce registration systems or to modify existing registers in the years of military government in Southeast Asia. Achievements were limited at the time and there is no evidence of technical or administrative residues.

The general paucity of modern demographic data in the period prior to independence does not preclude some analysis of population distribution and of geographic, economic, social, and political interrelations. However, despite a major historic literature and numerous on-going studies, there have been a few comprehensive and intensive approaches to the demographic reconstructions of the type that would be needed to measure population change and the components of that change between the late colonial and the early national periods and the present.[b]

The recognition of the importance of censuses and surveys for development planning is widespread in Southeast Asia. The priority accorded vital registration remains limited, however, despite the great need for data to project population growth, to measure and plan migration and redistribution, and to plan, operate, and evaluate family planning programs. International and national activities have been substantial, but achievements have been less than anticipated from the late 1940s to the present. Time is required for the achievement of complete and accurate census enumeration and vital registration since such systems rest ultimately on individual knowledge and compliance. Southeast Asian countries have not yet had the time to develop the organization and procedures and, more importantly, time for the evidentiary value of such records to become established. Moreover, there have been many unfortunate incidents in which statistical activities have become associated with disorders and political instability.

In most countries of Southeast Asia the sample survey is a necessary adjunct to the census or may even substitute for it. Thus, in this volume great reliance is placed on survey data, for example in establishing fertility rates for the Philippines, or in describing social and economic characteristics of the population in Thailand and Malaysia. Particularly difficult is the case of Indonesia where census and vital registration data are limited and where multi-purpose sample surveys of national scope are nonexistent. This situation has forced analysts to rely on techniques of estimation which utilize incomplete and faulty data. However ingenious such techniques may be they cannot provide estimates of high precision.

The continuing and increasing use of the sample survey has led to a growing awareness of its limitations. There are major difficulties in the reliability of responses and in the causal indeterminancy of cross-sectional data. These problems are amenable to solution through improvements in design and analytical technique. Through sequential questioning responses can be activated that

---

[b]The analysis of the 1939 census of the Philippines and the 1930 census of Indonesia as well as the historic analyses for Singapore and West Malaysia affirm the current relevance of the data and the increasing sophistication of analysis in the countries. There are also probing studies of the course of death rates and the variations in birth rates. Traditional reconstructions of growth are being subjected to close scrutiny.

otherwise would lie dormant; sequential analysis of survey data designed to move from concomitance to causation is another significant advance. Both of these topics are discussed elsewhere in this volume (see Chapter 15).

Population Growth in Southeast Asia

Today, the major factor associated with variations in natural change within and among most of the Southeast Asian countries is fertility. In North Vietnam, South Vietnam, Laos, and the Khmer Republic, though, mortality remains a major determinant of changes in growth. Increased hazards of death, flight, malnutrition, and severe living conditions influence marriage, the survival of spouses, and fertility. There are hazards in the achievement and preservation of low mortality among some groups in peripheral or isolated areas in these and other countries. There are occasional conflicts that result in elevated mortality for some groups at some time periods. Natural cataclysms such as the floods of 1972 increase mortality, deplete living facilities, and retard economic development. In some of the larger countries of Southeast Asia, as in some of the countries of South Asia, general levels of mortality remain unacceptably high. Even the maintenance of these levels is dependent on internal stability and rates of economic growth at least commensurate with those of population.

The prevalent balance of the factors of growth in Southeast Asia yields substantial and accelerating rates of natural increase. Mortality has declined to relatively low levels and is still declining. Fertility has remained at or near traditionally high levels. Differences in fertility and in growth within and among the countries form intricate patterns that are related to the indigenous culture or subcultures, age at marriage, the stability of marriages, socioeconomic status, type of economic activity, and rural, urban, or regional area of residence. This mosaic of relationships is modified by differences in country or culture of origin, status in the political hierarchy, and religion.

Relief from high rates of population growth cannot be obtained by removing populations to less dense areas. In Indonesia, transmigration, long a favored solution to the crowded conditions of Java, is now tied to development programs rather than to rural resettlement as a goal in and of itself. In the Philippines, the expansion of settlement cannot remain a safety valve for the more densely occupied areas. As Francis C. Madigan of the Mindanao Center for Population Studies observed, "Mindanao can hardly be longer conceived as a reservoir into which surplus population from the rest of the Philippines may be safely diverted while the traditional birth rate churns away producing ever larger generations of children."

Urban-Rural Balances and Social Transformation

Historically, the demographic transition from high to low fertility has been geared to a process of development which encouraged migration in response to a gradient of opportunity from rural to urban areas. The process was complex involving changes in fertility, increased levels of literacy and education, transformations of the occupational structure and social mobility. Simple repetition of the demographic adjustments of the West are unlikely in Southeast Asia, now or in the future. The new programs that are imperative for the 1970s find neither precedent nor models in the countries now developed. The populations are too massive, the rates of increase too high, to permit the development of the patterns of the West. Japan, the one country in Asia to complete its demographic transition, does not appear to be a model for Southeast Asia in the future, although analysis of the Japanese case can provide, as in the case of the West, clues to association, interrelations and dynamic factors.

The case of Thailand is instructive: the urban population increases 5 percent annually necessitating a much greater rate of development to prevent deterioration in the average level of living. At the same time the rural population, the source of much of the urban growth grows at a rate of 3 percent per year, signifying very high levels of fertility. In short, the urban areas are being overwhelmed while the population mills churn on in the countryside. At the same time in Thailand there is a growing demand for education and new manpower requirements to be met through education. But since social mobility and social status are associated with education, there are inflexibilities in the utilization of those who are educated. There are major shortages in training for doctors and nurses, and there are also difficulties with the quality of the high school graduates. The numbers of students completing high school and aiming at university education pose problems of institutional expansion now and the threat of unemployment at professional levels later.

In considering the dynamics of urban growth and urbanization in Southeast Asia, it is necessary to recognize that rates of urban growth and urbanization are related both to migration and to the high fertility both of the indigenous urban people and of the migrants. Natural increase and migration, growth and distribution, are associated—rather than separable—processes. The relations of urban growth or urbanization to development may be positive or negative, and the assessment may differ according to whether the focus is the short run or the long run.

There is in Asia one country, Sri Lanka, which has so far managed to avoid the drift of large masses from the country to the city and such concomitant urban pathologies as high unemployment, crime, shanty towns, and substandard housing. This is the case despite high levels of natural increase and despite sluggish rates of economic growth. The factors that combined to maintain the rural-urban equilibrium with low levels of economic activity and growth involve the history of Ceylon in the last quarter century, perhaps earlier. The direct program was the rehabilitation and resettlement of the cultivatable land in the thinly populated Dry Zone, with rural settlement possibilities for the impoverished and the landless. The dispersal of economic activity in agriculture and the slow growth of economic activity in the urban sector minimized both the push from the rural areas and the pull to the cities. "The retentive capacity of the rural sector owes much to the social welfare policies that were followed by the Government after independence and the pattern of income transfers that took place during this period . . . The pattern of income distribution in which sharp sectoral and regional differences were contained at tolerable levels was principally due to the social and welfare programs followed by the State." There were consumer subsidies, health services, free education from the primary to the tertiary levels, and a system of guaranteed prices to stabilize farm incomes. Unemployment which increased throughout the last decade, will have its full impact in the 1970s.

There are plans for a new urban configuration to draw the Dry Zone into the mainstream of economic activity and to alter the rural-urban mix of the country. The present development strategy is the modernization of the traditional sector. This is a development to be pondered and studied by those concerned with balanced growth in Southeast Asia. The major question to be resolved concerns the relative advantages of rapid economic growth and urbanization with their many problems in contrast to slow economic growth and slow urbanization in a more equalitarian milieu.

Rapid population growth, ever larger cities with limited urbanization of their inhabitants, and mounting numbers in rural areas are present hazards to social and economic development and political stability in Southeast Asia. Population growth in the less developed countries today is much higher than any experienced in the West in past periods, and there are no chances for emigration of any magnitude. Growth from natural increase hinders development in urban as in rural settings. The reduction of the rate of natural increase must be the underlying strategy in urban and in rural areas.

In most of the countries of Southeast Asia, natural increase is high in urban as in rural areas and the migrants who add so substantially to urban populations are relatively small portions of the rural increase. The simple demographic transition through "natural" declines in fertility that are associated with rapid industrial development and swift urbanization are unlikely to occur. Policies and programs to spread family planning are essential; the priorities accorded them must be far higher than they now are. But small family ideals and effective contraceptive practice are associated with social structures and social transformations, with educational aspirations and economic opportunities, with advancing status for girls and women, and with actual or anticipated rises in real income. Can social transformations stimulated at low levels of economic development speed the transitions in family ideals and control practices that are essential to slowing population growth in cities as in rural areas?

Cities and urban areas are sectors in nations, components of national status and dynamics. The acute problems of increasing manpower prevail in urban and in rural areas. The goals of declining fertility and slowing rates of population growth pertain to total populations. Social and economic developments that are simply urban are unlikely to achieve urban goals or resolve national demographic difficulties when the majority of the people remain rural. The transformations in urban and in rural areas are intertwined. In countries now modernized, the peoples of the cities were initiators, carriers, and stimulators of change. Demographic and social transitions moved outward along the continuum from great city to remote rural areas. Is this, too, the pattern of present and future in Southeast Asia? What of the human aspect of urban-rural interrelations, migration? How intensive can or should it be? How selective? What are its impacts on the areas of origin? What happens to migrants in cities and what impact do they have on life there? Do migrants serve as conduits of change? Do they diffuse urban values and altered reproductive mores to the countryside? Or do they perpetuate rural ways and reproductive levels in the cities? Can urban growth be made to siphon off rural increase or must the flow of migrants be stemmed in favor of rapid, direct social and demographic transformations in rural society? It is a measure of the enormity of the research task that lies ahead, that answers to these questions are wanting.

Adaptation to Growth[c]

Studies of local areas reveal a varied repetoire of adaptive practices to population growth. Some of these, for example labor recruitment from Central Luzan to Hawaii and Guam, blur recognition of growth as catastrophic and preclude assessment of the implications of increasing numbers. As opportunities for international movements decline, as the limits of land expansion impress themselves, other adaptive responses emerge. Again in Luzan recent studies show some increase in the age at marriage; the *dasel* or male dowry is disappearing; wedding feasts are less elaborate. Perhaps because the adaptive repetoire is so varied there is no strong evidence of a relationship between high fertility and high levels of outmigration from rural areas.

Frequently found at the other end of the migration stream are the squatters, who find in the social dynamics of their communities the means of survival and often avenues to upward social mobility. These communities, which from the outside may appear to be the last stop on the road to social oblivion, may actually be stations on the way up. In Lapu Lapu village, a squatter settlement in Davao, the migrants came largely from the central slums and were above the average of those areas in education, skill, occupation, wealth, and income. They

---

[c]This section has been rewritten by the editors but includes observations and points made in Dr. Taeuber's above cited paper.

were not, however, more interested in fertility regulation, perhaps for the very reason that their life adjustment patterns appeared to be working for them. However, since the official government family planning program was introduced only recently, their ultimate and comparative acceptance of the programs may well be different.

A major type of adjustment to growth throughout Southeast Asia involves greater implication in the market economy. This is strikingly true where developments such as the Mekong Project fosters innovation in agriculture, transportation, and marketing. In this respect the essential adaptive mechanism is the social system itself. But such projects are apt to become sources of population displacement as large areas of fertile lowlands are flooded and as massive resettlement schemes break the bonds that traditionally hold agrarian and even nomadic populations to their accustomed habitats. The big dam on the Mekang will flood large areas in Northeast Thailand and Laos and require the relocation of some 300 thousand persons—a process which will swell the supply of casual labor in Bangkok.

Possibly the most celebrated adaptation to population growth which has been described is the process of cultural involution in Indonesia, examples of which have been found in other parts of Southeast Asia. The process is characterized by an elaboration of social rules and prescriptions and may be accompanied by retrogression in productive technology. At the base of involutionary change on the failure of labor demand is the urban economy and an intensification of labor demand in agriculture. Thus population is retained in rural areas with consequent increases in density. In an effort to balance survival and equity, the opportunities of earning a livelihood are spread thinly and the tensions created by increased pressure on the sustenance base are buffered by new social forms. This system roots the rural population while it continues to grow. Even today in Java, sample surveys indicate that 98 percent of the population were born in their district of residence. But there are signs that this sytem is reaching its limits. In some areas where the limits of rice cultivation have been surpassed cassava is now the staple food. Ecological limits too are being pushed hazardously as cultivation pushes up the mountain slopes and deforestation threatens the eventual destruction of lands vulnerable to monsoon rains. The system of mutual aid which was basic to traditional Indonesian enterprise is yielded to greater use of hired labor in order to escape the obligations for the provision of sustenance that the older system required. As this happens much of the resilience that characterized Indonesian rural society will have disappeared. Such a development was inevitable. Development and the cash nexus is inextricable. The old system still asserts itself, however. It is still not considered proper to accept pay from friends or relatives, and especially for male villagers there are still time consuming family and social obligations which are incompatible with strict labor discipline. Professor Koentjaroningrat, Coordinator for Social Sciences in the Indonesian Institute of Sciences, has observed in seeking male migrants for industrial labor, employees prefer those from some distance away so that considerations of this type will not complicate labor-management relations.

Policies of intervention have frequently been lacking in coordination. Side by side with attempts to establish barriers to further immigration to cities and efforts to remove those already there are proposals to deal with the problems of rural growth through increase rural to urban migration. Programs to encourage people to stay where they are by expanding local opportunities have not been notoriously successful. Land reform measures have generally been disappointing in their results. Programs to provide credit to farmers so that they can participate in the Green Revolution have, if anything, worked against the retention of agricultural labor.

Land resettlement has been for years a favorite solution to population-resource imbalance. With little understanding of the process, this solution has been proposed, as Carlos Fernandez of the Institute of Philippine Culture notes, "with every crisis situation—the Huk insurgency, the Taal volcano eruption, dislocation of squatters from Manila and Quezon City, displacement of agricultural tenants in the untested hopes that population movement might be a solution." Resettlement projects, hopeful for the landless and the poor in an abstract view, merely transplant old ways of life to new areas. Land acquisition is not sufficient as a stimulant to agricultural production, social development or upward social mobility. Furthermore, land settlement schemes may be so in name only. A field study of a resettlement project in Central Palawan found that two-thirds of the settlers were not on farms. If they left their original settlement they were most likely to be in a town.

The tentative hold on subsistence which perceptibly grows worse under increasing population densities and the inability of central governments to initiate substantial development leads to a constant threat of insurgency in many parts of Southeast Asia. The standard government responses to insurgency, i.e., counterinsurgency, leads often to massive population displacements, sometimes as in the case of Indonesia with severe and lasting ecological damage and a diversion of national resources and energies away from development.

The problem facing planners dealing with population growth is formidable. Paraphrasing Gavin Jones, Population Council Advisor at the Lembaga Demographic, University of Indonesia, there is no alternative to simultaneously attempting to control population growth, aim for a balanced pattern of economic development and for a pattern of economic development that stresses equality of income distribution and opportunities for personal development at modest levels of material consumption. If this were not enough, there are serious constraints imposed by financial considerations and the level of governmental competence and complexity added by cultural and ethnic diversity. It is possible that ancient arguments of resistance to change will be validated in a slowly declining fertility, the consequence of which is a population cumulation that places economic and social development, political stability, and the preservation of achieved levels of mortality at hazard. It is also possible that here, as elsewhere in Asia, swift declines in fertility will occur in presumably traditional peasant societies and confound both the social scientists and the demographers.

Notes

1.   Tomas Frejka, *The Future of Alternative Paths to Equilibrium* (New York: Wiley, 1973).

2

A Statistical Profile of the Countries of Southeast Asia

John F. Kantner and *Lee McCaffrey*

As those who live there and those who travel there know, Southeast Asia is a mosaic of cultures. National boundaries, which to a considerable degree are the morains of former foreign invasions, are superimposed on culture areas. The map of Southeast Asia appears, in some instances, to have been drawn by a geographer named Procrustes.

On the rim of mainland Southeast Asia, Chinese culture and influence is firmly established in Korea, Taiwan, Hong Kong, Singapore, and China itself. In these areas the demographic transition is well along and the pace of economic development is well ahead of the rest of Asia. The severe problems of population growth and economic development are not found here but in Indonesia, the Philippines, Indochina, and Thailand. In Malaysia there are some hopeful signs of demographic change for though the rate of population growth remains high because of low mortality, the birthrate appears to have begun its descent. Economic development in Malaysia also has been impressive compared to the non-Chinese areas of Asia. However, the strains of ethnic diversity are a constant threat to further economic development and to population programs in Malaysia. Moreover, the large numbers coming into adulthood—the births of the post-insurrection years—will exert an upward pressure on the birth rate in the years immediately ahead.

It is this group of Southeast Asian countries with annual rates of population growth in excess of 2.5 percent with which this volume is essentially concerned. The statistics presented here are for the purpose of providing perspective. Since the basic data are often of questionable quality, there is ample room for disagreement among experts over certain figures. Therefore, we have not attempted to reconcile these figures with similar figures scattered throughout the book.

Table 2-1

Total Population and Intercensal Growth Rates for Selected Countries of Southeast Asia

	Census Population (ca. 1970)	Estimated Population (Jan. 1970)	Estimated Annual Growth Rate (1970)	Years to Double
	(Population in Millions)			
Cambodia	–	7,102	2.2	32
Laos	–	2,985	2.4	29
N. Vietnam	–		2.0	34
S. Vietnam	–	39,106	2.6	27
Indonesia	119,232	121,198	2.6	27
Malaysia	10,537	10,787	2.9	24
Philippines	37,008	38,114	3.4	20
Thailand	34,152	36,161	3.3	21

Source: 1970 Census figures and annual growth rates from International Demographic Statistics Center, U.S. Bureau of the Census; estimated population, UN Population Division.

Table 2-2

Vital Rates for Selected Countries of Southeast Asia, 1970

Country	Births Deaths (per 1,000 pop.)		Infant Deaths per 1,000 births	Life Expectation at birth*
Cambodia	42	20	159	50.0
Laos	42	17	137	47.5
N. Vietnam	37	17	N.A.	50.0
S. Vietnam	43**	12**	N.A.	50.0
Indonesia	44	19	140	45.1
Malaysia	36	7	79	57.2
Philippines	44	11	82	56.1
Thailand	42	9	68	59.1

Source: International Demographic Statistics Center, U.S. Bureau of the Census.
*1965-1970, UN Monthly Bulletin of Statistics, April 1971.
**Estimates for 1972.

Table 2-3

Age Composition for Selected Countries of Southeast Asia (Percentage)

Age	Cambodia	Laos	Vietnam*	Indonesia	Malaysia	Philippines	Thailand
0-14	44.8	42.5	41.2	44.6	44.0	46.3	45.5
15-39	37.0	37.9	35.7	38.2	38.2	37.2	36.6
40-64	15.5	16.7	19.3	14.7	14.8	13.9	14.9
65 and over	2.7	2.9	3.8	2.5	3.0	2.6	3.0

Source: UN Population Division, Population by Sex and Age by Regions and Countries 1965-1985.
*North and South

Table 2-4

Characteristics of the Population of Selected Countries of Southeast Asia, ca. 1970

Country	Percentage Urban	Percentage of Labor Force in Agriculture	Percentage Literate	Per Capita GNP ($U.S.)
Cambodia	12	80	41	$111
Laos	13	81	15	73
N. Vietnam	N.A.	N.A.	N.A.	100
S. Vietnam	24	65	60	175
Indonesia	17	70	43	104
Malaysia	40	55	43	352
Philippines	34	53	72	219
Thailand	15	78	68	173

Source: International Demographic Statistics Center, U.S. Bureau of the Census.

Table 2-5
Projected Populations (Medium Variants) for Selected Countries of Southeast Asia

		(in Millions)		
Country	*1970*	*1980*	*1990*	*2000*
Cambodia	7.1	9.7	13.1	16.8
Laos	3.0	3.9	5.0	6.2
N. Vietnam		25.6	30.9	35.7
	39.1			
S. Vietnam		21.8	26.2	30.3
Indonesia	121.2	161.4	207.4	255.3
Malaysia	10.8	14.3	18.6	22.6
Philippines	38.1	54.1	74.9	98.1
Thailand	36.2	49.8	66.2	83.2

Source: UN Population Division, Population by Sex and Age by Region and Countries 1965-1985; UN Monthly Bulletin of Statistics, April 1971.

Part II

Fertility in Southeast Asia

Introduction to Part II

In the complex demographic situation of Southeast Asia great interest centers on the analysis of fertility trends and on the search for portents of change. Much hangs in the balance. There is increasing demand for education among the populations of the area in the belief, often belied, that this is the surest route to economic and social advancement. Yet during the 1960s progress in education merely managed to keep even with the growth of the school age population. On another front, national economic planning has to contend continually with the ever larger shipments of new manpower recruits. They are both too numerous and lacking in the skills most in demand. In only about ten years from now, by 1985, men aged fifteen to sixty-four in Southeast Asia will be 60 percent more numerous than the same group in 1970! The list of problems that are exacerbated by the unrelenting growth of population is readily extended to the areas of health, housing, urban development, and even more subtle aspects of the quality of life.

At the same time there is much social and economic change in the region. Urban populations are ever larger proportions of the total population, to a large extent owing to the net outflow of population from rural areas. Modernization in various guises—from the seemingly superficial diffusion of new types of consumer goods to more profound modifications of the infrastructure, is evident everywhere. Even though the benefits of modernization are not as uniformly distributed as the costs, there would seem to be much to entice the population, especially the young, into new patterns of behavior.

And indeed in some quarters behavior is changing, even those private forms associated with fertility. At the same time, however, the traditional levels of fertility display impressive resistance to change. Prachuabmoh, Knodel and associates,[a] in their discussion of Thai fertility, noted that "low" fertility rates are to be distinguished from "lower" rates. The former must be preceded by a fundamental revision of notions about the family—its size, composition, and economic role. In Southeast Asia some rates have become lower; few are low.

---

[a]Limitation of space required us to exclude several excellent papers from this Part. This includes a substantial paper on Thailand by Visid Prachuabmoh, J. Knodel, and S. Prasithrathsin. *The Rural and Urban Population of Thailand; Comparative Profiles,* Research Report no. 8, Institute of Population Studies, Chulalonghorn University, Bangkok, 1972, and an important study by Wilhelm Flieger and Peter C. Smith of trends in Philippine marital fertility. *Demographic Patterns to Modernity: Patterns of Early-Transition in the Philippines,* Quezon City: The University of Philippines Press, 1974.

In most countries of the region, birthrates are high although by no means reaching unimpaired levels of natural fertility. Paired against low mortality however these birthrates yield rates of natural increase sufficient to double a population in a little more than a generation. The potential for further growth is also enormous owing to the fact that typically two-fifths of the population is under fifteen years of age. Thus the parents of the next fifteen years or so are now on hand and they are a large group. Besides this there is the prospect of further reductions in mortality, the direct effect of which will be to increase the rate of natural increase. If mortality reduction involves an upgrading of levels of nutrition and the adoption of modern practices for the care and feeding of infants, the effect, at least in the short run, could be to shorten birth intervals and so offset the factors tending toward lower fertility.

So far in Southeast Asia there is little evidence of fertility decline outside the areas of Chinese cultural influence. The number of births per thousand of the population (the Crude Birth Rate) did decline in all countries for which reasonable estimates can be made. However, in contrast to countries like Taiwan and Korea, which showed declines of 30 percent or more in their crude birth rates, due mostly to declines in marital fertility, the non-Chinese populations of Southeast Asia for which we have data show much smaller declines and these are due, more than anything else, to changes in marriage patterns. For this reason the decline is greatest among women under the age of thirty whereas in countries that are farther along in their transition to low fertility the incidence of decline is more widely spread over the reproductive ages. The dynamics of the marriage market have been more important to the observed drop in birth rates in Malaysia and the Philippines than a decline in the pace of reproduction within marriage.[b] In fact, it appears that fertility within marriage may have increased somewhat in the decade of the 60s in the Philippines and among the Malay population of West Malaysia.[1] Most women in these populations start to reproduce soon after marriage and continue having babies right through their reproductive period. There is no indication of early termination of childbearing among women over thirty as one finds in populations where a downward revision of marital fertility schedules is underway.

William Flieger's seminar presentation provided data to show that over the decade ending in 1968 those who were married tended to have more children than in the past; Cho and Retherford attribute all of the decline in the Malay crude birth rate to changes in age structure and marital composition. Marital fertility by their estimates tended to increase between 1960-1969.[1]

The change in the percentage of young females who are married has been quite dramatic throughout the region (Table II-1). It is evident that there is

---

[b]Whether this is also true of Indonesia, Thailand, and other non-Chinese areas is uncertain since data are lacking for adequate analysis.

Table II-1
Percentage of Young Females Currently Married

		(selected countries in selected years)	
		15-19 Years	*20-24 Years*
Indonesia	1964	34.2	73.8
	1969	29.5	73.1
W. Malaysia			
Malays	1960	42.9	79.9
	1969	21.4	66.8
Chinese	1960	9.0	52.1
	1969	5.4	40.0
Indian	1960	43.5	81.9
	1969	17.7	62.8
Philippines	1960	12.4	54.5
	1968	10.6	47.7
Thailand	1960	12.5	56.2

Source: Lee Jay Cho and Robert Retherford, "Comparative Analysis of Recent Fertility Trends in East Asia, *International Population Conference,* Vol. 2 (Liege: International Union for the Scientific Study of Population, 1973).

great diversity among the countries of Southeast Asia in the extent to which they have moved from traditional patterns of early marriage toward modern patterns of delayed marriage. As Smith shows in his detailed analysis of the Philippines, a change in the timing and prevalence of marriage commenced in the previous century and was well along by the end of World War II. Thailand appears also to have reached by 1960 about the same point in its nuptiality transition as the Philippines. The Chinese of West Malaysia by 1969 had advanced to the point where only about one in twenty females 15-19 years of age were married and only two in five of those in the next higher age group. Malays of West Malaysia and Indonesians show signs of new patterns emerging but, especially in the case of Indonesia, have a way to go before their nuptiality patterns take on a modern aspect. The demographic impact of these changes are thoroughly explored for the Philippines in Chapter 3, by Peter Smith, who also attempts to isolate the determinants of the shift away from early marriage. It is essential, as he points out, to understand the complex dynamics of the birth rate in order to get a correct notion of what is accomplished through direct intervention in the form of national fertility regulation programs.

The Malaysian case, which is the subject of Chapter 4, by James Palmore et al., presents some unique features. Like the other countries of Southeast Asia, it is culturally diverse with ethnic tensions very close to the surface and embroiled at times with issues of population policy. But unlike other Southeast Asian countries a strong and sustained frontier movement since early in the nineteenth century gave Malaysia a rate of growth that other countries of the region have achieved only in recent decades. In more recent years Malaysia has been the beneficiary of remarkable improvements in mortality. Life expectation at birth has increased by about one year each year since 1947. It was not until 1967 that the annual rate of population growth showed any diminution despite the fact that the crude birth rate began its descent as early as 1961. The decline in the birth rate and in fertility, Palmore demonstrates, is the consequence not only of changes in age composition and marital status, both of which tended to have a nega- tive effect, but also of declines in marital fertility. These changes he shows occurred across all ages and were as great or greater in rural as in urban areas. These are the hall- marks of genuine changes in fertility and they can be seen also in a doubling in recent years in the level of birth control acceptance, especially noticeable outside metropoli- tan areas. Although the fertility transition appears to have taken hold firmly and reli- ably, large ethnic differences in fertility and contraceptive practice remain. Moreover, the population is still very young as the result of past high levels of fertility. For this reason the momentum of population growth is still substantial.

The largest country of Southeast Asia, Indonesia, which has great potential for development is among the most demographically backward. Its mortality rates, as best they can be guessed, are high relative to other countries yet its rate of natural increase is high both in historical terms and in comparison to other countries with lower levels of mortality.

There is great debate about the age structure of the Indonesian population. The distribution reported in the 1961 Census showed Indonesia with an excep- tionally small proportion of its population between the ages of ten and twenty. An echo of the turbulence of the period of the Japanese occupation and the postwar struggle for independence, some thought; a typical pattern of mis- reporting characteristic of non-numerate populations, thought others. The argument was waged between academics but the question was not academic. If the first interpretation was largely correct, the country was experiencing a calm before the demographic tidal wave that in another ten years would inundate the country with adolescents and young adults demanding an educa- tion, a livelihood, formenting unrest and embarking on their own reproduc- tive careers which would produce their own echoes a generation later. If the "hollow age groups" instead were artifactual, the whole issue with its frighten- ing implications would turn out to be phantasmagoric. In Chapter 5, on the Indonesian demographic situation, McCaffrey provides the latest evidence on this question which indicates that the truth falls somewhere between the opposing arguments.

To all appearances Indonesians, or more exactly the residents of Java and Bali, are responding in surprising numbers to the national family planning program. That program is not only vigorous but also relatively young, which may have something to do with its vigor. Still some informed observors are impressed by what they see in the statistics on acceptors of contraception and in the seemingly high rates of continuation among acceptors.[c] The program is now being extended beyond Java and Bali to the Outer Islands where the rates of growth appear to be greater. In 1973 the national program was reaching an estimated 13 percent of the fertile women of Java and Bali.[2] While this is lower than the available estimates for other large countries of Southeast Asia in which approximately 20 to 25 percent of eligible couples currently use contraception, it is a respectable showing for a new program. If Thailand is an indication of what can happen, one might expect that the rate of acceptance in Indonesia would continue a rapid rise. In Thailand, a survey in 1969 by investigators from Chulalongkorn University found that only 11 percent of rural wives under age forty-five were currently using some method of birth control. Three years later this percentage had doubled.[3]

Whether these levels of contraceptive practice will have much impact on population growth in Southeast Asia depends on the effectiveness and consistency with which contraception is used, the role of abortion (a subject about which little is said officially), and, of course, the extent to which the programs hold together administratively. These factors, together with the pace and equity of social and economic development and that-not-to-be-counted-on-sine-qua-non, the political situation, will determine the demographic future of Southeast Asia and to a considerable extent the welfare of those who live there.

Notes

1. Lee Jay Cho and Robert D. Retherford, "Comparative Analysis of Recent Fertility Trends In East Asia," *International Population Conference* Vol. 2 (Liege International Union for the Scientific Study of Population, 1973).
2. *Agency for International Development Population Program Assistance Annual Report 1973*, (Washington, D.C.: U.S. Government Printing Office, 1974), p. 65. Suwardjono puts the estimate at "around 15 percent of the eligible population," *Studies in Family Planning* 5, 5 (May 1974).
3. Institute of Population Studies, Chulalongkorn University, Working Paper, No. 1 (Revised), August 1973, p. 18.

---

[c]To be impressed one has to read charts and tables with their bouyant percentages and sharply ascending curves rather than to observe the patient flow in an average clinic which on average amounts to two per day. Relative to the number of clients Indonesia has a very large number of outlets for contraceptive supplies and services. It has the installed capacity for a much expanded program.

3

Philippine Nuptiality in the Twentieth Century

Peter C. Smith

Introduction

In the face of dramatic economic, social, and spatial change in the Philippines during the last seven decades, the observer with a concern for demographic processes is led to inquire if traditional patterns of population movement, marriage, and reproduction have shown any response, been altered in any way. Certainly the impact of the economy on population distribution is immediately evident (Pascual 1966; Simkins and Wernstedt 1963; Vandermeer and Agaloos 1962; Wernstedt and Simkins 1965; Wernstedt and Spencer 1967). And recent data suggest that fertility and marriage patterns too have not been entirely immune to modernizing forces, though the responses have been muted and, in part, countervailing.[a] Two broad changes in family formation are indicated: on the one hand, there has been a gradual but accelerating movement toward later marriage for females; on the other hand, and in sharp contrast, there is some evidence that marital fertility has *risen* slightly. Indeed, given known changes in nuptiality, childbearing within marriage must have quickened somewhat since there is little indication of fertility decline overall (Smith 1974).

Apart from population movement, therefore, the principal demographic response to social and economic change has been with respect to nuptiality: the timing of marriage and its prevalence. It is important—for the policymaker as well as for the social scientist—that this demographic response be examined and its ramifications understood. This chapter, then, investigates the role of nuptiality in twentieth century Philippine demography. The approach is geographic, disaggregative, and to some extent, historical. We explore the national pattern by considering nuptiality variations across areal units as well as over time.

Focusing first on province-level patterns, we examine census data describing a set of forty-five units with constant territory over the 1903-1970 period. There were fifty provinces in 1903 (including nine comandancia, excluding Manila). Political reorganization has eliminated four of these while

---

Parts of this chapter appear in Chapters 2 and 9 of Wilhelm Flieger and Peter C. Smith. *A Demographic Path to Modernity: Patterns of Early-Transition in the Phillipines.* Quezon City: University of Phillipines Press, 1974.

[a]We refer to series of analyses of the 1968 NDS by the staff of the Population Institute, University of the Philippines (Flieger and Smith 1974). Support for the statements in this paragraph is found here.

creating a number of new ones. The forty-five units examined here differ from
the contemporary provinces as follows. In 1903: Mountain Province combines
Benguet and Lepanto-Bontoc; Palawan combines Paragua and Paragua Sur; Sulu
combines Basilan, Jolo, Siassi and Tawi-Tawi; Camarines was called Ambos
Camarines; Misamis Occidental was Misamis; Misamis Oriental was Dapitan;
Quezon was Tayabas. In 1939: Cotabato combines Cotabato, Bukidnon and
Lanao; Quezon was called Tayabas. In 1939 *and* 1960: Cagayan combines
Cagayan and Batanes; Camarines combines Camarines Norte and Camarines Sur;
Surigao combines Surigao and Agusan. In 1960: Albay combines Albay and
Catanduanes; Capiz combines Capiz and Aklan; Cotabato combines Cotabato,
Bukidnon, Lanao del Norte and Lanao del Sur; Mindoro combines Occidental
Mindoro and Oriental Mindoro; Zamboanga combines Zamboanga del Norte
and Zamboanga del Sur. In 1970: Agusan combines Agusan del Norte and
Agusan del Sur; Cotabato combines Cotabato and South Cotabato; Davao com-
bines Davaos del Norte, del Sur and Oriental, Leyte combines Leyte and
Southern Leyte; Misamis Oriental combines this province and Camiguin; Mountain province includes Benguet, Ifugao, Kalinga Apayao and Mountain Province;
Samar includes Eastern, Northern and Western Samar; Surigao includes Surigaos
del Norte and del Sur. Throughout this chapter the term province refers to these
units rather than the contemporary administrative divisions.

The data allow us to consider the seven decades in three parts: 1903-1939
(the American period to the beginning of the Second World War); 1930-1960
(essentially the postwar period political independence); and 1960-1970, a period
of especially rapid demographic change.

The analysis moves to a further disaggregation when we examine local-area
data, available most recently from the 1939 census enumeration. The two sources
of data prove complimentary: province data, available for several points in time,
provide important insights into spatial-temporal changes in nuptiality; the municipal data describe only a single point in time, but do so in depth. And 1939
is an important juncture in Philippine history—it marks the end of several decades
of substantial change and the beginning of a series of major military, political,
and social upheavals. As we shall see, it also proves to be a useful breaking point
for separating periods of contrasting demographic processes.

Seventy Years of Demographic Response

For a long-run perspective on twentieth century Filipino nuptiality we must
rely upon census distributions on marital status.[b] A significant long-term trend

---

[b]It is fortuitous for our purpose that census questions concerning marital status
have, since the first modern census in 1903, all incorporated a "de facto" conceptual
framework. Thus the 1903 census questionnaire asks interviewers to determine for each
person "whether married or single, widowed or divorced," and further specifies: "The

Table 3-1

Percentage of Females Single by Age and Singulate Mean Age at Marriage, 1903 to 1970

Age Group	YEAR				
	1903	1939[a]	1948[a]	1960	1970
	Percentage Single				
15-19	73.6	80.3	85.1	87.3	89.2
20-24	33.3	36.2	40.7	44.3	50.3
25-29			18.8	19.5	21.5
	15.6	15.7			
30-34			12.6	11.6	11.7
35-39			9.5	8.1	8.0
	9.4	7.4			
40-44			8.7	7.6	7.3
45-49[b]	7.8	5.4	6.9	7.0	6.7
SMAM	20.9	21.9	22.1	22.3	22.8
	Proportion of Total Change: 1903-1970				
15-19		.43	.31	.14	.12
20-24		.18	.26	.21	.35
25-34		.08	.14	.07	.71
SMAM		.52	.11	.11	.26

[a]Women with marital status not reported have been removed from the total.
[b]45-54 in 1903 and 1939.

for females is immediately evident in table 3-1, which shows percentage of females single (never married) by age and singulate mean age at marriage (SMAM) for available census years from 1903 to 1970[c]. The percentage

---

married may be divided into two classes, those legally married and those living together by mutual consent, or as they will be spoken of hereafter, consensually married." In 1960 married persons were: "all persons living together as husband and wife whether legally or consensually (without benefit of marriage) . . ." The married population in 1970 included ". . . a person who lives with someone as man and wife, whether legally married or not." See USBC (1905: Vol. II, 10, 69ff.), BCS (1963: Vol. I, xvii) and BCS (1970).

[c]The Singulate Mean Age at Marriage or SMAM (Hajnal 1953), is computed from proportions single in successive age groups. This index takes advantage of the fact that the

never married has increased steadily for all except the oldest age groups. The percentage single at 15-19 rose by 15.6 points over the period or by about one-fifth of its 1903 level; the percentage single at age 20-24 increased by one-half of its level in 1903.

The timing of these changes over the first seventy years of this century is also shown in table 3-1. Nearly one-half the shift in the percentage single for the youngest age group had occurred by 1939; almost three-fourths had taken place by 1948. In contrast, the shift for women aged 20-24 occurred later—only one-fifth by 1939, and more than half *since* 1948. The singulate mean age at marriage (SMAM) rose by 1.9 years over the period, with more than one-half of this increase coming *before* World War II. Change was slowest over the 1948-1960 period (Smith 1968). Although it may not be large in absolute terms, or in comparison with changes for certain other societies (Agarwala 1962; Freedman, Hermalin, and Sun 1972; Hajnal 1965), this shift in age at marriage is a significant one, especially when viewed in terms of the relatively advanced age at marriage already achieved for women by 1903. The observed changes in the timing of marriage for females are persistent over time; moreover, the tempo and age-pattern of the changes clearly suggest the gradual diffusion of a late-marriage norm from younger to older age-groups over the period. A national nuptiality trend of some magnitude is clearly evident.

Interprovincial Variations in Nuptiality

Overview

While the percentage single and the mean age at marriage indicate a steady trend over the 1903-1970 period, the timing of marriage has pursued a more varied course at the provincial level (cf. table 3-2.[d] Interprovincial differences

---

mean age at marriage is the mean duration of single (never married) life. Where s_x is the proportion single in the age group x to $x + 5$,

$$\text{SMAM} = \sum_{x=0}^{50} \left(s_x - 50 s_{50} \right) / \left(1 - s_{50} \right).$$

For other applications, see Hajnal (1953) and Dixon (1971). For a population with a sustained, positive rate of growth, SMAM overstates the true mean somewhat. Singulate means around 1960 for some Asian female populations are: South Korea, 21.3; India 16.8; Pakistan, 16.5; Taiwan, 21.0 Malaya, 19.3; Sabah, 19.4; Sarawak, 19.8; Japan, 24.7; Thailand, 21.9; Ceylon, 22.0; Singapore, 20.5; Hongkong, 22.3 (Dixon 1971).

[d]The index of marriage pattern or I_m, devised by Ansley Coale and others for a study of the fertility transition in European provinces, is simply a weighted average of proportions married by age, with a standard schedule of very high fertility rates by age as the weights.

Table 3-2
Measures of Level and Interprovincial Dispersion for Selected Indexes of Male and Female Marriage Patterns, 1903, 1939, 1960, and 1970: 45 Provinces

Indexes of Marriage Pattern	MEAN				STANDARD DEVIATION			
	1903	1939	1960	1970	1903	1939	1960	1970
Female								
% Single 20-24	33.3	36.2	44.3	48.8	9.05	9.76	9.31	9.82
SMAM	20.7	–	22.2	22.7	1.34	–	0.98	1.07
I_m *	0.787	0.760	0.703	0.624	0.059	0.069	0.066	0.063
% Ever-Married	92.2	94.6	93.0	93.5	3.22	2.94	4.08	4.22
Male								
% Single 20-24	55.4	–	63.9	–	10.58	–	7.34	–
SMAM	24.4	–	24.8	–	1.48	–	0.80	–
% Ever-Married	94.0	–	96.9	–	4.63	–	1.22	–

*I_m expresses the implication of a schedule of percentages single for fertility. A maximum value of 1.0 indicates no loss of fertility due to marriage pattern. See footnote *d*, p. 34.

were generally more pronounced in 1939 than at the turn of the century but
diminished in the postwar period to 1960, only to increase again thereafter.
On balance for females there was somewhat *more* variation in 1970 than seven
decades before. Changes in the variability of age at marriage and the percentage
single have been greater for men than for women, and have led to a reduction
in interprovincial differences.

The changing provincial distribution of relative levels on I_m is shown in
table 3-3. Over the 1903-1939 period twenty-five provinces experienced *rising*
female ages at marriage while the remaining twenty experienced *declines*. In
the postwar period to 1960, on the other hand, all provinces except the three
Ilocos provinces experienced delayed marriage. In the 1960-1970 period all
provinces experienced substantial delay, especially those which had lagged
behind before 1960.

Regional Patterns

When we collapse the provinces into a smaller number of regions which
have had a broadly homogeneous experience, distinct regional patterns emerge
(cf. table 3-4).[e] The island of Mindanao, especially its southern part, was
characterized by very early marriage in 1903, reflecting both its frontier status
and the presence of upland and coastal non-Christian populations. With the
heavy in-migration of the twentieth century the age at marriage (after declining
marginally before 1939) had risen substantially by 1970. The total downward
shift in I_m over seven decades was nearly 20 percent. Apparently prewar in-
movement was dominated by single males and to a lesser degree early-marrying
settler females, while the postwar period saw later marriage due to normalizing
sex ratios (in the south) and in-movement of older married women to the north.[f]

See Coale (1969). $I_m = (\Sigma\ m_i F_i)/(\Sigma\ w_i F_i)$, where w_i, m_i, and F_i are all women, married
women, and the standard fertility rates, respectively, for successive age groups. Summation
is over the age range 15 to 49. Across the forty-five provinces the correlation coefficient
relating I_m and SMAM in 1960 is -.94. Both these indexes are based on cross-section percentages single by age. They differ in that SMAM reflects years lived single among those
in an hypothetical cohort who eventually marry, while I_m, by using a set of fertility rates
as weights, indexes the impact of the schedule of per cents single on fertility.

[e]The broad sub-areas given in table 3-4 were derived informally by considering
patterns of change in nuptiality (I_m), the sex ratio and intercensal rates of growth. They
do not represent a formal regionalization of the forty-five original units. Ten of the
original provinces have not been placed in any of the sub-areas.

[f]The age-sex information for 1903, 1939, 1960 and 1970 strongly suggests that
frontier movement should be seen as a two-stage demographic process. For further support for this view, see the analysis of Mindanao's 1960 age structure in Wernstedt and
Simkins (1965: 99-102). The early stage would seem to involve very early marriage for
females and the later stage delayed entrance into marriage. Whether the shift in female
age at marriage is due to declining frontier sex ratios as a consequence of postwar female

Table 3-3
Indexes of Marriage Pattern (I_m) for Females, 1903, 1939, 1960 and 1970: 45 Provinces

Province	I_m 1903	1939	1960	1970	Index Numbers (1903 = 100) 1903	1939	1960	1970	Index Numbers (1939 = 100) 1903	1939	1960	1970
1. Abra	0.755	0.731	0.719	0.599	100	97	95	79	103	100	98	82
2. Albay	0.735	0.751	0.683	0.621	100	102	93	84	98	100	91	83
3. Antique	0.745	0.713	0.635	0.574	100	96	85	77	104	100	89	81
4. Bataan	0.809	0.765	0.760	0.616	100	95	94	76	106	100	99	80
5. Batangas	0.760	0.697	0.669	0.575	100	92	88	76	109	100	96	82
6. Bohol	0.625	0.678	0.651	0.572	100	108	104	92	92	100	96	84
7. Bulacan	0.755	0.675	0.614	0.576	100	89	81	76	112	100	91	85
8. Cagayan	0.868	0.756	0.750	0.665	100	87	86	77	115	100	99	88
9. Capiz	0.721	0.724	0.698	0.608	100	100	97	84	100	100	96	84
10. Camarines	0.788	0.791	0.717	0.634	100	100	91	80	100	100	91	80
11. Cavite	0.809	0.758	0.651	0.575	100	94	80	71	107	100	86	76
12. Cebu	0.670	0.683	0.632	0.572	100	102	94	85	98	100	93	84
13. Cotabato	0.847	0.867	0.758	0.680	100	102	89	80	98	100	87	78
14. Davao	0.832	0.869	0.771	0.662	100	104	93	80	96	100	89	76
15. Ilocos Norte	0.773	0.603	0.633	0.581	100	78	82	75	128	100	105	96
16. Ilocos Sur	0.726	0.593	0.629	0.587	100	82	87	81	122	100	106	99
17. Iloilo	0.776	0.691	0.606	0.538	100	89	78	69	112	100	88	78
18. Isabela	0.893	0.801	0.802	0.728	100	90	90	82	111	100	100	91
19. Laguna	0.811	0.773	0.702	0.599	100	95	86	74	105	100	91	77
20. La Union	0.755	0.609	0.667	0.572	100	81	88	76	124	100	110	94
21. Leyte	0.713	0.768	0.737	0.661	100	108	103	93	93	100	96	86
22. Manila	0.797	0.670	0.492	0.470	100	84	62	59	119	100	73	70
23. Marinduque	0.688	0.766	0.747	0.663	100	111	108	96	90	100	98	86
24. Masbate	0.782	0.862	0.787	0.716	100	110	101	92	91	100	91	83
25. Mindoro	0.845	0.834	0.800	0.696	100	99	95	82	101	100	96	83

Table 3-3 (cont.)

Province	I_m				Index Numbers (1903 = 100)				Index Numbers (1939 = 100)			
	1903	1939	1960	1970	1903	1939	1960	1970	1903	1939	1960	1970
26. Misamis Occ.	0.743	0.790	0.669	0.578	100	106	90	78	94	100	85	73
27. Misamis Or.	0.792	0.785	0.705	0.606	100	99	89	76	101	100	90	77
28. Mountain Prov.	0.813	0.858	0.763	0.662	100	106	94	81	95	100	89	77
29. Negros Occ.	0.860	0.798	0.683	0.599	100	93	79	70	108	100	86	75
30. Negros Or.	0.699	0.753	0.694	0.625	100	108	99	89	93	100	92	83
31. Nueva Ecija	0.840	0.761	0.695	0.631	100	91	83	75	110	100	91	83
32. Nueva Viscaya	0.907	0.820	0.782	0.678	100	90	86	75	111	100	95	83
33. Palawan	0.758	0.837	0.817	0.724	100	110	108	96	91	100	98	86
34. Pampanga	0.761	0.704	0.659	0.595	100	92	86	78	108	100	94	84
35. Pamgasinan	0.873	0.722	0.676	0.592	100	83	77	68	121	100	94	82
36. Quezon	0.815	0.827	0.772	0.681	100	101	95	84	98	100	93	82
37. Rizal	0.812	0.727	0.574	0.533	100	90	71	66	112	100	79	73
38. Romblon	0.804	0.772	0.728	0.660	100	96	90	82	104	100	94	85
39. Samar	0.796	0.806	0.772	0.712	100	101	97	89	99	100	96	88
40. Sorsogon	0.783	0.807	0.734	0.649	100	103	94	83	97	100	91	80
41. Sulu	0.827	0.853	0.746	0.648	100	103	90	78	97	100	87	76
42. Surigao	0.765	0.805	0.724	0.669	100	105	95	87	95	100	90	83
43. Tarlac	0.873	0.748	0.700	0.616	100	86	80	70	117	100	94	82
44. Zambales	0.844	0.785	0.688	0.603	100	93	82	71	108	100	88	77
45. Zamboanga	0.768	0.830	0.761	0.681	100	108	99	89	92	100	92	82
PHILIPPINES												
Unweighted	0.787	0.760	0.703	0.624	100	96	89	79	104	100	93	82
Weighted[a]	0.770	0.705	0.647	0.614	100	92	84	80	109	100	92	87

[a]Weighted by provincial population totals.

On balance marriage came later in the south throughout the century. Northeastern Luzon (the Cagayan Valley) has been similarly characterized by an early but rising age at marriage, again due to an initial frontier situation (high sex ratios) to which families (married women) and older single women have been migrating. The total downward shift in I_m in this area has also been about one-fifth, a third or so of which, in contrast to Mindanao, occurred before 1939.

In the Bicol Peninsula the trend overall has been toward later marriage, but this movement lagged far behind the national trend until an acceleration occurred in the sixties. In 1960 Bicol was characterized by early marriage relative to all other areas except the frontiers, yet by 1970, after a decline in I_m of more than one-tenth in the decade, Bicol's I_m was below the national average.

Ilocos is a complex and fascinating region with respect to both population movement and nuptiality, and we shall be returning to it below. Broadly, out-movement of males before 1939 (principally to Hawaii; see the sex ratios in table 3-4) caused delays in female age at marriage, but the predominantly female out-movement, largely single, since then has led to a rising I_m over 1939-1960. This contrary trend was reversed again in the sixties. The I_m for Ilocos declined rapidly over 1960-1970 to fall below the national average.

The Manila region (Manila, Rizal, Bulacan, Pampanga, Cavite) and Central Luzon as a whole are extremely important areas—they carry the brunt of the national trend toward later marriage. The index of marriage pattern has declined sizably and steadily in both areas, by 32 percent in the metropolitan zone and by 29 percent in the Central Plain. The long-term decline in I_m in these zones is no doubt the direct consequence of rapid economic and social change in the urban zone and beyond (Fuchs and Luna 1972; 37-39; Smith 1970).

Sex selective migration has also played a role. Central Luzon has sent some males to other regions, and the Manila sex ratio has declined markedly since the turn of the century. Also, Manila increasingly has been the destination of young, and apparently single, female migrants.

The islands of the Visayas fall into several groups. Panay, Cebu, and Bohol have had a similar experience: persistent out-movement of males throughout the century (as indicated by their growth rates and sex ratios) and an overall shift toward later marriage. This trend probably reflects the relative development of these provinces (except for Bohol) as well as the effects of migration: Panay (with Iloilo City) and Cebu (with Cebu City) are the regional foci of the Visayan cultural area, and have been centers of economic change as well (Sicat 1972:366). The I_m index for the island of Panay has declined by fully one-fourth since 1903, much of this occurring since 1960.

---

in-movement, and what form the later female in-movement takes (single women, married women with husbands, married women following after husbands, etc.) are matters for investigation. Are local (frontier) girls marrying later, or are older single males recruiting older brides among single women elsewhere?

Table 3-4
Sex Ratios, Rates of Intercensal Population Change and Indexes of Marriage Pattern (I_m) Groups of Provinces, 1903-1970

AREA	SEX RATIO				ANNUAL POP. CHANGE[a]			I_m			
	1903	1939	1960	1970	1903-1939	1939-1960	1960-1970	1903	1939	1960	1970
Southern Mindanao	1342	1120	1098	1030	3.57	4.94	3.95	0.822	0.856	0.761	0.674
Northern Mindanao	1055	1035	1038	1008	3.12	2.54	3.41	0.770	0.795	0.707	0.634
Northeast Luzon	1136	1018	1032	1012	2.35	2.39	3.24	0.856	0.806	0.772	0.684
Bicol Peninsula	999	1044	1047	1018	1.86	2.68	1.95	0.766	0.780	0.709	0.632
Ilocos Coast	936	896	961	952	1.02	1.20	1.84	0.751	0.615	0.651	0.582
Manila Region	1094	1034	963	952	2.10	3.50	4.31	0.783	0.700	0.576	0.534
Central Luzon	1007	992	1000	987	1.91	2.13	2.81	0.862	0.743	0.691	0.609
Panay Island	915	961	978	956	1.54	1.24	1.87	0.754	0.704	0.638	0.564
Cebu and Bohol	974	944	962	953	1.47	1.01	0.96	0.657	0.681	0.638	0.572
Negros Island	1070	1102	1042	985	2.45	2.21	1.37	0.796	0.783	0.686	0.607
Philippines	1002	1016	1018	990	2.08	2.52	2.97	0.770	0.705	0.647	0.614

[a]Exponential r.

The island of Negros has had a different history. The sugar industry opened Negros to rapid colonization over the second half of the nineteenty century.[g] Before then it was not heavily populated. Early in-movement was to both the eastern and western halves, while the 1903-1939 period saw continued in-movement to western Negros. There has been net out-movement from both halves since 1939. Negros Oriental has received most of its migrants from Cebu whereas the flow to Negros Occidental largely has originated on Panay.

Of the migrant population of Negros Occidental in 1960 52.3 percent were born on the island of Panay, only 27.5 percent on the islands of Cebu or Bohol. In contrast, Panay contributed 8.3 percent of the migrants to Negros Oriental, while Cebu and Bohol contributed 46 percent. In 1960, 75 percent of Negros Occidental was Ilongo speaking, while Cebuano was mother tongue for 94 percent of Negros Oriental's population.

Negros Occidental has had higher sex ratios and rates of growth throughout this century. As a consequence of these divergencies in ethnicity and migration experience, Negros Occidental has seen continuing marriage delay in this century as it has moved from frontier to more normal conditions. Thus, although Negros Occidental exceeded the national level on I_m in 1903 and Negros Oriental was well below it, in 1970 both provinces fell near the national average.

In overview, first, it is evident from the data presented thus far that population movement has a complex impact upon nuptiality in receiving and sending places, depending upon the marital status of migrants when they migrate (we lack direct information on this), the timing of marriage after migration, the sex selectivity of migration, and age, sex, and marital status differences between early and late-migration streams.

Second, the areas of heavy in-movement saw increases in I_m (movements to earlier marriage) before 1939 and delayed marriage afterward. The large prewar frontier movements introduced complexity into the national situation and counterbalanced what would otherwise have been a widespread, major prewar shift toward later marriage.

Third, the Philippines' core region—defined here as (a) the Manila Region (five provinces), and (b) the remainder of Central Luzon (five additional provinces)—has shown a major, sustained shift toward later marriage. It is tempting to suggest that delayed marriage to a degree has substituted for out-migration as a response to rural population pressure in the *barrios* on the central plain.

---

[g]The principal event was the opening of the port of Iloilo to foreign shipping (De la Costa 1965: 152ff.). See also Wernstedt and Spencer (1967).

Of the migrant population of Negros Occidental in 1960 52.3 percent were born on the island of Panay, only 27.5 percent on the islands of Cebu or Bohol. In contrast, Panay contributed 8.3 percent of the migrants to Negros Oriental, while Cebu and Bohol contributed 46 percent. In 1960, 75 percent of Negros Occidental was Ilongo speaking, while Cebuano was mother tongue for 94 percent of Negros Oriental's population.

Clearly, however, two important forces are at work: rural densification with attendant rising tenancy rates and declining farm sizes, and urbanization, with all its ramifications. The latter is the dominant factor close to Manila—say within 50 kilometers (Smith 1970)—while rural population densities may be the major force farther away.

Two other areas, the islands of Panay and Cebu, also show shifts of substantial magnitude toward later marriage though sex ratios seem to play a more important role than rising pressure on resources. Of several leading areas of late marriage, easily the most important—because it apparently reflects the joint impact of rural population pressure and urbanizing economic change—is the Manila-Central Plain region.

Components of Intercensal Change

The combined effects of provincial nuptiality trends and interprovincial migration can be elucidated in another way: by decomposing the overall shift in nuptiality into additive components indicating the effects of changing provincial patterns, the changing distribution of population across provinces, and the interaction of these.[h] This decomposition of nuptiality change is illustrated in table 3-5 using the percentage single among females age 20-24. When we separately decompose changes before 1939 and over 1939-1960 the components reflecting changing province means and changing population distribution prove to have opposite signs. Also, the interaction effect is nearly as important as the effect of population redistribution. Moreover, it reverses sign between the two periods.[i] The same decomposition of 1960-1970 changes yields a contrasting result.

Table 3-5
Change in Percentage Single, Females Age 20-24

Source of Change	1903-1939	1939-1960	1960-1970
Change in Province Means	5.07	7.73	6.15
Shift in Population Distribution	-1.08	-1.38	0.02
Interaction	-0.78	1.01	-0.15
Total National Change (Observed)	3.23	7.35	6.02

[h]In decompositions of this kind the interaction term is positive when changes in sub-unit means are positively correlated with changes in sub-unit shares of total population. The decomposition formula and its rationale are given in Duncan et al. (1961: 62-64).

[i]The same configuration is observed when we decompose I_m. National changes over the two periods are -21 and -60, respectively, while the components reflecting changes in province means are -34 and -64. The distribution components are 7 and 10, the interaction components 6 and -6.

Shifting population distribution no longer has a negative effect, and the inter-action term reverses its sign again.

These patterns restate in a concise fashion the observations that were offered above. The early-marriage provinces, largely the frontier territories, steadily increased their relative shares of population over 1903-1960. More-over, increasing percentages single occurred, before 1939, in provinces with *diminishing* shares of population (the negative interaction term), while the postwar pattern until 1960 involved rising percentages single for areas with *increasing* shares of population. Put another way, prewar high-growth prov-inces (the frontiers) were areas with declining ages at marriage, while 1939-1960 high-growth provinces tended to be areas of rising age at marriage. Over the 1960-1970 period the effect of redistribution was negligible, but provinces with delayed marriage tended to be those with net out-movement.

A strategic point is highlighted by these decompositions: the actual prov-ince-by-province shifts in the timing of marriage over 1903-1970 were actually of greater magnitude than is suggested by the observed national pattern. This carries important implications for the future path of nuptiality which will be considered below.

Changing Sources of Variation

We have noted a complex pattern of relationship linking nuptiality changes with sex and marital status-selective population movements and the relative availability of potential spouses. To examine these relationships further while introducing several new explanatory variables we now turn to a multiple regres-sion analysis of nuptiality variations on each of the four dates. (By utilizing unweighted province data in these regressions we deliberately focus upon province-level variations alone, abstracted from the effects of redistribution.) To the sex ratio as an index of demographic influences on nuptiality we add four other explanatory variables: a measure of economic level, a measure of population pressure, an index of the level of modernization among females, and ethnicity. Specifically, the variables are the percentage of families living in homes of durable construction (percentage of households in 1960 and 1970), density, the percentage of females age ten and over who are literate, and dominant mother tongue. Only the following mother tongue categories are available for each of the four dates: Ilocano, Visayan, Ilongo, Bicolano, Other.

Table 3-6 presents zero-order correlations between a series of nuptiality indexes and these five variables on each of the dates. In some instances data have been assembled for males as well as females. Regressions of I_m upon combinations of independent variables are reported in table 3-7.

We focus first on the timing of marriage for females. However, nuptiality

Table 3-6

Zero-Order Correlation Coefficients Relating Male and Female Marriage Indexes and Selected Independent Variables: 45 Provinces, 1903, 1939, 1960 and 1970

Independent Variable	Male			Female			
	1903	1939	1960	1903	1939	1960	1970
Percentage Single 20-24							
1. Sex Ratio	0.43	–	−0.42	−0.34	−0.28	−0.74	−0.65
2. % Durable Const.[a]	0.36	–	0.48	0.06	–	0.54	0.38
3. Density	0.18	–	0.37	−0.05	0.25	0.47	0.31
4. Literacy, Female	0.46	–	0.21	−0.09	0.42	0.34	0.29
5. Ethnicity[b]	–	–	–	0.59	0.56	0.47	0.26
Mean Age at Marriage							
1. Sex Ratio	0.54	–	−0.44	−0.35	–	−0.67	−0.45
2. % Durable Const.[a]	0.45	–	0.54	0.08	–	0.56	0.32
3. Density	0.21	–	0.46	−0.09	–	0.53	0.38
4. Literacy, Female	0.51	–	0.33	−0.15	–	0.39	0.34
5. Ethnicity[b]	–	–	–	0.55	–	0.48	0.28
Index of Marriage Pattern (I_m)							
1. Sex Ratio	–	–	–	0.34	0.29	0.80	0.64
2. % Durable Const.[a]	–	–	–	−0.06	–	−0.53	−0.39
3. Density	–	–	–	0.01	−0.21	−0.50	−0.38
4. Literacy, Female	–	–	–	0.09	−0.38	−0.42	−0.50
5. Ethnicity[b]	–	–	–	0.57	0.59	0.51	0.24
Percentage Ever Marrying							
1. Sex Ratio	0.48	–	0.58	0.12	0.26	0.78	0.63
2. % Durable Const.[a]	0.62	–	0.37	0.20	–	0.23	−0.25
3. Density	0.57	–	−0.36	−0.12	−0.12	−0.13	−0.11
4. Literacy, Female	0.83	–	−0.24	−0.10	−0.08	−0.18	−0.26
5. Ethnicity[b]	–	–	–	0.40	0.56	0.61	0.14

– not computed or not available.

[a]Percentage of houses made of durable materials.

[b]Multiple correlation of five dummy variables. Signs are constrained to be positive.

is indexed, the correlation coefficients indicate a number of important changes over time. The significance of the availability of spouses (the sex ratio) for marriage timing has intensified over time: about one-tenth of total variation in nuptiality is accounted for in this manner in 1903 but about six-tenths in

1960,[j] with the shift coming after 1939. The importance of the sex ratio diminished somewhat in the sixties. The regression coefficient for this variable ([1], table 3-7) is large and significant in 1960 and 1970. Economic changes at the household level—crudely indexed by the dwelling materials measure—have grown in import, as have the roles of population density and individual level changes among females (educational and other kinds of exposure to new modes of thought and behavior). The heightened importance of literacy came largely before 1939. Note that the regression coefficient for density is at its maximum in 1939, while that for literacy grows (and is statistically significant) throughout. All variables decline in importance somewhat in the sixties. Ethnicity differentials have declined substantially in importance since 1939.

Nothing has been said thus far of the *universality* of marriage for females, an important facet of the overall role of nuptiality in fertility, especially with respect to replacement of generations. Panel 4 of table 3-6 indicates that female non-marriage tends to be most frequent where sex ratios are low and in relatively modern and dense (urban) provinces.

Male nuptiality is complimentary to female in most respects. Relatively modern or dense areas have later marriage. Interestingly though, especially in light of our earlier discussion of migration-sex ratio-nuptiality relationships, the effect of sex ratios on male nuptiality is strong but reverses itself before and after 1939. Later male marriage associated with a scarcity of females (the classic frontier phenomena) characterized the prewar period, but relatively early male marriage has been associated with high sex ratios since then. This unexpected result invites further investigation. Finally, there has been an important and growing association between late marriage for males and density—probably a reflection of the growing impact of rural population pressure on chances of obtaining farms for owner or even tenant operation.

The old frontier (prewar) milieu included low proportions of males ever-marrying—clearly a consequence of high sex ratios. The areas with high sex ratios in 1960, however, had high proportions ever-marrying. Modern, dense areas had low proportions ever-marrying, though this was of declining importance by 1960.

Focusing again on the timing of female marriage, the regression coefficients in table 3-7 suggest interdependencies between the effects of individual variables on I_m. The regression coefficients in 1903 for the sex ratio, for example, are greater when other variables are controlled. This is true of economic level in 1903 as well, but the same controls cause the regression coefficient for percentage durable construction to decline in 1960. This is an indication that the apparent intensification of the effect of economic level over

---

[j]The proportion of total variation in x which is held in common with y is given by $(r_{xy})^2$, the square of the zero-order correlation coefficient.

Table 3-7

Regression Coefficients and Coefficients of Multiple Determination for Regressions of Index of Marriage Pattern ($I_m \times 1,000$) on Selected Independent Variables: 45 Provinces, 1903, 1939, 1960 and 1970

			INDEPENDENT VARIABLES		
Combination	(1) Sex Ratio	(2) % Durable	(3) Density	(4) Literacy	R^2
			1903		
(1)	0.13*	–	–	–	0.10
(2)	–	−0.35	–	–	0.02
(3)	–	–	−0.05	–	0.02
(4)	–	–	–	0.84*	0.02
(5)	0.26*	−2.97*	–	–	0.22
(6)	0.16*	–	−0.12	–	0.12
(7)	0.24*	–	–	−3.47	0.14
(8)	0.24*	–	−0.08	−2.73	0.13
(9)	0.31*	−2.51*	−0.04	−1.85	0.21
			1939		
(1)	0.13	–	–	–	0.06
(3)	–	–	−0.64	–	0.33
(4)	–	–	–	−2.28*	0.12
(6)	0.11*	–	−0.62	–	0.38
(7)	0.11	–	–	−2.14*	0.17
(8)	0.10*	–	−0.56*	−0.61	0.37
			1960		
(1)	1.14*	–	–	–	0.63
(2)	–	−3.26*	–	–	0.26
(3)	–	–	−0.33*	–	0.56
(4)	–	–	–	−2.33*	0.16
(5)	1.00*	−1.56*	–	–	0.67
(6)	0.79*	–	−0.20*	–	0.78
(7)	1.05*	–	–	−1.05*	0.65
(8)	0.78*	–	−0.19*	−0.29	0.77
(9)	0.78*	0.54	−0.22*	−0.34	0.77
			1970		
(1)	1.07*	–	–	–	0.40
(2)	–	−1.10*	–	–	0.13
(3)	–	–	−0.05*	–	0.13
(4)	–	–	–	−3.14*	0.23
(5)	0.96*	−0.49	–	–	0.41
(6)	0.97*	–	−0.03*	–	0.44
(7)	1.05*	–	–	−3.06*	0.63
(8)	1.00*	–	−0.01	−2.89*	0.63
(9)	0.98*	−0.12	−0.01	−2.86*	0.63

*Coefficient is more than twice its standard error.

time is at least partially spurious; it cannot be separated from the growing effects of other changes. On the other hand, controls have little or no effect on the magnitude of the coefficients for density.

The four variables acting together account for 21 percent of the total variation in I_m in 1903, but 77 percent in 1960, a change due largely to the growth of density effects before 1939 and of sex ratio effects since then. The overall effect declines slightly by 1970, despite an increase in the impact of female literacy. Three variables together (combination 8) account for 13 percent of all variation in 1903, 77 percent in 1960, and 63 percent in 1970.

Thus far we have considered only the overall effect of ethnicity, without regard to patterns for specific ethnic groups. In a nation of several score unique mother tongues and at least eight major language groups (Pascasio 1967), ethnicity is likely to be an important factor explaining inter-area differences in behavior. Because it is an important variable, and because ethnicity is poorly specified on so gross a level of aggregation as the province, we now turn to an examination of data for local administrative units—municipalities.

Sources of Local-Area Variation

Seeking a marriage partner can be viewed as a kind of market activity, carried out within a market area linking buyers and sellers of a specific kind of commodity. This supply and demand perspective (eg. Caldwell 1963) immediately suggests that for examining marriage behavior, local areas are much more appropriate units of analysis than are provinces. Localities probably correspond more closely to actual market areas—delimited territories within which most transactions or matches are carried out—than do larger units. The local sex ratio, for example, clearly is of greater relevance to available females in a locality than is the provincial ratio.

Also, municipalities are much more homogeneous than are provinces with respect to mother tongue. It is not unreasonable to conceive of an Ilocano or a Tagalog town as a social system creating pressures on individuals to conform to local prescriptions with respect to the timing of marriage.[k]

Another important reason for shifting the analysis to the municipal level is demonstrated by a simple exercise in analysis of variance. The province units conceal much internal spatial variation. Of the total intermunicipal variation (SS_T) in I_m, 42.2 percent is within-province variation (SS_W) which cannot be accounted for by province-level characteristics.

Nuptiality information for municipalities is only available for 1939. The local-area analysis that follows is confined to that date therefore, it describes

---

[k]Even more appropriate as analytic units defining social-normative systems would be *barrios* or even *sitios*. Data are not available for these units, however.

patterns and conditions in the first four decades of this century, and especially
in the decade or two preceding 1939. The dominant ethnic group in each
municipality, determined on the basis of 1939 census data on mother tongue,
is taken from Philippine Studies Program (1956: Vol. I, 265-81). The distribution of the 1,178 towns in 1939 by dominant mother tongue is given in
table 3-8 column 2.

Ethnic Differences Across Local Areas

The basic patterns of ethnic variation in nuptiality (I_m) are presented in
table 3-8.[1] The entries in columns 3 and 6 are mean values on I_m and mean
age at marriage (SMAM) within ethnic categories.[m] Deviations from the
national means in 1939 are shown in columns 4 and 7. These gross deviations
(no controls have been introduced as yet) indicate empirical differences across
ethnic areas arising from differences in cultural-social milieu in combination
with extant economic and other variations across areas.

The largest deviations are for towns dominated by Ilocanos, Pampangueños,
Pangasinan and the heterogeneous non-Christian ("Other") category. The two
Central Luzon minorities (rows 6 and 7) marry relatively late. Late marriage is
most pronounced among Ilocanos, where I_m falls to 10 percent below the
national level and SMAM is 1.8 years above the national means. The "Other"
category includes upland and mountain tribal groups for which we have only
ethnographic commentary, generally suggesting early marriage. The category
average for this group of towns corroborates this qualitative evidence. Only
three category means on I_m exceed the national: "Other," Bicolano and towns
dominated by Samar-Leyte speakers. These towns have mean ages at marriage
below the national level.

Do these gross deviations from national averages change in any substantial
manner (especially, do they diminish) when other potential correlates of ethnicity and marriage pattern are considered? Controls on the sex ratio, economic
level and educational level-literacy are introduced in columns 5 and 8.[n] The

---

[1]Note that on the municipal level we are able to deal with the eight major languages
and a heterogeneous category labeled "Other" (see table 3-9, column 1). The latter is
comprised largely of towns dominated by upland non-Christian tribes or Muslim cultural
groups.

[m]These values were obtained through dummy variable regression (Suits 1957).
Regression coefficients have been transformed manually to deviations from the overall
mean using the procedure described in Melichar (1965).

[n]The economic index (ECON) is the unweighted average of four related measures:
the percentages of families with a radio, electric lighting, piped water supply, and homes
of durable construction. Averaging proportionally reduces the error component, so that
ECON has a higher correlation with I_m than does any of its components. The same
rationale underlies LIT, the average of percentage literate (all persons age 10+) and percentage attending school (all persons age 6-19).

Table 3-8
Gross and Net Effects of Ethnicity on I_m and SMAM: 1,178 Municipalities in 1939

Ethnic Category	I_m				SMAM		
	N	Mean	Mean Deviations (Gross Effects)	Adjusted Deviations[a] (Net Effects)	Mean	Mean Deviations (Gross Effects)	Adjusted Deviations[a] (Net Effects)
(1)	(2)	(3)	(4)	(5)	(6)	(7)	(8)
1. TOTAL TOWNS	1178	0.777	0.000	0.000	21.56	0.00	0.00
2. Tagalog	215	0.767	-0.010	0.010	21.77	0.21	-0.26
3. Ilocano	173	0.708	-0.069	-0.038	23.35	1.79	1.11
4. Cebuano	218	0.749	-0.028	-0.028	21.88	0.32	0.32
5. Ilongo	100	0.746	-0.031	-0.033	21.92	0.37	0.41
6. Pampango	27	0.721	-0.056	-0.042	22.83	1.27	0.95
7. Pangasinan	15	0.717	-0.060	-0.023	23.33	1.77	0.95
8. Bicolano	82	0.790	0.013	0.010	21.29	-0.27	-0.22
9. Samar-Leyte	56	0.795	0.019	0.000	20.96	-0.60	-0.20
10. Other	292	0.858	0.081	0.049	19.16	-1.60	-0.88
11. Percentage of SS$_{total}$			32.5	56.9		30.8	55.0

[a]With controls for Sex ratio, ECON and LIT. See text footnote *n*, p. 48.

entries here are adjusted deviations—net effects.[o] A number of changes result.
Tagalog marriage, late relative to the national pattern, is fully accounted for
by the sex ratios and socioeconomic conditions in Tagalog towns. Marriage
occurs slightly earlier, in fact, than these characteristics would suggest. Ilocano
late marriage, on the other hand, is only partially accounted for by the characteristics of Ilocano towns. Visayan deviations (Cebuano and Ilongo) are
largely unaffected by the controls, while Pampangueño and Pangasinan late
marriage primarily reflects attributes of these towns other than ethnicity.
Recall that the last two localities are within the emerging Manila-Central Plain
area of late marriage which was indicated above. Bicolano, Samar-Leyte, and
non-Christian early marriage patterns partially reflect the relatively backward
character of these areas. The large positive deviation for non-Christian towns
is cut nearly in half by the controls.

These shifts notwithstanding, ethnicity must be regarded as a persistent
factor in local area nuptiality variations. Nearly one-third of the intermunicipal variation in I_m (32.5 percent) was accounted for by ethnic differences
in 1939. Comparing this figure with variation accounted for by the three control variables in combination (45.6 percent) and by ethnicity together with
these characteristics (56.9 percent), the net or uncorrelated effect of ethnicity
proves by subtraction (56.9-45.6) to be 11.3 percent.[p]

Marriage, Migration and Mother Tongue:
Ethnic Responses to the Frontier

Two of the major Philippine ethnic groups have engaged in extensive
migration during the twentieth century: the Ilocanos and the Cebuano-speak-
ing people of the Visayas. Of the 173 Ilocano-dominated towns in 1939, only
88 are in the Ilocano home provinces (Ilocos Norte and Sur, La Union and
Abra). Thirty-five towns are in the Cagayan Valley and another fifty in the
Central Plain (especially in Pangasinan, Nueva Ecija, and Zambales). Of 218
Cebuano-dominated towns, 139 are in the Visayas source area while 79 are in
Mindanao.

The extensive dispersion of these two groups makes it possible to examine
the responses of these ethnic groups to movement into a new environment and
a new structure of opportunities. It is readily apparent from table 3-9 that the

[o]The dependent variable and the controls are continuous, while ethnicity is entered
into the model as a classificatory independent variable. The model therefore is that of
multiple covariance analysis (Blalock 1972). See Blau and Duncan (1967: 128-52) for
a discussion of multiple regression, multiple covariance and multiple classification
analysis and the relationships among them.

[p]For another example of partitioning of variation in this way see Blau and Duncan
(1967: 132 ff.).

Table 3-9
Nuptiality Indexes for Ilocano and Cebuano Towns in Home and Frontier Areas: 1939

Ethnic Group and Location	N	I_m GROSS Mean	I_m GROSS Ratio: Frontier/Home	I_m NET[a] Mean	I_m NET[a] Ratio: Frontier/Home	SMAM GROSS Mean	SMAM GROSS Ratio: Frontier/Home	SMAM NET[a] Mean	SMAM NET[a] Ratio: Frontier/Home
(1)	(2)	(3)	(4)	(5)	(6)	(7)	(8)	(9)	(10)
1. ILOCANO	173	0.708	–	0.739	–	23.35	–	22.67	–
2. Home	88	0.659	1.000	0.703	1.000	24.32	1.000	23.47	1.000
3. Cagayan	35	0.772	1.170	0.770	1.100	21.96	0.900	21.99	0.940
4. Other Frontier	50	0.747	1.130	0.772	1.100	22.60	0.930	22.04	0.940
5. CEBUANO	218	0.749	–	0.749	–	21.88	–	21.88	–
6. Home	139	0.708	1.000	0.716	1.000	22.58	1.000	22.43	1.000
7. Frontier	79	0.819	1.140	0.803	1.120	20.65	910	21.00	0.940

[a]Controlling for sex ratio, ECON and LIT. See text footnote n, p. 48.

overall means for Ilocano and Cebuano towns in 1939 conceal major home-
frontier differences. Ilocano towns in frontier areas have an average I_m about
15 percent higher than that for Ilocano towns on the Ilocos Coast. There is
somewhat less difference in the mean age at marriage, indicating that the
frontier effect on proportions married is greatest at the most fertile ages. The
Cebuano home-frontier effect is quite similar: 14 percent for I_m, somewhat
less for the mean age at marriage. It is perhaps significant that the Ilocano and
Cebuano "responses" to their respective frontiers are so similar in magnitude
despite the fact that their initial (home) levels on I_m are different.

What are the factors at the root of this response to the frontier environment: demographic (the sex ratio), economic, social? The question is not
readily answered with the data at hand, but table 3-9 offers some clues. The
"net" values on I_m are adjusted means reflecting statistical controls on sex
ratio differences and on levels of ECON and LIT. Note that home-frontier
differences diminish when these factors are taken into account. Also notice,
however, that much of the empirical difference remains. Ilocano home-frontier
differences on I_m, for example, are only partially accounted for by differences
in the sex ratio and in economic level. These controls are even less effective
with Cebuano towns. An important research task for the future is to identify
the characteristics of frontier towns and of the frontier environment generally
which seem to promote early marriage.

A Prospectus

The central question about Philippine nuptiality necessarily focuses on the
likely course of female proportions single over the remainder of the twentieth
century. Will the trend we have described here continue?; at what pace, and
with what impact on the level of fertility?

Data from the NDS of 1973 indicate that the long-term trend in nuptiality
accelerated in the early 1970s. By 1973 the percentage single at age 20-24 had
reached 57.4, well above the 1970 level and nearly three-fourths again the proportion in 1903. The index of marriage pattern had reached .577, only three-
fourths its 1903 level. About one-third of the 1903-1973 change in I_m came in
the short period after 1960.

For a number of reasons this continued trend in the 1970s should not be
surprising. The social and economic forces operative throughout the century
have continued to gather momentum. The literacy level, for example, already
high in 1960, had increased by another 11 points by 1970. Of major importance is a continuing transition in female labor force participation,[q] especially

___
[q]See Rañoa (1972) and BCS (1972) and other years. Female labor force participation rates have risen between 1958 and 1968 (survey data are not available for earlier

in the white collar occupations. That this extra-familial activity has been a very important deterrent to early marriage is clear in the following figures from the 1968 NDS. Among women aged 30-59 in 1968 the mean age at union for those who had not had any work experience before marriage (about three women in ten) was 0.7 years below the mean for all women. Women who had been employed in a family enterprise (about four in ten) also married early—0.1 years below the average. However, those whose employment before marriage had drawn them outside the context of family and family enterprise into the non-familial world of wages and salaries married significantly later—1.7 years later than the overall average and 2.4 years later than women who had not worked before marriage at all. One married women in six in 1968 had had a wage or salary job before marriage. And the proportion of women currently with such a job continues to rise.[r]

While economic and social change of this kind is proceeding apace, the forms and consequences differ from place to place. The key early marriage areas of the past—the Mindanao and Cagayan Valley frontiers—are changing in character; by and large they are disappearing. Most of the open territory has been filled and rates of in-migration have tapered off. And, where in-movement continues a second stage has been reached, characterized by growing female in-movement, declining sex ratios, and later marriage for females.

The key late marriage areas, especially the Manila Region, the Central Plain, Cebu, and Iloilo, are expanding and intensifying their semi-modern character. The Manila Region, especially, is expanding outward quite rapidly. Metropolitan definitions now include from twenty to thirty or more munici-palities—extending from Malolos in Bulacan to Los Baños in Laguna. The planning region includes all the territory surrounding Laguna de Bay. Age at marriage throughout this area is rising rapidly. And in the remainder of the Central Plain age at marriage is rising nearly as fast. Here, as well as on the islands of Panay and Cebu, the determining factor may be modernizing change, or rising rural densities, or both these forces in combination. Whatever the mix of causal factors, the impetus for later marriage will surely grow throughout the remainder of the century. Marriage patterns can be expected to respond.

The Philippines is not the only country in Asia with changing fertility levels that must be attributed, wholly or in significant measure, to delayed marriage

---

dates), especially for women aged 25-44 (Rañoa 1972:5). The female shares of exper-ienced workforce and of higher-level occupational categories (professional and techni-cal, proprietors, white collar) have risen as well (Rañoa 1972: 14, 21).

[r]Compare BCSSH survey rounds for May of 1961 and 1971 (BCS 1961, BCS 1971). Employed women with wage or salary occupations were 29.9 percent of all employed women in 1961, 39.8 percent a decade later. The share of women self-employed or working as unpaid family workers declined from 68.9 to 60.1 percent. Professional or technical women reached 7.8 percent of the employed in 1971, up from 4.4 percent in 1961.

(Cho and Retherford 1973). There are two kinds of implication for policy. First, the possibility is raised of explicit policies to influence age at marriage— policies designed to accelerate the delay. In the Philippines programs directed toward generating female wage and salary employment are an attractive prospect. Second, whatever the impact of deliberate programs, a significant trend is already in progress. The impact of the national family planning program— directed as it is exclusively toward reducing rates of marital fertility—cannot be assessed adequately until nuptiality effects on overall fertility have been taken into account.

References

Agarwala, S.N. *Age at Marriage in India.* Alahabad: Kitab Mahab Private Ltd., 1962.

Blalock, Hubert M. *Social Statistics.* Second edition, New York: McGraw-Hill Book Company, 1972.

Blau, Peter M. and Otis Dudley Duncan. *The American Occupational Structure.* New York: John Wiley and Sons, Inc., 1967.

Caldwell, J.C. "Fertility Decline and Female Chances of Marriage in Malaya." *Population Studies* 17, 1 (July 1963): 20-32.

Carroll, John J. *Changing Patterns of Social Structure in the Philippines 1896-1963.* Quezon City: Ateneo de Manila University Press, 1968.

Cho, Lee-Jay and Robert D. Retherford. "Comparative Analysis of Recent Fertility Trends in East Asia." Paper prepared for the 1973 meeting of the International Union for the Scientific Study of Population, 1973.

Coale, Ansley J. "The Decline of Fertility in Europe from the French Revolution to World War II." In S.J. Behrman, Leslie Corsa Jr., and Ronald Freedman (eds.), *Fertility and Family Planning: A World View.* Ann Arbor: University of Michigan Press, 1969, pp. 3-24.

De la Costa, S.J., Horacio. *The Jesuits in the Philippines 1581-1768.* Cambridge: Harvard University Press, 1961.

De la Costa, S.J., Horacio. *Readings in Philippine History.* Manila: The Bookmark, Inc., 1965.

De la Costa, S.J., Horacio. *Asia and the Philippines.* Manila: Solidaridad Publishing House, 1967.

Dixon, Ruth B. "Explaining Cross-Cultural Variations in Age at Marriage and Proportions Never Marrying." *Population Studies* 25, 2 (July 1971): 215-233.

Duncan, Otis Dudley, R.P. Cuzzort, and B. Duncan. *Statistical Geography: Problems of Analyzing Areal Data.* Glencoe: The Free Press, 1961.

Flieger, Wilhelm and Peter C. Smith (eds.). *A Demographic Path to Modernity: Patterns of Early-Transition in the Philippines.* Quezon City; University of the Philippines Press, (in press).

Freedman, Ronald, Albert Hermalin, and T.H. Sun. "Fertility Trends in Taiwan: 1961-1970." *Population Index* 38, 2 (April-June 1972):141-166.

Fuchs, Roland J. and Telesforo W. Luna Jr. "Spatial Patterns of Socio-Economic Structure and Change in the Philippines, 1939-1960." Working Papers of the East-West Population Institute, No. 26. East-West Center, Honolulu, 1972.

Golay, Frank H. "The Philippine Economy." In George M. Guthrie (ed.), *Six Perspectives on the Philippines.* Manila: The Bookmark Inc., 1968, pp. 199-279.

Hajnal, John. "Age at Marriage and Proportions Marrying." *Population Studies,* November 7, 1953, pp. 111-36.

Hajnal, John. "European Marriage Patterns in Perspective." In D.V. Glass and D.E.C. Eversley (eds.), *Population in History: Essays in Historical Demography.* Chicago: Aldine Publishing Company, 1965, pp. 101-143.

Hooley, Richard W. "Long-Term Growth of the Philippine Economy, 1902-1961." *The Philippine Economic Journal* 7, 1 (First Semester, 1968): 1-24.

Kintanar, Agustin Jr., R.M. Bautista, M.B. Concepcion, J. Encarnacion Jr., M. Mangahas, V.B. Paqueo, and P.C. Smith. *Studies in Philippine Economic-Demographic Relationships.* Quezon City: Economic Research Associates Inc. and Institute of Economic Development and Research, 1974.

Larkin, John A. *The Pampangans: Colonial Society in a Philippine Province.* Berkeley: University of California Press, 1972.

Melichar, Emanuel. "Least Squares Analysis of Economic Survey Data." In *1965 Proceedings of the Business and Economic Statistics Section,* American Statistical Association. Washington: American Statistical Association, 1966, pp. 373-85.

Nag, Moni. *Factors Affecting Human Fertility in Nonindustrial Societies: A Cross-Cultural Study.* Yale University Publications in Anthropology, No. 66. New Haven: Human Relations Area Files Press, 1968.

Owen, Norman G. "The Principalia in Philippine History: Kabikolan, 1790-1898." IPC Papers, Quezon City: Ateneo de Manila University Press, (forthcoming).

Pascacio, Emy M. "The Language Situation in the Philippines from the Spanish Era to the Present." In Antonio G. Manuud (ed.), *Brown Heritage: Essays on Philippine Cultural Tradition and Literature.* Quezon City: Ateneo de Manila University Press, 1967, pp. 225-252.

Pascual, Elvira M. *Population Redistribution in the Philippines.* Manila: University of the Philippines, Population Institute, 1966.

Philippine Studies Program, University of Chicago. *Area Handbook on the Philippines,* Subcontractor's Monograph HRAF-16, Human Relations Area Files, Inc., 1956.

Philippines (Rep.), Bureau of the Census and Statistics [BCS]. *Census of the Philippines: 1960, Population and Housing.* Manila, 1963.

Philippines (Rep.), Bureau of the Census and Statistics [BCS]. *The BCS Survey of Households Bulletin.* "Labor Force," 1956-1972.

Rañoa, Milagros. "An Analysis of Working Force Activity in the Philippines, 1948-1968." Ph.D. dissertation, Department of Sociology, University of Chicago, 1972.

Sicat, Gerardo P. "Dimensions of Regional Growth, 1948-1966." In Gerardo P. Sicat, *Economic Policy and Philippine Development.* Quezon City: University of the Philippines Press, 1972, pp. 347-387.

Simkins, Paul D. and Frederick L. Wernstedt. "Growth and Internal Migrations of the Philippine Population, 1948 to 1960." *The Journal of Tropical Geography* 17 (May 1963): 197-202.

Smith, Peter C. "Age at Marriage: Trends and Prospects." *Philippine Sociological Review* 16, 1-2 (January-April, 1968): 1-16.

Smith, Peter C. "Areal Differentiation and Urbanization Process in Lowland Luzon." Ph.D. dissertation, Department of Sociology, University of Chicago, 1970.

Smith, Peter C. "Changing Nuptiality." In Wilhelm Flieger and Peter C. Smith (eds.). *A Demographic Path to Modernity: Patterns of Early-Transition in the Philippines.* Quezon City: University of the Philippines Press, (in press).

Suits, Daniel B. "The Use of Dummy Variables in Regression Equations." *Journal of the American Statistical Association* 52, (December 1957): 548-551.

United States Bureau of the Census [USBC]. *Census of the Philippine Islands.* Washington, D.C.: U.S. Government Printing Office, 1905. English and Spanish.

Vandermeer, Canute and Bernardo C. Agaloos. "Twentieth Century Settlement of Mindanao." *Papers of the Michigan Academy of Science, Arts, and Letters* 47 (1962): 537-548.

Wernstedt, Frederick L. and Paul D. Simkins. "Migration and the Settlement of Mindanao." *Journal of Asian Studies* 25, 1 (1965):83-103.

Wernstedt, Frederick L. and Joseph E. Spencer. *The Philippine Island World: A Physical, Cultural, and Regional Geography.* Berkeley: University of California Press, 1967.

Wickberg, Edgar. *The Chinese in Philippine Life: 1850-1898.* New Haven: Yale University Press, 1965.

4

The Demographic Situation in Malaysia

James A. Palmore, Ramesh Chander,
and *Dorothy Z. Fernandez*

For 150 years, heterogeneity and rapid change have characterized the demography of Malaya, Sabah, and Sarawak. In fact, the present demographic situation in Malaysia can only be understood by reference to this dynamic past. The present ethnic composition of the nation and its urban and rural distribution results from a long history of heavy immigration and from important ethnic differentials in fertility and mortality patterns.

Sustained rapid population growth is a recent phenomenon for much of the developing world. For West Malaysia rapid population growth has been evident since at least 1891, and probably started even earlier. Combined data from censuses and early estimates suggest that West Malaysia's population has been growing at yearly rates in excess of 2 percent since the early nineteenth century. Rapid population growth has also been occurring in Sabah and Sarawak, although it is difficult to establish exact dates for the onset of rapid growth.

Because of boundary changes and poorer data quality, East Malaysian long-range growth rates are likely to be more seriously in error than the rates for West Malaysia. Nevertheless, it does seem likely that high growth rates (averaging above 2 percent a year) did characterize Sabah prior to 1911 and Sarawak prior to 1947.

Determinants of Population Growth

Malaysia's population has grown quickly for so many years because the 1820-1970 period witnessed both heavy immigration and high rates of natural increase, with immigration playing a major role prior to World War II and natural increase playing a major role only from sometime after the 1920s.

Complete and accurate immigration figures for the entire 1820-1970 period are not available. Nevertheless, some knowledge of net migration can be found in census data and estimates that report separate totals for the major community groups of each area in Malaysia. Additional information is available from data on yearly arrivals and departures at the major Malaysian ports. Accurate data on fertility and mortality are only available for very recent years (table 4-1), and complete registration has still not been obtained in Sabah and Sarawak. However, some knowledge of fertility and mortality conditions can be obtained from other sources including survey data and estimates from censuses.

Table 4-1
Crude Birth, Death, and Natural Increase Rates Based on Registration for West Malaysia, Sabah, and Sarawak: 1911-1970[e]

Year	West Malaysia			East Malaysia-Sabah			East Malaysia-Sarawak		
	Crude Birth Rate	Crude Death Rate	Crude Rate of Natural Increase[c]	Crude Birth Rate	Crude Death Rate	Crude Rate of Natural Increase	Crude Birth Rate	Crude Death Rate	Crude Rate of Natural Increase
1911	n.a.[b]	46.3[a]	n.a.	n.a.	n.a.	n.a.	n.a.	n.a.	n.a.
1921-1925	28.5[b]	26.4[b]	2.1[b]	n.a.	n.a.	n.a.	n.a.	n.a.	n.a.
1926-1930	34.6[b]	28.7[b]	5.9[b]	n.a.	n.a.	n.a.	n.a.	n.a.	n.a.
1932-1935	37.2	21.7	15.5	n.a.	n.a.	n.a.	n.a.	n.a.	n.a.
1936-1940	40.7	20.5	20.2	n.a.	n.a.	n.a.	n.a.	n.a.	n.a.
1941-1945	n.a.	n.a.	n.a.	n.a.	n.a.	n.a.	n.a.	n.a.	n.a.
1946	36.8	21.0	15.8	13.1	11.9	1.2	n.a.	n.a.	n.a.
1947	43.2	19.5	23.7	20.0	15.5	4.5	13.7	6.2	7.5
1948	40.5	16.3	24.2	19.8	13.4	6.4	11.5	5.2	6.3
1949	44.0	14.3	29.7	23.3	12.3	11.0	16.9	6.4	10.5
1950	42.3	15.9	26.4	28.0	11.9	16.1	21.3	11.2	10.1
1951	44.0	15.4	28.6	30.7	13.2	17.5	23.4	8.6	14.8
1952	45.0	13.8	31.2	32.7	12.6	20.1	25.9	9.3	16.6
1953	44.4	12.6	31.8	31.0	12.2	18.8	25.1	8.4	16.7
1954	44.6	12.4	32.2	32.7	10.6	22.1	23.5	7.2	16.2
1955	44.0	11.7	32.3	31.0	10.8	20.2	21.3	6.7	14.6
1956	46.7	11.6	35.2	31.1	9.8	21.3	23.4	6.1	17.3
1957	46.2	12.4	33.7	36.1	9.1	27.0	22.2	6.2	16.0
1958	43.3	11.0	32.3	38.4	7.6	30.8	26.3	5.7	20.6
1959	42.2	9.7	32.4	30.4	7.3	23.1	25.3	5.7	19.6
1960	40.9	9.5	31.4	35.3	8.3	27.0	25.1	5.8	19.3
1961	41.9	9.2	32.7	35.6	6.6	29.0	25.9	5.2	20.7
1962	40.4	9.4	31.0	34.7	6.9	27.8	29.0	5.0	24.0

Table 4-1 (cont.)

Year	West Malaysia			East Malaysia-Sabah			East Malaysia-Sarawak		
	Crude Birth Rate	Crude Death Rate	Crude Rate of Natural Increase[c]	Crude Birth Rate	Crude Death Rate	Crude Rate of Natural Increase	Crude Birth Rate	Crude Death Rate	Crude Rate of Natural Increase
1963	39.4	9.0	30.5	33.9	5.8	28.1	25.8	5.5	20.3
1964	39.1	8.1	31.1	35.4	5.5	29.9	27.3	5.1	22.2
1965	36.7	7.9	28.8	35.8	5.5	30.3	28.0	5.0	23.0
1966	37.3	7.6	29.7	36.9	5.9	31.0	28.9	4.8	24.1
1967	35.3	7.5	27.8	36.9	5.9	31.0	27.8	4.8	23.0
1968	35.2	7.6	27.7	39.1	5.0	34.1	29.0	4.8	24.2
1969	33.0[d]	7.2	25.8[d]	37.0	4.9	32.1	28.5	4.8	23.7
1970	33.8[d]	7.3[d]	26.5[e]	35.7	5.6	30.1	n.a.	n.a.	n.a.

[a] Penang and Malacca only

[b] Six states only (Penang, Malacca, Perak, Pahang, Negri Sembilan, and Selangor). These figures are weighted averages of separate rates reported separately for Penang, Malacca, and Singapore and for Perak, Penang, Negri Sembilan, and Selangor.

[c] Differences due to rounding.

[d] Adjusted to use 1970 census total as denominator.

[e] Sources are United Nations 1951, United Nations 1955, United Nations 1970, MacGregor 1948, and Department of Statistics 1972.

Before the Second World War, international migration was the primary cause of rapid population growth in Malaysia. Most of Malaysia's present population are either immigrants or the descendants of immigrants who arrived between the middle of the eighteenth century and 1940. During the years covered by census data, most of the immigrants were Chinese, Indians, and Pakistanis, although more limited immigration of Malays also occurred. Heavy immigration into Malaysia was very much tied to British colonial interests; Chinese and Indian laborers were encouraged to come to Malaya to exploit the agricultural and mining resources of the sparsely settled peninsual. As the British oversaw the development of the Straits Settlements in the early 1800s, substantial immigration occurred. As British interests extended to the Federated Malay States in the late 1800s, migration accelerated there to supply labor for rubber estates and tin mining (Ginsburg and Roberts 1958: Chapters 2 and 3). Later, Chinese and Indian labor was also imported into the Unfederated Malay States, and Chinese labor into Sabah and Sarawak.

The heavy migration covered many years and the timing varied for the different regions and ethnic groups. For Malaya, Smith distinguishes two broad phases of migration. From the beginning of the British period to World War I, migration was the primary cause of rapid population growth as death rates were high and high sex ratios led to low fertility. Between the two World wars, significant migration continued but contributed proportionately less to population growth when death rates declined and fertility increased as sex ratios generally approached a more normal balance (Smith 1952: 1-2). With the beginning of the Second World War, the period of significant migration ended and large-scale migration has not resumed since then. The exact migration volume is impossible to establish.

While accurate measurement of immigration is not feasible, it is somewhat easier to measure the effects as reflected in the composition of the population. As late as 1921, almost half of Malaya's population was foreign born, with three-fourths of the Chinese and nine-tenths of the Indians and Pakistanis having been born outside Malaya or Singapore. More recently, a higher percentage of the population was native born, although almost a third of the Chinese, Indians, and Pakistanis in Malaya in 1957 and a fifth of the Chinese in Sabah and Sarawak in 1960 were foreign born.

By 1970, the effect of heavy immigration was evident only in the resultant ethnic composition of the nation. Sex ratios were only slightly higher than one would expect for a population unaffected by migration; the age distribution showed effects of migration only in the oldest age groups; and the percentage foreign born had declined to lower levels. While tangible social and political effects undoubtedly remain from the heavy migration periods, the demographic effects of the migration are no longer critical except insofar as the ethnic composition of Malaysia is unusual and the fact that these ethnic groups do have distinctly different fertility and mortality patterns.

Mortality Levels

Between the First World War and 1947, the primary cause of rapid population growth shifted from immigration to natural increase as death rates declined.
In the period before vital registration statistics were available, mortality was
undoubtedly high. Even the first registered figures record high rates: the
registered crude death rate for the Straits Settlements was 46.3 in 1911 and
rates close to thirty were reported in six states between 1921 and 1930 (table
4-1).

By 1970, the West Malaysian crude death rate was 7.3, and the United Nations
Population Division estimates a crude death rate of 12.5 and a life expectancy at
birth of 55 for East Malaysia in 1965-1970 (United Nations 1972: 127). While it
is clear that mortality has declined from pre-transition levels, the precise rate of
decrease and the dates of the onset cannot be accurately ascertained. This is
especially true for East Malaysia.

Recent mortality trends for West Malaysia are more definitively established.
Registered crude death rates from 1946 to 1970 show a steady decline from 21.0
to 7.3. Using the registration and census data, we have also prepared a new series
of life tables.[a] These newly calculated life tables for 1947, 1957, and 1970 show
an increase in female life expectancy at birth from forty-six to sixty-six over the
1947-1970 period. Life expectancy for the combined male and female population
increased from forty-six to sixty-four (table 4-2). All these data show a very rapid
mortality decline.

While mortality was already low by 1970, it is likely to decline even further.
The 1970 life expectancies still showed significant differentials between the major
ethnic groups (female life expectancies at birth were seventy-one Chinese, sixty-
three for Malays, and sixty-one for Indians or Pakistanis). Moreover, life expectancies in the four largest cities were somewhat higher than those for the whole of
West Malaysia (male and female life expectancies at birth of sixty-four for all West
Malaysia and expectancies of sixty-five to sixty-nine for the major cities—see
table 4-2). If one assumes at a minimum that the groups with lower life expectancies will attain the mortality levels of the groups with the highest expectancies,
then mortality will decline even further.

In the twenty-three year period covered by these life tables, there has already
been some convergence in mortality conditions for the three ethnic groups: The
1947 difference between the lowest and highest female life expectancies at birth

---

[a]Previous life tables include those in Fell (1960) and in annual vital statistics reports
from the Department of Statistics beginning with 1966. The new life tables use a consistent methodology (Keyfitz 1966) to maximize comparability over time and hence
differ somewhat from earlier reported figures. For 1947, Smith's age-specific death rates
were used with the 1947 census base population. For 1957 and 1970, the basic data were
registered age-specific deaths and census base populations (the adjusted census age distribution for 1957). The authors are indebted to Ward Mardfin for assistance in preparing
these new life tables.

Table 4-2
Mortality Rates and Life Expectations, West Malaysia 1947-1970 and Major Cities in West Malaysia, 1970: By Community Group[a]

Mortality Rate and Community Group	West Malaysia			Major Cities: 1970			
	1947	1957	1970	Kuala Lumpur	Georgetown	Ipoh	Johore Bahru
Crude Death Rate							
Total	19.5	12.4	7.3	4.9	7.1	5.1	4.4
Malays	24.6	15.0	7.6	3.7	5.7	3.8	3.9
Chinese	14.3	9.7	6.5	5.1	7.1	5.2	4.6
Indians or Pakistanis	15.7	11.1	8.2	5.7	8.1	5.7	7.1
e_0 *for Females*							
Total	46.4	55.9	65.8	n.a.	n.a.	n.a.	n.a.
Malays	40.6	51.2	63.4	n.a.	n.a.	n.a.	n.a.
Chinese	56.8	63.3	70.7	n.a.	n.a.	n.a.	n.a.
Indians or Pakistanis	45.3	53.2	61.4	n.a.	n.a.	n.a.	n.a.
e_0 *for Males and Females*							
Total	45.7	54.6	63.7	67.6	64.7	69.0	68.6
Malays	40.4	50.5	62.5	66.1	64.5	68.4	67.8
Chinese	52.6	59.8	67.0	69.4	65.9	70.3	70.6
Indians or Pakistanis	48.5	55.0	59.6	64.5	61.1	64.9	(62.5)[b]

[a]Basic data from Smith, 1952, Fell, 1960, Del Tufo, 1949, Department of Statistics, 1972, MacDonald, 1959, and unpublished preliminary tabulations of the 1970 Census. These are from newly prepared life tables calculated using techniques suggested by Keyfitz (1966).
[b]1970 figures for Indians and Pakistanis in Johore Bahru based on relatively few cases.

was sixteen years whereas the 1970 difference was nine years. Additional convergence in the future is likely to mean lower mortality rates for all West Malaysia.

Fertility Levels

As mortality declined it is likely that Malaysian fertility rates first showed an increase before beginning to decline. This assertion must be viewed as tentative, however, as data on Malaysian fertility before very recent years must be interpreted with caution.

For East Malaysia, little can be said. In the 1956-1960 period, the official registration system recorded an average crude birth rate of 34.3 for Sabah and 24.5 for Sarawak. For the same years, estimates using the Bogue-Palmore regression equations (Bogue and Palmore 1964) range from 41.8 to 43.4 for Sabah and from 40.1 to 46.0 for Sarawak. These figures suggest that 1956-1960 birth registration was no more than 83 percent complete in Sabah and 61 percent complete in Sarawak. For more recent years, the United Nations Population Division has estimated crude birth rates of 48.0 for both Sabah and Sarawak in the 1965-1970 period (United Nations 1972: 127).[b] Their estimates suggest even more extreme under-registration as late as 1965-1970: 77 percent completeness in Sabah and 58 percent in Sarawak.

For West Malaysia also, long-run fertility trends are difficult to evaluate because of under-registration and past heavy immigration. The immigrants were primarily young males for early periods, leading to very imbalanced sex ratios for both the total population and for the childbearing years.

Smith (1952) and others have asserted that crude birth rates increased in the early part of this century as imbalanced sex ratios moved towards a more usual balance of men and women. If this is true, it cannot be easily documented. Malaya's registered rates do show an increase from 28.5 (six states only) in 1921-1925 to 37.2 in 1932-1935 (the first period of registration figures for all Malaya) to 46.7 in 1956. Most of this measured increase is probably due to improving registration and perhaps some of the increase is due to a changing sex ratio. After 1931, however, little of the increase can be attributed to the age and sex distribution. The proportion of the total population who were women aged 15-49 was higher in 1931 than it was in 1970: fully 50 percent of the women in the 1931 population were in the childbearing years (as compared to 41 percent in 1970), and the percentage currently married in the young ages was higher in 1931 than in later years (see table 4-3). Unless one makes the unlikely assumption that marital fertility rates decreased between 1931 and

---

[b]The 1970 age distribution for East Malaysia is unavailable at this time. As a consequence, Bogue-Palmore estimates cannot be prepared for the 1960-1970 period.

Table 4-3
Percentage of West Malaysian Women Currently Married By Five-Year Age
Groups: 1957, 1966-1967, and 1967

	Ages of Women						
Year	15-19	20-24	25-29	30-34	35-39	40-44	45-49
Percent Currently Married:							
1931[a]	49%	85%	91%	89%	85%	75%	68%
1947[b]	38%	79%	88%	87%	84%	75%	68%
1957[c]	35%	75%	90%	91%	88%	81%	72%
1966-1967 (Family Survey)[d]	24%	65%	86%	90%	84%	86%	74%
1967-1968 (Socio-Economic Survey)[e]	18%	59%	85%	91%	90%	85%	78%

[a]Calculated from Vlieland, 1933, pp. 232-233.
[b]Calculated from Del Tufo, 1949, pp. 206-259.
[c]Calculated from Fell, 1960, Table 6, p. 72.
[d]Source is Cho, Palmore, and Saunders, 1968, p. 739.
[e]Sources are Chander, 1973, p. 12 and Cho, 1969, p. 7.

1970, it is clear that crude birth rates were severely under-registered before recent years. As a consequence, the increase in fertility that may have accompanied improving sex ratios was unrecorded and can only remain a plausible speculation.

In more recent periods, West Malaysian fertility becomes easier to trace. While registration was still incomplete in 1947, estimates combined with the registration system do permit an analysis of the beginning fertility decline in Malaysia. Rates appear to have increased slightly from 1947 to 1957 (table 4-4), but fertility began to decline in 1956 or 1957. Since census data allow calculation of important age and marital status measures, the present analysis of the decline starts with 1957.

West Malaysian Fertility from 1957 to 1970

Between 1957 and 1970, the West Malaysian crude birth rate declined by at least 27 percent—from an officially recorded figure of 46.2 in 1957 to

Table 4-4
Fertility Rates for West Malaysia: 1957-1970

Year	Crude Birth Rate	Crude Birth Rate Adjusted for Under-Registration	Gross Repro-duction Rate	Total Fertility Rate[a]	Age-Specific Fertility Rates for Woman of Ages:[g]					
					15-19	20-24	25-29	30-34	35-39	40-44
1947[b]	43.2[c]	47.2[f]	3.28[f]	n.a.	n.a.	n.a.	n.a.	n.a.	n.a.	n.a.
1957	46.2[d]	—	3.23[h]	6660	123	329	347	272	182	79
1957	—	49.1[f]	3.59	7255	145	371	371	297	187	80
1960	40.9[d]	n.a.	n.a.	6110	125	278	323	257	154	85
1962	40.4[d]	n.a.	n.a.	5860	103	277	333	237	154	68
1965	36.7[d]	n.a.	n.a.	5515	83	265	292	241	157	65
1967	35.3[d]	n.a.	n.a.	5230	71	231	289	221	166	68
1970	33.8[e]	n.a.	n.a.	4975	57	235	277	225	143	58

[a]Rates for women 45-49 have been omitted because they are unavailable in estimates for 1960, 1962, 1965, and 1967.

[b]Table 4-1 utilizes Saw's (1967b) estimates for 1947. Tables 4-12 and 4-13 utilize Smith's (1952) estimates for 1947. Saw does not present 1947 estimates by community group. Smith does not present 1947 estimates for the total population.

[c]Source is MacGregor, 1948. p. 9.

[d]Source is Department of Statistics, 1972, p. 5.

[e]Adjusted to use 1970 census total as denominator instead of 1970 estimates as previously published in official department of statistics publications.

[f]Source is Saw, 1967b, p. 118.

[g]TFR and ASFR for 1957 calculated from Fell (1960) and from Saw (1967b); for 1960-1967 from Cho (1969); 1970 by Palmore, Chander, and Fernandez.

[h]Calculated from Fell, 1960, p. 42, by combining the age-specific rates for each community group and multiplying by the proportion of births female in 1957.

33.8 in 1970. Since estimates by Saw and Cho indicate that the completeness of
the birth registration system was improving during the same time period, official
figures understate the decline.

One estimate for 1957 (Saw 1967) was that birth registration was only 92.3
percent complete. For 1967, Cho (1969) estimated 98 percent completeness.
Assuming that vital registration was essentially complete by 1970, the crude
birth rate declined by over 30 percent between 1957 and 1970. The decline has
resulted primarily from the combination of two factors: a decline in the proportion of women married in the ages 15-24 and declines in the fertility of currently
married women. This conclusion is based on a rather extensive set of calculations
using several different data sources.

The 1957-1970 decline in the crude birth rate is reflected in an almost equally
large percentage decline in the total fertility rate. In fact, age-specific fertility
rates declined at all ages between fifteen and forty-four (table 4-4). The actual
percentage decline depends on whether we use Fell's estimates of 1957 age-specific rates (Fell 1960), which do not correct for under-registration or those of
Saw (1967b), who corrected for both under-registration and estimated undercounts in the 1957 census. Either set of figures is an estimate, since tabulations
of live births by age of mother did not begin until after the census and 1958
was the first full year for which the tabulations are available. For the 1970
rates, the present authors have chosen to calculate rates with no adjustments
to either the 1970 registration or census data. While both under-registration of
births and census undercounts are likely, good estimates of the extent of these
errors are not yet available. The unadjusted 1970 calculations are likely to overstate the fertility rates, since the percentage of undercounting in the census
undoubtedly exceeds the percentage of birth under-registration. As a consequence of these methodological decisions, the data reported here understate
the 1957-1970 fertility decline. The minimum decline in the total fertility rate
was somewhere between 24 and 31 percent, from a high in 1957 of 6,660 (Fell)
or 7,255 (Saw) to 4,975.

The 1957-1970 fertility declines are not due to changes in the age structure
of the population. Between 1957 and 1970, there was no substantial change in
the proportion of women in the childbearing ages. In both 1957 and 1970, 41
percent of the female population was between the ages of fifteen and forty-five.
As a percentage of the total population, women 15-44 years old were roughly
20 percent in both 1957 and 1970. Within the 15-44 year age range, however,
the 1970 population did have somewhat more concentration in the 15-24 age
range. A series of standardizations reported in table 4-5 show that less than a
twentieth of the fertility decline can be attributed to age structure changes.
For example, if one assumes the 1957 (adjusted) age distribution had prevailed
into 1970, the crude birth rate would have been 34.4 in 1970 instead of 33.8,
leading to an estimated 26 percent decline instead of the actual 27 percent
decline. Changes in marital patterns, however, have contributed substantially.

Table 4-5
West Malaysian Crude Birth Rate Standardized on the Age Distributions of 1957 and 1970: By Community Group

| | All West Malaysia | | | | Malaya | | | | Chinese | | | | Indians or Pakistanis | | | |
| | Crude Birth Rate[c] | CBR Directly Standardized on Basis of: | | | Crude Birth Rate[c] | CBR Directly Standardized on Basis of: | | | Crude Birth Rate[c] | CBR Directly Standardized on Basis of: | | | Crude Birth Rate[c] | CBR Directly Standardized on Basis of: | | |
Year		1957 Age Distribution (adjusted)[a]	1957 Age Distribution (unadjusted)[b]	1970 Age Distribution		1957 Age Distribution (adjusted)[a]	1957 Age Distribution (unadjusted)[b]	1970 Age Distribution		1957 Age Distribution (adjusted)[a]	1957 Age Distribution (unadjusted)[b]	1970 Age Distribution		1957 Age Distribution (adjusted)[a]	1957 Age Distribution (unadjusted)[b]	1970 Age Distribution
Birth Rates:																
1957	46.2	46.2	46.2	46.2	48.1	48.1	48.1	43.3	43.3	43.3	43.3	47.2	49.7	49.7	49.7	54.2
1960	40.9	42.1	42.7	42.4	43.3	47.9	47.4	43.6	37.5	34.9	36.4	39.9	43.4	43.0	45.2	47.3
1962	40.4	40.4	41.0	40.4	43.0	45.5	45.1	41.1	37.3	35.0	36.6	40.0	41.5	37.8	39.8	41.5
1965	36.7	37.9	38.4	37.9	39.1	45.2	44.7	40.7	34.1	29.7	31.0	34.2	37.8	33.8	35.6	36.5
1967	35.3	35.6	36.1	35.4	38.2	42.8	42.4	38.3	32.5	26.6	27.7	30.5	35.3	31.8	33.4	34.7
1970	33.8	34.0	34.4	33.8	35.3	39.5	39.1	35.3	31.9	27.8	29.1	31.9	32.2	29.8	31.3	32.2

[a] Source is Fell, 1960, p. 45.

[b] Source is Fell, 1960, p. 58-61.

[c] Crude Birth Rates for 1957-1967 are taken from Department of Statistics, 1972. 1970 rates are adjusted to use 1970 Census totals as denominators instead of the 1970 estimates as previously published in official Department of Statistics publications.

The proportion of women married in the younger age groups has been declining since 1931 (table 4-3). Between 1957 and around 1967, declines in the percentage married in the youngest age groups (and rising ages at marriage) have been especially swift. Since marital status data from the 1970 census have not been tabulated to date, survey estimates must be used. The most recent estimates precede the census by three to four years. Unfortunately, two surveys taken twelve months apart give different estimates of the marital structure. The 1966-1967 West Malaysian Family Survey recorded as currently married 24 percent of the women aged 15-19 and 65 percent of those 20-24. The 1967-1968 Socio-Economic Survey reports figures of 18 percent and 59 percent for the same age groups. While the difference of one year in the reference period and sampling error in both surveys may account for part of the difference, non-sampling errors may be more significant.

Between 1957 and around 1967, the percentage of women currently married decreased between 31 and 49 percent for women aged 15-19 and between 13 and 21 percent for women aged 20-24, depending on which survey estimate is used. Smaller decreases occurred in the ages 25-34 and small increases occurred in the later years of the reproductive period (table 4-3).

Using the two sets of survey data to provide a range, we estimate that 30 to 53 percent of the 1957-1967 crude birth rate decline can be accounted for by changes in the marital structure. These estimates are based on standardizations using the 1957 age and marital status distribution and two separate estimates of 1967 marital fertility. For both estimates of marital fertility, Cho's 1967 age-specific estimates were used (Cho 1969) and only the percentage married in each group was varied to fit the estimates from the two different surveys (table 4-6).

With either survey estimate, the effect of changes in the proportion married is clearly a significant one, but it is still true that at least 40 percent (using the Socio-Economic Survey data) of the 1957-1967 fertility decline was due to changes in marital fertility. Part of this marital fertility decline may be due to the increasing use of family planning, although this is hard to substantiate prior to 1967. The West Malaysian Family Survey, the baseline survey for the national family planning program which began in 1967, was not taken until 1960-1967. By that date, only 14 percent of the currently married women 15-44 years old had ever used contraception or sterilizaton and 8 percent were currently using contraception or were sterilized. There were indications, however, that the potential demand for family planning information and services was extensive (see table 4-7). Little diffusion of family planning had occurred by 1966-1967 (see Palmore, Hirsch, and Ariffin 1971). Both ever use and current use were somewhat higher (16 percent and 11 percent respectively) for women in the 25-34 age range.

Between 1966-1967 and 1970, family planning use increased significantly. The Post Enumeration Survey of the 1970 census included some indicators of

Table 4-6

1967 West Malaysian Crude Birth Rate Standardized on the 1957 Age and Marital Status Distribution, Percentage Change in the Rates 1957-1967 and Percentage of Decline 1957-1967 Due to Changes in the Age and Marital Status Distribution

| | YEAR | | | Percentage Change 1957-1967 | |
| | 1957 | 1967 | | | |
Birth Rates and Percentage of Decline Due to Changes in the Age and Marital Status Distribution		Using 1967-1968 Socio-Economic Survey Estimates of % Married to Estimate 1967 Marital ASFR[a]	Using 1966-1967 Family Survey Estimates of % Married to Estimate 1967 Marital ASFR[a]	Using 1967-1968 Socio-Economic Survey of % Married to Estimate 1967 Marital ASFR[a]	Using 1966-1967 Family Survey Estimates of % Married to Estimate 1967 Marital ASFR[a]
Crude Birth Rate	46.2	35.3	35.3	-24	-24
Birth Rates Standardized on Unadjusted 1957 Census Age Distribution[b]	46.2	36.1	36.1	-22	-22
Birth Rate Standardized on 1957 Census Age and Marital Status Distribution[b]	46.2	41.9	39.4	-9	-15
Percentage of Decline in the birth rate due to changes in:					
Age distribution				7[c]	7[d]
Marital status distribution				53[c]	30[d]
Age and marital status distribution				61	38

[a]The implied marital age-specific fertility rates are as follows:

Ages	1967-68 SES % Married	1966-67 FS % Married
15-19	397	295
20-24	390	355
25-29	341	336
30-34	242	246
35-39	185	198
40-44	80	79

[b]Source is Fell, 1960, p. 72. Using the adjusted 1957 census figures gives lower percentages of the 1957-1967 decline due to changes in the age and marital status distribution.
[c]Do not add to 61% due to rounding.
[d]Do not add to 38% due to rounding.

Table 4-7

West Malaysia, 1966-1967: Proportion of Wives 35-44 Who Approve of Family Planning, Who Have Heard About One or More Methods of Family Planning, and Who Know Where to Get Information, by Stratum and Other Characteristics[b]

(All figures are expressed in percentages)

Age and Selected Characteristics	Metropolitan			Non-Metropolitan Urban			Rural			Total West Malaysia		
	Approve of family planning	Have heard of one or more methods	Know where to get information	Approve of family planning	Have heard of one or more methods	Know where to get information	Approve of family planning	Have heard of one or more methods	Know where to get information	Approve of family planning	Have heard of one or more methods	Know where to get information
A. Previous Fertility												
0-2 children	61	74	55	70	45	32	49	14	10	54	28	20
3-5 children	71	78	51	76	65	42	63	19	14	66	34	24
6 or more children	69	82	61	74	72	49	68	26	11	69	43	26
B. Race of Respondent's Father												
Malay	59	67	62	74	56	42	64	20	11	65	26	17
Chinese	70	86	56	76	72	41	71	46	21	73	72	43
Indian or Pakistani	67	60	43	69	56	53	38	7	3	50	27	21
C. Education of Respondent												
No formal education	60	72	43	68	49	31	63	19	10	64	27	15
1-5 years of school	71	82	61	82	80	57	58	30	22	67	53	39
6 or more years of school	78	89	72	81	95	65	a	a	a	76	86	62
D. Respondent's Desires for More Children												
Wants more children	64	72	51	71	51	24	55	15	11	57	22	15
Does not want more	70	80	58	75	67	47	69	28	13	70	46	29
All wives 35-44	68	79	56	74	64	43	62	21	12	65	37	24

[a]Fewer than twenty cases.
[b]Source is Palmore, 1969.

family planning knowledge, attitudes, and practices (KAP) for comparison with the 1966-1967 baseline data. Early tabulations show that three times as many currently married women 15-44 years old were using oral tablets in 1970 (12 percent) than were using them in 1966-1967 (4 percent). By 1970, a fifth of the women aged 25-34 were currently using some contraceptive method (table 4-8.

Differentials in Fertility and the Fertility Decline in West Malaysia

The recent fertility decline has not occurred uniformly among different segments of the population. Cho estimated a 10 percent decline in the total fertility rate for rural areas from 1958 to 1967 as compared to declines closer to 30 percent for metropolitan and urban areas (table 4-9). Both before and after the decline, urban fertility was substantially lower than rural fertility. Our own calculations show that significant urban-rural fertility differentials remain in 1970.

There were also ethnic differentials in the decline and 1970 data still show substantial fertility differences between the Chinese, who have the lowest fertility rates (a total fertility rate of 4,745), and the Malays with the highest (a total fertility rate of 5,150—see tables 4-10, 4-11, and 4-12). Between 1957 and 1970, Indian fertility declined most, Chinese second most, and Malay the least. The differential participation in the decline completely altered the rank order in fertility rates. In 1957, Indian fertility was highest, Chinese second, and Malay third. In 1970, Malay fertility was highest, Indian fertility was second, and Chinese fertility was lowest.[c]

For the separate ethnic groups, we must modify our earlier statements (for the total population) about the effects of changes in the age, sex, and marital status distribution on fertility. Changes in the age distribution between 1957 and 1970 were different for each ethnic group. For the Malays, a substantial percentage of the 1957-1970 fertility decline was due to changes in age structure (approximately one-third). For the Chinese and Indians, the 1970 age distribution was favorable to high fertility (relative to the 1957 age distribution) and age standardized crude birth rates indicate greater declines than the unstandardized rates (table 4-5). It is likely that changes in marriage ages have also differed by ethnic group (Palmore and Ariffin 1969; Chander 1973), but a full assessment of these effects must await publication of the 1970 census marital status data.

---

[c]Note, however, that this ranking does not hold for all areas in West Malaysia. For example, this rank order holds for only two of the four largest towns (table 4-13).

Table 4-8
West Malaysia, 1966-1967 and 1970: Mean Number of Live Births, Mean Number of Children Wife Wants, Percentage Who Have Ever Used Contraception, and Percentage Who are Currently Using Contraception: By Age and Place of Current Residence[a]

Age and Selected Fertility and KAP Indicators	All West Malaysia		Place of Current Residence Metropolitan		Other Urban Areas		Rural	
	1966/7	1970	1966/7	1970	1966/7	1970	1966/7	1970
Ages 15-24								
Mean No. of Live Births	1.9	1.6	1.6	1.4	1.6	1.5	1.9	1.6
Mean No. Children Wife Wants[b]	4.4	4.1	3.8	3.6	4.2	4.0	4.5	4.1
% Ever Used Contraception[c]	10%	20%	30%	35%	17%	28%	7%	16%
% Currently Using Contraception[c]	5%	12%	22%	19%	11%	16%	3%	10%
Ages 25-34								
Mean No. of Live Births	4.3	4.1	3.5	3.4	4.1	3.7	4.5	4.4
Mean No. Children Wife Wants[b]	5.3	4.5	4.3	3.9	4.9	4.3	5.6	4.8
% Ever Used Contraception[c]	16%	33%	43%	51%	34%	41%	6%	27%
% Currently Using Contraception[c]	11%	20%	33%	32%	26%	25%	3%	16%
Ages 35-44								
Mean No. of Live Births	5.8	6.0	5.6	5.3	6.0	6.0	5.8	6.2
Mean No. Children Wife Wants[b]	5.3	4.9	4.4	4.3	4.9	4.8	5.6	5.1
% Ever Used Contraception[c]	14%	26%	41%	37%	25%	34%	6%	21%
% Currently Using Contraception[c]	9%	14%	32%	20%	19%	19%	1%	12%

[a]Sources are: Department of Statistics, 1971, pp. 35 and 37, and National Family Planning Board of Malaysia, 1968, p. 25.

[b]Comments on the validity of this index are found in National Family Planning Board of Malaysia, 1968, Chapter 2. The index is included here partly because it is one of a very few indices available for both 1966-1967 and 1970.

[c]For 1966 and 1967, figures include those currently sterilized. For 1970, it is not stated in source whether sterilization is included or excluded.

Table 4-9
West Malaysia, 1958-1967: Estimated Total Fertility Rates and Age-Specific Fertility Rates for Metropolitan Areas, Other Urban Areas and Rural Areas[a]

Area and Year	Total Fertility Rate	Age-Specific Fertility Rates for Women of Ages:					
		15-19	20-24	25-29	30-34	35-39	40-44
Metropolitan Towns[b]							
1958	5,385	67	246	284	235	160	85
1960	5,235	75	257	293	230	121	71
1962	4,920	44	245	271	204	148	72
1965	4,375	52	201	262	207	110	43
1967	3,970	44	195	210	196	113	36
Other Urban Areas[b]							
1958	5,950	104	272	326	242	175	71
1960	5,440	76	256	305	209	122	120
1962	5,960	85	290	376	243	121	77
1965	4,295	43	175	265	197	148	31
1967	4,065	43	141	259	196	125	49
Urbo-Rural Areas[b,c]							
1958	5,410	85	235	321	204	193	44
1960	6,240	96	260	368	223	171	130
1962	5,490	88	206	358	268	115	63
1965	5,725	62	283	304	186	199	111
1967	5,720	64	266	351	212	141	110
Rural Areas[b]							
1958	6,345	147	305	345	245	148	79
1960	6,390	147	288	329	271	163	80
1962	6,145	125	290	343	242	162	67
1965	5,965	99	293	304	260	167	70
1967	5,690	83	252	312	231	185	75
Percentage Change in Fertility Rates, 1958-1967:							
Metropolitan Towns	−26	− 34	− 21	− 26	− 17	− 29	− 58
Other Urban Areas	−32	− 59	− 48	− 21	− 19	− 29	− 31
Urbo-Rural Areas[c]	+ 6	− 25	+ 13	+ 9	+ 4	− 27	+150
Rural Areas	−10	− 44	− 17	− 10	− 6	+ 25	− 5

[a]Source is Cho, 1969, pp. 14-15.

[b]"Metropolitan Towns" are cities having populations of more than 75,000 in the 1957 census and the State Capitals; "Towns" are places with population of 7,670-75,000 in the 1957 census; "Urbo-rural Areas" are those areas which do not fall into any of the categories above but have urban characteristics and where the population dependent on non-agricultural occupations is likely to be more than 60% of the total population; and "Rural Areas" are all others.

[c]The sample size for urbo-rural areas was small. These estimates are of questionable reliability.

Table 4-10
Fertility Rates for Malays in West Malaysia: 1947-1970

Year	Crude Birth Rate	Crude Birth Rate adjusted for Under-Registration	Gross-Reproduction Rate [f]	Total Fertility Rate [a,g]	Age-Specific Fertility Rates for Women of Ages: [a,g]					
					15-19	20-24	25-29	30-34	35-39	40-44
Fertility Rates:										
1947	41.8[b]	48.1[e]	2.67	5,495	172	308	263	196	113	47
1957	48.1[c]	—	2.97	5,965	163	342	279	208	146	55
1957	—	53.7[f]	3.53	7,110	209	407	339	250	162	55
1960	43.3[c]	n.a.	n.a.	6,070	177	287	312	243	130	65
1962	43.0[c]	n.a.	n.a.	5,800	144	287	306	219	153	51
1965	39.1[c]	n.a.	n.a.	5,835	119	298	292	240	151	67
1967	38.2[c]	n.a.	n.a.	5,640	97	260	296	224	170	81
1970	35.3[d]	n.a.	2.56	5,150	75	251	267	227	151	59

[a]Rates for women 45-49 have been omitted because they are unavailable in estimates for 1947, 1960, 1962, 1965, and 1967.

[b]Source is MacGregor, 1948, p. 9.

[c]Source is Department of Statistics, 1972, p. 5.

[d]Adjusted to use 1970 census total as denominator instead of 1970 estimates as previously published in official Department of Statistics publications.

[e]Source is Smith, 1952, p. 59.

[f]Source is Saw, 1967a, p. 642.

[g]Source of estimates for GRR, TFR, and ASFR: 1947, Smith (1952); 1957, Fell (1960), and Saw (1967a); 1960-67, Cho (1969); 1970, Palmore, Chander and Fernandez.

Table 4-11
Fertility Rates for Chinese in West Malaysia: 1947-1970

Year	Crude Birth Rate	Crude Birth Rate adjusted for Under-Registration	Gross Repro-duction Rate[g]	Total Fertility Rate[a,g]	Age-Specific Fertility Rates for Women of Ages:[a,g]					
					15-19	20-24	25-29	30-34	35-39	40-44
Fertility Rates:										
1947	44.0[b]	44.7[e]	3.37	6,880	107	333	354	286	208	88
1957	43.3[c]	–	3.56	7,205	38	280	412	355	239	117
1957	–	43.6[f]	3.68	7,460	48	307	417	360	242	118
1960	37.5[c]	n.a.	n.a.	6,045	51	241	324	272	202	119
1962	37.3[c]	n.a.	n.a.	6,040	37	245	378	268	169	111
1965	34.1[c]	n.a.	n.a.	5,135	30	222	286	254	165	70
1967	32.5[c]	n.a.	n.a.	4,610	25	177	288	228	153	51
1970	31.9[d]	n.a.	2.34	4,745	26	200	293	229	141	60

[a]Rates for women 45-49 have been omitted because they are unavailable in estimates for 1947, 1960, 1962, 1965, and 1967.
[b]Source is MacGregor, 1948, p. 9.
[c]Source is Department of Statistics, 1972, p. 5.
[d]Adjusted to use 1970 census total as denominator instead of 1970 estimates as previously published in official Department of Statistics publications.
[e]Source is Smith, 1952, p. 73.
[f]Source is Saw, 1967a, p. 642.
[g]See note g, Table 4-10.

Table 4-12
Fertility Rates for Indians and Pakistanis in West Malaysia: 1957-1970[a]

Year	Crude Birth Rate	Crude Birth Rate adjusted for Under-Registration	Gross Reproduction Rate[f]	Total Fertility Rate[a,f]	Age-Specific Fertility Rates for Women of Ages:[a,b,f]					
					15-19	20-24	25-29	30-34	35-39	40-44
Fertility Rates:										
1957	49.7[c]	—	3.92	7,905	209	429	441	283	159	60
1957	—	49.8[e]	3.92	7,890	242	429	408	288	159	52
1960	43.4[c]	n.a.	n.a.	7,110	147	375	393	309	131	67
1962	41.5[c]	n.a.	n.a.	6,145	126	361	353	223	128	38
1965	37.8[c]	n.a.	n.a.	5,680	98	268	323	214	189	44
1967	35.3[c]	n.a.	n.a.	5,330	100	270	250	200	193	53
1970	32.2[d]	n.a.	2.42	4,920	72	280	266	203	118	45

[a]Smith (1952) did not prepare 1947 fertility estimates for the Indian population.

[b]Rates for women 45-49 have been omitted because they are unavailable in estimates for 1947, 1960, 1962, 1965, and 1967.

[c]Source is Department of Statistics, 1972, p. 5.

[d]Adjusted to use 1970 census total as denominator instead of 1970 estimates as previously published in official Department of Statistics publications.

[e]Source is Saw, 1967a, p. 642.

[f]See note g, Table 4-10.

Table 4-13
Total Fertility Rates for Each Community Group in the Four Largest Cities of
West Malaysia: 1970

| City | All Community Groups | Community Group | | |
		Malays	Chinese	Indians or Pakistanis
Kuala Lumpur Municipality	3,550	3,890	3,325	3,805
City of Georgetown	2,145	1,750	2,100	2,805
Ipoh Municipality	3,470	3,725	3,365	3,655
Johore Bahru Town Council	3,960	4,165	3,830	5,035

Different levels of contraceptive use have also undoubtedly contributed to both the differential fertility decline and current fertility differentials. While the exact quantitative effects of contraceptive use are difficult to determine, urban women have used contraception more than rural women and Chinese women have used it more than the other ethnic groups (4-14).

The future prospects for Malaysia's population growth and ethnic balance clearly depend primarily on what happens to fertility, but prediction of future fertility levels is hazardous with several competing influences evident. For at least the next fifteen years, Malaysia's present age structure means that increasingly large female cohorts will be entering the reproductive years. While a trend towards rising age at marriage has been established, marriage ages are already attaining levels that make it unlikely much additional decreased fertility can be expected from that trend. Contraceptive use, on the other hand, is clearly increasing rapidly. Further, additional urbanization may lead to higher proportions of the population attaining the lower urban fertility levels. Since urban-rural differentials are critical to the prospects, some discussion of the urbanization data is required.

Urbanization and Internal Migration

Malaysia in 1970 was still very much a rural nation. In more highly urbanized West Malaysia, less than a third of the population lived in towns of 10,000 or more persons. In East Malaysia, less than a sixth lived in such towns. In the whole nation, only eight towns had more than 75,000 people. While the largest towns were growing more quickly than the rural areas, recent urban growth rates do not indicate massive rural to urban migration.

Table 4-14

West Malaysia, 1966-1967: Percentage Who Have Ever Used Contraception or Sterilization and Percentage Currently Using Contraception or Sterilization Among Currently Married Women 15-44 By Age, Community Group and Place of Residence[a]

Ages and Contraceptive Use Indicator	All West Malaysia Community Group				Metropolitan Towns[b] Community Group				Other Urban Areas[b] Community Group				Rural Areas[b] Community Group			
	All Community Groups	Malays	Chinese	Indians or Pakistanis	All Community Groups	Malays	Chinese	Indians or Pakistanis	All Community Groups	Malays	Chinese	Indians or Pakistanis	All Community Groups	Malays	Chinese	Indians or Pakistanis
Ages 15-24																
Percentage who ever used contraception or sterilization	10	9	18	12	30	30	33	22	17	12[c]	21[c]	23[c]	7	7	4[c]	8[c]
Percentage currently using contraception or sterilization	5	3	12	9	22	20	27	13	11	4[c]	14[c]	23[c]	2	2	0[c]	5[c]
Ages 25-34																
Percentage who ever used contraception or sterilization	16	7	37	20	43	28	48	41	34	16	49	30[c]	6	5	13[c]	9[c]
Percentage currently using contraception or sterilization	11	4	26	14	33	22	37	31	26	12	38	28[c]	3	2	5[c]	5[c]
Ages 35-44																
Percentage who ever used contraception or sterilization	14	8	34	9	41	27	47	28	25	14	36	19[c]	6	6	11[c]	0[c]
Percentage currently using contraception or sterilization	9	2	27	7	32	16	38	20	19	9	28	16[c]	1	1	7[c]	0[c]

[a]Source is National Family Planning Board of Malaysia, 1968, pp. 268, 275, 282, and 289.

[b]Metropolitan towns are Kuala Lumpur, Georgetown, Ipoh, Klang, and Johore Bahru. All places of 7,500 population or more in 1957 and not one of the metropolitan towns are designated other urban areas. The remaining places are defined rural.

[c]Sample base for percentage is less than 100 cases.

Aside from what can be inferred from census tabulations, Malaysian data on internal migration is extremely limited, perhaps with some justification. Until recent years, international migration was so dominant that internal movements probably seemed relatively unimportant. Further, Malayan tabulations of place of birth by current residence showed relatively small flows across state boundaries. The 1957 tabulations, for example, showed net migration above thirty thousand persons only for Singapore, Selangor, Malacca, Perak, and Penang.

The 1970 census was the first to include additional migration questions beyond the place of birth questions so important in earlier history. Unfortunately, tabulations of these data are not yet available. However recent survey data indicate that internal migration may now be important.

The 1967-1968 Socio-Economic Survey for West Malaysia included a question on place of residence at the 1957 census. Due to sample size limitations, 1967-1968 residence by 1957 residence data were only tabulated for five zones (combinations of the eleven states) and nine of the larger towns. With such inclusive boundaries, there was still substantial internal movement in ten years. Three hundred six thousand persons crossed zonal boundaries and 550 thousand persons crossed either a zonal boundary or the boundary of one of the eight largest towns (population of 75,000 or more). Surprisingly, however, the net migration figures deduced from these data do little to support a prediction of accelerating urbanization, as they report a net outmigration from the eight largest towns (table 4-15).

The finding is not entirely believable because the intercensal growth rates for those eight towns were higher than the West Malaysian average. Since fertility is lower in these towns than elsewhere, it is hard to account for higher

Table 4-15

West Malaysia: Estimated Net Migration 1957 to 1967-1968[a]

| | Number of Migrants (in 1000s): | | |
	In	Out	Net
Panel A: Metropolitan Migration			
Metropolitan areas	136.6	193.5	−56.9
Non-Metropolitan areas	193.5	136.6	+56.9
Panel B: Zonal Migration			
Selangor and Negri Sembilan	138.2	57.6	+80.6
Kelantan, Pahang, and Trenggannu	44.5	34.8	+ 9.8
Kedah, Penang, and Perlis	37.1	59.3	−22.2
Johore and Malacca	33.7	56.9	−23.2
Perak	52.6	97.5	−45.0

[a]Calculated from previously unpublished tables from the 1967-68 Socio-Economic Survey.

town growth rates unless there was net in-migration. Perhaps the 1970 census migration data will permit a sensible explanation. Until these data become available, however, present data resources do not encourage a prediction of increasingly rapid urbanization. Perhaps that will occur only when rural population densities reach higher levels and urban opportunities exceed those available from the rural economy.

Future Population Growth

For at least the next decade, it is hard to imagine that Malaysian annual growth rates will decrease below 2 percent a year unless there is vigorous intervention by the government and private sectors into programs designed to change demographic behavior. In East Malaysia, even an incipient fertility decline is not yet evident. Admittedly, West Malaysia has already undergone a significant fertility decline. A substantial proportion of this decline, however, was occasioned by changes in marital patterns which are not likely to contribute much to future declines. Low rates of urbanization, an unfavorable age structure and the prospect of further decline in mortality give added strength to a prognosis of continued rapid growth.

References

Bogue, Donald J. and Palmore, James A. "Some empirical and analytic relations among demographic fertility measures with regression models for fertility estimation." *Demography* 1, 1 (1964): 316-338.

Chander, Ramesh. *Field Count Summary,* 1970 Population and Housing Census of Malaysia. Kuala Lumpur: Jabatan Perangkaan Malaysia, 1971a.
___ *Urban Connurbations-Population and Households in Ten Gazetted Towns and Their Adjoining Built-Up Areas.* 1970 Population and Housing Census of Malaysia. Kuala Lumpur: Jabatan Perangkaan Malaysia, 1971b.
___ *Community Groups.* 1970 Population and Housing Census of Malaysia. Kuala Lumpur: Jabatan Perangkaan Malaysia, 1972.
___ "Family planning and fertility trends in West Malaysia." *Proceedings of the Combined Conference on Evaluation of Malaysian National Family Planning Program and East Asia Population Programmes.* Kuala Lumpur: National Family Planning Board of Malaysia, (in press).

Cho, Lee-Jay. *Estimates of Fertility for West Malaysia: 1957-1967.* Research Paper No. 3, June 1969, Department of Statistics. Kuala Lumpur: Jabatan Perangkaan Malaysia, 1969.

Cho, Lee-Jay, James A. Palmore, and Lyle Saunders. "Recent fertility trends in West Malaysia." *Demography* 5, 2 (1968): 732-744.

Del Tufo, M.V. *Malaya: A Report on the 1957 Census of Population.* London: Crown Agents for the Colonies, 1949.

Department of Statistics, Malaysia. *Interim Report on Family Survey – A KAP Study 1970.* Kuala Lumpur: Jabatan Perangkaan Malaysia, 1971.

___ *Monthly Statistical Bulletin of West Malaysia.* Kuala Lumpur: Jabatan Perangkaan Malaysia, 1972.

Fell, H. *1957 Population Census of the Federation of Malaya. Report No. 14.* Kuala Lumpur: Department of Statistics, Malaysia, 1960.

Ginsburg, Norton and Chester F. Roberts. *Malaya.* Seattle: University of Washington Press, 1958.

Jones, Lawrence W. *Sarawak: Report on the Census of Population Taken on 15 June 1960.* Kuching: Government Printer, 1962a.

___ *North Borneo: Census of Population Taken on 10th August, 1960.* Kuching: Government Printer, 1962b.

Keyfitz, Nathan. "A Life Table that Agrees with the Data." *Journal of the American Statistical Association* 61, 1 (1966): 303-312.

MacGregor, R.B. *Report on the Registration of Births and Deaths for the Year 1947.* Kuala Lumpur: Government Press, Malayan Union, 1948.

McDonald, E.M. *Population, Births, Deaths, Marriages and Adoptions (Malaya) 1957.* Kuala Lumpur: Government Press, Federation of Malaya, 1959.

Nathan, J.E. *The Census of British Malaya, 1921.* London: Waterlow and Sons, 1922.

National Family Planning Board of Malaysia. *Report on the West Malaysian Family Survey: 1966-1967.* Kuala Lumpur: Government of Malaysia, National Family Planning Board of Malaysia. (by James Palmore with the assistance of A. Schnaiberg, C.M. Langford, and D. Fernandez), 1968.

Newbold, T.J. *Political and Statistical Account of the British Settlements in the Straits of Malacca.* Vols. I and II. London: John Murray, 1839.

Noakes, J.L. *Sarawak and Brunei: A Report on the 1947 Population Census.* Kuching: Government Printer, 1950.

Palmore, James A. "Malaysia: The West Malaysian family survey, 1966-1967." *Studies in Family Planning* 1, 40 (1969): 11-20.

Palmore, James A., and Ariffin bin Marzuki. "Marriage Patterns and Cumulative Fertility in West Malaysia, 1966-1967." *Demography* 6 (1969): 383-401.

Palmore, James A., Paul M. Hirsch, and Ariffin bin Marzuki. "Interpersonal Communication and the Diffusion of Family Planning in West Malaysia." *Demography* 8 (1971): 411-425.

Sandhu, Kernial Singh. *Indians in Malaya.* Cambridge, England: Cambridge University Press, 1969.

Saw, Swee-Hock. "Fertility Differentials in Early Postwar Malaya." *Demography* 4 (1967a): 641-656.

___ "A note on fertility levels in Malaya during 1947-1957." *Malayan Economic Review* 12, 1 (1967b): 117-124.

Smith, T.E. *Population Growth in Malaya: An Analysis of Recent Trends.* London: Oxford University Press, 1952.

United Nations. *Demographic Yearbook 1951.* New York: United Nations, 1952.

___ *Demographic Yearbook 1955.* New York: United Nations, 1955.

___ *Demographic Yearbook 1971.* New York: United Nations, 1972.

Vlieland, C.A. *British Malaya: A Report on the 1931 Census and on Certain Problems of Vital Statistics.* London: Crown Agents for the Colonies, 1933.

5

The Demographic Outlook in Indonesia
Lee McCaffrey

Introduction

Despite the limitations of the available data, it is obvious that Indonesia
faces grave population problems.

Indonesia, the most populous country in Southeast Asia, had a reported
1971 population exceeding 119 million. The true population was perhaps
greater by 6 or 7 million. According to U.S. Bureau of the Census estimates,
the crude birth rate (CBR) stood at 44 and the death rate (CDR) at 19 per
1,000 in 1970.[1] Since these estimates are based on data of poor quality, the
birth rate actually may be somewhat higher. The death rate, high by Asian
standards, reflects the per capita declines in food production and the reemer-
gence of malaria, smallpox and plague during the 1960s, the prevalence of
cholera and TB, and the deterioration of public health services up until 1968.

McNicoll,[2] using intercensal (1961-1971) cohort survival rates, estimates
a CDR for the country as a whole in excess of 25. He regards this as unrealistically high, attributing the inaccuracy to large errors in age reporting in both
the 1961 and 1971 censuses. McNicoll also derived mortality data from
census retrospective data on children ever born and children still living classified by age of mother. This procedure is less affected by inaccurate age
reporting and yields estimates, which are "plausible and substantially better
than those derived from the intercensal survival rates of cohorts."[3] Given
a population growth rate above 2 percent, the relatively small proportion of
the population in low mortality ages, and the generally poor economic and
health conditions, McNicoll feels that a CDR much below 20 per 1,000 is
not reasonable.

According to UN estimates since 1950 the CDR has declined more per-
ceptably than the CBR, resulting in rising rates of natural increase. If the
Indonesian death rate were to fall to the level of the Philippines, Malaysia
or Thailand with no change in the birth rate, the rate of natural increase
would rise well above 3 percent, which if continued would double the population in a bit over two decades. The Indonesian population has within
it enormous potential for growth.

Early Population Estimates

Even population estimates for early nineteenth century Java and Madura

83

Table 5-1
Crude Birth, Death, and Natural Increase Rates in Indonesia

	Birth	Death	RNI
1950-55	48.8	29.1	19.7
1960-65	46.6	23.6	23.0
1970	44	19	25

Sources: 1950-55 and 1960-65, U.N. Population Division *Working Paper No. 38,*
1971. AID *Population Program Assistance, 1971.*

provided some idea of Indonesia's enormous growth potential. A census of Java
and Madura was taken by the British government in the year 1815 in connection
with the land revenue system introduced by Thomas Stamford Raffles, Lieu-
tenant Governor of Java during the British occupation (1811-1816). This system
was based upon the supposition that the government possessed proprietary right
to the soil with each cultivator expected to give part of his production to the
government, preferably in cash. A governor collector and his native assistant
obtained from village headmen the name of each male inhabitant and information concerning size and composition of each household, production from the
land, area cultivated, and number of cultivators. There was no actual enumeration, but rather a series of estimates provided by village heads based upon their
knowledge of the inhabitants and their willingness to provide complete information for purposes of taxation.[4]

Raffles' population count for Java and Madura for the year 1815 was 4.5
million. Concern began to be expressed regarding population pressures on this
small island even at this early date. Even so, Raffles' 1815 census appears to
have been a gross underestimate, as it would imply a population growth rate
for nineteenth century Java of 2.2 percent per annum, an unlikely possibility
considering the poor living conditions of the period.[5]

Bram Peper offers "a new interpretation" of nineteenth century growth
in Java, disputing the often cited improvements in living standards and health
conditions which supposedly led to a population explosion. According to
Peper, the indigenous population was not favorably affected by increased production and crop exportation which characterized the period, although colonial
wealth certainly increased. A smallpox vaccination program was the only major
public health improvement, and even this program covered small territories,
and failed to halt frequent epidemics.

While it is generally true that the Dutch exploited their colony's human
and natural resources, some measure of peace and order resulted from Dutch
administrative control, with favorable effects upon survival rates. Peper assumes

a fairly stable birth rate; however, a rising birth rate may have resulted from the Dutch "culture system," an extension of Raffles' "land revenue." Benjamin White has stated that although famine control, improvements in hygiene, and fewer wars cannot account for the very high growth rates of nineteenth century Java, Dutch economic policies, resulting in the removal of land and labor from the subsistence sector, forced the adoption of more labor intensive methods. Since a child's productive activities usually exceed his keep, White reasons that parents viewed children as valuable sources of labor and were inclined to have larger families.[6]

Current Data Quality

Indonesia's first modern census dates back only to 1930. Census legislation at that time provided for taking a census at ten-year intervals starting with 1930. However, the 1940 census was cancelled because of the war of the Netherlands against Germany. World War II, the Japanese occupation, then the revolution against the Netherlands, unrest, and economic disturbances followed.[7] The next census took place in 1961, but the planned tabulations and publications were never completed. Many census schedules were in fact lost.

The 1930 census provided a crude age classification,[8] i.e., (1) children who could not yet walk, (2) other children, (3) adults. The census report assumed that the first category above included persons up to ages fifteen or eighteen months and that the distinction between categories one and two presented no problems. However, Widjojo points out that a social value is connected with ambulation. This would tend to lead parents to overstate the age of their children. The distinction between other children and adults is even less certain.[9]

Census data became available by age and sex for the first time in 1961, providing minimal groundwork for demographic, economic, and social planning. However, the recorded age distributions are characterized by surpluses and deficits in certain five-year age groups. African censuses and surveys and those of India and Pakistan exhibit the same kinds of age misreporting. One plausible explanation for these similar distortions is that in all these cultures, accurate age determination is unimportant and for that reason largely unknown. The ages entered on the interview schedule may be interviewers' estimates rather than an exact age supplied by the respondent.

In an attempt to determine the underlying causes of these surpluses and deficits occurring in various five-year age groupings, studies were done using data from several African territories where retrospective data on children ever born, children still surviving, births, and deaths in the year immediately prior to the census were available. Using these data, fertility and mortality could be estimated and a corresponding stable population chosen. Census five-year cohorts were then compared with those of the stable population. In these

African territories, there is a tendency to overestimate the ages of young children, as well as the ages of girls 10-14 who have passed puberty. The former error combined with a tendency to underestimate the ages of girls 10-14 who have not reached puberty causes a peaking at ages 5-9. Deficits occur in the broad age group 10-19 and surpluses at 25-34. Overestimating the ages of young women may be caused by an upward bias associated with marriage and childbearing, an assumption that women marry at some conventional age and have a first birth after some prescribed interval.[10]

Iskandar and Etienne Van de Walle argue that the Indonesian population pyramid shows the typical age reporting errors of the African censuses, while Keyfitz and Widjojo ascribe the distortions from the stable distribution to abrupt changes in vital rates during the past decade. One method of evaluating the accuracy of a census age distribution is by comparing the actual percentage distribution with that of an appropriately chosen population model. Since many developing countries have nearly constant fertility and mortality conditions, and assuming that these conditions have remained constant over several decades, their age distributions should assume a stable form. Indonesia's 1961 10-19 age cohort occupies a disproportionately smaller part of the total age pyramid than would be expected if we were looking at a stable population. This is obvious when we compare the 10-19 cohort with the next younger and older groups. This small cohort may be the result of a sudden dip in the birthrate during the war of independence from 1945 through 1949. The Japanese occupation from the beginning of 1942 to the middle of 1945 was characterized by exorbitant demands for foodstuffs to aid the Japanese war effort as well as massive displacements of village populations, famine and sickness. Although data during this period are scarce, it is not improbable that total population size decreased as births fell below deaths.

Presumably, a comparison of the 1961 and 1971 age distributions would help determine if distortions of the 1961 population pyramid's shape are real or artifactual (table 5-2). The cohort aged 10-19 in 1961 becomes the 1971 20-29 cohort. Since the 1961 10-19 cohort was "hollow,"[a] the 1971 20-29 cohort should exhibit these same characteristics, if the "hollowness" is factual, that is, due to vital event changes in the past. This explanation would be even more convincing if the 1971 10-19 age group appears to comprise a normal proportion of the population. In other words, if each 10-19-year-old cohort is not being routinely subjected to an age misreporting bias, the 1971 10-19 cohort would occupy the same proportion of the population pyramid as it would in an appropriately chosen stable model.

McNicoll has tried to resolve the question of whether the "hollow" ages

---

[a]By "hollow", we are referring to a five-year age cohort which does not conform proportionally to the size that would be expected in a stable population, and which is disproportionately smaller than would be expected in relation to the adjacent age groups.

Table 5-2

Population by Sex and Age, Indonesia, 1961 and 1971 (in thousands)

	1961			1971		
	Males	*Females*	*Total*	*Males*	*Females*	*Total*
0-4	8,869	8,904	17,773	9,653	9,508	19,161
5-9	7,642	7,523	15,165	9,577	9,295	18,872
10-14	4,295	3,802	8,097	7,326	6,902	14,228
15-19	3,813	3,815	7,628	5,643	5,748	11,391
20-24	3,884	4,635	8,519	3,556	4,405	7,961
25-29	3,547	4,431	7,978	4,033	5,009	9,042
30-34	3,588	3,778	7,366	3,664	4,230	7,894
35-39	3,169	2,914	6,083	4,019	4,061	8,080
40-44	2,480	2,309	4,789	3,003	3,026	6,029
45-49	1,941	1,869	3,810	2,399	2,248	4,647
50-54	1,502	1,441	2,943	1,888	1,947	3,835
55-59	1,062	1,189	2,251	1,074	1,061	2,135
60-64	827	1,182	2,009	1,034	1,189	2,223
65-69	539	703	1,242	535	586	1,121
70-74	308	285	593	491	570	1,061
75+	373	400	773	379	391	770
Not Stated				4	4	8
	47,839	49,180	97,019	58,278	60,180	118,458

Source: Biro Pusat Statistik-Republic Indonesia Central Bureau of Statistics–Republic of Indonesia.

in the 1961 pyramid are real or artifactural, but has determined that the 1971 census age data are inconclusive in this respect.

> While the "hollow ages" in the pyramid (10-20 in 1961) have moved distinctly upward in the decade, the cohorts aged 20-30 in 1971 have shown remarkable powers of survival. It is very likely that both explanations are valid and the observed hollow should be split about equally between the protagonists.[11]

By protagonists, McNicoll is referring on the one hand to those who believe that the hollowness was real and caused by low birthrates in the 1940s followed by increased birthrates and reduced infant and child mortality in the 1950s and on the other to those who believe that adolescents and young adults are particularly subject to misclassification by age in nonnumerate populations.

Consequences for Future Population Projections

Insofar as the 1961 age distribution reflects the true situation, the relatively

large 5-9 cohort by 1971 began to progress through the reproductive years and
beginning around 1976 will contribute a large increment in the number of
births. If Iskandar and those who see both fact and artifact in the 1961 census
are correct, only a proportion of the cohort enumerated as 5-9 in 1961 was
actually 5-9; some were 0-4 and others 10-14. Were this the case, as these
people reach the reproductive ages and contribute births to an already over-
populated country, these births will be spread out over a longer time span. For
example, those persons enumerated as 5-9 in 1961 but who are actually 10-
14 have already had a proportion of their children, thus minimizing the anticipated upsurge in 1976.

Although Widjojo, by failing to concede a significant degree of age misreporting, may exaggerate the expected increase of the reproductive age groups
after 1976 and especially after 1981, it remains, as McNicoll has pointed out,
that "The implications of even a smaller rate of increase in cohort size for
employment, fertility, and migration are nevertheless considerable."[12] As the
large cohorts of the 1950s work their way up through the population pyramid,
a rejuvenation of the working population will occur during the 1970s, along
with increased pressure on education and job opportunities, all of which will
tend toward an imbalance of the existing social, cultural, economic, and political systems. Unless new methods of labor intensive farming are developed
or additional economic or educational opportunities become available, demands
upon the land, where 62 percent of the economically active population are
engaged, will be an irresolvable problem. Civil unrest and revolutionary threats
to political stability are not unlikely.

The latest Five Year Plan aims at achieving an annual economic growth rate
2.7 percentage points greater than the rate of population increase. While this
level of overall economic growth may appear to be a reasonable achievement, it
is not great enough to improve on present conditions even if one assumes quite
low capital-output ratios and the maintenance of stable and effective government.
Projected population growth (even in modified form) will divert economic gains
into additional schooling, housing, medical facilities, protective and administrative services, and other nonproductive activities, with negligible improvement in
the average Indonesian's standard of living.

The Indonesian population projections to the year 1991 by Iskandar and
Widjojo involve quite different underlying assumptions in terms of mortality
and fertility, but both project sustained rapid increase over the next seventeen
years. The lowest total, Iskandar's low figure, would represent the net addition of more than 65 million persons between 1971 and 1991.

Offsetting the staggering problem of accommodating population growth of
this magnitude is the recent rise in world oil prices which has greatly improved
the country's potential for development. Even though these prices will also
increase the cost of imports needed for development, the long anticipated take-
off of the Indonesian economy now appears closer at hand. Whether this

opportunity is realized, whether it will result in raising the level of average citizens' welfare rather than in increased disparity of income and opportunity, will depend largely on the administrative skill and idealism of those who run the country. Whatever the outcome, coping successfully with rapid population growth would vastly improve short-term and long-term prospects. There is no escaping the requirement that for all societies, population, resources, and economic and social organization set the terms for collective achievement. For Indonesia, the future outlook for resources is favorable; major problems remain regarding population, and economic and social organization which here is taken to include political organization.

Family Planning Program Efforts

The family planning program represents a major effort for limiting future population growth. Unofficial family planning efforts began as early as 1957 through the Indonesian Planned Parenthood Association. This organization was able to provide information only in the form of verbal encouragement of child spacing for health reasons. For ten years afterwards, the political climate remained hostile to the concept of family planning. When Sukarno fell from power, the official attitude changed and a National Indonesian Family Planning Institute was established in 1968 and given responsibility for coordinating family planning programs, making recommendations to the government concerning the national program, promoting international cooperation, and developing a generally broad, voluntary approach to family planning.[13]

In 1969, at the government's request, a joint UN-World Bank-WHO mission assisted in the formation of a national family planning program. By 1970, the National Family Planning Coordinating Board was established in the six provinces of Java and Bali with the task of clearly delimiting the policy-making and executive responsibilities of the national program and coordinating foreign aid. A five year plan (1972-1976) was developed (based on UN-World Bank–WHO recommendations), and a 1976 target of six million new acceptors established.

Recent reports from the National Family Planning Coordinating Board demonstrate that the clinics which are concentrated in Java and Bali have been attracting growing numbers of new acceptors and overall are achieving their targeted acceptance rates, i.e., 13 percent of their fertile women. In fiscal 1973, over one million women became contraceptive acceptors, over 90 percent of whom have chosen pills and IUDs. The current goal for fiscal year 1974 is 1,358,000[b] acceptors and expansion of the program to Sumatra, Kalimantan,

---

[b]The 1974 accounting year runs through March 1975. As of the end of December 1974 72 percent of the target was reported as fulfilled.

Sulawesi, and the other outer islands. The Bureau of Statistics and the Demographic Institute, University of Indonesia, have completed studies which suggest a remarkable decline in age-specific birth rates. While some experienced observers have expressed skepticism over the magnitude of decline shown by these data, some down-turn appears plausible. Most provinces of Java and Bali are developing evaluation projects to measure continuation experience of contraceptive acceptors. Early analyses of these data for an area of East Java indicate that the acceptor data are valid, and show an extraordinarily high rate of continuation among acceptor of the I.U.D. Continuation rates for other methods are about as would be expected. However, as yet a small percentage of total fertile women have been reached. The program is still tapping highly motivated segments of the population in the middle reproductive ages who already have large families. If the experience of other countries is any guide, a plateau may soon be reached in this regard with possible reductions in future acceptance rates.

It is difficult to present a succinct summary of the demographic outlook for Indonesia except to say that all the evidence is not yet available. It is obvious that growth potential is enormous, but starting from what base and modified by what economic, social, and political inputs remains to be seen.

Notes

1. *Agency for International Development Population Program Assistance* (Washington, D.C.: U.S. Government Printing Office, 1971).
2. Geoffrey McNicoll and Si Gde Made Mamas, "The Demographic Situation in Indonesia," Paper No. 28. East-West Population Institute, Honolulu, December 1973.
3. Ibid.
4. Nitisastro Widjojo, *Population Trends in Indonesia* (Ithaca: Cornell University Press, 1970). pp. 20-22.
5. Bram Peper, "Population Growth in Java in the 19th Century, A New Interpretation," *Population Studies* 24, 1 (March 1970).
6. Benjamin White, "Reply to Geertz and Van de Walle," *Human Ecology* 2, 1 (1974): 63-65.
7. Iskandar, *Some Monographic Studies on the Population of Indonesia* (Jakarta: Lembaga Demografi, Fakultas Ekonomi, Universitas Indonesia, 1970), p. 8.
8. Widjojo, *Population Trends,* pp. 79-80.
9. Ibid., p. 80.
10. U.N. Manual IV, *Methods of Estimating Basic Demographic Measures from Incomplete Data,* ST/SOA/Series A/42, No:67, XIII.2, pp. 19-21.
11. McNicoll and Mamas, "The Demographic Situation."

12. McNicoll and Mamas, "The Demographic Situation."
13. See Indonesia, *Country Profiles,* a publication of the Population Council, April 1971, p. 8.

References

Agency for International Development, Bureau for Population and Humanitarian Assistance, Office of Population. "Population Program Assistance, United States aid to developing countries, Annual Report." Fiscal Year 1973, pp. 65-68.

Central Bureau of Statistics—Republic of Indonesia. Censuses of 1961 and 1971.

Hanna, Willard A. "Population Review 1970: Indonesia." *American Universities Fieldstaff Reports* 19, 3 (1971).

Iskandar, N. *Some Monographic Studies on the Population of Indonesia.* Jakarta: Lembaga Demografi, Fakultas Ekonomi, Universitas Indonesia, 1970.

Keyfitz, Nathan. "Age Distribution as a Challenge to Development." *American Journal of Sociology* 70 (1965): 659-668.

McNicoll, Geoffrey and Si Gde Made Mamas. "The Demographic Situation in Indonesia." Paper No. 28. East-West Population Institute, Honolulu, December 1973.

Peper, Bram. "Population Growth in Java in the Nineteenth Century." *Population Studies* 24 (1970): 71-84.

Ryder, Brooks. "Indonesia." *Studies in Family Planning* 3, 7 (July 1972): 128-132.

United Nations. *Methods of Estimating Basic Demographic Measures from Incomplete Data.* Series A, *Population Studies,* No. 42. New York, 1967.

Universitas Indonesia, Fakultas Ekonomi, Lembaga Demografi. *Demographic Factbook of Indonesia.* Jakarta, 1973.

Van de Walle, Etienne. "Some Characteristic Features of Census Age Distributions in Illiterate Populations." *American Journal of Sociology* 71 (1966): 549-555.

White, Benjamin. "Reply to Geertz and Van de Walle." *Human Ecology* 2, 1 (1974): 63-65.

Widjojo, Nitisastro. *Population Trends in Indonesia.* Ithaca: Cornell University Press, 1970.

Zaidan, George C. and Peter C. Muncie. "Indonesia: Launching a National Program." In "The Population Work of the World Bank" *Studies in Family Planning* 4, 11 (November 1973): 296-300.

Part III

**Population Distribution
and Development**

Introduction to Part III

Population size, the level of social and economic development, and the constraints of the environment imply a pattern of spatial organization. As populations grow, as the nature of social organization changes[a] or the environment is modified, population is redistributed. The most visible aspect of redistribution is migration but redistribution can and does occur as the result of differential rates of natural increase between regions and between urban and rural sectors.

The process of population redistribution is seldom smooth or efficient—even when attempts are made to organize and channel it. Some of the liveliest (and most misery filled) pages in the history of the currently advanced countries relate to the period in their history when a new spatial morphology was being formed. By comparison, however, the problems faced then were simple and less urgent than those now facing the countries of Southeast Asia as they work out their new spatial orders. Here the growth of population is greater, rural land hunger often more extreme, opportunities for a better life in urban areas more constricted, alternative areas for expansion less abundant, and the export of population either through conquest or treaty less feasible. (What export there is tends to be of the wrong kind from the point of view of the sending country—the better educated and more skilled.) As Gunnar Mydral has observed of urban growth in Asia, it is less a response to vigorous economic growth and beckoning opportunity than a reaction against lack of economic opportunities in the rural sector.[1]

The root problem of development in Southeast Asia indeed has been the economic malaise of the countryside. The countries of Asia that have developed at a pace sufficient to sustain widespread expectation for a better life have either been those such as Singapore or Hong Kong, which did not have to contend with a rural undertow, or those like Japan, Taiwan or Korea, where peasant productivity was raised through an ingenious combination of new technology with labor intensive modes of production. Instead of viewing human resources as the primary basis for development, the tendency in most of Southeast Asia has been to adopt Western or Soviet models of development in which primary emphasis is given to the productivity of capital. Against this criterion

---

[a]This includes not only changes in modes of production, institutional structure and normative orientations but also changes in territorial limits of effective organization. Insecurity in rural areas is or has been characteristic of much of South East Asia and has been responsible for large demographic dislocations.

for investment allocation, the mass of small holders in rural areas fare badly, even as residual claimants of large-scale agricultural schemes.

But problems at the rural end are not the only ones that have to be confronted. Urbanization that is not accompanied by significant industrial development leads to social unrest and political instability. The capital requirements for urban construction including the provision of infrastructure and industrial development are immense. Failing this the accretions of population flowing in from the country are not absorbed into the urban economy in such a way as to, in Professor Hauser's borrowed phrase, make urbanism a way of life. They become part of a service structure that is marginal to basic urban functions. The great primate capitals of Southeast Asia would lose some of their distinctiveness if there were no more street vendors, pedicab drivers, porters, and various profferors of personal service, jobs to which migrants typically gravitate, but they would continue to operate. The fact that urban centers have so little capacity to absorb new populations is what leads Professor Hauser and others to declare that "More misery will result from rural-urban migration in the next decade than from high fertility."[2] More than economic friction is implied in this prediction since population redistribution is often associated with communal tension and conflict and a rise in various forms of social pathology.

Urban life is a recent experience for many of the residents of Southeast Asian cities. In Bangkok for example, two-thirds of the family heads were born outside of the city, many of course in rural areas. This is an inevitable concomitant of the myriad growth in recent years of Asian metropoli: Djakarta grew from around 800,000 in 1948 to around 5 million in 1970; Manilla attained comparable size in the postwar period; Bangkok now stands close to 3 million. Moreover, because of the weak economic development of the hinterland, the network of urban places outside the primate center is underdeveloped. This can be seen in the fact that Manilla contains over one-third of the urban population of the Philippines or the fact that Bangkok is thirty times larger than Chiengmai, the second largest city in Thailand. One result of this top heavy urban structure is that rural-urban migration, instead of being ladder-like as is the case of urbanization in the West, involves the inflow of great numbers of migrants unprocessed by the experience of living in lesser towns and cities along the way. Thus they are suddenly exposed to high density living, making of the city a crucible for rapid social change. This process also produces the social pathology and misery to which Hauser alludes.

Despite the magnitude or urban growth, which is one of the main aspects of population redistribution in Southeast Asia, the pace of urbanization is not of unprecedented proportions. In Chapter 6 Gavin Jones puts this development in perspective both in historical terms and in relation to the fact that however impressive the pace of urban growth, Southeast Asia remains overwhelmingly rural. It is worth noting also that population distribution is never unidirectional.

Not only is there return migration but the process of development leads to new patterns of exchange within the expanded territory over which the urban center is dominant. To the centripetal pull of the urban growth poles are added strong centrifugal forces which are most evident in rapid suburbanization and in frontier movements. These are all part of a single process of redistribution with the same root cause—rural distress.

Hendershot, in Chapter 7, looks into the question of whether the high fertility of rural areas promotes outmigration. Were this to be the case, it would follow that fertility regulation programs might, if successful, be a useful means to stem the tide of migrants which the cities are ill equipped to handle. His analysis indicates that the problem is essentially one of differential opportunities—actual and perceived—and thus a problem which involves more fundamental solutions in terms of new patterns of development which would create new opportunities in rural areas and in regional urban centers. He believes that the rural population would be responsive to such programs and notes that the more cognizant migrants from the areas he studied are now going to smaller urban centers rather than to Manilla.

The creation of economic opportunities to divert migrants from the primate cities has been discussed for many years with little result. The case of Ceylon, in various respects a demographic oddity, is sometimes cited in demonstration of the point that rapid urbanization need not accompany rapid population growth. It is true that Ceylon has experienced very rapid population growth as the result of its highly effective assault against infectious disease. And it is also true that the rate of urbanization has been modest—in just over the past twenty years there has been no perceptible increase in the relative size of the urban population. In a paper on "Rural-urban Balance and Development: the Experience of Ceylon," which we had to omit from this volume for reasons of space, Godfrey Gunatilleke notes that in part this happy outcome results from the perhaps less happy fact that Ceylon's economy has been unusually sluggish. However he states also that "the retentive capacity of the rural sector owes much to the social welfare policies that were followed by the Government after independence and the pattern of income transfer . . . during this period." Sharp disparities in income distribution between sectors and regions "were contained at tolerable levels . . . principally due to the social and welfare programs followed by the state." These included consumer subsidies, health services, free education through the tertiary level, and stabilization of farm incomes through a system of guaranteed prices. It is worth commenting that even without large-scale urbanization new patterns of delayed marriage have emerged in Ceylon which have helped it achieve one of the lowest birth rates in Asia outside of the Chinese fringe areas.

Development is a value ladened idea. What are the goals which development schemes aim to achieve? Is an urban society with Western style consumerism the objective? Is the concern about "overurbanization" merely a question of how fast the process should proceed, not where it should lead? It is clear that

most generally these questions are begged. The processes we are talking about
are long range. They develop their own imperatives and points of no return as
they continue. Yet nowhere in Southeast Asia are there development plans
that extend even to the end of the present decade. According to Gavin Jones
the goals of development in Southeast Asia cannot be to duplicate Western
consumer economies. "It remains highly doubtful whether the developing countries as a whole can reach Western levels of living, though they will certainly
produce many contributions that match the size of the largest Western cities of
today . . . One is inclined to argue that failure by Southeast Asian countries to
reach Western levels of living would not be an unmitigated disaster . . . the best
the planner can do is to strive . . . to control population growth, aim for
balanced urban development and for a pattern of economic development that
stresses equality of income distribution and appropriate opportunities for personal development at a lower level of material consumption than in the West."
In a less Western vein Puey Ungphakorn advocates the kind of development
in Southeast Asia that would achieve:

1. security from war, robbery, assault, hooliganism, and administrative and
   political tyranny;
2. good health, physical and mental; good and accessible medical care;
3. freedom from hunger;
4. gainful, interesting, and secure employment, providing adequate earnings;
5. clean and comfortable housing;
6. the right to the fruit of one's savings;
7. freedom of faith and worship; freedom not to conform;
8. opportunities for cultural, aesthetic, and other recreation;
9. a sense of community with the neighborhood;
10. protection and improvement of the environment;
11. self-reliance and mutual help.

The growth, composition, and distribution of population are interwoven with
each item in this list. How and with what effect we have yet to discover.

Notes

1.   Gunnar Myrdal, *Asian Drama: An Inquiry into the Poverty of Nations*
     (New York: Pantheon, 1968), pp. 470-471.
2.   Statement to the Population Panel Seminar, Pattaya, Thailand, June
     11-14, 1972.

6 Implications of Prospective Urbanization for Development Planning in Southeast Asia

Gavin W. Jones

At the outset of this chapter, it is necessary to put to rest one important misconception: namely, that rapid urbanization (that is, an increase in the proportion of population living in urban areas) is occurring in Southeast Asia. The main sources of this misconception would seem to be three:

1. Most people who write about the problem live in the capital city of their country, which tends to be growing rapidly in population (often by more than 5 percent per annum), and more rapidly than the urban population as a whole, which is itself increasing quite rapidly.
2. Personal income levels in the capital cities tend to be rising, with the result that the more visible signs of urban expansion such as increasing traffic congestion, and the mushrooming of speculative shophouse developments tend to be very much in evidence.
3. A great deal is written about those areas of the developing world where rapid urbanization *has* been occurring (Latin America, Korea, Taiwan, and, to a lesser extent, the Middle East).

As a result, many have been misled into thinking that Southeast Asia has been undergoing rapid urbanization. Yet, the fact is that urbanization has proceeded slowly in Southeast Asia during the past twenty years compared with Latin America, Africa, East Asia, and the Middle East (see table 6-1).

If Kingsley Davis' estimates are correct, the percentage of Southeast Asia's population living in rural areas has only fallen from 86 percent in 1950 to 80 percent in 1970. Results of the 1970 round of censuses for the major countries of the region confirm that the rate of urbanization increase has been slow during the 1961-71 census period, though slightly faster than estimated by Davis.

There is, of course, considerable inter-country variation within Southeast Asia. Fairly rapid urbanization has been occurring in Malaysia, for example. But this is not the typical Southeast Asia experience.[1]

The columnist or planner, trapped in his air conditioned car in a Djakarta, Bangkok, Saigon, or Manila traffic jam, is also prone to blame his city's problems on the massive influx of rural poor. He is partly correct. Rural-urban migration is indeed contributing to the growth of these cities. But the often drawn inference that there is a substantial exodus of people from the rural areas seeking to better their prospects in the towns is most misleading. In most countries of Southeast (and South) Asia net rural-urban migration is

Table 6-1
Trends in Proportion Urban, 1950-70, Various Developing Regions

	Percentage Urban			Change in Percentage Urban	
	1950	*1960*	*1970*	*1950-70*	*1960-70*
Northern Africa	24.6	29.6	34.6	10.0	5.0
Western Africa	10.6	14.7	19.7	9.1	5.0
Eastern Africa	5.5	7.5	9.9	4.4	2.4
Middle & Southern Africa	6.6	11.6	15.4	8.8	3.8
Middle America	39.2	46.2	53.0	13.8	6.8
Caribbean	35.2	38.5	42.5	7.3	4.0
Tropical South America	35.8	44.7	53.1	17.3	8.4
East Asia (excl. Japan)	12.1	18.0	25.3	13.2	7.3
Southeast Asia	13.6	16.6	20.1	6.5	3.5
Southwest Asia	24.3	29.5	35.5	11.3	6.0
South Central Asia	15.4	16.4	17.7	2.3	1.3

Source: Kingsley Davis, *World Urbanization 1950-1970. Volume I: Basic Data for Cities, Countries, and Regions*, Population Monograph Series No. 4 (Berkeley: University of California, 1969).

only a trickle. For example, in India, with a prospective "rural sending" population of 360 million, net rural-urban migration totaled six million over the ten year period 1951-61.

The point, of course, is that the urban population base in Southeast Asia as a whole is still very small. An insignificant level of outmigration, viewed from the rural sending side, can push up the growth rate of a primate city such as Bangkok from 3 percent (which may be the growth resulting from natural increase alone) to 5 or 6 percent.

The city-centric view of migration needs to be balanced against a rural-focused view. The one lends itself to visions of villages inhabited only by the old and the unadventurous. The other typically reveals the truth that once one leaves the extended rural fringe of the city (defined, say, as the area within two hours travel of the city) the amount of migration to the city is very limited. For example, in Thailand the city-centric view tells us that of Bangkok's total population, 5 percent had migrated from rural areas during the past five years.[2] The rural-centric view, based on a series of ten intensive village case studies in Thailand conducted during 1969-70, shows that Bangkok was the primary focus of the young people migrating away from home only in the case of villages in Ayuthaya province, which is very close to Bangkok. With regard to young people migrating from villages in

Chiang Mai and Kohn Kaen, in North and Northeast Thailand respectively, only about 8 percent had moved to Bangkok.[3] Analysis of census data reveals that these findings are consistent with the general patterns in the country as a whole.[4] Among the thirty-seven families from the villages studied who had moved during the previous three years only one had gone to Bangkok and only two others had migrated to other urban areas. Family migration from these villages was overwhelmingly motivated by the search for new, cheaper, or better land, not by the desire of urban employment.

In most of Southeast Asia, then, the growth of towns is rapid because the growth of the total population is rapid. Natural increase in the towns themselves ensures their rapid growth. On top of this, some "definitional urbanization" occurs as towns grow into the lower end of the population size spectrum defined as urban. Finally, limited additional urbanization occurs because of net rural-urban migration, often overwhelmingly focused on the country's primate city. We therefore have the phenomenon of rapidly growing urban populations which are only slowly increasing their share of total population because rural populations are also continuing to grow.

The Links Between Urbanization and
Economic Growth

Focusing for a moment on South and East Asia as a whole, there would appear to be a high degree of correlation during the past two decades between rates of urbanization and rates of economic development. Urbanization has been rapid in countries experiencing rapid economic development (Korea, Taiwan, Malaysia), and slow in countries experiencing slow economic development (India, Ceylon, Indonesia in the 1960s). The correlation between urbanization rates and patterns of economic growth appears to be high.

This does not answer the question of the direction or causation, but a good working hypothesis here is that the main factor operating is the movement to cities of substantial numbers of people when job opportunities increase rapidly and income differentials between farmers and employees of the larger manufacturing and trading enterprises in the cities continue to widen.

This leads us to the vexed question of the cause of urbanization in Southeast Asia. There has been a lengthy, and largely sterile, debate on the relative importance of "push" and "pull" factors influencing rural-urban migration. The common argument that rural migrants are being "pushed" by mounting poverty and population pressure rather than "pulled" into the urban areas of Asia, resulting in "over-urbanization,"[5] was effectively queried by Sovani as long ago as 1964.[6] He, among many others, suggests in effect that the sharp dichotomy often drawn between "push" and "pull" factors should be replaced by an approach that recognizes that at both the micro and the macro level a balance is established between the relative attractive and repellent characteristics of rural and urban residence.

In Southeast Asia, where a large proportion of rural dwellers are necessarily on the treadmill of day-to-day and season-to-season survival with little to spare for the comforts of life, it is not unreasonable to expect that in weighing the merits of moving to the city, economic factors will loom large. This appears to be true in western societies as well, but at least the option of giving less weight to economic factors is available to the man with a sizable bank balance and marketable skills behind him. The Javanese villager, facing the prospect of ending up unemployed on the streets of Djakarta, will perhaps be more willing to tolerate his nagging mother-in-law and his humdrum daily routine than will the Japanese or American farmer.

It would be unrealistic to discuss the economic motives for migration in Southeast Asia without mentioning the important migration stream of young people moving to the towns for secondary education. In much of rural Southeast Asia, secondary education facilities are not within commuting distance of most of the villages. (In parts of rural Thailand, even upper primary education facilities are not within commuting range of many villages. This is no doubt true of other countries as well.) Children wanting to pursue secondary education must actually move to the towns for extended periods, arranging to stay with relatives or friends or in hostels. Most commonly, they do not return permanently to their villages, both because jobs are not available there which reward the additional skills they have learned, and because their protracted stay in the towns changes their outlook and makes them less willing to tolerate the disadvantages of village life. Rural-urban migration based on an intervening period of education in a town can properly be considered primarily economic in motivation. Further education is pursued mainly for the economic rewards it promises, and economic considerations unquestionably loom large in the decision to remain in the town (or to move to a larger metropolis) once this education is completed.

These considerations, when added to the evidence that rates of urbanization in Asian countries *have* been closely correlated with rates of economic development and a shift in the industrial composition of employment, indicate that a model of migration that gives particular stress to economic objectives of migrants will be useful in the Asian context. It will not fit all countries equally well. South Vietnam, for example, seems to have been urbanizing more rapidly than its rate of economic development would warrant, but this is a fairly clear-cut case of economic motives for migration being overridden by insecurity and the fear of "death by napalm."

Todaro's model of labor migration is worth examining in this context.[7] According to this model, the spatial allocation of labor over time between a rural sector and an urban sector is primarily a function of the differential in the expected income between these two sectors. The "probability" of obtaining employment in the urban sector is seen as an important determinant of an individual's expected income and, therefore, of his decision to migrate.

$$\frac{M}{Lu}(t) = F\,\frac{V_u\,(t) - V_R\,(t)}{V_R\,(t)}$$

where

> M is the net number of rural-to-urban migrants
> Lu is the size of urban labor force
> Vu is the discounted present value of the expected urban real income over an unskilled worker's planning horizon

and

> V_R is the discounted present value of the expected rural real income stream over the same planning horizon.

Todaro does not completely ignore other elements in the decision to migrate. In fact, the final form of his overall migration model makes the percentage of people in a given area who choose to migrate vary directly not only with the relative urban-rural income differential, but also with the extent of clan contacts in the town, the relative index of per capita amenity levels and the size of the population of the urban center, and inversely with the cost of moving. But the expected (rather than actual) longer-run rural-urban earnings differential is given major emphasis. This is probably not unrealistic, even though to the cynic it may appear to imply that the villager is well versed in discount rate theory. Individuals are seen as taking a long-term view of their prospects in the city, as forming an opinion as to the income differential that is likely to obtain over the long run— and this, in a rough and ready fashion, is probably what they do. Thus, over the long run, a well-paying job preceded by a period of unemployment may be a more attractive prospect than continued low earnings in the rural sector.

The Todaro-type model, then, can explain in purely "rational economic man" terms the fact of high unemployment rates in many Asian cities that is sometimes attributed more to the attraction of the "bright lights" or the independent effect of "rural overpopulation" and rural poverty. It can explain it even more plausibly if we note:

1. the less-than-perfect knowledge available to many villagers about prospects in the cities, probably leading them to an over-optimistic assessment that gives more weight to the "bright lights" factor than would a state of more perfect knowledge;

2. the seasonal nature of much of the migration. For example, in Thailand

it appears that much of the migration to Bangkok begins as off-season migration, which shades into permanent migration over time if permanent work is found. Because of the limited income-earning opportunities in the villages in the off season, the opportunity cost of a period of unemployment in the city would tend to be lower for the seasonal migrant than for the permanent migrant;[a]

3. the documented tendency for the differential between modern-sector and rural earnings to widen. In terms of the Lewis-Ranis and Fei type of "unlimited labor supply" model such wide differentials should not exist, but there is growing evidence that very wide range differentials do tend to open up between the modern, large-scale manufacturing sector, often dominated by international firms, and the "traditional" sectors.[8] One important reason for this is the low resistance, for a variety of political and only quasi-economic reasons, to cost-push by international firms operating in the developing counties. Given a somewhat optimistic outlook on the part of the rural migrant, it is perfectly logical for him to tolerate a protracted period of unemployment in the city in exchange for the prospect that, by luck or good management, he can find a niche in the modern industrial sector at the end of that time, and the (relative) affluence such a prospect opens up for him.

It can be granted, then, that a balance exists between urban unemployment levels and the various attractive and repellent aspects of urban and rural life, as perceived by the individuals concerned. This balance at the moment is yielding rates of urban unemployment exceeding 10 percent in countries such as Ceylon, the Philippines, and Malaysia, though apparently substantially lower in Thailand. And because the earnings gap between the modern industrial sector and the agricultural sector is unlikely to narrow, high rates of urban unemployment are likely to be with us for a long time. This would be true even in countries which experienced a spectacular growth of manufacturing and service industries; more rapid expansion of job opportunities in the cities would only serve to encourage more rural dwellers to migrate so that unemployment rates would be unlikely to fall until the point was reached of incipient labor shortage in the rural areas which, together with rising agricultural productivity, would begin to drive up earnings of peasants and of agricultural labor. Such a point is a long way off in most Asian countries, faced as they are with a very rapid increase in the labor force through the 1970s and beyond. Southeast Asia faces an increase of more than a quarter in its labor force during the 1970s.[9]

[a]I am well aware that points 1 and 2 may seem to contradict each other, i.e., if much of the migration to the city begins as seasonal migration, how can we claim that the villagers concerned have only limited knowledge about prospects in the cities? But the seasonal migrants may be drawn from particular regions of the country, whereas in other areas knowledge about prospects remains much more limited. This appears to be the case in Thailand, where seasonal migrants to Bangkok are drawn heavily from the northeast and central plain areas.

The prognosis would seem to be for the pace of urbanization to be linked closely with the pace of industrialization, for levels of urban unemployment to remain high in both rapidly and slowly urbanizing countries for a lengthy period, and for such levels to fall substantially after a time only in those countries where both a decline in the growth rate of labor force and sustained rapid industrialization and rural development occur. Korea, Taiwan, and Singapore are three candidates for inclusion in the latter group of countries, but, unfortunately, it is not difficult to think of countries which are *not* candidates.

It could be argued that the foregoing analysis ignores the fact of increasing rural population pressures and the closing of the "land frontier" in a country such as the Philippines. Will this not cause a discontinuity in the process of urbanization, leading to faster rates of urbanization due to land hunger? Probably not. For one thing, the closing of the frontier is something that occurs gradually as marginal land is brought into production. Moreover, even where new land has been unavailable for decades, the capacity of at least some Southeast Asian societies to absorb more and more rural dwellers in a process of "static expansion" has proved to be very great.[10] This is not meant to deny that limits exist, or that serious problems may result from encroachment onto marginal land, but only to stress that the limit to available land is not reached suddenly, in the space of a year or two.

One thing is certain. The absorptive capacity of the rural sector will be put to the test in the coming decades in countries such as Indonesia, Philippines, Ceylon and, to a lesser extent, Thailand and Malaysia. It requires only simple arithmetic to demonstrate that the alternative to increasing rural populations would be rapidly growing levels of urban unemployment. The percentage rate of increase in employment in the non-agricultural sectors necessary to prevent the agricultural labor force from increasing is given by the following relationship:

$$r = t \times \frac{100}{d}$$

where

r = % rate of increase in employment in the non-agricultural sector.
t = % rate of increase in the total labor force.
d = non-agricultural labor force as percentage of total labor force.

Applying this formula to Indonesia, where the non-agricultural share of the labor force is, at most, 35 percent and the annual rate of growth of the labor force is approximately 2.5 percent, then $r = 2.5 \times 100 / 35$ or 7.1 percent. Even if the non-agricultural share of the work force rises to 50 percent, *r* would fall only to 5 percent. Given the continuous increases in labor productivity expected in parts of the non-agricultural sector,[b] the growth of non-agricultural output necessary to sustain these increases in employment would be of the order of 10 percent or more. The likelihood of sustaining such increases over a long period is remote, particularly in view of the serious foreign exchange constraints faced by many countries and the unfriendly trading stance adopted by many of the major western countries.

As a rough rule of thumb, we can say that in a situation of rapid population growth, not until the urban proportion of the population has climbed to about 40 percent (implying non-agriculture's share of the workforce is about 50 percent) can growth in the number of rural dwellers be halted, because it would require an impossibly rapid increase in production in the non-agricultural sector.

For countries such as Indonesia and Thailand, which still have more than 80 percent of their population living in rural areas and almost 70 percent of their work force in agriculture, this implies that rural population growth will continue for a considerable period, along with rapid growth of the urban population and a continued balance between levels of underemployment and low-productivity employment in urban and rural areas.

Long-term Perspectives

If it is true that urbanization is an inexorable process, then some plausible projections of urbanization in the Southeast Asian region can be made based on recent trends and likely developments. Such projections show that, despite the probability of a relatively slow pace of urbanization in many countries, a number of metropolitan areas will have grown into very large cities by the end of the century. The Bangkok-Thonburi metropolitan area will probably have grown from its present 3 million to between 10 and 13 million by that time;[c] Djakarta should be even larger, with some 12 to 16 million;[d] Manila should also be in the "10 million plus" range; Singapore, because it lacks a rural population reservoir and is reaching a very low rate of natural population increase,

---

[b]Particularly in manufacturing, transport and electricity supply; in East and Southeast Asia, during the 1955-65 period, output growth in manufacturing of 8.1 percent per annum was accompanied by employment growth of 5.0 percent per annum (United Nations, *The Growth of World Industry*, 1967 Edition, Vol. I).

[c]This estimate is based on a set of detailed projections computed at the National Economic Development Board in Bangkok; in all projections a decline in population growth rates is assumed, and Bangkok's share of Thailand's total urban population is held constant, although it had been gradually increasing during the decade of the 1960s.

[d]This estimate assumes that the 4.4 percent average annual growth rate recorded by Djakarta's population in the 1961-71 period will slacken considerably to an average of 3 to 4 percent per annum during the remaining decades of the century.

will number only about 3½ million very prosperous citizens unless its migration policy is drastically altered.

Cities such as Djakarta, Bangkok, and Manila, then, can be expected to attain a population by the end of the century as large as that of the largest cities in the world at the present time. Their growth, and that of many other large cities through the developing world, will be unprecedented. Viewed from the vantage point of Southeast Asia in the 1970s, the great cities of Europe were virtually static during their growth phase,[e] allowing time for each evolutionary step to be observed, measured, and, at least to some degree, planned. The doubling of the size of Southeast Asian cities in fifteen or twenty years, or even less, raises planning problems of an unparalleled kind, and demands techniques which have not yet been developed, let alone tested and accepted as valid. Moreover, these cities are projected to reach the New York-Tokyo size at much lower levels of per capita income than the United States and Japan enjoy. How, then, will the massive infrastructure investment needed to make these cities livable be financed? One reaction to this question is to conclude that growth cannot possibly take place, because the highly industrialized and sophisticated economy supporting the massive conurbations of New York and Tokyo certainly will not be reproduced by Indonesia, Thailand, and the Philippines by the year 2000; growth of their primate cities toward the size of present-day New York and Tokyo will be halted by such disasters as breakdown of transport systems, water supplies, and telephone systems, and by the sheer inadequacy of the administrative apparatus to implement the necessary long-range planning schemes that would be a precondition for making these cities habitable at three or four times their present size.

This argument is initially plausible, especially to those who have experienced the many frustrations of working in these large Southeast Asian cities. But before concluding too hastily that "it just can't happen" one might be forgiven for asking where the people will live, if not in these conurbations—in the rural areas, which in the Philippines and Java-Bali are already crowded to bursting point? . . . or in smaller cities, which will no longer be small if they receive the massive population increments projected? The dilemma is posed most sharply when we consider Java, where even the relative successes achieved in agricultural production during the past few years cannot alter the basic problems of mini-holdings, landlessness, and extreme poverty. Movement to the cities holds out the greatest long-term hope for millions of Javanese rural dwellers; moreover, the whole strategy of the country's economic development program is directed towards the sort of industrial development that goes hand

---

[e]Madrid appears to be the only European city to have doubled its population in less than twenty years at any time after reaching a population of one million. Other major Cities in the Western world to have achieved such a high growth rate include New York, Los Angeles, Moscow, and Leningrad.

in hand with urbanization. It is hard to see how the strategy could be otherwise; and yet the implications of taking this road are chilling, when viewed from the perspective of the environmentalist.

Table 6-2 shows a possible hierarchy of Javanese cities in the year 2000, assuming a highly successful industrial development program in the meantime and a gradual slowing in the Indonesian rate of population growth. The assumptions are made explicit in the footnote to the table, but it might be emphasized here that the 30 percent of population projected to be living in towns with populations exceeding 100,000, while well above the 13 percent in such towns in 1971, is well below the proportions at present living in such towns in countries such as Australia (65 percent), Britain (71 percent), the United States (58 percent), and Japan (55 percent).

I am not suggesting that the city populations shown in table 6-2 will actually be reached in Java by the year 2000. But they are indicative of the city size that will have to be reached eventually if Java progresses along the road towards a western pattern of economic development. Full success in attaining a

Table 6-2
A Hypothetical Projection of the Population of the Largest Cities in Java in the Year 2000 Given a Highly Successful Economic Development Program (in thousands)

1.	Djakarta	17.300
2.	Surabaja	5.760
3.	Bandung	3.840
4.	Semarang	1.642
5.	Surakarta	1.280
6.	Malang	1.152
7.	Jogjakarta	1.047
8.	Kediri	886
9.	Tjirebon	823
10.	Bogor	768

Assumptions

1.   Substantial decline in fertility in Indonesia as a whole. Indonesia's population reaches 215 million in year 2000.

2.   Percentage of population in towns above 100,000 rises from about 13 percent in 1971 to 30 percent in year 2000.

3.   City size distributions follow the Zipf rank-size rule except that, in the line with 1971 city-size distributions, the population of the largest city, Djakarta, is reduced by one third before calculation of other city sizes.

4.   Most cities of Java grow more slowly than other Indonesian cities, so that (for example) Semarang is passed in size by Palembang and Makassar before the year 2000.

As a matter of interest, the fourth, fifth, and sixth cities of Indonesia according to these calculations would be Medan (2.9 million), Palembang (2.3 million), and Makassar (1.9 million).

Japanese-style economy in Java would imply still more people living in the "million-plus" cities, particularly if population continues to climb after the turn of the century. Indeed, achievement of Zero Population Growth in the year 2020 together with a Japanese level of urbanization and perpetuation of the present urban size hierarchy would yield populations of about 31 million for Djakarta, 10 million for Surabaja, and 7 million for Bandung.

Present development strategy leads to a Java, with an area less than a quarter that of France and about a third that of Japan, sustaining about 7 "million cities" and two massive "urban corridors," one from Djakarta through Bogor to Bandung (comparable in population to the present Boston-to-Washington megalopolis in the United States) and the other in the Surabaja-Malang-Kediri triangle. A third agglomeration could well develop linking Jogjakarta and Surakarta in Central Java. And it is important to recognize that despite such massive urban development, the rural population of Java would be still larger than it is at the moment, barring catastrophes or highly unlikely trends in fertility.

The Japanese pattern would be more relevant to Java than, say, the U.S. pattern, not only because of its successful integration of intensive agriculture, large-scale industry, and small-scale, more traditionally-structured manufacturing industry, but also because of its heavy reliance on imported raw materials, a prospect that also faces Java if it is to industrialize successfully. But because of its extreme population density, Java would have to sustain a denser clustering of massive cities than Japan does at the moment, well before reaching present Japanese standards of affluence. Java has roughly the same population as Japan's main industrial island of Honshu on little more than half the area of the latter. Given the serious pollution problems now facing many parts of Honshu, the ecological problems facing an industrializing Java will be immense. The raw material requirements of an industrialized Java would be enormous, as would the volume of waste products generated. To reach present Japanese levels of per capita income, the people of Java would be producing (and presumably throwing away) twelve times more than they are at present. This is assuming no population increase. With a 50 percent increase in population, the figure would rise to eighteen times its present level.

That population density is a factor in environmental degradation is generally recognized, but its relative importance is very imperfectly understood. ECAFE has developed a crude Index of Pollution Potential[11] based on the formula

$$IPP = DP^2 \times PI : K,$$

where

IPP is index of pollution potential;

DP is density of population;
PI is per capita income and
K   is constant : 100.

This index is not very illuminating when applied at the national level. For example, it gives a much higher figure for Hong Kong than for Indonesia for any given future levels of per capita income and population. It has more meaning when applied to smaller areas: for example, a comparison between West Java and Selangor state in Malaysia. But to be really meaningful, it would have to specifically take account of the spacing and relationship of cities in a given area rather than crude population density as such. For example, the "Pollution Potential" of the Djakarta-Bogor-Bandung urban corridor that will probably develop may be much higher than that of the same population living in a number of large cities more evenly spaced throughout West Java.

The Javanese case is extreme, though with a quarter of Southeast Asia's population it deserves more than a cursory treatment. In Southeast Asia as a whole, there is no question that levels of consumption and production (and hence of raw material utilization and waste disposal) will be very much greater by the end of the century than they are at present. Attainment of a 6 percent economic growth rate (a rate that ECAFE planners believe can be attained by the region)[12] would yield a total regional product in the year 2000 almost six times its 1970 level. The share of product emanating from the major conurbations of the region will go up even faster, implying that problems such as air and water pollution (already severe in a city such as Bangkok) will greatly intensify unless (and probably even if) serious control measures are taken. In the enormous spate of literature on environmental problems during the past few years, there is no unanimity on the question of how far it is possible for the developing countries to progress towards western standards of living. The gulf between publications such as Forrester's *World Dynamics* or the British Movement for Survival's *Blueprint for Survival* or the Club of Rome's pronouncements, and the more optimistic assessments of other experts appears almost unbridgeable.[13] However, the less strident claims of the "prophets of doom" and the warnings that even the optimist finds necessary to make would both appear to be consistent with at least two conclusions:

1. If the developing countries hope to attain western levels of living, they had better get there with the minimum possible population growth;[f]

---

[f]Not that population growth will contribute anywhere near as much to resource depletion and pollution as will economic development; but a reasonable answer to the question, "What would cause more environmental damage than 300 million affluent Southeast Asians?" is "600 million affluent Southeast Asians."

2. It remains highly doubtful whether the developing countries as a whole can ever reach *present* western levels of living; though they will certainly produce many conurbations that match the size of the largest western cities of today.

Does Urban Growth Aid or Hinder Development in Southeast Asia?

If we are to develop a strategy for influencing the urbanization process, we must first decide whether urbanization is a good or bad thing. In facing this question, I think we must first ask: What is the possible and desirable development of the economic structure in Southeast Asian countries? And in facing *this* question, we must note the most basic and important difference between Southeast Asian countries today and western countries when they experienced their industrial revolutions: that population growth rates are much higher in Asian countries than they were in the west, and the escape valve of international migration is not available. Rapid population growth, as already pointed out, implies that both rural and urban populations will continue to grow for some time, and it adversely affects the possibility of transforming the industrial structure of the countries of the region.[14]

Let us separate urban growth into its two main components: natural increase and migration. I would argue that urban growth resulting from high rates of natural increase hinders development just as rural population growth resulting from high rates of natural increase does. If natural increase of population in both areas can be slowed we will be better off, and reduction of natural increase must be the underlying strategy which affects rural and urban development alike.

However, given the fact that, do what we might to reduce fertility, population will continue to grow rapidly for some time yet, there is the further question of whether we should look favorably on the rural-urban migration flow which is boosting urban growth rates. We are faced with the fact that for the next thirty years, which is well beyond the length of the time for which we can really do meaningful planning, the employment structure of Southeast Asia will remain predominantly agricultural and the agricultural workforce will continue to grow. There will be a gradual shift of the industrial structure towards industry and services, *but in this context of a still-increasing agricultural work force.* The history of western industrialization, then, is not the model for these countries to follow. The point at which a decline in the absolute number of workers in agriculture was reached was a key event in the economic history of the western countries. But such a point cannot be reached in Asia in the foreseeable future and perhaps never will be except in a few individual countries. Agricultural population densities will reach staggering proportions in parts of Asia. If a situation of calamity is to be avoided (and I think we must face the possibility of calamity in an area such as Java if rural populations increase much more) not only must the birthrate be lowered, but the whole of agriculture must be transofrmed in a labor-intensive fashion: the Taiwan example rather than the western example. Modernization of all kinds must be brought about *within the rural sector*. We cannot afford the luxury of waiting for the slow transformations that accompanied urbanization in the West; parts of Southeast Asia face a grim future unless the modernizing influences usually associated in some way with urbanization can be made to operate in the rural context as well. This applies particularly to fertility; it is essential that birthrates be lowered in Southeast Asia while the population remains predominantly rural and agricultural.

Viewed in this light, what should be our attitude to that part of urban growth that results from rural-urban migration? One of its benefits is clearly that it slows the growth of the agricultural work force and allows a better chance of achieving the increased productivity in agriculture so vitally needed. How well these opportunities in agriculture are grasped will then have a major effect on the future transformation of the economic and social structure of Southeast Asia.[g]

To the extent that the shift of the industrial structure away from agriculture is inevitably accompanied by urbanization, I would argue that urbanization is part and parcel of the process of transforming the economic structure and therefore a good thing. But obviously *not all* paths and patterns of urbanization are necessarily good, and here is where policy measures designed to channel urbanization into the most desirable pattern enter the picture. Of course, there are limits, such as the siting of agro-based industries in rural areas, within which the transformation of the economic structure is possible without the accompaniment of urbanization. But it is doubtful that the links between the shift in the sectoral structure of employment and urbanization can be broken to any great extent.

What of the political and social implications of urban growth? If the predilection of the Bangkok and Seoul populations for consistently voting against the government are any indication, then those who take the line that existing governments must be overthrown by a mass movement before any chance of *real* development is possible could argue that urbanization will help achieve this end. Those, on the other hand, who see political stability as consistent with economic and social development and therefore desirable, could argue

----

[g]Some people, of course, including Colin Clark and Esther Boserup, would argue that increasing population pressures in rural areas are a useful stimulus to productivity—increasing agricultural change. In reply to this, I would argue that even if this argument has some validity, rural population densities will still increase substantially *even if* part of the increase is drained off into urban areas.

that people be kept down on the farm. Yet, voting patterns do not necessarily lead to some kind of mass popular uprising. And the assumption that rural areas will remain quiet and a-political in the context of rapid population growth and rapid social change is also a dangerous one, as the recent experience of Ceylon might indicate. This whole question requires country-by-country study; no broad generalizations are possible.

Urban Development Strategy: Can and Should the Government Influence Urbanization Patterns?

Although migration to the town may be a rational step for some individuals to take in the circumstances prevailing in many Southeast Asian countries, it can be argued that such undesirable "externalities" as the political dangers inherent in the existence of masses of young urban unemployed and the burden of providing infrastructure in the cities may give sufficient grounds for government intervention to reduce the inflow. If continued migration and continued high levels of urban unemployment and underemployment are seen to be highly undesirable, the question remains whether there are policies related to urban development (as distinct from policies designed to foster rapid economic growth, which we can assume will be carried out anyway) that might have the effect of reducing these levels of unemployment, and whether a government would be justified in implementing such policies.

Before discussing the role of urban development strategy, it is necessary to emphasize the great constraints within which all development planning works. Development planning should be seen, not as the prime mover in development, but rather as an attempt to channel the powerful forces at work (many of them exogenous to the planner's equations) in ways that will result in the greatest advantage, or, at worst, the least disadvantage, to the country's development efforts.

One of the "great forces" that is pretty much exogenous is the legacy of past inertia or past misguided policies, which is no less of a straight jacket now than are problems resulting from some "act of God" or one of the major world powers. To illustrate simply, the problems faced by Indonesia and Ceylon because they let Malaysia "get the jump on them" in rubber research and replanting in the 1950s and 1960s (problems resulting from defective development planning and administration in these countries) are no less constraints on present development efforts than are the problems faced by South Korea, Taiwan, and Hong Kong because Mr. Nixon decided to woo the Southern vote and impose textile quotas (a decision which they are presumably powerless to influence).

Powerlessness to influence world economic trends that have a crucial bearing on their development efforts is a fact of life for Southeast Asian countries. If people increasingly prefer coffee to tea, there is little that Ceylon can do about it. If new breakthroughs in synthetic rubber occur, there is little that Malaysia can do about it. I would argue that these countries are also relatively powerless to influence the pattern and pace of urban development. Certainly prudence suggests limited expectations of success for urban development strategy. Western city planners seem to be coming more to the view that "town planning has claimed greater impact and range for its operations in dealing with the 'total man' than its delivery capability can justify. Over time this leads to lack of credibility . . ."[15] Or, as stated more succinctly by an Australian transport economist, "Whenever . . . (town planners) . . . try to fly in the face of political and economic forces, which is most of the time, they just screw things up."[16] It would be presumptuous to expect that planners in most Southeast Asian countries, working with a normally inadequate planning apparatus and (though it is unfashionable to mention it) often in a context of corruption and divided interest among political leaders, would be any more successful. In one Southeast Asian country that can remain nameless, careful selection of appropriate sites for a satellite city by the government's town planners was no more than a charade; final site selection appears to have satisfied the criterion of profitability for certain government officials rather than accepted town planning norms. On another plane, when Djakarta, or any other major Southeast Asian city, tries to halt the migrant inflow through a system of registration certificates it is attempting, like Canute, to hold back the tide. Such a policy can be operated successfully only by a strong, corruption-free, totalitarian government.

If, as I have argued, planning will have limited effect on the pattern and pace of economic development, which is the primary determinant of the pattern of urbanization, it is hard to imagine that planning designed specifically to alter the pace of urbanization will fare any better. There is simply little room for Asian countries to maneuver in terms of policy to affect overall rates of urban growth. The basic aim must be reduction of population growth rates in both rural and urban areas, recognizing that net rural-urban migration is inevitable if the industrial structure is to be modernized and the agricultural sector is to be given a chance of transformation into a high-productivity sector.

There is, I think, much more room to maneuver the pattern of city size distribution and the regional distribution of urban population, with the aim of a more balanced social and economic development for the country as a whole. For example, it is not difficult to suggest some steps that could be taken in Thailand to make for a more balanced development of urban centers: increasing the unrealistically low land taxes in Bangkok, alteration of outmoded legislation on location of abbatoirs and sawmills, adjustment of freight rates, creation of a new administrative capital away from Bangkok, development of a new port with a transport network bypassing Bangkok, plus a variety of measures (subsidies, zoning regulations, tax holidays, etc.) that in greater or lesser degree would weigh in favor of the location of industry in provincial towns rather than Bangkok. Even a policy of informing rural dwellers about urban employment opportunities—or lack of opportunities—perhaps through developing a system of employment exchanges, would have an effect. But what we are woefully ignorant about is the extent to which such measures, singly or in combination, would modify the pattern of urban development that will result from continuing with present policies and laws. And without any clear idea of the extent to which present trends would be altered, it is quite impossible to conduct any meaningful cost-benefit studies on the effects of various possible measures.

Conclusion

A key argument of this chapter has been that Southeast Asia is going to produce western-type megalopolises without the accompanying advantage of western-type affluence. City growth will be accompanied, not by rural depopulation, but by continuing expansion of rural populations. And income levels, though increasing, will remain far below those already existing in the West.

One is inclined to argue that failure by Southeast Asian countries to reach western levels of living would not be an unmitigated disaster. For one thing, indicators of levels of living are notoriously misleading. On the one hand, technological developments are not adequately reflected in per capita income measurements; on the other, much of what passes for higher income levels in the West is merely the superfluous trappings of a life style that is no more satisfying than the life style available to many lower-income groups. In other words, the quality of life is greatly variable at any given level of per capita income, as conventionally measured. It is not necessary for the developing countries to reach American mass-consumption levels, or even Japanese levels, to provide the *possibility* of a satisfying life for their populations.

The sort of rewarding life at lower per capita income levels that I am arguing is theoretically possible is a life that will have to be lived, for a considerable part, by people clustered together in cities and massive conurbations, some of them in the "10 million plus" population league. The daunting task facing the Asian planner is to fashion a better life, at relatively low per capita income levels, for a growing population distributed (eventually in roughly equal numbers) between traditional rural, urban, and major metropolitan areas. As I have argued earlier in this chapter, the resources available to the planner are limited, and he can hope to exercise only limited control over patterns of economic development and patterns of urbanization. The best he can do is to strive within these limits to control population growth, aim for balanced urban development, and for a pattern of economic development that stresses equality of income distribution and adequate opportunities for personal development at a lower level of material consumption than in the west. It would be tragic if some of the dissatisfaction currently expressed in the west about the defects of the mass-consumption society were not absorbed in a constructive way by planners in the developing countries, and used to modify the picture of the kind of society that they ultimately aim to create.

Notes

1. Analyses of urbanization in Thailand and Ceylon have recently been published: Sidney Goldstein, "Urbanization in Thailand, 1947-1967," *Demography* 8, 2 (May 1971); Gavin W. Jones and Selvaratnam, "Urbanization in Ceylon, 1946-1963," *Modern Ceylon Studies: a Journal of the Social Sciences* 1, 2 (1970); Godfrey Gunatilleke, *Rural-Urban Balance and Development: The Experience in Ceylon,* paper presented to the SEADAG seminar on Population and Development, Pattaya, Thailand, June 11-14, 1972.
2. Sidney Goldstein, "Interrelations between Migration and Fertility in Population Redistribution in Thailand," Chulalongkorn University Institute of Population Studies, Research Report No. 5 (1971), p. 15.
3. These findings are reported in F.W. Fuhs and J. Vingerhoets, "Rural Manpower, Rural Institutions and Rural Employment in Thailand," Manpower Planning Division, National Economic Development Board, Bangkok (July 1971, mimeo), pp. 88-91. A fuller report is in preparation.
4. Goldstein, "Interrelations between Migration and Fertility," pp. 7-24.
5. "The rather high rate of urban growth," Gunnar Myrdal writes, "is due more to the push of rural poverty than to economic dynamism in the cities;" Gunnar Myrdal, *Asian Drama* (New York: Twentieth Century Fund, 1968), Vol. III, p. 2131; see also Vol. I, p. 467-71.
6. N.V. Sovani, "The Analysis of Over-Urbanization," *Economic Development and Cultural Change,* Vol. XII, No. 2 (Jan. 1964).
7. See M.P. Todaro, "A Model of Labor Migration and Urban Unemployment in Less Developed Countries," *American Economic Review* (March 1969).
8. H.A. Turner and D.A.S. Jackson, "On the Determination of the General Wage Level—A World Analysis"; or "Unlimited Labor Forever," *Economic Journal* (Dec. 1970).
9. J.N. Ypsilantis, *World and Regional Estimates and Projections of Labor Force,* in Sectoral Aspects of Projections for the World Economy, First International Seminar on Long-Term Economic Projections, Elsinore, Denmark, August 14-27, 1966. Vol. III. Discussion papers. (United Nations, 1969 ST/TAO/Ser.c/105, Vol. III).

10. See Clifford Geertz, *Agricultural Involution: The Processes of Ecological Change in Indonesia* (Berkeley and Los Angeles: University of California Press, 1963).

11. ECAFE secretariat, *Man and the Ecosystem and the Scope of the Seminar*, paper prepared for ECAFE Regional Seminar on Ecological Implications of Rural and Urban Population Growth, Bangkok, August-September 1971, p. 8.

12. See U.N., *Economic Survey of Asia and the Far East, 1970* Table II-116.

13. Joseph L. Fisher and Neal Potter, "The Effects of Population Growth on Resource Adequacy and Quality," in National Academy of Sciences, *Rapid Population Growth: Consequences and Policy Implications* (Baltimore: Johns Hopkins Press, 1971); S. Fred Singer (ed.), *Is There an Optimum Level of Population?* (New York: McGraw Hill: A Population Council Book, 1971); Ansley Coale, "Man and His Environment," *Science* 170 (October 9, 1970).

14. See Theodore Ruprecht and Carl Wahren, *Population Programs and Economic and Social Development* (Paris: O.E.C.D. Development Center, 1970), pp. 28-34.

15. Raymond Bunker, Town Planning Department, Sydney University, quoted in *The Bulletin* (an Australian weekly), April 15, 1972, p. 21.

16. Nicholas Clark, also quoted in *The Bulletin* (April 15, 1972) p. 21.

7

Fertility, Social Class, and Out-Migration from Two Rural Communities in the Philippines

Gerry E. Hendershot

Introduction

In its "Statement on Population Policy and Program" the presidentially appointed Commission on Population of the Philippines recommended the adoption of a national population policy including the following elements:

> To promote the broadest understanding by the people of the adverse effects on family life and national welfare of unlimited population growth and to provide the means by which couples can safely, effectively, and freely determine the proper size of their families. . . .
> To adopt policies and establish programs guiding and regulating the flow of internal migration, and influencing spatial distribution in the interest of development progress. (Commission on Population 1970: 254, 256)

While the Commission explicitly recognized both rapid population growth and maldistribution of population as national problems, and recommended programs of fertility and migration control, it did not explicitly recognize that the two problems may be causally interrelated. Its recommended programs of fertility control (dissemination of family planning information and services) and migration control (resettlement and "provision of facilities such as safe water supply and other amenities to make rural life more attractive") (Commission on Population 1970: 257) do not seem to be interrelated solutions.

The views of eminent social scientist Gunnar Myrdal illustrate the interrelationships between rapid growth and maldistribution of population:

> Despite the roughness of the data and the varying conceptions of "urban" and "rural" among the countries, the evidence supports a relatively rapid increase in urbanization in South Asia. Yet the sex composition and mortality differences between urban and rural areas yield lower rates of natural population growth in urban centers than elsewhere. It is clear, then, then, that *net migration from rural to urban areas is the main reason for the more rapid growth of the latter.* But the movement cityward is largely unrelated to any vigorous expansion of urban employment opportunities, for, as

will be discussed later, the cities are beset by serious unemployment
and "underemployment" problems of their own. And in view of the
squalor, overcrowding, inadequate housing and sanitation in urban
centers, the movement toward the cities cannot in general be motivated by any increase in their "net attractiveness"; recent studies
indicate the reverse.

If this is so, then *the principal cause of South Asian urbanization
must be an increase, relative to urban areas, in rural poverty and
insecurity, at least in certain strata of the rural population, which
creates a "push" toward the cities. The dynamic element would
therefore appear to be the very rapid growth of population in the
region; this, in the first instance, presses on the lower strata in the
rural sector and then spills over, as it were, into the towns and cities.*
Urbanization is thus more a reaction *against* the lack of vigorous economic growth than a response to rising levels of income per head.
Indeed, much of it is due to factors inhibiting economic development,
such as civil wars, instability, and crop failures, as well as to excessive
rates of population growth. Instead of standing as a symptom of
growth, as it was in the West, urbanization in South Asia is an aspect
of continued poverty (Myrdal 1968: 470-471; emphasis added).

A similar argument is made by some students of Philippine society; Carroll
(1970), for instance, writes:

> [The high rate of population growth] is one of the major causes
> of pressure on the agricultural resources of the nation, fragmentation
> of land holdings and the increase of tenancy, destructive farming
> methods, *migration, urbanization,* unemployment, pressure on the
> educational system and on other public services (p. 12; emphasis
> added).

Put more concisely: (1) high fertility in rural populations causes poverty;
(2) the impoverished migrate to the cities in search of a livelihood; and (3) the
influx of migrants creates overurbanization, a maldistribution of population
which impedes economic development. While all of these propositions and
their underlying assumptions require testing in many cultural settings, it is
the more limited task of this chapter to test one derivative hypothesis in a
single culture. Using data from two rural communities in the Philippines, a
test will be made of the hypothesis: *the higher the level of fertility, the
greater is the rate of out-migration.*

The following situation is hypothesized. As the children of married
couples in the rural Philippines reach maturity, some decision must be made
about their futures, a decision in which the affected children, their parents,

and perhaps other family members may actively participate. The choices open for the children are basically two: (1) marry and set up housekeeping in the vicinity with a farm acquired from or through the parents or other family members; or (2) migrate to the city or another rural area where land is more easily accessible to individuals. It is assumed that the former is the preferred outcome; therefore, the real determinant is the accessibility of land in the vicinity of the family home. That accessibility depends largely on the land held—owned or securely tenanted— by the parents, and the number of siblings who have some legitimate claim to that land. In general the greater the amount of land held and the fewer the number of siblings, the higher the probability that the children can—and therefore will—remain near the family home on reaching their majority.

This is a simplified description of a very complex process with many variations in particular cases. Nevertheless, if the views expressed by Myrdal and Carroll are correct, this situation—or something like it—must occur with sufficient frequency to produce the hypothesized relationship between fertility and out-migration.

Data

The data for this study come from sample surveys conducted by the University of the Philippines Population Institute in the communities of Calasiao and Miagao. Murphy (1968) provides the following brief descriptions of each community.

> *Calasiao* is in the north central part of Pangasinan province. It is bounded on the north by Dagupan City, the provincial city of the province, on the south by the municipality of San Carlos, on the east by Binmaley, and on the west by Santa Barbara. The 1960 Census counted 29,330 residents; the municipality has an area of approximately 4,340 hectares and a population density of about 5.5 persons per hectare. It contains 19 barrios and the poblacion. Calasiao is one of 45 municipalities in the province.
>
> Pangasinan is a relatively prosperous area that has attracted migrants from neighboring regions. It has been, and still is, a melting pot for the Pampangos, Ilocanos, and Tagalogs who have built its essentially agricultural economy. The main crops are palay, coconuts, tobacco and sugar cane. Widespread cottage industries produce bamboo crafts, maguey and buri rope, nipa shingles for roofing, and coconut candy or "bocayo." Hats made from buri are also a major

establishments in Calasiao. Because it is near to Dagupan City, communications are good. In general, Calasiao is a prosperous agricultural
area (pp. 1-2).

Iloilo is one of three provinces on the Island of Panay in the Western
Visayas, and *Miagao* is one of 42 municipalities in Iloilo. Located in the
center of the province, Miagao is bounded by the province of Antique
of the northwest, by the municipalities of Igbaras and San Joaquin on
the northwest and southeast, respectively, and by Iloilo Strait on the
southwest. It comprises the remarkable number of 111 barrios plus
the poblacion. Miagao had a populaton of 32,114 in 1960 residing in
an area of 13,208 hectares; its population density was 2.4 persons per
hectare.
Iloilo has small net inmigration, and the population of Miagao
includes the native Ilongos, others from the Visayas, as well as immigrants from Luzon. The terrain varies from level plains to rolling
hinterlands, and the economy is largely agricultural. Rice and sugar
are the major crops although corn and mangos are also grown. There
is little industry, and what home industry exists is centered around
weaving.
Miagao is about 42 kilometers from Iloilo city which is the principal urban city of Panay. Transportation is by bus or train (p. 4).

The purposes and procedures of the surveys in Calasiao and Miagao have
been described by Concepcion and Flieger (1968). In each survey a 25 percent
random sample was drawn from a census listing of ever married women over
fifteen years of age, stratified by age and presence or absence of spouse. Home
interviews were conducted with sample women beginning in September (Calasiao) and October (Miagao) of 1967; the KAP-type interview schedule used in
both communities was identical, except that different local dialects were used.
Response rates were very high—99 percent in Calasiao, and 94 percent in Miagao.
The present study focuses attention on out-migration of children from the
parental home at the time of reaching their majority. This focus makes some
parts of the community samples irrelevant, namely those women either too
young or too old to have children in their late teens and twenties. For that
reason women under forty and women sixty or over were excluded from the
analysis. Also, women whose husbands were no longer living were also excluded;
the division of property and relocation of family members which might follow
the death of the household head are possibly related to out-migration, but in
ways probably different from those hypothesized here; to have included
widowed women would have confused the two sets of factors. Thus, the
sample for the present study consists of ever married women between the
ages of forty and sixty and living with their spouses. There were 469 such

women in Calasiao, about 31 percent of the total sample; in Miagao the number was 505, about 37 percent of the total.

Definition of Migrant

Near the end of the interview, women were asked the following question:

> We would like to know if you have had relatives, 10 years old and over, who had lived with you till 1960 but have since left for another barrio, province, or abroad.

If the answer was affirmative, then the number of such persons was ascertained as well as certain additional information—age, sex, marital status, destination, reason for leaving, etc.—for a maximum of three relatives. In this study all persons named in response to this question will be called "migrants" or "outmigrants." If the destination of a migrant were Manila or its suburbs, or any other chartered city in the Philippines (regardless of size or other characteristics), he will be called an *urban* migrant; a migrant to any other destination will be called a *rural* migrant.

Several features of this definition have a bearing on the interpretation of our findings. Although migrants are relatives of the respondent, the nature of the relationship is not known; more specifically, it is not known whether or not the migrants are children of the respondent. Much of the interpretation which follows will assume that migrants *are* the respondent's children. Two facts provide indirect support: (1) by far the most common household residence pattern in the rural Philippines is the nuclear family—father, mother, and unmarried children—which makes it unlikely related outmigrants would be anything but children of the respondent (Carroll 1970: 11); (2) other known characteristics of the migrants—such as age—are consistent with this assumption.

Migrants had to be at least ten years old at the time they migrated. This criterion seeks to exclude most moves by children accompanying relatives since the presence of such "epiphenomenal" migrants in the sample would make it more difficult to determine underlying causes of migration.

Persons who moved both very short and very long distances are defined as migrants. They had to have moved outside the barrio, but that might be a very short distance, especially in Miagao with its 111 or more barrios; at the other extreme, some migrants from Calasiao (11 in number) were destined for foreign lands. The distributions of migrants by broad geographic destinations are shown in table 7-1. Large majorities of the migrants in both municipalities did move at least to another municipality, and most of those moved outside of their own geographical region; on the other hand, some migrants

Table 7-1

Distribution (Percentage) of Outmigrants by Geographic Destination by Urban-Rural Destination: Calasiao and Miagao

Geographic Destination	Calaciao to			Miagao to		
	Total	Urban	Rural	Total	Urban	Rural
	Desti-nation	Desti-nation	Desti-nation	Desti-nation	Desti-nation	Desti-nation
(Number)	(225)	(140)	(85)	(382)	(244)	(138)
Total	100	100	100	100	100	100
Municipio[a]	17	2	41	8	3	17
Region[b]	35	26	51	24	9	51
Greater Manila[c]	36	59	0	47	73	0
Other[d]	12	13	8	21	15	32

[a]Within Calasiao for Calasiao outmigrants; within Miagao for Miagao outmigrants.

[b]Outside the municipio, but within the geographic region; the region for Calasiao includes the provinces of Bataan, Bulacan, Nueva Ecija, Pampanga, Pangasinan, Tarlac and Zambales; for Miagao the region includes Aklan, Antique, Capiz, Iloilo, Romblon, and Negros Occidental

[c]Includes the City of Manila and its suburbs—Caloocan, Pasay, Quezon, Makati, Mandaluyong, Paranaque, San Juan, Las Pinas, Malabon, Marikina, Navotas, Pasig, Pateros, and Taguig.

[d]Includes all domestic and foreign destinations not elsewhere classified.

in both municipalities—including substantial numbers among those classifed as "rural" migrants—"only" moved to another barrio within the municipality. There would probably be little disagreement with defining persons who moved outside the municipality as migrants, but there may be disagreement about so defining persons who moved to a nearby barrio. This is the problem Goldscheider (1971: 59-64) has called "the minimum question"—what is the minimum travel distance or social change which must occur in order for a move to be called migratory? Goldscheider concludes that "all residence changes—from one domicile to another" should be included within the concept of migration (p. 64). Such changes, he argues, require the migrant to reorganize his total round of activity. If that is true generally, then it must certainly be true in the case of a Filipino who moves to another barrio, because the barrio is the most important "container" of life activities in the rural Philippines (Eggan 1968). All persons who moved outside the barrio, even those who moved to an adjacent barrio, are defined as migrants in this study.

Finally, some data are lost because personal information was obtained for a maximum of three migrants from each household; thus, if a household had, say, five migrants, information on age, sex, destination, etc., was obtained for only three (which three is not clear). About 10 percent of the migrant cases in Miagao are lost for this reason, while only about 3 percent are lost in Calasiao.

Characteristics and Motivations

In table 7-2 the migrant samples are described with respect to age, sex, and marital status so that the reader may form more specific ideas of their characteristics. The migrants are predominantly young; most were in their twenties at the time of the interview, and would have averaged three to four years younger when they left the barrio. (The migration occurred between 1960 and the date of the interview in late 1967; if the annual rate of

Table 7-2

Distribution (Percentage) of Outmigrants by Age, Sex, and Marital Status by Urban-Rural Destination: Calasiao and Miagao

Age, Sex, and Marital Status	Calasiao to			Miagao to		
	Total	Urban	Rural	Total	Urban	Rural
	Desti-nations	Desti-nations	Desti-nations	Desti-nations	Desti-nations	Desti-nations
(Number)	(225)	(140)	(85)	(382)	(244)	(138)
Current Age of migrants*						
Less than 20	13	16	8	23	25	20
20-29	65	70	67	56	55	59
30 or more	22	14	35	21	20	22
Sex						
Male	49	56	39	50	47	54
Female	51	44	61	50	53	46
Marital Status						
Single	31	44	11	67	80	45
Married	69	56	89	33	20	55

*Would have been about three years younger, on the average, at the time of migration.

migration was about equal over that period of time, and if there is no serious memory bias in recalling the migration, then it can be assumed that the sample migrants are evenly distributed across the annual departure dates.) The youth of the migrants is circumstantial evidence in support of the assumption that they are the respondents' sons and daughters leaving home for the first time.

The sex ratio of the total migrant samples in the two communities is near unity. Among urban migrants males dominate in Calasiao, females in Miagao; among rural migrants females dominate in Calasiao, males in Miagao. Thus, both males and females are well represented in both urban and rural migration, and such differences in sex composition as occur are not consistent across the two communities.

The migrants in the two communities differ markedly with respect to marital status; while more than two-thirds of the migrants from Calasiao are married, only one-third of those from Miagao are married. Although the rural migrants in both communities are more likely than urban migrants to be married, the greater prevalence of marriage in Calasiao is found among migrants to *both* rural and urban destinations. This difference between the two communities is consistent with the findings of Smith (1971), who reports both earlier mean age at marriage and higher proportions married at age fifty for the region around Calasiao than for the region around Miagao. Smith suggests that such differences in marriage patterns "may be the product of imbalanced sex ratios, rather than underlying cultural prescriptions" (p. 167).

Out direct approach to uncovering the underlying causes of migration is to ask informants—the migrants themselves or others who know the circumstances—why migration occurred. The sample women in Calasiao and Miagao were asked for each migrant: "Why did he leave this place?" Responses were coded by the interviewers into one of seven categories. Marriage and work reasons (table 7-3) account for 95 percent of the migrants from Calasiao and 80 percent of the migrants from Miagao; each other reason accounted for less than 10 percent of the migrants in either community. Only 2 percent of the migrants from Miagao were reported to have left for "lack of land," and *none* of the migrants from Calasiao is reported to have left for that reason.

The infrequent mention of lack of land as a reason for migrating may be regarded as evidence against the fertility-migration hypothesis under examination in this chapter, but Gugler (1969) suggests that such evidence should not be weighed too heavily since recall of motivations for past actions, especially those of other people, may not be accurate. Also, there is a tendency for past actions to be attached in memory to culminating events, rather than to known causes which built up to them; thus, an occasion such as a marriage or a reported job opportunity in the city may be remembered as the "reason" for a migration actually caused by land shortage. Even though the "real" reason may be accurately remembered, it is the "cause" of only one incident of migration, while what is wanted is a class of causes which can explain variations in rates of

Table 7-3

Distribution (Percentage) of Outmigrants by Reason[a] for Leaving by Rural-
Urban Destination: Calasiao and Miagao

Reason for Leaving	Calasiao to			Miagao to		
	Total	Urban[b]	Rural	Total	Urban[b]	Rural
	Desti-nations	Desti-nations	Desti-nations	Desti-nations	Desti-nations	Desti-nations
(Number)	(225)	(140)	(85)	(381)	(244)	(137)
Total	100	100	100	100	99	99
Marriage	56	39	84	19	8	39
Work	39	53	15	61	74	39
Education	3	5	0	8	9	5
Family and Health	1	1	0	1	1	*
Land	0	0	0	2	*	6
Others	2	2	1	9	9	10

[a]As supplied by the respondant about the migrant

[b]Chartered cities

migration independently of such incidental causes. Finally, the individual may
be an inappropriate unit of study for migration; while it may indeed be the
individual who migrates, the underlying causes of his migration—despite the
motives imputed to him—may be factors affecting the family which he leaves
behind. Thus, it may be the *family* which is short of land, and this may be the
underlying reason for his moving to Manila "to find a better job"; in this case
his motive, even when accurately reported, is immaterial for present purposes.

A "Rate" of Out-migration

The measure of migration to be used in testing the fertility-migration hypothesis is a quasi "rate" of out-migration for each household formed by dividing
the reported number of outmigrants (urban or rural) by the number of children
even born to the respondent. This ratio is an attempt to approximate with the
available data the rate of out-migration among children of the respondents
between 1960 and 1967. It is only an approximation since, as noted earlier,
the migrants in the numerator are not *known* to be children of the respondents,
although it may be assumed that most are. Also, other unknown factors may

exist which would make this measure less than a perfect approximation to its intended referent.

Basing the ratio on the number of children ever born to the respondent has theoretical advantages over alternative possibilities. First, it makes the measure of migration a property of a family, rather than some class of individual; this is congruent with the theoretical assumption that population growth effects outmigration through the family, and permits the use of family characteristics as predictor variables. Second, children ever born is a commonly used measure of cumulative fertility; its presence in the ratio emphasizes the hypothesized relationship between fertility and migration. Alternative bases, such as the number of household members or the number of living children, while perhaps being better estimates of the population at risk, would not have had this clear connection to fertility. In any case, children ever born, living children, and number of household members are so highly intercorrelated as to make the distinction among them of only theoretical interest for present purposes.

Distributions of sample women by the ratio of outmigrants to children ever born (multiplied by 1,000) are presented in table 7-4. It will be noted that in about four-fifths of the Calasiao households the migration ratio is zero;

Table 7-4
Distribution (Number and Percentage) of Respondents by Urban and Rural Migrants Per 1,000 Children:[a] Calasiao and Miagao

| | Calasiao to | | | | Miagao to | | | |
| | Urban Destinations | | Rural Destinations | | Urban Destinations | | Rural Destinations | |
Migrants per 1000 Children	No.	%	No.	%	No.	%	No.	%
Total	469	100	469	99	505	100	505	101
None	380	81	414	88	345	68	395	78
1-99	7	1	11	2	10	2	9	2
100-199	45	10	29	6	51	10	48	10
200-299	25	5	11	2	56	11	28	6
300-399	4	1	3	1	23	5	11	2
400-499	3	1	0	0	7	1	3	1
500-599	3	1	1	*	8	2	9	2
600 or more	2	*	0	0	5	1	2	*

[a]Distribution of sample women by the ratio of outmigrants from the household to children ever born (multiplied by 1,000).
* = less than 0.5%

that is, it was reported that *no* related household member had left the barrio between 1960 and the date of the interview. In Miagao out-migration was more common, however, more than two-thirds of the respondents reported no outmigrants. It is apparent that in these communities large majorities of families had not experienced out-migration; conversely, the migration which did occur was concentrated among a minority of the families. This skewed distribution of families by migration ratios should be kept in mind while interpreting the mean migration ratios presented below.

Social Class and Children Ever Born as Predictors

It is hypothesized that fertility and migration, as measured by the household migration ratio, are positively related. Fertility will be measured by the number of children ever born to the respondents; since all of the women in this sample were forty or over at the time of the interview, it is a measure of *completed* fertility. (Only one of the sample women was pregnant at the time of the interview.) Distributions of sample women by number of children ever born—grouped into small, medium, and large numbers—are given in table 7-5.

Fertility is not the only theoretically significant determinant of propensity to migrate; the accessibility (to children) of farm land might also be hypothesized

Table 7-5

Distributions (Number and Percentage) of Respondents by Age, Social Class, and Children Ever Born: Calasiao and Miagao

Characteristics	Calasiao		Miagao	
	Number	Percentage	Number	Percentage
Age				
40-44	178	38	161	32
45-49	117	25	133	26
50-54	93	20	127	25
55-59	81	17	84	17
Social Class				
Non-farm	179	38	104	21
Small tenant	84	18	91	18
Medium tenant	19	4	79	16
Small owner	132	28	133	26
Medium owner	55	12	98	19
Children Ever Born				
0-4	128	27	136	27
5-7	143	31	177	35
8 or more	198	42	192	38

as related to the migration ratio, negatively in this case. This measure of accessibility to land was suggested by the work of Anderson (1962) on land tenure in a Pangasinan community. Anderson observes that:

> Earning a living in the barrio under study is dependent upon one's relationship to the land, the primary means of production and source of wealth. The type of relationship that one has to this primary resource largely determines his standing in the community. (p. 45)

> A number of analytically derived but empirically verifiable vertical categories stood out on the basis of occupation and access to the land. This categories corresponded to certain behavioral differences among barrio members, and certain cultural symbols seemed to be associated with them. Furthermore, families so categorized could be ranked consistently by a sample of community members. Analytically I found them to be characterized by a progressive weakening of a claim to derive a living from the land. (p. 46)

In order of descending access to land, the categories identified by Anderson (and their approximate numbers as a percentage of the total) are as follows: medium landowners (2 percent); small owners and secure tenants (17 percent); insecure tenants (44 percent); agricultural laborers (32 percent); and those regularly employed in non-agricultural work (5 percent). These categories are basically determined by access to land, but their social meaning is much broader; belonging to a category is an important determinant of the persons's social status within the community and has the character of social class.

While no attempt was made in this study to exactly replicate the social class categories identified by Anderson, the broad outlines of his analytical distinctions were followed. Two characteristics of the respondent's household were used in constructing social class categories: tenancy status and farm size. Respondents who reported that neither they nor their husbands owned or were tenants of any farm land were classified as "non-farm." If either spouse or the family owned any farm land at all, they were classified as "owners." If either spouse or the family were farm tenants but owned no farm land, the family was classified as "tenant." With respect to size, farms of less than 2 hectares were classified as "small"; farms of 2 hectares or more were classified as "medium." (Since fewer than 2 percent of the families owned more than 5 hectares, no "large" farm size category can be said to exist.) The "non-farm" category and the cross-classification of the tenant status and farm size variables yields five categories. The distributions of sample women among the five categories, ordered from low to high by presumed degree of access to land, are given in table 7-5. These figures are not comparable to those of Anderson since different definitions have been used and also because our data refer to only part of the total community. Inter-community comparisons are possible, the most striking of which is Calasiao's much higher proportion in the non-farm category. Whether this is due to a greater demand for non-agricultural laborers in Calasiao, or to the formation of a surplus labor force (Takahashi 1969: 140-43) cannot be determined with the available data.

One other variable, age, was introduced into the analysis as a control. The propensity to migrate is much higher in the young adult ages than in any others (see, for instance, Morrisson 1971); age, in fact, is one of few variables which are consistently and significantly related to the probability of migration. For that reason, a statistical control on age seems necessary in testing out fertility-migration hypothesis. Unfortunately, the ages of the respondents' children are not known; instead, the ages of the respondents themselves are used, it being assumed that the ages of mothers and their children are highly intercorrelated. The distributions of sample women by age groups are also shown in table 7-5.

The statistical technique of Multiple Classification Analysis is used to test our hypothesis (Andrews, Morgan, and Sonquist 1969). This technique is useful when dealing with several ordinal variables—such as age, social class, and children ever born—as predictors of an interval variable—such as the migrant ratio. We assume that the effects of the predictor variables on the dependent variable are additive. In other words, the total effect on the dependent variable of the predictor variables is simply the sum of their individual effects.

Table 7-6 presents age, social class, and children ever born as predictors of urban and rural migration ratios. The mean migrant-children ratios for the categories of each variable have been adjusted for the effects of the other two variables in the analysis. The results are briefly summarized as follows: (1) the relationship between age and migration is positive, but not consistently linear; (2) the relationship between social class and migration is not linear, as expected, but curvilinear, with "lower" and "higher" social classes having the higher migration ratios, and the "middle" classes having lower migration ratios (cf. Lee 1966: 56); and (3) the key relationship between fertility and migration is positive and linear in Calasiao, as hypothesized, but slightly curvilinear in Miagao. Thus, there appears to be limited support for the principal hypothesis under investigation.

Table 7-7 presents additional results from the analysis using age, class, and children ever born as predictors of the migrant ratio. The betas are standardized measures of the strength of the relationship between each predictor variable and the migration ratio, adjusting for the effects of the other predictor variables. The R^2 is the square of the multiple correlation coefficient, adjusted for loss of degrees of freedom. In no case is children ever born more strongly related to migration than age, and in only one case (rural migration from Calasiao) is it more strongly related than social class. Furthermore, in only one case (rural migration from Calasiao) does removing children ever born from the list of

Table 7-6
Urban and Rural Migrants Per 1,000 Children (Adjusted for Other Predictors)
by Age, Social Class and Children Ever Born: Calasiao and Miagao

	Calasiao to		Miagao	
Predictors	Urban Desti- nations	Rural Desti- nations	Urban Desti- nations	Rural Desti- nations
Age				
40–44	18	8	60	28
45–49	49	20	53	34
50–54	49	17	124	70
55–59	51	40	85	87
Social Class				
Non-farm	45	17	90	65
Small tenant	25	20	91	37
Medium tenant	12*	6*	39	40
Small owner	36	19	100	43
Medium owner	44	21	57	63
Children Ever Born				
0–4	25	4	74	50
5–7	37	17	73	41
8 or more	46	28	86	57

*Based on fewer than twenty cases.

Table 7-7
Betas and R-Squares for Multiple Classification Analysis Using Age, Social Class,
and Children Ever Born as Predictors of Urban and Rural Migrants Per 1,000
Children: Calasiao and Miagao

Municipality and Dependent Variable	Predictors	Betas			R^2
		1. Age	2. Class***	3. CEB	
Calasiao					
Urban migrants/CEB	1, 2, 3	0.16	0.10	0.09	0.02*
	1, 2	0.15	0.09	–	0.01
Rural migrants/CEB	1, 2, 3	0.20	0.05	0.17	0.05**
	1, 2	0.19	0.05	–	0.02*
Miagao					
Urban migrants/CEB	1, 2, 3	0.19	0.16	0.04	0.05**
	1, 2	0.20	0.15	–	0.05**
Rural migrants/CEB	1, 2, 3	0.19	0.10	0.06	0.03**
	1, 2	0.19	0.10	–	0.04**

* = $p < 0.05$
** = $p < 0.01$
***Nonfarm placed at the bottom of the S.E.S. ladder.

predictors reduce the total explained variance by a statistically significant amount. In other words, very little support is found here for the hypothesis that high fertility is related to high rates of outmigration.

Combining Social Class and Children Ever Born as a Predictor

It is possible that the effects of fertility and social class are not additive as has been assumed; rather fertility and social class may interact in their effect on migration. The effect of increasing family size might depend, on the social class level of the family, e.g., an increase in number of children which would force a radical change in the organization of a lower class family might be accommodated by a higher class family with little or no change. If such interactions do exist, then the assumption of additivity may be misleading. One solution to this problem is the creation of a new variable whose categories include all possible combinations of the interacting variables. This was done by simultaneously classifying respondents by the social class and children ever born variables already discussed, resulting in a fifteen-category combined variable (table 7-8). The numbers of sample cases in some categories are very small, making the mean migration ratios and the analyses based on them less reliable.

The mean migration ratios for categories of the combined social class-fertility variable, adjusted for age of respondent, are presented in table 7-9. Examination of these figures leads to no new conclusions regarding the hypothesized relationship between high fertility and migration; the most common pattern of relationship between children ever born and the migration ratio within classes, communities, and urban-rural destinations is positive, but this pattern is not consistent, especially in Miagao and among non-farm families.

Neither does table 7-10 lead to new conclusions. The combined social class-fertility variable is still less strongly related to the migration ratio than age of respondent. Also, the combined variable adds no significant amount of explained variance; that is, the amount of variance explained by age *and* the combined variable is not significantly different from that explained by age alone. Therefore, there is no significant interaction between class and fertility as causes of outmigration.

Summary and Conclusions

Since some scholars have argued that high fertility in rural populations leads to fragmentation of land holdings, poverty and economic insecurity, migration to the cities, and over-urbanization, this study has investigated the relationship

Table 7-8
Distributions (Number and Percentage) of Respondents by Social Class by
Children Ever Born: Calasiao and Miagao

Social Class and Children Ever Born	Calasiao		Miagao	
	Number	Percentage	Number	Percentage
Non-farm				
0–4	53	11	27	5
5–7	55	12	32	6
8 or more	71	15	45	9
Small Tenant				
0–4	16	3	20	4
5–7	21	5	42	8
8 or more	47	10	29	6
Medium Tenant				
0–4	2	*	9	2
5–7	7	2	27	5
8 or more	10	2	43	9
Small Owner				
0–4	38	8	49	10
5–7	45	10	42	8
8 or more	49	10	42	8
Medium Owner				
0–4	19	4	31	6
5–7	15	3	34	7
8 or more	21	5	33	7

* = less than 0.5%

between fertility and out-migration in two Philippine rural communities. Using
the number of children ever born as a measure of fertility, and the ratio of outmigrants to children as a measure of migration, little support was found for the
hypothesis that high fertility is related to high levels of out-migration, either
to urban or rural destinations.

Despite the lack of support for our hypothesis, rejection without further
consideration would be premature. It is possible that the two study communities are not typical of the thousands of Philippine rural communities, or of the
smaller number from which there is unusually large out-migration. In this
connection it may be noted that rates of farm tenancy are lower in the two
study communities than in those areas of the nation which have experienced
the greatest amount of agrarian unrest. It is also possible that the pressures
of high fertility operate in different ways than those hypothesized here; for
instance, population pressure may be a characteristic of whole communities,
in which case it is inappropriate to look for its operation at the family level
of social organization.

Table 7-9

Urban and Rural Migrants Per 1,000 Children (Adjusted for Age) by Social Class by Children Ever Born: Calasiao and Miagao

Social Class and Children Ever Born	Calasiao to		Miagao to	
	Urban Distinations	Rural Distinations	Urban Distinations	Rural Distinations
Non-farm				
0–4	52	6	85	88
5–7	49	15	99	54
8 or more	37	26	88	62
Small Tenant				
0–4	4*	2*	62	29
5–7	1	13	91	41
8 or more	47	33	110	31
Medium Tenant				
0–4	−11*	1*	− 6*	− 8*
5–7	− 4*	17*	45	32
8 or more	32	7	48	58
Small Owner				
0–4	13	10	105	36
5–7	33	22	77	41
8 or more	53	21	115	52
Medium Owner				
0–4	6*	− 7*	68	75
5–7	73*	15*	44	31
8 or more	52	47	59	82

*Based on fewer than twenty cases.

However, if our conclusions are generally valid—that is, if high fertility is *not* related to high levels of out-migration from rural areas in the Philippines, what are the implications for a national population policy? Programs of fertility control, even if successful, will not do much to alter the existing pattern of large scale rural-urban migration. Of course, reducing fertility will make the absolute number of migrants smaller than otherwise even if the *rate* is unchanged.

Programs of migration control treating other "causes" of rural-urban migration should be considered. On the basis of previous analyses of the sample survey data from Calasiao and Miagao, I had argued that rural-urban migrants in the Philippines are above the rural average with respect to aspirations and potential for upward social mobility; moreover, many realize their ambitions in the city (Hendershot 1970, 1971). If rural-urban migration leads to maldistribution of

Table 7-10

Betas and R-Squares for Multiple Classification Analyses Using Age and Social
Class–Children Ever Born as Predictors of Urban and Rural Migrants Per 1,000
Children: Calasiao and Miagao

| Municipality and Dependent Variable | Predictors | Betas | | R^2 |
		1. Age	2. Class-CEB	
Calasiao				
Urban migrants/CEB	1, 2	0.17	0.19	0.03*
	1	0.15	–	0.02*
Rural migrants/CEB	1, 2	0.20	0.20	0.04**
	1	0.19	–	0.03**
Miagao				
Urban migrants/CEB	1, 2	0.20	0.18	0.04**
	1	0.20	–	0.03**
Rural migrants/CEB	1, 2	0.20	0.16	0.03*
	1	0.20	–	0.03**

* = $p < 0.05$
** = $p < 0.01$

the population, perhaps real or perceived opportunities are maldistributed. A
change in patterns of rural-urban migration would require some change in the
actual or understood distribution of opportunities. It is unlikely in the short
run that any substantial improvement in opportunities can be effected in the
thousands of communities from which rural-urban migration originates; but
perhaps development of opportunities in regional urban centers, or the wider
dissemination of knowledge about already existing opportunities would divert
some part of the rural-urban migration away from the metropolitan centers
such as Greater Manila, and thus mitigate the effects of overurbanization (cf.
Commission on Population Growth and the American Future 1972: 223-24).
The responsiveness of rural-urban migrants to such programs is suggested by
the fact that the "best" outmigrants from Calasiao and Miagao already seem
to be going not to Manila, but to smaller urban centers (Hendershot 1969:
21-22).

References

Anderson, James N. "Some Aspects of Land and Society in a Pangasinan Community." *Philippine Sociological Review* 10 (1962): 41-58.

Andrews, Frank, James Morgan, and John Sonquist. "Multiple Classification Analysis: A Report on a Computer Program for Multiple Regression using Categorical Predictors." Ann Arbor: Survey Research Centers, Institute for Social Research, 1969.

Carroll, John J. "The Family in a Time of Change." In John J. Carroll et al. (eds.), Philippine Institutions. Manila: Solidaridad Publishing House, 1970. Pp. 10-16.

Commission on Population. "Statement on Population Policy and Program." In Vitaliano R. Gorospe, S.J. (ed.), Responsible Parenthood in the Philippines. Manila: Ateneo Publications Office, 1969. pp. 253-257.

Commission on Population and the American Future. Population and the American Future. New York: The New American Library, Inc., 1972.

Concepción, Mercedes B. and Wilhelm Flieger. "Studies of Fertility and Family Planning in the Philippines." Demography 5 (1968): 714-31.

Eggan, Fred. "Philippine Social Structure." in George M. Guthrie (ed.), Six Perspectives on the Philippines. Manila: Bookmark, 1968. Pp. 1-48.

Goldscheider, Calvin. Population, Modernization and Social Structure. Boston: Little, Brown and Company, 1971.

Gugler, Josef. "On the Theory of Rural-Urban Migration: The Case of Sub-Saharan Africa." In J.A. Jackson (ed.), Migration. Cambridge, England: University Press, 1969. Pp. 134-55.

Hendershot, Gerry E. "Characteristics of Migrants to Manila and Other Urban Places from Two Rural Communities." Paper presented to the Third Conference on Population in Manila.

___ "Cityward Migration and Urban Fertility in the Philippines." Ph.D. dissertation, University of Chicago, 1970.

___ "Cityward Migration and Urban Fertility in the Philippines." Philippine Sociological Review 19 (1971): 183-91.

Lee, Everett S. "A Theory of Migration." Demography 3 (1966): 47-57.

Morrison, Peter A. "Chronic Movers and the Future of Population: A Longitudinal Analysis." Demography 8 (1971): 171-84.

Murphy, Edmund M. Four Fertility Surveys. Quezon City (Philippines): JMC Press, 1968.

Myrdal, Gunnar. Asian Drama: An Inquiry into the Poverty of Nations. New York: Pantheon, 1968.

Smith, Peter C. "Philippine Regional and Provincial Differentials in Marriage and Family Building: 1960." Philippine Sociological Review 19 (1971): 159-81.

Takahashi, Akira. Land and Peasants in Central Luzon: Socio-Economic Structure of a Philippine Village. Honolulu: East-West Center Press, 1969.

Part IV

Adaptation to Population Growth

Introduction to Part IV

"Traditional society" is an anthropological construct; the reality in Southeast Asia is change. The pressure of growing numbers on resources has challenged old, familiar practices and institutions. On the governmental level, new policies, and programs are brought forward; on the individual level, people take up new occupations, move to new places, listen to new voices of authority. In Part IV we are provided with a look at the process of adaptation at the level of individual response—responses made against the background of governmental efforts to modify environmental or organizational conditions so as to alleviate the imbalance between numbers and opportunities.

Three of the selections focus on village life—the problems found there and adaptations to them. Anderson's piece on "Social Strategies in Population Change" draws on findings from a study of a large rural village in Central Luzon (Sisya) which has been under observation for more than ten years. Life is hard in Sisya, according to Anderson, "still there is neither desperation nor hopelessness." In his view the high volume of out-migration from Sisya has obscured the nature of the growing imbalance from the average villager. Nevertheless as opportunities for migration to Guam and Hawaii decline, as it becomes more difficult to find jobs in cities or in frontier areas, responses to mounting population density can be observed in postponed marriages, the disappearance of the male dowry, less elaborate weddings, more doubling-up of families. Thus far fertility within marriage shows no tendency toward change, a phenomenon that is general throughout the Philippines. Adaptation thus appears to follow a course of least resistance, preferring a timing adjustment with respect to the entry into marriage to a more fundamental quantity adjustment with respect to the number of children born to a marriage.

Sisya was established as the result of migration to Central Luzon over a hundred years ago. The Thai village of Baan Dong Phong reported on by Lefferts is a second or third generation pioneer settlement which already is showing signs of ecological imbalance. As elsewhere in Asia the farmers of Baan Dong Phong are adapting in part by adopting new high yield grain varieties, by diversification of output (cotton, ducks, fish)[1] and production innovations like rice milling.[2] Exogenous change has a lot to do with these new practices as well as with the greater implications of Baan Dong Phong in the market economy of the nearby town. Flood control and irrigation encourage new types of production and the newly created canal banks provide the roads to move produce to market. Alongside these changes, which expand local opportunities and so help to retain population in the area, Lefferts notes that kin networks operate as a kind of labor exchange for the family based enterprise system. Together these two factors, changes in production and cooperative labor recruitment through kin networks, have prevented large-scale migration to Bangkok. However, Lefferts questions how long these arrangements can cope with the growing pressure of population on resources.

Retaining population by creating new opportunities for local employment is not a simple matter in the absence of the type of labor discipline required by nonfamily enterprise. For example, it was pointed out to the seminar by Dr. Koentjaraningrat, Coordinator for Social Sciences in the Indonesian Institute of Sciences, that labor recruits to the industrial penumbra of Jakarta are not drawn from nearby kampungs but come from farther away. One reason for this is that insofar as local entrepreneurship and family interrelationships are involved, it is difficult to establish the kind of impersonal monetary relationships that characterize modern enterprise and which are basic to labor discipline. Second, local labor finds it difficult to extricate itself from family and village responsibilities which compete for the time and attention expected by the employer. This problem is more severe in the case of the male labor force. Local female labor, to the extent it can be released from child care responsibilities, is more usable and with the decline in domestic rice processing, should become more available.

Conditions in rural Indonesia appear to be changing rapidly. Singarimbun's study of Srihardjo, a district near Jogjakarta, is based on field work carried out in the late 60s. The adaptation to increasing population density observed in Srihardjo involves the erosion of the traditional mutual aid system which while it assured a degree of equity, tended to weaken the motivation required for individual entrepreneurship. When all that can be shared is poverty, it is not surprising that a clean employer-employee relationship with limited liability for the welfare of others will appeal to those threatened under the old system with insupportable claims on the fruits of their labor. When rice gives way to cassava in the local diet the threat is plain for all to see. The implication of these recent changes in productive relations for development would appear to be far reaching.

With 98 percent of the population of Java resident in the same districts where they were born, mounting population density puts enormous pressure on traditional institutions and values. The lack of an escape through migration is basic to the thesis of agricultural involution propounded by Geertz.[3] But the elaboration of customary obligations and the retrogression of technology toward more labor intensive modes of production become nonadaptive when the absolute sustenance requirements of a growing population exceed the capacity of a highly involuted system of production. Thus in Srihardjo deepening poverty has led to a widening of class differences, a reorientation away from the values of the past toward present concerns, and an acceptance of subordination. One may see in this the kinds of changes required for a mobilization of the population along new lines of development. Given stable government, innovative and effective leadership, the rural population may prove to be ready for fundamental change to a surprising degree.

What of the other side of the problem—the urban areas to which many migrants find their way? Hackenberg's account of a squatter barrio (Lapu Lapu) in Davao City considers some of the issues involved in the transformation of rural folk into effective urban dwellers. She casts the process into a three-stage conceptualization which involves both upward social mobility and the acquisition of attitudes suitable for adaptation to the nonfamilistic institutions of the urban community. Migrants to Lapu Lapu manifest this transformation in most respects but as yet have not adopted modern practices relative to their own fertility. The proportion of married women practicing birth control (18 percent[a]) is about average for the Philippines and for Southeast Asia. Once again we have a demonstration of the resistant nature of the patterns of behavior associated with high fertility.

A favorite alternative to rural-urban migration is rural resettlement. Indeed, as Fernandez states in his chapter, "resettlement over the years has been a vaguely-defined and little-understood safety-valve measure which is handily revived with every crisis situation—the Huk insurgency, the Taal volcano eruption, dislocation of squatters from Manila and Quezon City, displacement of agricultural tenants—in the untested hope that population movement might be a solution. The time is ripe for a rethinking before the next revival." The Philippines of course is not the only country in Southeast Asia to have put its trust in resettlement. Fernandez's account of the Narra resettlement scheme brings out the problems and underscores the truth of Irene Taeuber's comment that resettlement projects, however hopeful for the landless and the poor in the abstract merely "transplant the old ways of life to new areas. Land acquisition is not sufficient as a stimulant to agricultural production, social development, or upward economic mobility."[4]

The chapter by Laquian considers broadly the question of encouraging, discouraging, and coping with migration. The importance of this question resides in the fact that migration is the adaptive response that typifies communities that are implicated in larger divisions of labor. Expansion of the area of interdependence with consequent redistribution of population is in fact what we call development. However population flows are dependent upon capital flows. Therefore the establishment of successful migratory streams in countries with low levels of personal savings requires planning and a collective investment effort which by default becomes a government responsibility.

The final chapter, that by Heer and Wu, takes up consideration of an

---

[a]There is virtually no difference by age in this percentage suggesting that new patterns are not setting in even among older, higher parity women.

adaptive response on which a good many hopes are centered. This is the so-called child-survival-hypothesis, the idea that as a consequence of the improved chances for child survival, married couples will decide to have fewer children without any loss of insurance for their own maintenance in old age. Thus low mortality, which is the major cause of rapid population growth and the consequent redistribution of population, may be self-adjusting in the long run. In the short run improved child survivorship can lower fertility without any necessary redefinition of the ideal family size. This comes about purely by an extension of birth intervals as the result of prolonged lactation by mothers whose babies survive. Changes in child care practices that would diminish lactation, for example, bottle feeding or solid food supplements that would require only partial breast feeding, would have the reverse effect. Reduction of fertility levels as the result of a conscious, planned reassessment of family size norms is however the ultimate adaptive response which sooner or later must occur. The alternative is a return to higher levels of mortality. The vital question is how long will this take? A clue perhaps is to be found in Heer's study in Taiwan, where compared to most other areas of Southeast Asia conditions are highly conducive to such change.

Notes

1. Writing of "China's Green Revolution," Ben Stavis notes that food grain production per capita has remained "about constant" whereas there is reason to believe that there has been a "diversification of the rural economy" in the form of increased production of vegetables, fruits, animals, fish, tobacco, tea, herbs, cotton, and other fibers, etc. *Monthly Review* 26, 5 (Oct. 1974).
2. Rice milling has caught on to a remarkable extent in Southeast Asia. In 1971 80 percent of Java's rice crop was hand pounded; estimates for the current period (1973) put the figure at less than 50 percent and possibly as little as 10 percent. See C. Peter Timmer, "Choice of Technique in Rice Milling on Java," *Bulletin of Indonesian Economic Studies* 9, 2 (July 1973).
3. Clifford Geertz, *Agricultural Involution: The Process of Ecological Change in Indonesia* (Berkeley: University of California Press, 1963).
4. Irene Taeuber, "Population Growth and Development in Southeast Asia." The Population Panel Seminars, 1972, Southeast Asia Development Advisory Group of the Asia Society

8

Social Strategies in Population Change: Village Data from Central Luzon

James N. Anderson

Introduction

This chapter reports some early findings of a ten-year study of population trends and social change in a barrio in the central part of Pangasinan province, Philippines. It describes the research project, the nature of the village studied, the principal features of population change during the period of study, the perceptions of population and resource trends (and of economic opportunities locally and elsewhere), and behavioral accommodations (personal, collective, and institutional) to these trends with particular attention to migration.

A focus of concern is whether there is a Philippine equivalent of the theme developed by Geertz in *Agricultural Involution.*[1] More specifically and with respect to provinces, it is important to determine "which elements of the population have tended to manifest explosive growth, and how has the additional stress on subsistence, social control, and the like been managed by the community?"[2] Considering the rate of population growth in the Philippines and the density of this part of Central Luzon, the expectation of massive population pressure and involuted social responses as described by Geertz for Java is appropos. As this chapter will show, however, our knowledge about population and social change at the microlevel in this and other specific regions of the Philippines is so poor that there is little factual basis for such a conclusion.

Objectives of the Research Project

My study of social demography in Central Pangasinan is part of a broader ongoing research entitled "Comparative Research into Philippine Economic and Social Organization and Change." This ambitious project involves the controlled comparison of four prominent types of socioeconomic adaptations within the provinces of Pangasinan, Nueva Ecija, and Tarlac. I identify these general ecotypes as: (1) small-holding diverse crop agriculture, (2) hacienda

I wish to acknowledge the support provided by grants from the Ford Foundation, by the Center for South and Southeast Asia Studies of the University of California, and by the National Science Foundation, which made this research possible. I also take this opportunity to thank my colleagues Ben Bautista, Floro Danao, Victor Garcia, and Julita Terrado who provided able field assistance and James Dobbins and Raymond Mitchell who painstakingly conducted the analysis of census data.

rice cultivation, (3) plantation sugar production, and (4) fish-gardening and fish pond management. In a collaborative effort involving several investigators, longitudinal microanalyses of economic and social organization and of demographic and ecological change in these four ecotypes will be accomplished in research sites representing each type. Research on the first type has been completed and is reported on in this chapter. Research on the second is underway. Perspectives concerning internal rural-rural migration developed in the course of research at the first two sites will be drawn upon for the present paper.

The Sisya Study—Saturated Small-Holding Diverse Crop Agriculture

The Sisya study was an intensive, decade-long study of a large rural village and its semi-urban solar town. Earlier research and publication focused upon aspects of the economy[3] and upon elite-peasant relations.[4] I am presently investigating the reciprocity of population and demographic changes and changes in organization and behavior.

Field work in Sisya and in Reina Maria covered the periods 1961-62 (fifteen months), 1966 (two months), and 1971 (three months). Population data were collected by four techniques: (1) by household census and interview, (2) by copying and analyzing parish records, (3) by consulting published and unpublished census materials dating from Spanish times to the present, and (4) by compiling genealogies. These data are supplemented with information collected by standard anthropological procedures: participant observation, journal field notes, nondirected interviewing, and mapping. In addition I carried out intensive study of selected households, collected life histories, and did settlement, land use, and land tenure reconstruction, ethnohistorical analysis, and nutritional surveys. Data included in this paper are based principally on the analysis to date of household censuses collected in 1961, 1962, 1966, and 1971.

Sisya: General and Unique Attributes

Sisya is a rural barrio composed of four *sitios*. The sitios, made up of kinsmen and neighbors, approximate natural social units. The oldest of these, Ilokandia, was settled by Ilokano-speaking migrants from Paoay, Ilocos Norte, sometime in the 1970s. Other migrants were "called" by relatives already established in Sisya. Some early migrants also made their way via Tarlac where they were unsuccessful in finding places to settle. By the 1880s Pangasinan elites had claimed ownership to unclaimed agricultural lands and subsequent migrants accepted the status of tenants. In sitios Sisya Center and Sisya West migrants were more heterogeneous than in the initially established sitios; fewer migrants were related or from similar places of origin. The four sitios reflect differences in the modes of their settlement even today. Ilocandia is 85 percent Ilokano speaking, East is 60 percent Ilokano, Center is 47 percent Ilokano, and West is 25 percent Ilokano. Almost all other residents are native Pangasinan speakers.

The sitios differ in the dates of their settlement and in ethnolinquistic composition and they also differ significantly in land use, land tenure, and degree of social homogeneity. Ilokandia in 1961 had a high proportion of owners, owner-cultivators, and owner-tenants (68 percent) and a low proportion of tenants (16 percent) and of irregularly employed (12 percent). By contrast Sisya East had a higher proportion of tenants (56 percent) and irregularly employed (15 percent), and a moderate proportion of small owner, owner-cultivators (26 percent). Sisya West is twice as populated as East but had, like the latter, a high proportion of tenants (38 percent) and irregularly employed (32 percent), and a low proportion of owners, owner-cultivators, and owner-tenants (22 percent). Sisya Center had a moderate proportion of tenants (29 percent) and irregularly employed (19 percent) to owners, owner-cultivators, owner-tenants (35 percent), and a high proportion of regularly employed persons holding jobs outside the barrio (15 percent).

Sisya is a migrant village. In the late nineteenth and early twentieth centuries central and eastern Pangasinan, Nueva Ecija, and Tarlac were "frontier" provinces much as Davao and Cotabato were in the 1950s and 1960s. Like the Ilokano and Pangasinan villages that spawned them, villages like Sisya have continued to send out migrants. Many Sisyano men have migrated abroad for employment. Others have migrated to Manila, Baguio, and Angeles. Many families have taken part in the pioneer settlement of first Eastern Pangasinan and Nueva Ecija, then Isabela and Nueva Viscaya, and finally Cotabato and Davao. Taking their places, immigrants, now nearly all relatives of barrio residents, still continue to trickle into Sisya.

Emigration and immigration aside, an extraordinary amount of spatial mobility characterizes the shifting population of Sisya. Individuals and households are constantly alert to new occupational opportunities, and four or five residence shifts in the domestic cycle of a family are not uncommon. These involve change of residence from one sitio to another, to neighboring barrios, or to neighboring towns where either member of the conjugal pair have close relatives. The construction of the Philippine house encourages local movements that permit families and individuals to test alternative socioeconomic options. The strategy of high mobility adopted by so many Sisyanos is related to three other factors: (1) the shortage of land resources and therefore of access to agricultural or residential land, (2) the high demand and limited opportunity for regular employment, and (3) the relatively high educational attainment among some groups. These factors promote high spatial mobility especially among the most insecure households and promote migration for employment and to the frontier among the most secure households in the barrio.

As implied in the foregoing, significant socioeconomic differences exist within the population of Sisya. These differences are based on the degree of access to land and on the regularity of employment of household heads. They are reflected in differential production, consumption, involvement in market transactions, participation in village social affairs, and in important cultural practices. Especially significant because of their marginal position relative to other Sisyanos, is the group I have called irregularly employed. Such people constituted 22 percent of the barrio population in 1961 (they constituted 32 percent of the population of Sisya West!). This expanding group of rural proletarians is involved with agriculture only as seasonal (and basically non-essential) wage laborers in rice planting and harvesting. Most of them are really unemployed, being supported mainly by tertiary occupations. All irregularly employed households are characterized to a greater extent than are other Sisyano households by multiple occupations by which they scratch out an existence.

Man-land and man-man relations with respect to land are extremely complex. Most of the fields within the barrio (total area, 247 hectares) and fields outside of the barrio (approximately 50 hectares) are cultivated by Sisya residents. In 1961, of the approximately 255 households, 92 (36 percent) held possessory rights over 141 hectares of agricultural land (another 11 percent held possessory rights over 7 hectares of residential property). Sisyano owners (and their tenants) retain the crop production of these fields. The remaining 95 hectares of agricultural land (and 4 hectares of residential property) are owned or held in pledge by people residing outside of Sisya. Because all this absentee owned or held land is sharecropped, one half of its production leaves the barrio. Most of its production (that of 64 hectares) goes as half share to landowners belonging mainly to the provincial elite class who reside in Reina Maria or beyond. Sixty-one Sisyano tenant households contribute to the provisioning of this elite group. Thus, although the ecological density for the village in 1961 was 1,468 people per square mile, the actual number of people who receive part of their sustenance from the 56 percent of households actually engaged in cultivation increases the effective pressure on resources to a considerably higher degree than this density figure would suggest.

Agricultural land is divided into holdings of various sizes, all astonishingly small when compared with holdings in most other regions in the Philippines. One landlord owns 10 hectares (the largest single holding) and, as with other relatively sizable holdings, there are numerous heirs awaiting its division. Three other individuals have holdings of more than 6 hectares. Five other holdings, which in the last generation were of comparable size or larger (one was 24 hectares, another 11 hectares), are now divided among heirs and average about 2 hectares each. Only about 51 percent of all agricultural holdings owned in the barrio are larger than 2 hectares.

The size of cultivators' farms is much smaller still, and is closely associated with tenure-occupational status. For the barrio as a whole, farms vary in size from an average of 0.94 hectares for tenants to 1.3 hectares for owner-cultivators and to 2.3 hectares for owner-tenants. The resulting differences in economic security for the different households are enormous when one takes into account the relative soil fertility, types of land areas involved, improvements made on them, their resulting differential productivities, and the fact that tenants share only one-half of most crops they produce. These differences can be expressed in rough annual cash earnings (1961) of from ₱30.00 for the poorest tenants to more than ₱1,000.00 for the richest owner-tenant, with owner-cultivator falling in between. The potential for cash earnings grew enormously with the advent of the government-subsidized Virginia tobacco market in 1956. The zenith of the tobacco market in Sisya came during the years 1960-63. With the decline of this market in 1964, cash earnings from tobacco, which had amounted to between 75 percent and 90 percent of most dry field cultivators' annual cash earnings during the peak years, declined drastically.

Sisya possesses certain physiographic features that permit relatively high agricultural productivity, and that provide barrio people with a good supply of aquatic fauna. These features allow higher population densities than could otherwise obtain in an area of comparable size. There are no less than three rivers and six creeks that water the area of central Pangasinan, endowing it with unusually good water conditions, in particular with a relatively high water table, and in earlier times laying down fertile alluvial soils. This situation favors Sisya in three ways: by permitting the year-round cultivation of crops, despite a long dry season; by providing the aforementioned possibilities for fishing and collecting; and by permitting potable domestic water to be drawn from constantly flowing artesian wells. However, most of the rivers and streams themselves are of little use for irrigation because they flow in deeply cut beds from three to five meters below the level of the land.

Though it is hardly perceptible, most of Sisya, like its neighboring barrios to the north and west, is elevated a meter or two above the areas to the south and northeast. Thus most of the lands in the barrios are dry uplands, slightly too high for sufficient water to collect or to be lifted by present techniques in order that irrigated rice may be grown. This feature, of course, has an important effect upon agricultural land use and productivity and restricts the hectarage of irrigated rice cultivation.

The composition of agricultural crops between 1961-71 changed drastically in response to changing market conditions, but the diversity of crops and the continuity of cropping (rotation) that are characteristic of this ecotype remained. The principal crops cultivated during the decade were rice, sugar (grown to supply the nearby sugar mill), vegetables (corn, mango, tomatoes, beans, and cassava), Virginia and native tobacco, and a variety of fruits.

The characteristic features of diverse crop land use, land tenure, population density, type of market involvement, elite-peasant relationship, and readiness to migrate shared by people living in this ecotype relate Sisya and other villages of central Pangasinan with villages in the Ilocos regions. These features contrast sharply with those characterizing the rice hacienda and sugar plantation types of eastern Pangasinan, Nueva Ecija, and northeastern and southcentral Tarlac, respectively.

Although Sisya is clearly rural in setting and in character, many in the population have little to do with agriculture (the irregularly employed) while 14 percent derive their principal support (and many others supplementary support) from the work of members who are regularly employed in jobs outside the barrio, in Reina Maria, Dagupan, Baguio, Angeles, Olongapo, Manila, Guam, Hawaii, or mainland United States.

In summary, life for almost all residents in Sisya is hard and opportunities are limited. Yet there is neither desperation nor hopelessness. Despite the precarious margin of existence, to which even the poorest Sisyanos have accommodated remarkably well, and in the face of clearly recognized evidence of diminishing resources and expanding numbers, hope persists that conditions will improve for one's own family or oneself if not for the larger collectivity. All Sisyanos aspire to and compete for higher social ranks. This goal is a constant concern, whatever one's position in the relatively continuous status hierarchy. Formerly rank and prestige were conferred almost exclusively by land ownership or by secure access rights to productive land, but in the last decade more alternative opportunities have become available in the form of new possibilities for employment. The constraints on education, nonagricultural employment, and professional status for barrio people have gradually loosened in the past two generations and this has begun to result in a broadened Philippine labor market. Nevertheless, despite alternate sources of rank and prestige, the ownership of 247 hectares of real property and the possession of strong claims to its use are still objects of major concern to Sisyanos. But land holdings and farm size are already small and are diminishing owing to increasing human pressure on the land. Moreover almost one-fourth of the population subsists mostly by largely superfluous labor in planting and harvesting. Therefore, no one is very secure in Sisya or, for that matter, even in the Reina Maria *Poblacion,* except the medium-scale or well-educated, upper-class landlords and professionals and those who have regular salaries.

Perceptions of "Population Pressure"

During the fieldwork of the summer of 1971 I heard many married Sisyanos express a desire to limit the size of their families. Generally they voiced the idea that it was difficult to raise a large number of children adequately. Others complained more bitterly than I remember they had in 1966, or in the early part of the decade, that the size of tenancies or owner-cultivated fields had grown too small to support their families. Still others referred to more diffuse indicators of a diminishing quality of life. Although my inquiry into these matters was not systematic, among the Sisyanos I spoke to only a few thought that conditions had not deteriorated during the 1960s. A life already hard seemed to be getting harder.

Perceptions of Population Change

Aside from their diffuse recognition of growth in the number of people and in the number of households, Sisyanos were aware of the increased size of families. This seemed especially acute to those old enough to consider from the perspective of three generations the size of the families they were born into and the size of those their grandchildren were born into. But this long-term perspective is rarely achieved, and even then may be blurred by the advent of deaths, secondary marriages, and step-siblings. The surest indicator of growth in family size to Sisyanos lies in the consequent fragmentation that occurs upon the division of inheritance of the always limited amount of property among numerous heirs. Other obvious indicators of growth to Sisyanos are the size of the school-age population and the expanding need for teachers and for facilities. More particularly, for parents having several children in school, the fact of growth is brought home by the additional cash demands to cover the costs of books, supplies, and donations.

Nevertheless, Sisyanos are happy about the large number of young people in their population. They are also proud that a large number of the senior generation have attained old age. However, miscarriages, infant and childhood deaths, and deaths to adults and to the aged occur often enough that the substantial advantages of births over deaths is not readily apparent to villagers. Emigration, as we shall see below, completely blurs any clear recognition of catastrophic growth. (See tables 8-1 and 8-2) For the intercensual period the surplus of births over deaths (149) is in large measure offset by net migration (116) for a net growth of 33 persons or 6 percent over the period.

Only one group in Sisya acutely recognizes the population imbalance in the sex ratio that occurs in the fourteen to twenty-four age group. These are the young males in their courting years who deplore the lack of barrio girls a few years their junior. A surprisingly high proportion of girls in their teens and early twenties live and work outside the barrio as housemaids and salesgirls. Substantially all of the out-migration is to other barrios and is equally divided between individual and family migration. Inmigrants, about half of whom are in late adolescent or young adulthood, also come preponderantly from other barrios. Of the outmigrants, 70 percent are from the group that was under eighteen years of age in 1962 and between nine and twenty-six years of age in 1971. Thus both in and out migration involves the young

Table 8-1
Sisya West: Population by Age and Sex and Percentage Change 1962 to 1971

Age	Female			Male			Total		
	1962	1971	Percentage Change	1962	1971	Percentage Change	1962	1971	Percentage Change
0-8	105	94	−10.5	100	103	3.0	205	197	− 3.9
9-17	61	58	− 4.9	61	68	11.5	122	126	3.3
18-26	21	40	90.5	30	42	40.0	51	82	60.8
27-35	34	24	−29.4	23	28	21.7	57	52	− 8.6
36-44	26	24	− 7.7	21	17	− 19.0	47	41	− 12.8
45-53	23	23	—	26	17	− 34.6	49	40	− 18.4
54-62	12	21	75.0	10	23	130.0	22	44	100.0
63+	8	10	25.0	10	12	20.0	18	22	22.2
Total	290	294	1.4	281	310	10.3	571	604	5.8

Table 8-2
Components of Population Change 1962 to 1971: Sisya West

| | 1962 Census Population | In-Migrants* | | Out-Migrants | | | | Birth | Death | 1971 Census Population |
		Within Barrio	Other	With Barrio Ind. Family	Ind.	Other Family				
Female	290	6	55	0	1	60	64	83	15	294
Male	281	1	43	1	5	44	46	90	9	310
Total	571	7	98	1	6	104	110	173	24	604

*Includes births to in-migrants subsequent to the 1962 Census.

members of the population predominantly. This is the case for both males
and females.

Sisyanos scarcely view themselves as a solidary population. They recognize that they are highly mobile people and they are not surprised by a rapid
turnover of neighbors or by drastic changes in the composition of their sitios
over time.

Perceptions of Resource Availability
and Opportunities

From the perspective of a casual observer it would be difficult to differ-
entiate Sisya from other peasant barrios in Central Luzon. This image of an
agrarian setting is not mistaken. The rhythm and style of life of Sisyanos are
definitely rural. Yet the casual observer would be wise to withhold judgment
about just how homogeneous its society is or how characteristically "peasant"
its culture. Half of the population of Sisya has at most only a seasonal connection with agricultural activity; many in the population have no connection
at all. Some Sisyanos draw their total support from resources external to the
barrio and almost everybody taps some external resources.

The point is that Sisya is very much an open system. Its inhabitants have
never been totally self-sufficient. Since the founding of the barrio, Sisyanos
have been, to some degree, involved in a national market network. By at least
the 1920s there existed a voluminous and continuous flow of people, goods,
and services across Sisya's boundaries.

Everyone in the barrio recognizes its boundaries, but these boundaries
have little ecological reality for them. Many Sisyano cultivators till fields outside the limits of the barrio, and cultivators residing in neighboring barrios
till some of its fields. Moreover, much of Sisya's agricultural produce flows
outside the barrio, to be consumed by landowners or pledgeholders residing
elsewhere, and by people who purchase that portion that enters the national
and international markets. Reciprocally, money flows back to the community
from outside employment.

Sisyanos have never had to think of relying totally on their restricted internal resources. Although barrio fields are highly productive (responding to
continuous crop rotation), only a few of the 56 percent of households that
engage in cultivation sustain themselves entirely by their agricultural production. Most cultivator households enter into a variety of supplemental, sometimes external, economic activities. The number of noncultivating households,
indicates that accommodations drawing upon resources beyond the narrow
resource base within the barrio began to be explored long ago. As we have
indicated, many Sisyanos gain their principal support from wage employment
outside the barrio. Almost all households show the general characteristic of

multiple occupational involvement in an attempt to attain some balance of subsistence and income producing activities. It is not that Sisyanos do not highly value local resources, principally land; rather, they recognize that resources and opportunities that exist outside the barrio are infinitely more expandable than those within its limits. Moreover, barrio people have evidence that external resources and opportunities can be exploited by villagers who take a proper approach to them.

The interactions of Sisyanos are thus bounded by a system much broader than that circumscribed by the barrio limits or by the barrio resource subsystem. It is a system that extends beyond the limits of province, island, or nation. By no means is this a system of limited good.[5] Most Sisyanos perceive the system to which they relate as an expanding pie, at least potentially. Opportunities are perceived to exist, and people are believed to be able (again, at least potentially) to alter their statuses and their life chances with proper actions and with luck. Such a perception, and the sustenance systems followed by Sisyanos over the past several decades, denies a simplistic concept of "population pressures."

Clearly the population of Sisya has grown well beyond the means of its one square mile of land to support its present residents and temporary out-migrants. If the external resources upon which so many Sisyanos presently depend were denied them, they would face a catastrophic crisis. But "population pressure" (or similar notion embodied in concepts such as "overpopulation" or 'carrying capacity') is relevant and perceptible only when expanding numbers of expanding needs are confronted with limitations of space or limitations of resources. To be sure, since the 1920s, Sisyanos have experienced a rapid growth of numbers and, particularly since the 1950s, they have growing needs reinforced by rising expectations. Even with their growing numbers and needs, however, Sisyanos have not yet experienced a critical limitation of resources or of space. Sisyanos have been so successful in exporting large numbers of their population, either temporarily or permanently, drawing upon external resources, and coping with changing economic conditions, that they have not found it necessary to face the implications of their growing numbers.

Personal, Collective, and Institutional Strategies in Population and Economic Change

Sisyanos frequently involve themselves in social negotiations to create new opportunities which will improve their socioeconomic status and the quality of their lives.[6] Sisyanos are highly familistic, yet it is through continuous social negotiations beyond the family that personal strategies are pursued. Neither familism nor other organizational commitments are serious impediments; that is, Sisyanos may be familistic but most of them are also remarkably individualistic. They show little of the local involutional tendency that has been observed elsewhere in Southeast Asia[7] except in the sense that their high dependence upon personal negotiations for social advantage can be said to be involutional. Most Sisyanos aspire to higher status and seriously work at strategies that will bring about that goal. Some of these strategies require considerable courage, adaptability, innovation, and deferred gratification. Few, if any, are directly or explicitly related to "population pressure."

Some personal strategies have important consequences for collective organization in Sisya and even have required accommodations or modifications in institutional arrangements. Of these personal strategies and collective and institutional accommodations, the most prominent is migration.

Migration

Three central elements of the peasantry subculture are reputed to be limited aspiration, lack of deferred gratification, and a limited view of the world.[8] The behavior of many Sisyanos clearly does not conform to these criteria. For instance, their migration behavior demonstrates considerable aspiration, willingness to defer gratification, and courage to leave their locality for distant and vastly different places.

International Migration

Four Philippine provinces provided the overwhelming majority of migrants to Hawaii in the first part of this century: Ilocos Norte, Ilocos Sur. Pangasinan, and La Union.[9] Ilokanos and Pangasinenses were especially responsive to labor recruiting efforts of the Hawaiian Sugar Planters Association throughout the period of active recruiting. Continuing migration after the 1920s was sustained by the successes of earlier migrants. A questionnaire distributed among teachers and students of the Pangasinan High School and Normal School by O.H. Charles, the District School Superintendent in the late 1920s, demonstrates that many persons in the sample had friends or relatives in Hawaii and the mainland and that a positive view was taken of the labor migration opportunity.[10]

In Sisya the major migration of workers to Hawaiian sugar and pineapple fields occurred in the period 1925-1929. Fourteen of the 305 household heads, according to the 1971 census, had worked in Hawaii. The majority of those who migrated remained there between twenty and forty years (sometimes without a single vacation home) and then returned to Sisya to live out their lives on their pensions. Most migrants were able to save enough money to buy agricultural land on their return. Heads of households also named twenty one primary relatives (parents, siblings, and children) born in Sisya who were in Hawaii. Many of these migrants send remittances to relatives in Sisya. Four residents of Sisya in 1971 were born in Hawaii.

Postwar Hawaiian migration was only two-thirds that of the earlier period and is not related to recruitment for field labor, but considerable Hawaiian migration continues today.

Guam has been the major target for overseas migration by Sisyanos since 1946. The principal period was immediately after the end of the war until 1954. Thirteen heads of household (a few of whom who had earlier worked in Hawaii) have worked from six months to ten years in Guam. Once again the income from this labor migration can be seen in the agricultural and residential land held and in the substantial houses built by those who migrated. In 1971 household heads listed eleven primary relatives who were born in Sisya working in Guam.

Migration to the mainland United States and elsewhere by Sisyanos is much more limited than to Hawaii or Guam. Only four household heads have worked in the United States. Nine primary relatives (born in Sisya) were named by household heads as living in the mainland United States. One more was in Sabah and one in England.

Sisyano families that have overseas migrants are among the most socioeconomically secure in the barrio. These families were secure before their members went abroad and they generally have reinforced their social positions upon the return of the former.

Internal Migration for External Employment

Migration for work outside the barrio is oriented in the same way as most international migration, as a temporary expedient, undertaken to gain a more secure living once one has returned to the barrio.

The 1971 census shows a rather remarkable total of 241 members of Sisyano households (validated by their remittances to those households) who work for wages outside the barrio (besides those who are employed overseas).[a] All but 11 percent of these externally employed Sisyanos (teachers, agricultural workers, poultrymen, and ministers) work in urban places. The largest number

---

[a]Actually, somewhat more Sisyanos work outside the barrio than our strict definition would indicate. Included in this figure are only those people who were working outside the barrio at the time of the (July) 1971 census and not those who worked portions of the last year outside Sisya. Excluded also were a large number of externally employed persons born in Sisya who are married and who presently reside elsewhere in Central Luzon. These people were excluded because they no longer contributed to their families of orientation. Finally another large group of Sisyanos who have in earlier years worked in Manila, Baguio, or Angeles are excluded in the above figure. It is indicative of just how extensive participation in wage work outside the barrio is that less than 15 percent of Sisyano households have not had some member at some time who worked outside the barrio.

are in the greater Manila area, a substantial number are in Baguio. The remainder
work in Angeles or Olongapo (U.S. bases), Dagupan, Reina Maria, or in Tiange
Poblaciones and a few of this group commute daily to their jobs; the others visit
their families only on weekends.

Detailed information on the kinds of jobs outside the barrio and the sex of
Sisyanos who hold them is provided by sitio for 1971 (and 1962) in table 8-3.
These data are arranged by sitio because they show certain striking differences
among the sitio populations. Several points reflected in the data are worthy of
emphasis since they affect the composition of the resident population and thereby put stress on institutional arrangements.

The largest job category of Sisyanos employed elsewhere is that of housemaid. Girls in this category, who work mainly in Manila but also in Angeles and
in Olongapo, practically all fall within the age group eleven to twenty-five. Most
of them come from economically insecure households in Sisya West and East, and
their absence has a profound impact on the age-sex composition of those sitios.
It should be noted that none come from Ilokandia. Parents do not take pride in
having daughters working as maids; the dangers of permitting young girls to live
far away from parental supervision are recognized. The chances that such girls
will make a customary marriage—including provision of a male dowry—are
much reduced, and they are permitted to undertake such work only because
the small earnings gained are so badly needed by the Sisyano household they
come from. From an analytical point of view, employment as a maid tends to
lower fertility as a result of later age at marriage. Occasionally, girls working as
maids become pregnant. Sometimes this may lead to an early marriage, although
more frequently the disgraced girl forfeits all prospects for a customary marriage.
At best, some years later, she may enter a common-law union. Low socioeconomic status is thus a principal factor associated with work as a housemaid.
The distribution of this and other categories of employment by sitios provides
some indication of the level of economic security enjoyed by some of the residents of these places. However, a more general principal is at work as well. The
number of people working in a particular job tends to be somewhat increased
by the size of the group in that job as employment is so importantly determined
by personal resource networks. When someone has a job she (or he) calls other
relatives or is sought out by them to help gain related employment. This is
true for practically all jobs (except those requiring a specific skill) which in the
Philippines are gained mainly through processes of personal intermediation.

The second largest category, factory worker, is overrepresented by Sisyanos
from Ilokandia and to a lesser extent from East. All these jobs are located in
Manila and most are held by males. Like the third largest job category, miner,
employment in these jobs tends to be quite steady and the pay is good as contrasted with most others. Almost all Sisyanos employed as factory workers or
miners secured their jobs through personal resource networks.

With regard to teachers, the sitio of Ilokandia is exceedingly well represented.

Table 8-3

Occupation, Age and Sex (by Sitio) of Residents Working Outside the Barrio in 1962 and 1971

OCCUPATION	SISYA WEST 1962 M	F	Total	1971 M	F	Total	SISYA CENTER 1962 M	F	Total	1971 M	F	Total	SISYA EAST 1962 M	F	Total	1971 M	F	Total	ILOKANDIA 1962 M	F	Total	1971 M	R	Total	TOTAL 1962	1971
Housemaid/Houseboy	1	26	27	1	24	25		3	3		7	7		3	3	1	9	10		3	3	5	4	9	36	52
Factory Worker				3	4		1			3	1			1		5	1	6	1		1	4	5		1	21
Teacher	1		1	6		5		1	2	3		4				2	2	4				1	2	6	4	17
Carpenter	3		3	6		6	3		3	5		6				6		6		4	4	2		2	8	14
Miner	2		2	6		6	1		1	4		5			1	3		3							6	13
Driver				2		2				4		4				3		3				1		1	2	10
Dressmaker/Tailor		1	1		4	5					1	1								1	1	1		1	5	10
Armed Forces	2		2	4		4	2		2	4		4				1		1		1	1	4		4	6	9
Laborer	2		2	5		5	3		3	2		1		6	6	4		4		1	1				5	9
Agricultural Worker										2		2							1		1	1		1	10	8
Mechanic	1		1	2		2				3		3				1	1	1				1		1	1	7
Guard	1		1	1		1				1		1				3		3				1		1	1	6
Sales Clerk	2	1	3	2	2	4										1		1							3	6
College Student	1	1	2		1	4	2	4	3	12	8	20		1		1	3	4		7	7	2	4	6	10	34
Cashier	1				1									1			5								7	0
Waiter/Waitress	1		1	3		4	1		1						1		1	1				1		1	1	4
Tricycle Cab Driver	2		2	4		4																			2	2
Shoe Repair	3		3																						3	4
Plumber	1		7	1		1	2		2	2	1	2													5	3
Clothes Vendor		6				1		4	4	1	1	2													11	3
Delivery Man	2		2	1		1																1		1	2	2
Malaria Control	1		1																						1	0
Bulldozer Operator	1		1																						1	0
Elevator Operator																									1	0
Insurance Agent	1		1																						1	0
Office Clerk		1	1		1	2																1		1	0	3
Poultryman	3		3			3																			0	4
Ice Plant Operator	1		1			1																			0	1
Warehouseman	1		1			1			1																1	2
Furniture Carver	1		1			1																			0	1
Radio Operator	1			1		1																1		1	0	2
Mason	1		1																						0	1
Lumberman	1																			1					1	1
Gardener	1																								1	0
Policeman	1															1		1				1		1	0	2
Welder			1			1	1		1																0	1
Hospital Attendant	1	1						1	1						1										3	0
School Janitor	1			1															1		1	1		1	2	2
Dishwasher	1		1																						1	0

Table 8-3 (cont.)

OCCUPATION	SISYA WEST 1962 M	1962 F	1971 M	1971 F	1962 Total	1971 Total	SISYA CENTER 1962 M	1962 F	1971 M	1971 F	1962 Total	1971 Total	SISYA EAST 1962 M	1962 F	1971 M	1971 F	1962 Total	1971 Total	ILOKANDIA 1962 M	1962 F	1971 M	1971 F	1962 Total	1971 Total	TOTAL 1962 Total	1971 Total
Palmist/Herbolario									1			1													0	1
Telegraph Operator									1			1													0	1
Accountant							1		1		1	1										1		1	1	2
Bus Conductor							2		1		2	1													2	1
Fisherman							1		1		1	1													2	1
Veterans Claims Agt.									1			1													0	1
Crane Operator									1			1													1	1
Machinist									1			1													0	2
Minister														1	1	1	1	2							2	2
Prison Supervisor														1	1		1	1							0	1
Baker														1	1		1	1							1	1
Storekeeper																									1	0
Hairdresser															1	1		1							0	1
Munic. Agric'lst																					1			1	0	1
Photographer																					2	1		2	0	2
Nun																				1		1	1	1	1	1
Engineer																					1			1	0	1
Barber																					1			1	1	0
Market Vendor																				1		1	1	1	1	0
Bank Clerk																				1			1		0	1
Nurse																						1		1	1	0
Wholesaler																			1				1		1	0
Looking for Work																									5	0
Total	30	36	56	41	66	97	27	10	49	18	37	67	13	5	33	31	18	64	15	16	29	19	31	48	152	276

The average level of education in this Ilokano-speaking sitio is somewhat higher than that of the other sitios. Many households in Sisya pursue an "education strategy" for their children's future—a strategy most successfully carried through by economically secure households. The households of Ilokandia have more than their share of heads who are landed, spinstered, in possession of pensions, who have worked and saved money abroad, or who receive remittances from relatives working abroad or in better paying jobs. The number of Sisyanos from Ilokandia in the armed forces of the Philippines and the number of skilled jobs that they hold relative to most of those held by wage workers from other sitios should also be noted.

Most of the remaining jobs held by Sisyanos are unskilled jobs which tend to be quite casual in nature, irregular, and unstable. Job holders in such employment usually held a different job prior to their present one and probably will go to yet another job when the current one is terminated.

From these data we can infer that there are really two very different classes of persons who work outside Sisya. One group is more secure with deeper roots in the barrio; they are better educated, can draw upon superior connections within their personal resource networks, and tend to hold skilled, secure, and well paid jobs. The other class is insecure, with residential histories full of movement; they possess minimal education and skills, have relatively weak personal resource networks, and tend to work in casual, unskilled, insecure, and poorly paid jobs.

However, one characteristic is common to the employed household heads of both these classes: while they are working outside the barrio, their families do not usually follow them but remain in Sisya where the household is maintained. Migrants for urban wage work explicitly recognize that the cost of living is much higher and the quality of life is much lower in the city than in the barrio. Therefore most of them choose to maintain their households in Sisya and to return two or three weekends a month for visits. Thirty-nine heads of households who are presently employed outside the barrio maintain residences for the remainder of their family in Sisya. Less than one-fifth of that number of household heads who were born or previously resided in Sisya and who work outside have settled their families with them in the city.

To many young Sisyanos, leaving the barrio to work in the city is a youthful adventure, marking the end of adolescence and the transition to adulthood. This orientation is most characteristic of girls, who hope not only to help their families but also to see a little of the other world of the city before they marry and settle down. For young men the wish for adventure is combined with the earnest desire to land a secure job. Most youthful female migrants return to Sisya after a shorter period away than their male counterparts, normally in two or three years. Not infrequently they return in the company of a husband, and occasionally (much more often than by chance) the husband is also a Sisyano or native of a neighboring barrio. In good time most of the young male migrants also return to Sisya to marry and take up farming or other employment, having failed to secure satisfactory employment outside the barrio. Fewer young males than females bring back spouses from Manila.

Marriage in the city sometimes results in what might be seen as urban-rural migration. Four girls from Sisya who married men born in Manila or in the Central Philippines, after several years of residence in Manila, returned with their husbands to Sisya. Two of the husbands have retained good jobs in Manila and have simply settled their households in Sisya; the other two men are now living and working in the barrio.

Internal Migration to the Agricultural Frontiers

Sisyanos have not only demonstrated their willingness to migrate overseas and to urban places for work, they also have contributed to the rural-rural migration to the agricultural frontiers. I already mentioned that Sisya was settled by migrants to the then frontier in parts of Central Pangasinan. The tradition of sending out migrants continued as first Nueva Ecija, then Nueva Viscaya, Isabela, and Cagayan provided the promise of land and a better life. In the past two decades forty-five Sisyanos have migrated, most of them as households but a few as sets of brothers to frontier areas. (I have not included migrants to other places in Central Luzon even though some areas in Western Pagasinan, Zambales, and eastern Nueva Ecija still have something of a frontier character.)

The largest number of migrants went to the southern Philippines. Eleven settled in Cotobato, five in Davao, two in Zamboanga, and one each in Basilan (Sulu) and Palawan. Eighteen Sisyano migrants settled in northeast Luzon: ten went to Isabela, four went to Cagayan, and four to other provinces. In addition three barrio households at present reside in Baler Quezon, two others are in Mindoro, and two are in interior Benquet.

Adapting to conditions in pioneer areas always requires hard work, sacrifice, determination, and courage. It also requires an initial investment in land and sufficient savings to support a family in the first few years. Migrants to the frontier from Sisya are all from among the more economically secure households in the barrio. It is interesting that once committed few have turned back; only three families have returned as far as I can determine. One family fled from their lands in Cotobato in May 1971; caught in the tragic outbreak of hostilities between Muslims and Christians over land, under threat of death they abandoned the land which they had purchased justly and legally and returned to Sisya. The second family abandoned its holdings in Isabela under harassment from both the New Peoples Army and the Philippine Constabulary. The third aborted migration scarcely got off the ground; the household head spent one year in Zamboanga trying to find a secure job and failing that returned to his family in Sisya.

Differences in Migration: 1962-1971

Differences in migration behavior between 1962 and 1971 in Sisya suggest an interesting story. Emigration in all categories is up. International migrants increased over two and one-half times between the two census periods. Many of the emigrants, most of whom in 1962 were near retirement age, had returned to Sisya as pensioners in 1971—the end of an era. Overseas migrants in 1971 are strikingly younger and include almost half as many females as males. Occupational categories have changed accordingly. The laborer category in 1971 includes mostly people in construction rather than in field labor.

Emigration for work outside the barrio increased as a whole from 152 in 1962 to 276 in 1971. Sitios East and West had the highest growth in the number of emigrants. The increase in East is the result mainly of the export of house-maids, who constitute one-third of the sitio total. The number of housemaids from West in 1971 is also significant but the proportion of maids in the migrant population has dropped sharply from 1962. The rise in the number of college students is very striking, especially in Center (see table 8-3).

Most females who emigrate for work are in the age group 11-25, and most male emigrants are in the age group 21-40. This pattern is discernible in all the sitios in 1971, whereas in 1962 most of the male emigrants were between the ages of sixteen and thirty, except in Ilokandia. As a result of these migrations, in Sisya East and West the age structure and sex ratios are notably skewed. Sitio Center has seven girls who emigrated to work as maids in 1971, and except for them emigration for employment from this sitio is almost totally male.

The second largest category of female migrants in 1962 was that of used-clothing vendors. Ten Sisyano women, most of them widows, bought bales of used clothing from the United States in Manila, washed it, resized it, repaired it, and sold it in various villages in Benquet Province. In 1971 this business was no longer possible because imports of used clothing had been stopped to protect the Philippine textile industry. Three barrio women who were formerly active in the used-clothing trade now make or buy and sell clothing to their former customers; others are employed as dressmakers.

A new and important category for male and female employment in 1971 is factory work, mainly in textile and shoe manufacture (see table 8-3). Early in the decade only one Sisyano was employed in such work. Also the number of males employed as miners, mechanics, drivers, carpenters, and security guards increased, and a number of new kinds of jobs appear to be growing.

Among the sitios, variation in the proportions of skilled and unskilled jobs is evident. Sitio Ilokandia is especially noteworthy for the number of its emigrants who hold jobs requiring education or skills (but note, for instance, the increase in teachers in all sitios except Center). The high level of education in Ilokandia is related importantly to savings accumulated from overseas migration for work. The migration of many people in this sitio is, like their concern for higher education, an indication of high achievement motivation. Emigrants from Sisya Center also hold more skilled jobs and better jobs than do migrants from Sisya West and East. Education and overseas migration for work are well appreciated as strategies for upward mobility and are utilized by Sisyanos in all the sitios but, as performance indicates, sitios Ilokandia and Center are a step ahead of sitios West and East. Members of the first two sitios seem to have had more collective resources to invest in education and international migration at an earlier point in time than members of the latter two. As one more indication of this advantage note the number of Sisyano college students from Center (20) and Ilokania (6) in proportion to their population numbers.

Hart's description of rural-urban migration, written from the perspective of a rural barrio (Caticugan) in Negros Oriental, provides the only data I know comparable to our Sisya material.[11] Before discussing similarities and differences, I must compare basic information about the two settings. Caticugan is about half the size of Sisya; its location is adjacent to Siaton *poblacion;* and it was founded about three decades earlier than Sisya.[12] Major differences in topography, land use, land tenure, settlement pattern, and economic orientation distinguish the two barrios. We will restrict the first part of our comparison to that between Caticugan and sitio Sisya West.[b]

Caticugano grew about twice as fast as did Sisya West during two recent periods for which data are available: 1951-65 for Caticugano and 1962-1971 for Sisya West. The annual flow of emigrants for work outside the barrio was quite similar when taken as a proportion of the estimated mid-period population and adjusted for the differing lengths of the two periods. Thus Sisya is experiencing less growth within its boundaries yet is exporting proportionately as many to live elsewhere.

Hart's data show that people under twenty-six years of age comprise the great majority of those working outside of Caticugan at the time of both censuses (76 percent in 1951 and 68 percent in 1965). In Sisya West the emigrants for work are not as youthful. Hart also notes that the majority of the group working outside Caticugan is female (in 1951, 53 percent of emigrants for work were females; in 1965, 62 percent were females).[c]

---

[b]I wish to call attention to the fact that Hart's enumeration of working emigrants includes international migrants, whereas our enumeration for Sisya counts international migrants separately. Comparability of the data presented are somewhat questionable because Hart's definition of what constitutes a Caticugano who works outside the barrio is unspecified.[13]

[c]Hart's attempt to clarify the sex ratio of Manila with data from Caticugan showing the dominance of female emigrants who temporarily migrate for work gives rise to misinterpretation. The Caticugan data demonstrate a spectacular rise (122 percent) in the number of young women employed as maids and sales clerks between 1951 and 1965 (27 to 75). Ninety-four percent of females working outside the barrio were employed in these two occupations at the time of the 1965 census. Some 20-25 percent of these young women were employed in Manila. Their employment obviously is not connected

The major differences between residents of Caticugan and Sisya who emigrated for work—taking the two barrios as a whole—are in age, sex, and type of work. More than half of the emigrants from Caticugan in 1951 were young people employed as maids, houseboys, or store clerks; such youthful emigrants increased to 65 percent in 1965. Contrast this with Sisya: in 1962, 26 percent of Sisyano emigrants worked as maids, houseboys, or store clerks; in 1971, although this group was still large, it represented only 21 percent of the total. Even more striking is the difference between the other kinds of jobs held. Hart states that occupations of externally employed Caticuganos in "1965 duplicate those of 1951."[15] New male occupations were those of driver and dock and factory worker. Almost all the jobs were in small urban centers (interestingly only eight Caticuganos were employed in Cebu and only nineteen in Manila— and only one or two were in jobs other than those of maid and houseboy). Emigrants from Sisya employed outside in 1962, by contrast, held a much wider variety of jobs, many of them requiring skills and education (see table 8-3) uncalled for in those held by Caticuganos. In 1971 skilled jobs held by Sisyanos working elsewhere increased tremendously (there were 21 factory workers, 17 teachers, 13 miners, 10 drivers, 9 members of the armed forces, 10 tailors/dressmakers, 7 mechanics, 4 shoe repairers, 3 office workers, and so forth). Most of these jobs were located in Manila, but some were in medium-scale urban centers (Baguio, Angeles, and Dagupan). Both males and females were represented in these skilled jobs, but males dominated.

In summary, Sisyanos, because of closer proximity to Manila and medium-scale urban places in Luzon, somewhat higher educational attainment, greater development of skills, and effective personal contacts, are a cut above Caticuganos in terms of the types of jobs they hold. Clearly Sisyanos have been able to take better advantage of new urban job opportunities. For them there also exist such possibilities as visiting families in Sisya each weekend or bimonthly. The advantages that Sisyanos have over Caticuganos in regard to secure employment in good jobs outside the barrios may make it difficult for the latter to close the gap.

I have stressed the high mobility of the people of this part of Luzon. For the largest sitio, West, only 57 percent of the 1962 census population was present in 1971. A good deal of this mobility consists of individuals who migrated for work or returned and of households that moved to the frontier or returned from Manila. Additional contributions to such movement occur with normal first residence change following marriage and with efforts to take advantage of

---

with any advance in industrialization, with preference for women in industrial jobs, or with employment as nurses and secretaries. Nor is it related to the pursuit of education (in most cases) or to greater equality of the sexes. The employment of these women is, rather, mainly related to the "needs" of upper and middle class Filipinos for lower class domestic help.[14]

a change in the opportunity structure (brought about by a reallocation of access to the use of land following the emigration or death of relatives).

One other major contribution to movement involves those Sisyano households that have no attachments or access to land resources and which fail to develop any regular employment. They are the lowest in socioeconomic status, float around the countryside doing occasional jobs, planting and harvesting, but also drawing on the support of their kinsmen and neighbors. These unfortunate people are really no more Sisyanos than they are active participant members of any other barrio. This category of "hopeless" people is growing both by natural increase and by default. Among the unemployed and the irregularly employed, migration serves little beneficial function except to enable a floating population to scratch out a bare existence.

Now, more briefly, I will sketch the outline of a few other prominent personal, collective, and institutional strategies adopted by Sisyanos in the face of population and socioeconomic change.

Alterations in Productive Strategies

The ten years that I have observed Sisya have left me highly impressed by its people, both residents and emigrants. Working within the limits of their resources, the parameters of which I am convinced they understand very well, Sisyano cultivators have exhibited great responsiveness to their own changing needs and to the changing whims of the national and international market.

One example is provided by the major shift to the cultivation of Virginia tobacco that occurred on Sisya's upland fields between 1957 and 1964. Some Sisyano cultivators previously had produced native tobacco (for cigars) as a dry-season crop, but Virginia tobacco cultivation and processing is entirely different, requiring a great deal of knowledge, skill, and labor. Also, planting time conflicts with the principal rice harvest and selling the crop required a new marketing network. Despite all these problems, within two years virtually all Sisyanos who tilled upland fields were producing an adequate grade of Virginia tobacco for a government subsidized market. Production of Virginia peaked in 1962 (it had already become the third ranking crop in the municipality by 1960). When I returned to Sisya in 1966 *no* Virginia tobacco was being grown. Instead many cultivators had responded to the declining price of Virginia, the increasing quota for sugar, and a new demand for cigar wrapper leaf. Although Sisyanos have also been responsive to the new technology of rice production, they learned not to overcommit themselves. This behavior stood them in good stead last fall when Tungro infection decimated much of the crop in fields sown to IR-5 and IR-24. The intensification of agriculture through continuous crop rotation, occasional multicropping, and through cautious experiments with new crops and technologies characterized Sisya in the 60s.

Creation of Non-Agricultural Means
of Support

The responsiveness of Sisyanos in generating new means of support is similar to their responsiveness in agriculture. One new gainful activity is the provision of transportation to town by motorcycle cabs, making the town accessible at any hour of the day or night. Most of the vehicles are owned by their drivers, and the eleven now being operated in Sisya earn each of their drivers about ₱4.00 or ₱5.00 a day.

Alertness to opportunities is widespread. In the early 60s rapidly growing *camachili* trees were cultivated and cut for sale as fuel for tobacco curing barns and as bark to leather tanners. In 1971 a major sideline of many men in Sisya East was acacia tree cutting. Now classified as a first class wood, acacia in and around Sisya have all been cut and transported to Benguet and Ifugao where the wood, also known as monkeypod, is carved, and barrio men scour the province looking for more. Several household heads in West are especially expert at working with bamboo; in their spare time they manufacture the large rice storage containers that each house requires. One Sisyano earned ₱500 last year from this supplemental activity. Another family manufactures bamboo trays used to smoke fish; a year ago they hardly knew what one looked like but today this craft provides them with income adequate to support themselves. These are not isolated examples.

Finally, the increase in teachers, either within the barrio (from two in 1962 to six in 1971) or outside it (from four in 1962 to sixteen in 1972), an increase of nearly 400 percent, is evidence enough of responsiveness to educational opportunity. (Note also the increase in nurses, midwives, accountants, agriculturists, and office workers.)

Most of these activities are supplemental rather than primary. They are performed mainly by tenants or irregularly employed persons during slack periods in the agricultural cycle. Tenants engaged in several such activities are seeking a balanced support strategy—in case of failure in one area they can still provide for themselves. The tenants of Sisya are by no means pure agriculturists, they are rural proletarians.

Marriage, Family Life, and Household Structure

During the 1960s the migration behavior of some young Sisyanos and the concern of others for higher education appear to have been associated with certain accommodations in marriage customs that apparently have consolidated.

Preliminary analysis indicates that the age at first marriage for males and females has risen since the 1930s and 1950s and that young Sisyano women who work outside the barrio for more than three or four years seriously jeopardize their chances of early marriage. (It remains to be seen if these factors will affect childbearing performance.)

The 1960s saw the virtual demise of an important institution—the *dasel,* the male dowry, or more accurately the initial fund of conjugal property provided by the groom and his family. With the fragmentation of property that occurs as a consequence of bilateral inheritance in a rapidly growing population. few potential heirs had any hopes of inheriting the land by the late 1950s. Thus the provision of anything resembling the traditional *dasel* concerned only a very select group of Sisyano landowners by the late 1960s. Dasel was irrelevant in the marriages of people from marginally (irregularly) employed households, and was all but irrelevant for most tenants. Regularly employed households modified the *dasel* to a cash fund or residential property. For proper marriages *albahiyas* continue to be used, but their function has become *pro forma.*

The elaboration of wedding feasts, which were such important social occasions in the past, was noticeably reduced also during the late 1960s. It is my impression that the number of customarily "proper" marriages also declined. Few disincentives exist today against civil marriages, elopement (usually later solemnized by church rituals), or consensual unions, and these marriages occur at approximately the same ages as do "proper" marriages and are just as stable. Therefore there is little in this change that is demographically significant.

Accommodations in patterns of family life and household structure by means of adaptation in inheritance and the increase in emigration to work are also associated with increasing pressure on internal resources in the barrio. The preferred household form is that of a nuclear family. The most prominent alternative pattern to the preferred nuclear-family residence is the stem family, which anticipates inheritance by likely heirs to the more substantially constructed houses in the barrio; in effect, one offspring (and his wife and children) takes care of his (or her) aging parents. The percentage of stem family households (almost 20 percent in 1962) has risen slightly over the decade. Most multifamily households constitute a similar response, but involve younger parents and an unresolved commitment regarding who will be responsible for their care in old age. Multifamily (and stem family) households are also a response to the near saturation of residence sites in the barrio.

Most households that are de facto headed by females are a consequence of male emigration for employment. No special problems are created by this household arrangement, since the household and normally the domestic budget is the domain of the Sisyano female and her role in the socialization of children is usually dominant. Most sitio neighbors have traditionally been highly interdependent, and emigration simply reinforces this interdependence. Several of the males who work outside the barrio try to arrange their visits home to coincide with the infertile period in their wives' cycles.

Occupations of Resident Sisyano
Household Heads

A brief consideration of the occupations of household heads who derive most of their livelihood from resources within the barrio will conclude this description of social strategies and population change. Understanding the dynamics of the internal economy gives us the best basis for projecting future trends and prospects.

Overall, the number of household heads who derive their livelihood mainly from internal resources has increased by fifty-five between 1962 and 1971 (from 221 to 276). Yet the general category of proprietors of more than one-half hectare of agricultural land has decreased by twenty (from eighty-five to sixty-five). The decrease of owner-tenants is particularly ominous since cultivators in this category are the best and most progressive farmers in Sisya. They cultivate the largest farms in the barrio. The reduction in their numbers from thirty-six to twenty-three signals a shift in barrio agriculture and life strategies away from farming. Many of their lands have been purchased by the Sugar Central in the past five years and are now planted exclusively to cane.

The number of household heads who derive their livelihood principally from share tenancy increased in nine years from eighty-eight to ninety-two. Seven owner-tenants in 1962 sold their land and were tenants in 1971. Other land was distributed by inheritance. The gains and losses by sitio are interesting. Center, with its large wage earning population, decreased sharply its number of owner-tenants and share-tenants; all other sitios increased their number of share-tenants.

The category of regularly employed household heads in all sitios increased mainly by virtue of the addition of locally resident teachers and of several returning (formerly regularly employed) pensioners from Hawaii.

A significant change toward greater insecurity is discernible in the category of household heads who have irregular means of support. The gross increase from 37 to 101 in nine years is shocking. The best represented category of household heads in Sisya (37 percent) are marginally employed. Especially significant as an index of declining economic opportunity are the striking increases in agricultural laborers, underemployed carpenters, persons dependent on relatives, sari-sari storekeepers, and the like. Most of these people are so marginally employed that they might be more accurately labeled unemployed. Many of them constitute a rootless population, moving from one place to another and from one activity to another in their attempts to scratch out a living. Some live on the margins of village society, relying heavily upon their kinsmen and neighbors, and contributing to high rates of theft of farm animals, rice, and valuables.

In general, the occupational trends within the Sisyano economy indicate

Table 8-4
Principal Occupation of Heads of Households Deriving Livelihood Within the Barrio at Time of 1961 and 1971 Census

Occupation	WEST 1962	WEST 1971	CENTER 1962	CENTER 1971	EAST 1962	EAST 1971	ILOKANDIA 1962	ILOKANDIA 1971	TOTAL 1962	TOTAL 1971
Proprietors of Land	21	16	23	20	12	8	29	21	85	65
Owners	6	3	4	8	2		7	3	19	14
Owner-cultivators	4	3	3	5	6	1	4	6	17	15
Owner-tenants	10	9	10	2	1	3	15	9	36	23
Owner-employed	1	1	6	5	3	4	3	3	13	13
Share Tenants	36	43	20	9	25	29	7	11	88	92
Regularly Employed	4	7	4	5	3	5		1	11	18
Teacher		3	1	3	1				2	6
Mill Operator			3	1		1		1	3	3
Pensioner	4	4		1	2	4			6	9
Irregular Means of Support	22	32	9	28	2	25	4	16	37	101
Agricultural Laborer	4	7	3	8		14	2	6	9	35
Smoked Fish Tray		2								2
Stovemaker		1								1
Tricycle Cab Driver		7		3				1		11
Carpenter	4	5	1	3	1	6		3	6	17
Contractor		1								1
Dried Fish Vendor		1								1
Gambling collector		2								2
Dependent on relatives		3		5		1		1		10
Buy and sell	6	2						2	6	4
Fireworks maker			1		1			1	2	1
Dressmaker/Clothes Vendor		1	1	2				1	1	4
Laborers	4		4						8	
Fisherman	1								1	
Washerwoman	1								1	
Grass gatherer	2		1						3	
Bus Driver				3						3
Radio mechanic				1						1
Rig Driver				2						2
Herbalist				1						1
Storekeeper						1		1		2
Tractor operator						1				1
Mason						1				1
Barber						1				1
TOTAL	83	98	56	62	42	67	40	49	221	276

that despite the remarkable ability of most Sisyanos to discover or create new niches, there has been a decline in control over internal resources, a decline in opportunities other than those provided by emigration or education, and a decline in the quality of life for an ever-increasing category of residents who are marginally employed (see table 8-4). Although almost all Sisyanos belong to a single social class, differences in socioeconomic stratification have increased since 1961-1962.[16] It is not so much that higher status families have become more secure as that lower status families have become more insecure. The latter benefit little from new opportunities. As things stand, they appear to have no future, and there is every indication that things will get much worse for them.

Notes

1. Clifford Geertz, *Agricultural Involution, The Processes of Ecological Change in Indonesia* (Berkeley and Los Angeles: University of California Press, 1963).
2. Robert Hackenberg, personal correspondence.
3. See James N. Anderson, "Land and Society in a Pangasinan Community," in S.C. Espiritu and C.L. Hunt (eds.), *Social Foundations of Community Development* (Manila: RM Garcia Publishing House, 1964), pp. 171-92; and James N. Anderson, "Buy and Sell and Economic Personalism: Foundations for Philippine Entrepreneurship," *Asian Survey* 9, 9 (September 1969).
4. James N. Anderson, "Personal Intermediation, Network, and Transactionally Generated Social Organization in the Philippines," paper presented at the 69th annual meeting of the American Anthropoligical Association, San Diego, California (November 1970); also, James N. Anderson, "Interpersonal Bridges Across Social Chasms: Personal Intermediation in Philippine Society," in manuscript.
5. G.M. Foster, "Peasant Society and the Image of Limited Good," *American Anthropologist* 67, 2 (1965).
6. Anderson, "Buy and Sell"; Anderson, "Personal Intermediation"; Anderson, "Interpersonal Bridges."
7. Geertz, *Agricultural Involution.*
8. See E.M. Rogers, *Modernization Among Peasants* (New York: Holt, Rinehart, and Winston, Inc., 1969).
9. See Bruno Lasker, *Filipino Immigration* (Chicago: University of Chicago Press, 1931), pp. 354-355.
10. Ibid., pp. 376-382.
11. See Donn V. Hart, "Philippine Rural-Urban Migration: A View from Caticugan, a Bisayan Village," *Behavioral Science Notes* 6, 2 (1971).

12. Donn V. Hart, *The Cebuan Filipino Dwelling in Caticugan: Its Construction and Cultural Aspects* (New Haven: Yale Southeast Asia Studies Cultural Report Series, 1959).
13. Hart, "Philippine Rural-Urban Migration."
14. Ibid., pp. 109, 110, and 119.
15. Ibid., p. 119.
16. Anderson, "Land and Society," pp. 175-192.

Change and Population in a Northeastern Thai Village
H. Leedom Lefferts, Jr.

Introduction

Studies of ecological change are concerned with an analysis of the population itself, the techniques the population utilizes to extract resources from the landscape, the nature of the resources, and how all of these have changed over a specified period of time. From December 1970 to June 1972, I analyzed the cultural ecological system of Baan Dong Phong, a Thai-Lao village 13 kilometers by paved and dirt road to the northeast of Khon Kaen City in Northeast Thailand (Isan). The more my study progressed, the more I became aware that the system I was studying was quite different from what had gone before. Since the village was in an irrigation project, the canal and attendant changes were new; however, other more subtle changes and processes had taken place over the fifty years since the village was founded, which began to impress me as being of greater importance in explaining what I saw, as well as in predicting what might be future modes of adaptation.

I found a continuing thread of adaptive response in the movement and placement of people on their resource base. In this chapter I wish to expose some possible facets of the man-resource relationship and the adaptive mechanisms that are available for the continuing survival of the system. The chapter is divided into two sections: the first on changes in technology and resources, the second on population dynamics. A conclusion redescribes the existing system, providing an idea of future problems. Statements of this system's operation are hypotheses based on impressions gained in field work and are as of this writing without statistical foundation.

Adaptive Mechanisms: Technology and Resources

If we exclude changes attributed to increased contact with Central Thailand and the West, resources and technology seem to be evolving very slowly in Baan Dong Phong. Since the village's founding, the same four tools have been used to cultivate rice: an iron-tipped plow, a harrow, a sickle, and two

For their support of this research, the Thai National Research Council and the U.S. National Institute of Mental Health deserve my gratitude and thanks.

pieces of wood tied with rope used to beat sheaves of rice and dislodge grain. All of these can be made in the village except for the iron tips of the plow and the sickle, which used to be made in nearby villages but are now produced at foundries. The cultivation of rice also does not seem to have changed. The villagers say that they have always used flooded rice paddies on land that, when first cultivated some fifty years ago, was forest. Over a much longer period of time, differentiation of rice varieties has occurred; in Baan Dong Phong some twenty-six different kinds of glutinous rice and twelve of regular (steamed) rice were used. Several of these were improved types coming from agricultural experiment stations, but the farmers themselves seem to have developed different varieties for specific situations.

Supplementary foods, such as fish, meat, and vegetables have always been a basic part of the balance of life. Perhaps the most dramatic change has come in vegetables, where many different types are presently cultivated. Thirty years ago, most vegetables were gathered from the land or planted and permitted to grow on their own. The great variety of what northeasterners call vegetables, ranging from corn to green onions and tomatoes, are the result of demands and opportunities placed before the villagers as a result of increased contact with the market of Khon Kaen.

This increased contact with the outside world also heightened the villagers' responsiveness to opportunities resulting in monetary benefits. Although rice has always been sold, the transactions previously involved fellow farmers who would transport the product by boat to Surin or Srisaket for selling. Now, rice is sold to a local rice mill. During World War II, when the importation of cloth to Thailand was banned, a concerted effort was made to produce and weave cotton cloth for sale; men traveled into the Central Plains to sell the product. For limited periods of time, kenaf production, cattle raising, duck egg production, and raising improved breeds of chickens also increased resources for a restricted number of villagers. These villagers became a very acquisitive people, always looking for a better opportunity to make money. Coupled with this flexibility is a realization that not all people are in a position to take advantage of every opportunity that comes along.

For purposes of analysis, it is possible to isolate technological and resource changes which result mainly from village initiative rather than outside influences. For example, rice varieties, cotton, stock and duck raising were independently adopted innovations. In addition, within the last ten years, Baan Dong Phong has been a beneficiary of several inputs traceable to the building of the Ubolratana Dam on the Nam Phong River, the subsequent establishment of the Nong Wai Irrigation Area, as well as the increasing access to market. These may be considered a single innovation package since each benefit was dependent on the other. They stem from technological and resource inputs which are under government control and much beyond the capabilities of the villagers. The dam has stopped floods, which regularly inundated at least one-half of the village's rice land, and has thereby increased productivity. The canal, as part of the irrigation project, supplies water to keep fishing pools filled, to sprinkle vegetable crops, to supplement rain for rice growing, and also provides a raised section of earth used as a road for all of the dry season and a large part of the wet season. Thus, commuting to Khon Kaen for wage labor and taking vegetables to market on a daily basis is now possible. Most of the benefits of this package seem to have been unintentional from the viewpoint of the planners. The purpose of the dam was to supply electricity, not increase productivity of the land. The primary purpose of the canal was rice irrigation, not increasing the available fishing grounds or the places for getting water for bucket irrigation of vegetables, or the provision of an embankment that could be made into a fairly decent road.

The cumulative result of these changes in technology and resources is greater complexity in landscape utilization. Continued refinement of certain techniques and crops, coupled with increasing contact with the outside world, permits a family to do more kinds of things on the same piece of land. We also find an increasing orientation to the market with reliance by the villagers on products that can only be obtained there. At the same time, contact with the outside world enables the people to have a greater degree of control over the vagaries of their environment.

Adaptive Mechanisms: The Social System

Population pressure on resources in a specific locale is a basic part of the ecological system of Northeastern Thailand. Specific methods have been adopted over a long period of time to redress the population-resources balance. Two basic mechanisms are available to villagers for controlling population in a specific area: (1) birth control and infant deaths and (2) migration.

It is difficult to estimate the degree of village consciousness with regard to birth control and infant deaths. Since Isan technological culture is labor intensive, parents want at least four children, even when artificial birth control methods are available. Presently, most of the women who practice contraception don't do so until they have six or more children. On the other hand, contraceptive and other population control practices were probably in existence before the coming of western medicine. There are numerous instances of babies dying at about two years of age when they were suddenly weaned, following the conception or birth of a younger sibling. Similarly, deaths of young children up to age ten or twelve were a fairly regular occurrence. This is not to say that completed families were small before western medicine affected individual life spans. It would be reasonable to expect that each family averaged four living children under natural conditions.

I hypothesize that the migratory system serves as the major redress of the man-resource relationship. It has probably been in existence for at least the last one-hundred-plus years and has operated to spread the Thai-Lao population over most of the Korat Plateau. Migration by Isaners can be typologically separated into two different modes: that of young adults, especially men, leaving their home villages to look for work and a bride, and that of families who leave the wife's home, moving either to a new house in the same village or another location altogether. Both of these modes stem from the same dynamics of family structure and are in response to a permanent localized population pressure on available resources. Specifically, two conflicting tendencies are interacting: first, the desire of parents to have their children live close, which is derived from the greater honor and prestige these parents will receive from having them around. In addition, there is the drive to form larger cooperative groups permitting greater resource exploitation and, thus, more family stability. Second is the counteracting force of insufficient command of local resources, tending to prohibit the formation of such a grouping. Coupled with these tendencies is the prevailing system whereby a male goes to live with his wife's family, taking a male dowry with him.

A system where young men look for brides necessitates some sort of search procedure. I found a few instances of arranged marriage, but by and large the young man and girl knew each other before wedlock. As the young man reaches sixteen, he begins seeking work away from home since there will probably be insufficient land to support him and his family. Methods of looking for work and for a bride are similar: the young man goes to his kinsmen or close friends to find a satisfactory situation. Before the growth of cities, most work took place at the home of a relative who had insufficient labor force for maximum utilization of his resources. Today there is considerable movement to Khon Kaen and other Northeastern cities for wage labor. In addition, at age twenty or older, the young man will spend time as a monk, which permits some time for travel and for finding situations of relative prosperity away from home. Marriage takes place within Baan Dong Phong if sufficient incentive, other than a bride price, is offered to a son by his parents. This incentive might take the form of land-holding expectations or a place on the work force for the young man's family. The type of migration discussed above cannot be described as an absolutely effective method of relieving population pressure since as one young man moves out another may move in on the occasion of a sister's marriage.

The migration of families tends to be more permanent. As parents produce children and as these children grow and are able to contribute in exploiting more resources, the family's relative wealth grows and perhaps escalates after the marriage of a daughter who brings a son-in-law into the family. Traditionally, as daughters marry, the elder daughter moves out of the parents' household. If adequate money is available, additional plots of land are purchased and families remain in the village, making the formation of larger cooperative units possible. Although only certain groups would be in a position to take advantage of some "free-floating" resources, the family moving out of the wife's parents' household usually begins a journey to new resources. As more children are produced by the new household and as its original resource allocation becomes less sufficient, inter-village migration takes place. As with the movement of young men looking for work and wives, search and actual migration occur along kinship lines. I found only one instance of a family moving into a previously unprepared resource base: a move to Bangkok by a man and his two children after the death of his wife. Although most migrants relocate in similar farming situations, there is increasing movement to Khon Kaen, to take advantage of wage labor. However, these migrants still depend on the village for rice resources.

A great amount of information transference occurs in Isan, particularly with the onset of the dry season and the holding of religious festivities by each village. At this time kin come to visit and spread the news of opportunities in new areas. Once a family from Baan Dong Phong moves, a continuing migration stream occurs for some years, consisting especially of other close relatives. This is to be expected since, if one family moves because of insufficient resources, other close kin are usually in similarly difficult straits and are also forced to move. In a village such as Baan Dong Phong, it becomes difficult to trace some kin groups when all close relatives have moved.

Under this system, extreme fragmentation of land does not occur. A situation has developed wherein there is an optimum amount of cultivable land (some 20 to 25 rai, 8-10 acres, or 3.2-4.0 hectares) for a basic household consisting of three to four laborers. As children are added, the potential for expanding this base increases, but it will never be expanded sufficiently to provide for all daughters with some space for sons. Expansion is stopped short of incorporating much land because each family establishes itself as a unit in its own right. We therefore have a system of expansion and contraction of the household's cycle which provides for the rational allocation of resources with specifications for migrants and an established pattern for the transfer of information and people.

Conclusion

Fifty years ago, Baan Dong Phong was established through migration: about thirty-five families, some 200 people, moved from three villages 30 kilometers to the south to the present village site, which at that time had a population of only three families. While such a massive migration seems rather unusual, it is probably normal in pioneer situations where no kin are already living at the destination. The present spot was selected because it was at the ecological border of more established villages whose land was too far away to be cultivated easily. The family and close kin of the leader of this migration were able to acquire a good quantity of land which has since maintained them in a preeminent position in the village. However, cooperation in this group is breaking down as the founding generation dies and their children's generation becomes older and less involved in the utilization of resources. Other families, with less land and consequently smaller cooperative groups, have been in a state of flux, with migration as a most important part of their existence. My census of the village, which attempted to include everyone who had ever lived there, involves approximately 1,800 individuals, with some 700 present residents. The village now includes 107 households, the aforementioned increase in resource availability resulting in increased density. As gardening, stock and duck raising, and wage labor appear, more households are staying, making possible the development of greater cooperative groups and the movement of goods and services between them in order to offset the vagaries of resource fluctuation. With this kind of situation, we can begin to talk of development and of specific kin groups building up to a take-off situation.

Thus, the picture of change in Baan Dong Phong is not totally of a "doom and gloom" nature. Up to the present, due to the ready availability of free-floating land and resources, places remain for migrants to settle. In addition, cooperation seems to be a part of the process, provided that individual households are related by kinship and depend on a number of different resource bases. I remain impressed by ingenuity of the Isaner in finding ways to subsist and increase their standard of living. Population pressure and migration remain the key to the system. In the past there have always been sufficient resources available—land, new techniques, or wage labor—to absorb the built-in tendency towards localized overutilization in the system. Whether sufficient resources remain on an areal basis is debatable.

10

Some Consequences of Population Growth in Java
Masri Singarimbun

The Problem in Outline

Java is a classic case of a large population living on a relatively small island in which all the available land has been cultivated for quite some time. Only East Pakistan, now Bangladesh, provides a similar example of over-population: Bangladesh is metaphorically an "island." As it had already experienced a "population explosion" (in the nineteenth century), Java has long occupied a special position in the demographic literature. The population problem that has arisen has created grave concern among government planners and social scientists for more than seven decades, but the problem is still very far from being solved.

In this chapter it is possible only to touch on a few of the many consequences of population growth in Java, but I have tried to mention those which are generally regarded as being most important, namely, the worsening of the man-land ratio, the effect on nutrition, and some of its social consequences. I have also included a section on the situation in the sub-district of Srihardjo (Jogjakarta) where I did my field work on family planning in 1969-70.

Raffles's "census" gave 4.5 million as the population for Java in 1815. In 1900 the population was recorded as 28.5 million, which means an extraordinary rate of natural increase of 2.2 percent during the nineteenth century. Some scholars, notably Peper and Widjojo, have questioned this in view of the conditions—level of living and health services—that prevailed in Java, in the first half of the nineteenth century in particular. "The view that there was an exceptionally rapid growth in Java is to an important degree the product of an ethnocentric European approach to the history of Java" (Peper 1970: 84). Raffles' estimate drew on figures reported by village heads and also involved guesswork for some regions and cities, and it seems safe to conclude that his "census" represents a gross underenumeration. Annual growth rates of 0.5 to 1.0 percent, in line with the estimates of Carr Saunders and Sauvy, seem more plausible. The population of Java may have been somewhere between 8 and 10 millions in 1800.

The first post-independence census of 1961 gave a total population of 63.1 million for Java (and Madura), an increase of 22.2 million from the 1930 census. The figures show a lower rate of population growth for Java than for the outer islands—1.4 percent per annum for Java and 1.9 percent per annum elsewhere in the period 1930 and 1961 (table 10-1). As migration was

Table 10-1
Physical Area, Population, Density, and Growth for Indonesia and Its Provinces, 1930-1961

Province	Square Kilometers	Population 1930 Number (1,000)	Population 1961 Number (1,000)	Density per sq. km. 1930	Density per sq. km. 1961	Average Annual Growth 1930-1961
Djakarta Raya	577	533	2,973	923.7	5,152.0	5.70
West Java	46,300	10,864	17,615	234.6	380.0	1.57
Central Java	34,206	13,707	18,407	400.0	538.0	0.96
Jogjakarta Special Region	3,169	1,558	2,241	492.0	707.0	1.18
East Java and Madura	47,922	15,056	21,823	314.0	455.0	1.21
Java and Madura	132,922	41,718	63,059	316.0	477.0	1.35
Outside Java	1,772,171	19,009	34,026	10.7	19.2	1.90
Indonesia	1,904,345	60,727	97,085	31.8	51.0	1.52

Note: 1 sq. mile = 2.6 sq. km; thus the 1961 population density for Central Java, 538 persons per km, would be 1,399 on a per sq. mile basis.

negligible the differential rate of natural growth between Java and outside Java, and between Provinces within Java, shows that there is indeed a close relationship between economic welfare and population growth.

The problems of poverty on Java are long standing. In the nineteenth century there had been an increasing awareness among Dutch social reformers of the adverse effects of colonial economic policy and population increase on native welfare. This growing awareness culminated in the publication of van Deventer's provocative article, "A Debt of Honor" (Een Eereschuld), in 1899 calling attention to the misery of the Javanese. The well-known ethical policy (1900 onward) was brought into being largely as a result of his argument that no lasting improvement in the economic situation of the natives was to be expected until the Netherlands' "debt of honor" to the Indies had been redeemed. The ethical policy was a development policy that involved the promotion of education, irrigation, and emigration (out-migration from Java).

In the years 1900 to 1924 approximately 158 million guilders in all (but excluding the wages for personnel and the value of compulsory labour) were expended on irrigation, drainage, and water-control works. This resulted in the irrigation of about two and a half million acres, which constituted approximately a third of the total wet rice-field (*sawah*) area for which *landrente* (land tax) was due on Java and Madura.

But the gains appear to have been eaten up by the growing numbers of people. J.H. Boeke, a well-known Dutch economist, asserted in 1927 that the ethical policy had failed to reach its objectives. His conclusion was based on "The Reports on the Economic Enquiries" of 1924 which, among other things, stipulated that cultivators now eat a bit more than before the First World War, but the food is of somewhat lower quality, and with its production surplus is able to buy slightly fewer imported goods than before the war (Boeke 1961: 268).

The situation has not changed much since then. Until recently the output of rice has not risen at a rate equal to the rate of increase in population despite considerable government efforts. In Indonesia as a whole, during the fifteen-year period 1953-1967, the output of rice, the preferred staple food, rose by 1.5 percent per annum whereas the population grew by 2 percent per annum or more. During this period the area under crops in Java hardly increased (in fact some quite unsuitable lands, for example, steep hillsides, came to be used for agriculture) and irrigation systems often fell into disrepair: it is therefore not surprising to find that the annual rate of increase in rice output in Java was no more than 0.2 percent. In the outer islands it was 3.3 percent during the same period.

In the last few years, in particular since the first five-year development plan (Repelita) was launched in 1969, the production of rice has grown at an impressive rate, in large part because massive programs have been mounted. It will probably not be long before the long-cherished goal of national self-sufficiency in rice will be achieved (Indonesia has been a net importer for

many decades), but it should not be concluded that the achievement of this
goal will automatically mean that everyone will then have enough rice to eat.[a]
At the family level the availability of rice and other foodstuffs is inevitably
"a function of the distribution of income, which in turn depends on the distribution of land and other wealth, the occupational structure and the social
stratification" (Sovanni 1972: 5). All the available evidence indicates that
ownership of the now very scarce agricultural resources of Java has also
become very unequal (see table 10-4 and 10-5).

Land and Population

Gradual fragmentation of land in Java began in the nineteenth century,
from the time when the rural population began to grow faster than new lands
could be opened for cultivation. All potentially arable land was already under
cultivation by about 1900, but economic hardship motivated the landless to
bring steep hillsides and other unsuitable areas under cultivation. This has
resulted in deforestation, floods, erosion, and a shortage of water for irrigation.

The process of deforestation is already far advanced. While a minimum of
30 percent of the land should be forest-covered in order to protect the water
supply vital to the wet rice lands, the forest area had decreased to 22.6 percent
by 1963.

In Java one *bau* (0.709 Ha) of wet-rice field, or 2 *bau* of unirrigated fields
is considered necessary to provide a reasonable livelihood for a farmer (Redmana 1970: 28). It appears that until the middle of last century most farmers
had at least that much land. Things have changed slowly and inexorably since
then as population has increased. Since the beginning of this century the
majority of farmers own less than a *bau*; and there are now many who own
very much less than this. But even in 1903 "of all those holding land in individual hereditary possession or having fixed shares of communal land, 70.8 percent had less than 0.7 Ha, another 18.2 percent from 0.7 to 1.4 Ha, 7 percent
from 1.4 to 2.8 Ha, and only 3.9 percent had more than 2.8 Ha" (Pelzer 1948:
166).

The Dutch author Burger has written comparing the situation in a village
near Pekalongan (North Coast of Java) in the years 1868 and 1928. He shows
how land has become relatively scarcer, and also illuminates a number of other
important results of continued population growth. The average peasant pro-
prietor in the *desa* (village) of Pekalongan owned from about 0.7 to 1.1 Ha

---

[a]There are quite a few people who cannot afford to buy rice or, if they grow it, to
eat it. Such people, of course, do not contribute to the demand for rice.

(1-1 3/5 *bau*) of wet rice-field in 1868 but only 0.5 Ha (4/5 *bau*) in 1928 (Burger 1971: 14).

During the same period the area of land used for housing (and for house-gardens) increased by 17 *bau*, thus reducing the area that could be sown to rice. Wages fell, too, as the result of the increase in population, and a decline in the (relative) availability of work opportunities. In 1868, a harvester was paid a share consisting of 1/5-1/3 of the rice harvest, whereas in 1928 this share had fallen to about 1/8-1/6, and in nearby villages was sometimes as low as 1/12.

It is a pity that the Agricultural Census of 1963 did not provide a full picture of the land-man ratio problem in Java, but, unfortunately, farms (or landholdings) of less than 0.1 Ha were not included in the census. Such information would be of inestimable value to our understanding of the land-man problem in Indonesia, and in Java in particular, where there are so many minute landholdings. Other useful information would be data on land ownership and tenancy, on landlessness and rural unemployment.

Research done in twenty-three villages in Java in 1954-56 showed that in half of the villages fully 20-50 percent of households owned less than 0.1 Ha of land (any land). In one village, Sukamanah, 72.0 percent of the households owned less than 0.1 hectare (Ismael 1960: 211). However, no information was provided on the question of actual landlessness.

Food and Population

Rice and maize were the staple food in Java until about the end of the nineteenth century. Since the turn of the century, with the worsening man-land ratio in Java, cassava, whose protein content (1.5 percent) is much less than that of rice (7½ percent) and maize (9 percent), has been increasingly consumed either as a supplement to or as a substitute for rice.

Cassava produces the most calories per hectare, but its low protein content makes it unsuitable as a staple food. People prefer rice, which is held in high esteem, but poverty forces many to eat the less expensive cassava.

The production and consumption of cassava are therefore important indicators of food problems for various regions in Indonesia:

> When a district produces more than 50 kg of cassava per head
> per year, it is very likely that many of the inhabitants use it as their
> staple food, which means that many will suffer from malnutrition.
> Of the eighty regencies (kabupaten) of Java, thirty-five produce
> more than 50 kg of cassava per head. (Some allowance must be
> made here for the possibility that cassava can be used in other ways,
> such as for starch, or it may be exported.) The most seriously

affected areas are the Southern Limestone mountains, from Gunung
Kidul to Malang Selatan, followed by the Northern Limestone mountains, from Corobojan regency in the west to the island of Madura.
Another centre is the Purworedjo, Kebumen, Wonosobo and Bandjar-
negara region. Many Madurese do not realise that in Madura cassava
is already the main staple food, not maize as is commonly said
(Napitupulu 1968: 65-66).

Malnutrition occurred first in Central Java, which is the most densely populated province, and later spread to East and West Java, but eventually to the
Lesser Sunda Islands outside Java.

On the basis of production data published by the Central Bureau of Statistics, Napitupulu calculated that daily per capita food consumption in Java
averages only 1,650 calories and 34 g. of protein, of which only 4 g. is animal
protein. These figures imply a deficiency of 300 calories and 14 g. of protein,
compared with the "standard" set by the Indonesian Nutrition Seminar of
1963 of 1,950 calories, and of 48 g. of protein (of which 12 g. should be animal
protein) per day. Napitupulu's conclusion should, however, be treated with
caution since, as he himself recognizes, Indonesian statistics are not yet very
reliable.

However, these estimates are broadly in line with the results of other surveys. Of the sixteen cases representing various places in Java (see table 10-2)
nine show an average intake of less than 1,700 calories per day, and ten a protein intake of less than 40 g.

The daily intakes in the limestone areas are even lower than those shown
in table 10-2. Gunung Kidul (1958-1959) in Jogjakarta Special Region had an
average daily intake of 1,350 calories per head. The protein intake of 15.6
g. per head in this regency "appears to be the poorest in the world, quantita-
tively as well as qualitatively" (Bailey 1961: I, p. 228). Dietary deficiencies in
the area, and in the other linestone regions in Java, are imposed by poverty.
"Taboos appear to have relatively little influence on the quality of the diet . . . .
Ninety-nine percent of the population are subsistence farmers who grow what
they eat, and eat most of what they grow" (Bailey 1961: I, p. 223). The
Gunung Kidul regency is the best known of the many *hunger oedema* districts
in Java; and it provides a fearful example of the great capacity of man to suffer
and to adapt himself to nutritional and agricultural adversities.

Many of the people of Java are forced, to some extent at least, to adapt to
dietary deficiencies. The careful and conservative calculations of Rose and
Gyorgy (1967) show that the caloric intake of the women in their Bogor
sample was only slightly above the basal metabolic requirement (adjusted for
height and weight). The results from their Central Java sample, drawn from
the Semarang area, indicate that the children, even as infants, were smaller than
the Djakarta standard, set by De Haas and his associates in 1935. "At the age

Table 10-2
Java: Per Capita Calorie and Protein Consumption

Region[a] and year of study	Place	Calories	Protein Animal g.	Total g.
Pati (1956)	Bulungan	1,741	11	42
	Ngurensiti	1,628	9	38
Semarang (1957)	Karanganjar — normal	2,095	7	47
	— poor	1,885	5	42
	Mangkangwetan	1,809	n.a.	38
	Wonoredjo	1,797	n.a.	41
	Pamongan	1,788	n.a.	38
	Sriwulan	1,559	n.a.	35
	Purworedjo — normal	1,471	9	35
	— poor	1,363	3	34
	Pudakpajung	1,420	n.a.	33
	Rajakusumo	1,419	n.a.	32
	Dempet	1,235	n.a.	31
Djakarta (1957)	(Workers' families)	1,537	7	41
Purwakarta (1959)	Gunung Tua	2,405	6	58
	Sukasari	1,680	6	46

Source: Post World War II nutrition surveys—reported by Napitupulu (1968, p. 64).
[a]Both Pati and Semarang are in North-Central Java; Purwakarta is in West Java.

of 5 they were one full year behind in both height and weight" (Rose and Gyorgy 1970: 149).

Clinical studies point in the same direction. Timmer's excellent study revealed that in Jogjakarta malnutrition was the most important cause of death for children from one to seven years old. Its contribution to mortality amounted to 9 percent in the group of infants, but increased to 36 percent in the second year of life; the share of malnutrition reached its peak, 40 percent, in the third year (Timmer 1961: 307). (Additional information on incomes—level of and distribution—will be found in the Appendix.)

The Situation in Srihardjo Subdistrict:
A Case Study

My first main impression of Srihardjo (a *kelurahan,* or subdistrict, which lies 10 miles south of Jogjakarta) was that the economic situation was by no means as bad as had been reported in the literature (for villages in this general region). I gained this impression because I could see people who owned such relatively expensive manufactured goods as motorcycles, scooters, bicycles, wristwatches, and radios. The latter were particularly noticeable because they could often be heard as one passed by a house. The people were also friendly and hospitable, even cheerful, and I saw no one who was suffering from starvation and who was thin like the people we see in many Freedom From Hunger Campaign posters. The artistic life of the village seemed flourishing—there was a group learning to play the *gamelan* (Javanese orchestra), and there were also three *djatilan* groups, who occasionally performed the amusing traditional horse dance. In addition, the countryside looked beautiful.

It was only after I had been in the village for sometime (in the course of my family planning research) that I slowly became aware of the existence and the extent of the problems of poverty, unemployment, and malnutrition that had arisen due to rural overpopulation. The two houseservants we engaged asked for extremely low wages—just food, and "it's up to you if you wish to give us a little something to buy clothes with." In the city a houseservant will get Rp. 600 (± $1.60) a month over and above his food. We found that our leftovers were used: they were taken home each evening by our houseservants to give to their parents. We found, too, that many of our neighbors were able to eat rice for only a few weeks after harvest. For most of the year they ate only cassava or other foods (which are cheapter than rice). If they did eat rice they ate it in the form of a porridge.

One of our house servants told us that it was relatively easy to get work for about a month at rice planting and harvest times. The wages, however, were very low, about Rp. 30 a day (0.75 kg rice, $0.08). A harvester was paid a small share consisting of one-twentieth of the rice harvest. At other times, work of any sort was very hard to get. In our servant's household there were three people of working age, himself, his elder brother, and his father, and all were frequently unemployed. His mother had occasionally been able to trade in bananas, which she sold in Jogja; the work was heavy, and she was able to earn no more than enough merely to cover the cost of the food she consumed on the trip. A picture of just how low their real incomes must be can be seen from the following prices: 1 egg Rp. 12; 1 kg rice Rp. 40; 1 kg beef Rp. 160; one visit to a doctor Rp. 150; to extract a tooth Rp. 1,000; a flashlight battery Rp. 50; 1 pair of sandals (Bata) Rp. 170; 1 pair of shoes (Bata) Rp. 750; transistor radio Rp. 4,000–Rp. 10,000; second-hand bicycle Rp. 5,000–Rp. 12,000; motorcycle Honda 125 cc. Rp. 155,000; one round-trip to Jogjakarta by bus Rp. 80. To become the owner of a transistor radio, not to mention a motorcycle, is far beyond the means of most people.

Both morbidity and mortality remain high, in part because diets are poor, and also because modern medicine is very expensive in relation to income. In February 1970, a neighbor of ours, an agricultural laborer, got the flu. To go to the doctor (twice) and to get some medicine he needed Rp. 300, which he borrowed from a neighbor. At the same time he promised to repay 10 kg of

coconut sugar (Rp. 500). I cannot imagine his ever being able to repay. Many
of the very poor are in debt—and if they don't pay they are unable to borrow
again. There are also beggars.

It is not possible for me to say whether these sorts of things are in any way
typical of what is happening elsewhere in Java. There is, however, a strong likelihood that the various "problems of poverty" of which I have written are
indeed faced everywhere by the people who are in the poorest class. The pre-
harvest period (patjeklik) has long been known as a very hard time of the year
for them.

Miri is one of the four villages in Srihardjo sub-district in which my intensive study was done in 1969-1970. The physical and socioeconomic conditions
of the average village reflect, to a large degree, the general condition of the
average village in Bantul Regency of which Miri is administratively a part. Miri
has easy access to road and markets, it has a Maternal and Child Health (MCH)
clinic, and its terraced wet-rice fields are well-watered. Bantul Regency may be
regarded as an average regency in the Jogjakarta Special Region: its inhabitants
are in general better off than those of Kulonprogo and Gunung Kidul Regencies,
but not as well off as those in Sleman.

The Jogjakarta region has a very high population density, and there is a
strong correlation between soil fertility and population density. In 1930 the
average density per square km was 492. It has risen to 707 by 1961; and to
784 by 1970. The Kabupaten (regencies) of Sleman and Bantul have the best
land, and also the highest population density, 1,028 per square km and 1,126
per square km respectively (1971). The sub-district (Srihardjo) had a population
density of 1,480 persons per square km. of all land in 1970, and in Miri, one of
its villages, and located wholly on the fertile, well-irrigated lowland soils (much
of Srihardjo land is dry land) had a population density of 2,350.

The 164 families (694 people) that live in Miri have access to 29.52 hectare
of land; land per head is thus 0.0425 hectare. The geographical area of Miri
land is a little less, only 27.15 hectares, but some of the Miri residents own land
elsewhere. Over 90 percent of the people earn their living from agriculture.

Average holding (any land) in Miri is 0.243 Ha *per owner.* As shown in
table 10-3, 37 percent of the families own no irrigated land whatever and
another 30 percent own irrigated land of 0.1 Ha or less in size. Fewer than 5
percent possess the "ideal" amount of 0.7 Ha of irrigated field.[b] The figures
given here include the *tanah pelungguh* and tanah pengarem-arem, i.e., the land
allotted to village officials and ex-officials in lieu of salary and pension. (About
20 percent of arable land in Jogjakarta Special Region fall under these categories.) In order to have an average of 0.7 Ha of irrigated land per family, there
should only be about 30 instead of 164 families in Miri. The trend suggest that

---

[b]0.7 Ha of irrigated rice-fields can be worked by the average family with hand tools
alone and without the use of any hired labor

Table 10-3
Miri: Land Ownership of 164 Families[a]

Land Type	Number of Families	Proportion in Each Category Percentage	Average Holding Per Owner Hectare[b]
Irrigated land	104	63	0.196
House compound	123	75	0.087
Any land	128	78	0.243

Source: D.H. Penny and H. Singarimbun, "A Case Study of Rural Poverty," *Bulletin of Indonesian Economic Studies* 8, 1 (March 1972): 79-88.

[a]*Tanah pelungguh* and *tanah pengarem*[2] have been classified as "owned land."

[b]1 hectare is 2.5 acres (approx.).

any further increase in population and of the number of families will further widen the gap between the very modest ideal of 0.7 Ha and reality.

Table 10-4 shows three striking features: the diminution of holdings, the relatively large proportion of the landless, and the concentration of ownership of irrigated land.

According to the Land Reform Law (1960) no person was allowed to own more than 5 hectares of rice-land in the densely populated regions. Strictly speaking, there is not a single family in the village that owns 2 hectares of land, specified as the minimum in the same law. There is, however, one man in Miri, a village official, who controls a little more than 2 hectares by virtue of the fact that he has some *tanah pelungguh*. However he has no hereditary rights, nor any right of disposal over such land.

The data on land controlled for the 116 family sample show a situation that is in no way different from the data given in table 10-4. Land controlled by each family was calculated by adding to the figure for land owned half the area of land rented from others, and then subtracting half the area of owned land rented to others (table 10-5). Other data show that 67 percent of the families control less than 0.20 Ha of land and that 5 percent have no access whatever to land. The average amount of land controlled per family is 0.217 hectare, of which 0.078 Ha is house-compound (31 percent).

Another important source of income is the coconut-sugar industry. It provides more income and more employment per hectare than rice. Tapping coconut trees, twice a day, is hard work, and over 40 percent of all labor time in the village is spent in coconut-sugar production. Women and children spend much of their time collecting fuel in the form of small branches and leaves, both from the house garden and from the hills. Their urgent need for firewood means that

Table 10-4
Miri: Ownership of Irrigated Land[a]

Area Owned	Number of Owners	Percentage of All Owners	Percentage of All Land Owned
None	60	37.0	0.0
Under 0.2 ha	77	47.0	33.3
0.201-0.8 ha	24	14.6	39.4
0.801 and over	3	1.8	27.0
TOTAL	164	100.0	100.0

Source: D.H. Penny and H. Singarimbun, "A Case Study of Rural Poverty," *Bulletin of Indonesian Economic Studies* 8, 1 (March 1972): 79-88.

[a]Includes *tanah pengarem-arem* and *tanah pelungguh*. Land owned is slightly larger than land controlled.

Table 10-5
Miri: Land Controlled, Irrigated Land, and House Compound

	Total ha.	House Compound ha.	(%)
Largest single farm	2.26	0.37	16
First quintile (top 20%)	0.67	0.18	27
Village average	0.22	0.08	36
Fifth quintile (bottom 20%)	0.05	0.03	59

Source: D.H. Penny and H. Singarimbun, "A Case Study of Rural Poverty," *Bulletin of Indonesian Economic Studies* 8, 1 (March 1972): 79-88.
Note: Omits twelve families who own no house compound.

the reforestation program for the eroded hills has not succeeded. Indeed deforestation is still proceeding.

Although a tapper can handle thirty trees, the average number of trees per tapper is eight. The average daily income per tapper (family) is Rp. 50, or the equivalent of 1.3 kg of rice. The nature of the enterprise makes a tapper and his family immobile both economically and geographically, but it does provide him and his family something to cling to in life. In general, tappers have no alternatives.

Other sources of wage, or quasi wage employment in the village include collecting wood and leaves for the coconut industry, itinerant selling, bicycle repair, etc. As a rule wage work pays about Rp. 30 a day, when work is to be had.

Unemployment is high, higher than reported in the studies done by Dutch scholars between 1920 and 1935. In Srihardjo people work, on the average, fewer than 90 days in the main rice season (180 days).

Some Social Consequences

The poverty that has arisen as a result of overpopulation has had deleterious social effects: the number of people in the lowest economic and social category has grown, and there has been a great increase in the number of people who have little hope for a brighter future. In this group "present-time orientation" is strong. It is not uncommon, for example, for a farmer who has some land, but whose rice output is not enough to meet his own requirements, to sell a large part of his meagre crop immediately after it has been harvested. He will do so even though he knows that rice prices are very much lower at harvest time and that he will be forced to buy food later at a relatively higher price. He does this because, at harvest time, he values cash more highly than the rice he has produced and knows he will need at some time in the future. He is influenced by consumption and social needs such as buying something nice for the children, giving a *selamatan* (feast), etc. There are others, of course, who must sell at harvest because they have debts to repay; and same too, who must sell even before harvest (*idjon*).

This economy of scarcity, seems to offer the poor a specific role in their relationships with the people in the upper economic strata. "Scarcity found the 'worker seeking humbly any kind of toil'. As a suppliant to his superiors, the worker under scarcity accepted the principle of authority; he accepted his own subordination and the obligation to cultivate the qualities appropriate to his subordination, such as submission, obedience, and deference" (Potter 1954: 205).

Ten Dam's description of the life style of the people in the lowest income group in Tjibodas village (West Java) provides a good illustration of this point. Some 40 percent of the families were completely landless. (He was writing of the situation in 1954.) They earn their living primarily by working for landowners or those who are fortunate enough to be able to rent land. The majority of these poverty-stricken people work only on a short-term basis, hired and dismissed from day to day. They also engage in petty trade, selling small quantities of bananas, tobacco, etc., on a commission basis.

Ten Dam (1961: 351) writes:

In his behaviour towards people outside his own group, the farm

hand is resigned to his fate: he would like to improve his situation
but does not know how, and acquiesces. He does tend to show an
interest in political movements which promise a great deal and in
messianic movements of the *ratu adil* type, but the interest is only
fleeting: in the long run such movements fail to yield results. The
group is inclined to be suspicious of everything coming from outside
its own sphere. However paradoxical it may sound, when all is said
and done the farm hands place most confidence in the judgments
of their employers. It is not unlimited confidence, of course, but
with regard to them the farm hands at least know where they stand.
That is the only reality (often quite harsh reality) on which they
can build, anything else is for them an unattainable chimera.

There are cases where the enduring patron-client relationship, with its social
concomitants, is extended to the next generation, as if it is part of the inheritance of both sides. My observations support those of Franke, who has recently
concluded an anthropological study in a village in North-Central Java. Franke
writes that there has arisen

a set of primarily economic fusion [between groups], based mainly
around rice field ownership but including all economically well-off
families around which primarily landless, under- or unemployed
families have gravitated seeking some degree of work and security,
while these same wealthy families are able to acquire dependable
labor accompanied by local neighborhood and family sanctions
which reduce the possibility of protest, disorder, corruption, and
the like" (1971: 22).

Java's social organization has long been characterized by rigid social stratification. The landless represent the lowest stratum, and there have always been
some landless people even in the days before Java "filled up." The ever-increasing popoulation has caused the number of people who are landless, or almost
so, to increase substantially; and this has tended to reinforce the longstanding
rigidities in the social system, and to offset the efforts that have been made to
dynamize village life.

Appendix 10A: Incomes in Jogjakarta
Special Region; Some Survey Results

Two major income studies have been done in recent years at the Faculty of Economics, Gadjah Mada University. Results from the first have been published by Sukamto (1962) and Mubyarto and Fletcher (1966); and results from the second will be found in Deuster's dissertation (1971). These studies give invaluable information on income levels and distribution and on consumption patterns. They show that the incomes of many families are very low.

Discussion

If we use an estimated average family size of about 4.5 persons, and if we assume that the rice consumption per family is 450. kg rice a year, i.e., 100 kg per person per year, and that about 20-25 percent of total income must inevitably be used for items other than food, then we can see from table 10A-1 that about 50 percent of the families had incomes of 500 kg of rice or less per year, and thus not enough to enable them to eat rice, the preferred basic food, the year round.[c] In all income groups, including the groups with the highest income, over 50 percent of income was spent on food (table 10A-2). Table 10A-2 and part of table 10A-3 (1959) are drawn from the same data, but the occupational classifications were changed by Dr. Deuster in his study; and table 10A-3 indicates that there was a decline in (median) income in the sixties and that income was less equally distributed at the end of the period than it had been at the beginning.

References

Bailey, K.V. "Rural Nutrition Studies in Indonesia: Background to Nutritional Problems in the Cassava Areas." *Trop. geogr. Med.* 13 (1961): 216-233.
Boeke, J.H. "Objective and Personal Elements in Colonial Welfare Policy."

---

[c]100 kg per head is a conservative figure, as it would provide only 780 calories per day, and minimum average daily requirements are at least 1600 calories. By contrast the average rice consumption of the Javanese farmer families in North Sumatra is about 125 kg per head per year (M. Singarimbun and D.H. Penny, *The Population Problem: Some Economic Arithmetic,* 1972, draft); while the second National Socio-economic Survey gives an estimate of rice consumption of 140 kg per head per annum for Sumatra Mubyarto, "Persoalan pembangunan pertanian di Sumatera, Jogjakarta, 1971 (mimeo.).

Table 10A-1
Jogjakarta: Income Distribution, 1959

Category	Annual Income per Family	Average Income per Family in Rice Equiv.	Number of Families
	Rupiah	Kg/family/year	Percentage
1.	0- 1,199	138	7.4
2.	1,200- 2,399	320	23.1
3.	2,400- 3,599	466	22.7
4.	3,600- 4,799	640	13.8
5.	4,800- 5,999	819	8.9
6.	6,000- 8,399	1,047	10.3
7.	8,400-11,999	1,455	7.8
8.	12,000-17,999	2,318	4.3
9.	18,000-23,999	3,235	0.8
10.	24,000 & over	5,617	0.8

Source: Sukamto, "Laboran penjelidikan biaja hidup untuk Daerah Istimewa Jogjakarta: 1954-61." *In Laporan Kongres Ilmu Pengetahuan Nasional* II, Djilid ke-9, 1962, p. 343.
Note: Milled rice Rp; 6.50/kg.

In W.F. Wertheim (ed.), *Indonesian economics: the concept of dualism in theory and policy.* The Hague: W. van Hoeve Publishers, Ltd., 1961.

Burger, D.H. *Laporan mengenai desa Pekalongan dalam tahun 1868 dan 1928.* Bhratara, Djakarta, 1971.

Deuster, P.R. "Rural Consequences of Indonesian Inflation: A Case Study of the Jogjakarta Region. Ph.D. dissertation, University of Wisconsin, 1971.

Franke, R. *The Javanese Kangen Family,* 1971 (preliminary draft).

Ismael, J.E. "Keadaan penduduk di duapuluh tiga desa di Djawa." *Ekonomi* 2, 3 (1960): 197-223.

Mubyarto. *Persoalan pembangunan pertanian di Sumatera.* Jogjakarta, 1971 (mimeographed).

Mubyarto and L.B. Fletcher. *The Marketable Surplus of Rice in Indonesia: A Study in Java-Madura.* International Studies in Economics, No. 4, Department of Economics, Iowa State University, Ames, 1966.

Napitupulu, B. "Hunger in Indonesia." *Bulletin of Indonesian Economic Studies,* No. 9, (1968).

Pelzer, K.J. *Pioneer Settlement in the Asiatic Tropics.* International Secretariat, Institute of Pacific Relations, New York, 1945.

Penny, D.H. "Review of Paul R. Deuster, "Rural Consequences of Indonesian Inflation: A Case Study of the Jogjakarta Region, 1971." *Bulletin of Indonesian Economic Studies* 8, 1 (March 1972): 93-95.

Table 10A-2
Jogjakarta: Income Distributions, by Occupations 1959

Occupation	Annual income per family		Expenditure on food as proportion of income
	Cash equiv.	Rice equiv.	
	Rp.	kg	percentage
Farmer-laborer	2,956	455	75
Farmer-tenant	3,296	507	68
Trader	3,610	555	70
Farmer-owner	3,803	585	64
Laborer	4,240	652	64
Transfer receiver (pensioner, etc.)	5,592	860	60
Other	5,800	892	65
Self-employed, n.e.i.	6,190	952	55
Cottage-industry (own business)	7,537	1,159	63
White collar	12,742	1,970	54

Source: Sukamto, "Laboran penjelidikan biaja hidup untuk Daerah Istimewa Jogjakarta: 1954-61." *In Laporan Kongres Ilmu Pengetahuan Nasional* II, Dijilid ke-9, 1962, p. 233.

Table 10A-3
Medium Household Incomes in Rice Equivalents, by Occupational Groups (kg per year)

Occupational Group	Proportion of all families		Kg per year	
	1959	1968	1959	1968
Small farmer	12.1	17.1	352	266
Farmer-laborer	10.2	12.5	500	448
Medium farmer	12.7	11.4	689	766
Farmer-other	13.5	11.1	706	621
Laborer	9.9	11.8	725	489
Transfer Receiver	9.7	6.8	825	565
Other	13.1	11.8	974	957
Large farmer	11.0	11.1	1,237	1,411
White collar	7.8	6.4	1,970	1,435

Source: Derived by D.H. Penny, "Review of Paul R. Deuster, *'Rural Consequences of Indonesian Inflation: A Case Study of the Jogjakarta Region 1971'*," *Bulletin of Indonesian Economic Studies* 8, 1 (March 1972): 93-95, from data provided by P.R. Deuster, "Rural Consequences of Indonesian Inflation: A Case Study of the Jogjakarta Region," Ph.D. dissertation, University of Wisconsin, 1971. The 1971 data cited by Deuster are from the earlier Consumption Survey (see tables 10A-1 and 10A-2).

Penny, D.H. and M. Singarimbun. "A Case Study of Rural Poverty." *Bulletin of Indonesian Economic Studies* 8, 1 (March 1972): 79-88.

Peper, B. "Population Growth in Java in the Nineteenth Century." *Population Studies* 24 (1970): 71-84.

Potter, D.M. *People of Plenty*. Chicago: The University of Chicago Press, 1954.

Redmana, H. *Beberapa persoalan ponduduk di Indonesia*. Djakarta: Lembaga Ilum Pengetahuan Indonesia, 1970.

Rose, C.S. and P. Gyorgy. "Malnutrition in Children in Indonesia." In H.W. Beers (ed.), *Indonesia: resources and their technological development*. Kentucky: The University Press of Kentucky, 1970, pp. 143-164.

Sovanni, N.V. *Population Change, Food Supply and Nutrition*. Paper for LCAFE Regional Seminar on Population Aspects of Social Development, Bangkok, January 11-20, 1972.

Sukamto, "Laporan penjelidikan biaja hidup untuk Daerah Istimewa Jogjakarta: 1954-1960." In *Laporan Kongres Ilmu Pengetahuan Nasional* II, Djilid ke-9, Seksi E-3, 1962, pp. 329-78.

Ten Dam, H. "Cooperation and Social Structure in the Village of Chibodas." In W.F. Wertheim (ed.), *Indonesian Economics: The Concept of Dualism in Theory and Policy,* The Hague: W van Hoeve Publishers Ltd., 1961, pp. 345-382.

Timmer, M. *Child Mortality and Population Pressure in the D.I. Jogjakarta, Java, Indonesia*. "Bronder-offset," Rotterdam, 1961.

Widjojo, Nitisastro. *Population Trends in Indonesia*. Ithaca: Cornell University Press, 1970.

11

Social Mobility and Fertility Control in a Squatter Barrio of Davao City, Philippines

Beverly Heckart Hackenberg

Introduction

This study examines the hypothesis that the squatter settlements of the world, both past and present, have functioned as the institutional agents of change, transforming peasant immigrants into urbanites with all of the accompanying changes in attitude and behavior.

> Thus the ancient city was transformed by degrees. In the beginning it was an association of some hundred chiefs of families. Later the number of citizens increased, because the younger branches obtained a position of equality. Later still, the freed clients, the plebs, all that multitude which, during the centuries, had remained outside the political and religious association, sometimes even outside the sacred enclosure of the city, broke down the barriers which were opposed to them and penetrated into the city, where they immediately became the masters. The entry of this inferior class into the city was a revolution, which, from the seventh to the fifth century, filled the history of Greece and Italy. (de Coulanges 1956: 274-275).

Throughout history, wherever towns ceased to be the domain of a few, the less privileged intruded. The more able among them wrested property, privilege, and franchise from the reluctant citizens. Their presence and power transformed feudal manors into the cities of the world. The processes by which people moved from peasant status to become legitimate citizens of the city have been discussed by many from Aristotle and Livy through Thomas and Znaniecki to Redfield and Oscar Lewis. Most writers have tended to view the situation of the immigrant from their own middle or upper class background. Thus we have the social disorganization and degradation of the slums and the wretched squalor of the squatter areas. For a long time there was little effort to compare the present situation of the inhabitants of these places with their former lives and understand the shrewd calculations of the individuals as they worked to maximize the advantages of their positions.

The great disorganization of the Polish peasant immigrant may better be interpreted as a temporarily unorganized state during which he quickly substituted fraternal organizations for those familial insitutions from which he came

(Wood 1955) in much the same way that the inhabitants of the Lima's barriadas established their associations (Doughty 1970). Much of Lewis's culture of poverty is not significantly different from conditions in the peasant village, "the constant struggle for survival, unemployment and underemployment, low wages . . . child labor, the absence of food reserves in the home . . . living in crowded quarters, a lack of privacy, gregariousness, a high incidence of alcoholism . . ." (Lewis 1961: xxvi-xxviii). Perhaps the migrant does not regard these negative factors with the same loathing displayed by the authors, but concentrates on the positive characteristics of the city such as a wider variety of employment, educational possibilities, and the excitement of city life.

The present movement of peasants into slums and beyond them into squatter settlements is obviously a twentieth century survival of the ancient process of city building and urbanization which is only now being blocked in the western countries by rigid enforcement of property laws. Squatter settlements are a phenomena of any rapidly growing city and are especially associated with industrialization. Western-world cities passed through this phase at a time when there were not many differences in the amenities of life; all streets were mud filled, there were no sewers, everyone had diseases; and no one really cared how others suffered. Sjoberg (1960: 97-98) has described the squatter settlements of medieval Europe,

> The disadvantaged members of the city fan out toward the perphery,
> with the very poorest and the outcasts living in the suburbs the
> farthest removed from the center. Houses toward the city's fringes are
> small, flimsily constructed, often one-room hovels into which whole
> families crowd.

Following the rapid industrialization and expansion of western-world cities there was a change in attitude toward the working and living conditions of the urban poor. Great reforms were instituted and people became sensitive to situations which had gone unnoticed for centuries. Housing standards were set and enforced, and labor laws prohibited unhealthful and dangerous working conditions. Since the major rural-urban migration had passed, these new laws did not discriminate severely against the western poor who followed the upward mobility channels of former migrants. The twentieth century wars with accompanying labor shortages forced a temporary relaxation of regulations, thus assisting the wartime and immediate postwar migrants to move through the system and into the suburbs. It is only recently, with the added burden of racial discrimination, that the process has broken down, especially in American cities.

At the end of World War II the industrialization of the Third World began, accompanied by the explosive growth of cities whose inevitable slums and squatter districts brought shivers of horror from the worldwide community of social scientists, city planners, police, government officials, and United Nations experts. Their critical opinion, formed from viewing the problem at a discreet and safe distance, was that these lawless and desperate people had created a crisis and had made the city, "a poor habitat, not only for man but for industry and trade. Chaotic in form and destructive socially" (Weissman 1966). Something had to be done to remove the sufferers to a more suitable place. Perhaps it did not occur to these onlookers that the squatter settlements had *prevented* a crisis and that no chaos existed except in their perception. The movement of people without capital into industrializing cities cannot effectively be controlled except in police states. These people display the revolutionary, lawless tendencies so often ascribed to them only when they are unable to utilize their newly acquired, modest wealth to satisfy basic needs for security and living space. The "riots of Watts" will not take place where slum leaders plot their next *barriada* invasion.

More recent writers have attempted to interpret the life styles of the slum dwellers and squatters from a less ethnocentric middle class position and have begun to provide more valid insights into the manner in which the immigrant manipulates his environment, given his capabilities and perceptions of his situation. The first descriptions of the slum-squatter situation as an orderly process were made by Mangin and Turner in papers resulting from their ten-year study of the barriadas of Lima, Peru.

The Turner Model of Urban Settlement

Turner has presented a model of urban settlement in terms of the immigrant's priorities as they relate to the functions of the transitional city. Housing is defined environmentally rather than structurally: "in terms of performance or functional relationships between habitat and the inhabitant .... there are three basic functions of the dwelling environment: location, tenure, and amenity. For any place to function as a dwelling it must have accessible location, it must provide secure, continued residence for a minimum period, and it must provide a minimum of shelter from hostile elements . . . whether climatic or social" (Turner 1968: 356). Each of these three functions are variables related to the social situations of the inhabitant through time. These social situations are those of the *bridgeheader*, the *consolidator*, and the *status seeker*.

A migrant begins as a bridgeheader when he enters the city. His priorities are a location immediately adjacent to the central city, where casual jobs are plentiful, and a cheap rented room which can be given up quickly if the occupant wishes to move. He has little interest in the overcrowding, discomfort, and lack of security usually associated with this area.

As the ambitious bridgeheader acquires capital, his priorities change. By this stage he has probably begun a family, increasing his need for space and therefore his rental costs; his slowly acquired material possessions are endangered by thievery. Job security and income have improved sufficiently, enabling his wife and children to leave their casual employment. Thus, as a consolidator, he is looking for housing he can afford in an area away from the high crime rate and crowding of the slum, but within cheap transportation distance of his work. At this time he becomes interested in more space, congenial neighbors, and in the availability of social services such as schools, clinics, and religious facilities. The consolidator has two courses open to him. He may move into an established squatter settlement as a renter, hoping to obtain a site for a house at a later date, or he may join a group in planning and invading a new squatter area.

Turner's highest social level is that of the "status seeker," whose highest priorities are involved with amenities. A rented apartment in a socially acceptable location is preferable to a squatter house in the wrong location. These people will frequently rent or allow a relative to live in their house in the squatter village.

This model documents the spatial movement of the peasant from entry into the city until he has become an established urbanite. As he struggles through the years to achieve a secure foothold in the city, the peasant is also acquiring an urban set of attitudes and values.

One index of modernization universally recognized is controlled fertility behavior. The country whose population exhibits a low death rate and birth rate is accepted as having completed the demographic transition into a modern westernized nation. Most Third World countries are still in the transition, with a falling death rate but a high birthrate. If it were possible to document a change in fertility behavior as the urban immigrant achieves his status changes, there would be reason to postulate a favorable future of controlled growth for these countries rather than the crisis and chaos now envisioned.

Turner proposes and preliminary evidence supports the notion that a change in life style occurs for those immigrants who negotiate the change from the first to the second stage of urban residence. With Macisco, Bouvier, and Weller (1970), Hendershot (1971) and older writers, we submit that this change in life style embodies a change in attitudes toward fertility.

If the new arrival in the central city perceives a child as an income producer, and pregnancy exerts minimum interference with a wife's earning capacity, there is little motivation for family planning. In the squatter barrio, the position of the child changes from producer to consumer. Family savings must be invested for education if the family is to secure further upward mobility.

This study is a preliminary report, testing the hypothesis that squatter settlement provides an institutional context favorable to fertility control, and encompasses a clientele more receptive than that of the central city slums where the majority of family planning programs are located.

Empirical Background

The city of Davao, Republic of the Philippines, was chosen for the study because of its extremely high in-migration and large slum and squatter populations. Davao was the third largest metropolitan area in the Philippines in 1960, with a population of 225,712. An annual rate of increase in excess of 5.5 percent was recorded over the intercensal decade 1960-1970; the population reached 389,312 in the terminal year. Davao's growth rate has been remarkably constant. For the intercensal interval of 1948-1960, the city displayed an annual increase of 5.75 percent. At the present rate (5.5 percent), the city population will reach 758,000 by 1980, and will pass the *one million* mark by 1988.

Sectoral Growth of Davao City

The city consists of a *poblacion* (City Proper), and four adjacent districts containing residential and industrial concentrations (Bunawan and Toril) and primarily agricultural communities (Tugbok and Calinan). Inner city slums (Piapi, Bolton, Agdao, Bucana) are confined to the poblacion, while squatter barrios (Buhangin, Lanang, Talomo, Garcia Heights) are located in Toril (older squatter settlements) and Bunawan (newer squatter barrios). It is immediately apparent from table 11-1 that Toril and Bunawan, the two districts containing squatter settlements, outdistanced the growth of the city as a whole, and the poblacion. The locus of population growth in Davao is represented by the newer squatter colonies extending northward.

The Squatter Settlement of
Lapu Lapu Village

The first squatter settlements in Davao City were occupied during the immediate postwar years, but they have been extended continuously to the present time. The squatter settlements of Lanang in the northeast sector of the city's coastal zone were first invaded in the 1950s by people working in the coconut haciendas there. They were later joined by the families of workers from the timber processing and exporting firms of Alcantara and Sons and South Bay Lumber Company which bound the squatter settlement on the north and east sides. In 1963, these squatters were getting so numerous that the hacenderos and lumber firms on whose land they had settled began a process of eviction. With

Table 11-1
Davao City Intercensal Comparison

| | 1960-1970 | |
	1960	1970
Poblacion (City Proper)	82,720	119,808
Tugbok	29,462	31,416
Calinan	36,617	55,055
Toril	47,301	85,845
Bunawan	29,612	97,188
DAVAO CITY	225,712	389,312

1960-1970 Increase as Percentage of 1960

	Net Increase	% of 1960
Poblacion (City Proper)	37,808	31.5%
Tugbok	1,954	6.6
Calinan	18,438	50.3
Toril	38,544	81.4
Bunawan	67,576	228.2
DAVAO CITY	163,600	72.4%

this impetus a group of 288 banded together and successfully invaded some adjacent government land and built Lapu Lapu Village.

The site of the village is a marshy area surrounded by coconut groves. The residential tract occupied by the squatters consists of 2 hectares which had been leased before the war by a Captain Rivera for fish ponds for raising *bangos*. The leaders of the group were able to choose land on the edges of the coconut groves but the rest of the settlers had to contend with house lots which were frequently under water. Their ingeneous solution to the problem, considering their lack of capital to purchase dirt fill and have it transported to the site, was to approach the South Bay Lumber Company and to have them dump truck loads of sawdust into the marsh. Many of the homes were built on this insubstantial base.

Following the rapid erection of wooden houses built from scrap lumber which was collected from the nearby sawmills, the legal battles for legitimate possession of the land began. Captain Rivera (now residing in the United States) and his relatives attempted to evict the squatters who claimed they had a legitimate right to the areas.

Regardless of the merit of the squatters' assertions, the Lanang Homeless Association was formed for the purpose of contesting the ownership of the occupied tract. It was initiated at least eight years ago with the area's most important leader as president. Through attorneys, it filed a protest to force the release of the land for private titles. Embodied in this petition, prepared in January 1964, is a survey of the settlement giving locations and sizes of lots, and streets dividing them.

Attached to this petition was a list of 288 claimants, who were supposedly inhabitants of Lapu Lapu. In reality almost a third of them had only put up frames of houses in order to establish their rights while they acquired more capital for building. This led to disaster in the courts. When the case was brought before the judge in 1970 he made an inspection of the village and ruled against the squatters because too many of the people named in the petition did not reside in Lapu Lapu. This led to an overthrow of the old leadership. A new leader was elected and the by-laws amended requiring the owner to complete his house or sell his rights to someone who would.

Visual impressions of Lapu Lapu Village are somewhat mixed. The usual plants and trees surrounding Filipino houses are missing since nothing will grow in sawdust. The heat from the sun on sawdust is intense and on a rainy day it is almost impossible to enter even with a jeep. There are the usual small front-room Sari-Sari Stores but there is no market place in the area. The appearance of the village is constantly changing as the residents complete new houses or improve their old ones. Several families have built new homes on their lots and have torn down their old shacks. As in squatter areas all over the world, there is a continual upgrading of the village.

Lapu Lapu had no school when we began our surveys in early 1970, but an efficient committee was formed, materials were collected, and the squatters built their own three-room school which opened for grades 1-3 in July 1970. It now has six grades and eight rooms. The first teachers were volunteers from among the educated squatters since the city would not provide teachers to a school built on private land. However a sufficient amount of cajoling and pressure in an election year forced the mayor to attend the dedication of the school and city teachers were soon assigned to it. One of the squatters is the principal teacher and several of the teachers are residents.

Although the other most needed facility according to responses on our survey was electricity, the privately owned Davao Light Company was reluctant to place their poles on private land. This too was overcome with numerous meetings and petitions, and in July 1970 electricity was brought into the village. The majority of the homes now have electric lights and some even have TV.

The present concern of the inhabitants is to obtain adequate drainage to keep from floating away in the rain. There are no sewers and there probably never will be any. Rain water, caught in tanks as it drains from the roof, is the customary drinking water source for all of Davao. Transportation by jeepney is readily available to all points of Davao and many of the men work in the lumber companies nearby. Obviously, by many criteria of adjustment, Lapu Lapu Village is a success and its occupants, many of whom arrived there from the slums of Davao, take great pride in the peace and quiet of their new "suburban residence."

Descriptive data on Lapu Lapu Village were obtained through identical surveys repeated at two different points in time; the first survey was conducted in March 1970 and the second in December 1971, approximately twenty-one months later. Both surveys were conducted under the sponsorship of the Davao Research and Planning Foundation with the participation of our office staff at the Mindanao Development Center.

Lapu Lapu Village is a component of the evolving urban social organization of Southeast Asia. It illustrates the position of the organized squatter community in the process of urban growth, upward social mobility, and incipient fertility control. To indicate these aspects of life in the village, the following data are presented from a preliminary tabulation of the December 1971 survey data on 228 households.

Demographic and Socioeconomic Characteristics

The information presented here concerns the rate of growth, size, and composition of Lapu Lapu Village, together with enough household data to permit a socioeconomic classification of the community. Against this classification, some preliminary data on fertility and family planning practises are presented and examined.

The Origin and Growth of Lapu Lapu Community

The village is almost entirely a product of the last decade: only forty-two households, 18 percent of the present number, were established before 1965 (table 11-2). By 1969, the community had expanded to 127 households, or 56 percent of present resident strength. The remaining 44 percent of the community — 101 households — represent new arrivals during 1970-1971.

The mushrooming growth of Lapu Lapu Village during the latter half of the last decade is part of the general trend toward expansion in the Bunawan sector of Davao City (see table 11-1). Since 1964, however, the annual growth rate of the village has been 27.5 percent per year, or approximately five times the 5.5 percent annual growth rate registered by Davao City between 1960-1970.

Should this rate continue, and it obviously cannot continue for very long before available lots are exhausted, the population of Lapu Lapu would exceed 1,000 households in 1977, and would reach the 2,000 mark in 1980. The obvious inference is that other target areas will be chosen by the unaccommodated hordes of homeseekers, and new squatter associations and duplicate villages will soon be appearing elsewhere in Bunawan.

Table 11-2

Household Arrival Year in Lapu Lapu Village: All Households Present
in December, 1971

| | Households | |
Arrival Year	N	%
1960	2	1.0
1963	9	3.9
1964	31	13.6
1965	18	7.9
1966	18	7.9
1967	14	6.1
1968	11	4.8
1969	24	10.5
1970	53	23.2
1971	48	21.1
TOTAL	228	100.0

The growth rate of Lapu Lapu Village in recent years serves as an indicator
of the growing demand for the life style which it represents rather than as a projection of the anticipated population of the village itself.

The growth of Lapu Lapu Village is not some sort of inexorable response to
demographic imperatives. It has been conditioned and shaped by historical circumstances; an initial growth spurt accompanied the filing of a petition for release of the land in 1964, and the more recent avalanche of new households was
immediately preceded by the establishment of the elementary school within the
community and the arrival of electricity.

We may conclude that population growth and movement provides a more
than ample supply of new city-dwellers to Davao, but that features of a particular destination operate to select the portion finding its way to Lapu Lapu Village. We will seek these selective factors in our review of the characteristics of
community residents.

First of all, the ultimate origin of household heads and spouses is overwhelmingly rural; 188 (85 percent) of the householders originate in rural areas, while
only 33 (15 percent) have spent their entire lives in urban surroundings. Heads
and spouses of only 17 households claim Davao City as their home community.

Secondly, for 188 (85 percent) of the 221 householders responding to this
item, paths of migration have taken them to intervening destinations prior to
their arrival in Lapu Lapu Village. Examination of these intervening destinations

Table 11-3
Intervening Destinations of Households Residing in Lapu Lapu Village,
December, 1971

	Percent	*Households*
No Intervening Destination		33
Intervening Destination by Type:		
A. Rural Residence Only	9.0	17
B. Central Slum Only	33.5	63
C. Central Slum & Squatter Village	17.0	32
D. Other Squatter Village Only	40.5	76
TOTAL		221

(see table 11-3) permits us to offer an observation with direct bearing upon the
Turner hypothesis: 91 percent of the Lapu Lapu Village dwellers with intervening destinations resided previously in a slum or other squatter area, and 51 percent of them were definitely central city slum dwellers at some stage in their
pattern of movement. We may conclude that Lapu Lapu Village, as a final destination, represents the achievement of upward socioeconomic mobility for a
substantial proportion of the present residents.

Age-Sex and Household Composition of
Lapu Lapu Village

The demographic composition of the community as of December 1971 is
given in table 11-4. Adequate comparative data are not available, but when the
distribution is matched with that of Davao City for 1960 (as published in the
Census of the Philippines for that year) some minor differences are apparent.
The largest of these is a 3.6 percent excess of pre-school children, and a 3.1 percent deficiency in the population 20-29, in the squatter barrio.
Inspection of table 11-4 discloses an interesting feature of the sex ratio
which may explain these deviations. There is an excess of females fifteen through
twenty-nine over males, and an excess of males thirty through sixty-four over
females. The data suggest a marked tendency for older males to marry younger
females who are in their peak reproductive years. This tendency is compatible
with the excess of pre-school children and the deficiency of young male adults
in the village population.

Table 11-4
Age-Sex Composition of Lapu Lapu Village. Population of December 1971

| | Males | | Females | | Total | |
	N	%	N	%	N	%
9-4	165	11.7	137	9.7	302	21.4
5-9	120	8.5	117	8.3	237	16.8
10-14	92	6.5	77	5.5	169	12.0
15-19	63	4.4	81	5.7	144	10.1
20-24	40	2.8	54	3.8	94	6.6
25-29	47	3.5	61	4.3	108	7.8
30-34	64	4.5	49	3.5	113	8.0
35-39	46	3.3	44	3.1	90	6.4
40-44	29	2.1	20	1.4	49	3.5
45-54	36	2.5	30	2.2	66	4.7
55-64	15	1.1	9	0.6	24	1.7
65+	6	0.4	8	0.6	14	1.0
TOTAL	723	51.3	687	48.7	1,410	100.0

Household composition of the Lapu Lapu Village population in 1971 is illustrated in table 11-5. The mean number of persons per household was 6.12 – slightly below the 6.4 persons per household disclosed in the 1970 Davao City Census. In short, examination of age-sex and household data discloses that the Lapu Lapu Village population is only slightly different from the larger community of which it is a part.

Table 11-5
Household Composition of Lapu Lapu Village. Population of Residents in December 1971

Members in Each Household	Frequency N	%
1	1	0.4
2	11	4.6
3	23	9.8
4	33	13.9
5	27	11.4
6	44	18.6
7	29	12.3
8	27	11.4
9	20	8.5
10	13	5.5
11	4	1.8
12	4	1.8
TOTAL	236	100.0

Socioeconomic Characteristics of
Lapu Lapu Village

The illusion of sameness is destroyed when we examine the education, employment and income data for the occupants of this squatter barrio.

The average educational attainment for household heads and spouses is one and one-half years of high school (7.5 years of education). There is an expected sex differential. Males have completed two years of high school while the female average falls in the sixth-year level (completion of elementary school).

This level of educational attainment among an adult population of primarily rural origin is exceptional. In the adult population of Davao Province (made up of those twenty-five years of age and over in 1960), over one-half had never attended school (table 11-6).

The occupants of a squatter barrio do not consist of the dregs of rural society cast out into an inhospitable and unreceptive urban setting. The impression of better-than-average socioeconomic status will be further confirmed by a glance at the occupational distribution provided in table 11-7.

To those familiar with the economic structure of Southeast Asia, one of the striking features of the occupational distribution is the absence of low-status, low-paying positions such as driver, laborer, household helper, agricultural worker, security guard or tailor-dressmaker. These categories combined comprise only 29.6 percent of the labor force. Other indications of relative affluence are the low rate of unemployment and the very small number of women in the labor force (less than 30 percent of all housewives making their homes in Lapu Lapu Village).

Table 11-6
Education of Parents in Lapu Lapu Village

	Male		Female	
	N	*%*	*N*	*%*
Attended College	41	18.1	28	12.2
Attended High School	87	38.3	68	29.7
Attended Elementary	96	42.3	129	56.3
No Education	3	1.3	4	1.8
TOTALS	227	100.0	229	100.0

Table 11-7
Employment Patterns in Lapu Lapu Village

	Male	Female	Total	%
Artisans and Craftsmen[a]	55	1	56	16.7
Commercial[b]	19	41	60	17.9
Clerical	16	1	17	5.0
Laborer	37	0	37	11.1
Industrial[c]	57	3	60	17.9
Farm and Stock	10	0	10	3.0
Driver	31	0	31	9.3
Professional-Managerial	16	11	27	8.1
Tailor-Dressmaker	2	6	8	2.5
Business	2	2	4	1.2
Personal Service	2	2	4	1.2
Security Guard	8	0	8	2.5
Retired	4	0	4	1.5
Government Service	3	0	3	0.9
Unemployed	5	0	5	1.5
TOTALS	267	67	334	100.0

[a]This category includes predominantly auto mechanics, carpenters, and factory-employed carpenters, i.e., highly skilled workers.

[b]Males in this category are primarily salesmen paid a basic monthly wage. Women are sari-sari store operators, earning much lower income.

[c]No distinction is made here between skilled machine operators and unskilled workers, however, the highly skilled are in the majority. All are paid substantial wages and employment is permanent.

The primary criterion for assessment of socioeconomic status in occupational terms, however, is the large proportion of better-paying jobs held by male household heads in the community. The highly remunerated categories of employment in table 11-7 include artisans and craftsmen, industrial wage workers, professional-managerial and government workers. These positions, taken together, comprise 50 percent of the male labor force.

The inferences made from educational and employment data concerning the relatively acceptable circumstances of life in Lapu Lapu Village will be tested using the income distribution provided in table 11-8. The income distribution reveals that the average monthly household income in the village is ₱ 312.44, with one-fifth of the households earning monthly incomes of ₱ 400 or more. Looked at from the other side, less than one-fifth of the households in the community earned less than the minimum wage of ₱ 240 per month.

A final index of both social stability and socioeconomic status related to the Turner hypothesis may be formulated from (1) the proportion of

Table 11-8
Household Income in Lapu Lapu Village. Resident Population of
December 1971

Monthly Income	Number	Percentage
0- 99	6	2.7
100-199	34	15.4
200-299	96	43.4
300-399	40	18.1
400-499	14	6.3
500-599	16	7.2
600-699	9	4.1
700-799	4	1.8
800-899	2	1.0
TOTAL	221	100.0

homeowners among the residents of Lapu Lapu Village, and (2) the estimated
cash value of the residential property owned and occupied by them. Of the
233 households for which data were secured, 160 or 69 percent, were owner-
occupants of residences in the community while another 55 households, or
24 percent, were renting. A final 18 households, or 8 percent, consisted of
occupants who were administering the property for others. Such "administrators" may best be defined as caretakers or watchmen who occupy property for
the owner while he is absent.

The financial security represented by the owner-occupants making up two-
thirds of the households in Lapu Lapu Village may be further supported by
data regarding the cash value of their residences in table 11-9. While values of
individual dwellings ranged from below ₱ 500 to above ₱ 25,000, the average
dwelling was valued at ₱ 3,100. Since the cheapest low-cost commercial
housing available in Davao City costs about three times that figure, the dwellings are not sumptuous. The area is subdivided and lots are surveyed and sold
by the Lanang Homeless Association. If not occupied, they may be repos-
sessed and sold again by the Association. An improved lot remains in the
possession of the owner, however, and he may sell it, together with its improvements, to a subsequent occupant. These simple considerations are
apparently enough to create a market in Lapu Lapu Village real estate. And,
once established, the market continues to function under circumstances where
demand exceeds supply. The consequence, apparently, is to drive prices up
and to discriminate against low income persons who may seek entry into the
community. These considerations provide a partial explanation of the

Table 11-9
Estimated Sale Value of Houses and Lots in Lapu Lapu Village:
December 1971

Valuation (Press)	Frequency
0- 500	44
501- 1,000	31
1,001- 1,500	12
1,501- 2,000	12
2,001- 2,500	16
2,501- 3,000	9
3,001- 3,500	21
3,501- 4,000	11
4,001- 5,000	7
5,001- 6,000	7
6,001- 7,000	4
7,001- 8,000	9
8,001- 9,000	7
9,001-10,000	3
10,001+	16
No Estimate	24
TOTAL	233

unusually high levels of education, employment, occupational status, and income found in the community.

To summarize, the Turner hypothesis concerning upward social mobility associated with the formation of squatter associations and the seizure and occupation of new residential areas is applicable to Lapu Lapu Village. The rural origins and intervening destinations of the present residents define the steps up the ladder leading to eventual entry into Lapu Lapu Village or some equivalent squatter barrio.

The capital requirements for admission to the community insure that only persons who are securely employed at better-than-average salaries are accepted. Once these people become occupants, they tend to invest a portion of their earnings in community development and home improvement. Consequently, property values tend to increase and entrance requirements for the next group of applicants become even more rigorous.

Implications for Fertility Control

For many families with agricultural backgrounds who manage to negotiate
the transition to urban life, success and security are accompanied by "seizure"
of a place in a squatter community such as Lapu Lapu Village. The conventional
wisdom surrounding demographic transition theory would suggest that an up-
wardly mobile cluster of households of this sort should provide an ideal clientele
for fertility control.

Empirical support for this notion is forthcoming from survey items in the
Lapu Lapu interview schedule which deal with favorable attitudes toward, and
present utilization of family planning services. Of 192 married women between
the ages of seventeen and forty-four, which we shall take as an approximation of
the population at risk, thirty-five, or 18 percent, were using a contraceptive
method at the time of the survey, and another 71 women, or 37 percent, expressed definite interest in learning about a family planning method. These two
groups, the contraceptors and those interested in family planning constituted
55 percent of the married women in the fertile age range. Further analysis of
interest in family planning may be made from the vantage point of the age composition of married women, reproductive experience, and socioeconomic status
within the community.

Interest in family planning is strongest in the age groups seventeen through
thirty-four, and weakest in those above age thirty-five (table 11-10). Since the
target population for family planning programs corresponds with the group of
women who seem most favorably disposed, our initial impression is that a substantial population reduction might be achieved by providing adequate services
to the village.

Table 11-10
**Age Composition of Married Women in Lapu Lapu Village by Attitude Toward
Fertility Control**

Age	Acceptors	Interested	Not Interested	Total
17-19	1	3	1	5
20-24	7	12	9	28
25-29	8	21	26	55
30-34	12	15	16	43
35-39	6	16	21	43
40-4	1	4	13	18
TOTAL	35	71	86	192

Table 11-11

Socioeconomic Characteristics of Married Women in Lapu Lapu Village by Family Planning Attitude

		Acceptors	Interested	Not Interested
1.	*Education*:			
	A. Elementary	37.0%	54.0%	62.0%
	B. High School and College	63.0%	46.0%	38.0%
2.	*Income*:			
	A. Below ₱ 300/mo.	45.7%	64.8%	61.6%
	B. Above ₱ 300/mo. (to ₱600/mo.)	45.7%	28.2%	27.9%
3.	*Employment*:			
	A. Permanent	83.4%	79.4%	70.5%
	B. Impermanent	16.6%	20.6%	29.5%

This impression is heightened when we turn our attention to the socio-economic characteristics of married women, classified by their attitude toward family planning, presented in table 11-11.

Women defined as acceptors have the highest level of education and the households to which they belong have the highest concentration of incomes in the ₱ 300-600 range. Heads of their households have the highest proportion of permanent employment with major factories and corporations in Davao City.

Favorable attitudes and strategic socioeconomic position with regard to family planning must be translated into effective behavior if the upward social mobility of Lapu Lapu families is to be used as a predictor of fertility control. The fertility performance of the married women of the community is examined in table 11-12. The measure of fertility performance is average number of children ever born to women in each five-year age group from fifteen through forty-four.

The obvious conclusion from table 11-12 is that those women using contraception are also those whose fertility has already proven to be excessive by community standards *at every age level*. For them, interest in contraception might be characterized as "too little and too late." Interest in family planning, like acceptance of a contraceptive method, appears to be directly related to fertility performance. Those uninterested in family planning are the married women with the fewest children.

Despite these less than encouraging conclusions regarding reproductive performance, only one-half of the present acceptors have reached the age of

Table 11-12
Children Ever Born to Married Women in Lapu Lapu Village by Age Group and Family Planning Attitude

Age	Acceptors	Interested	Not Interested	All Women
17-19	2.0	1.0	1.0	1.4
20-24	2.7	1.8	1.7	2.3
25-29	3.3	2.6	2.6	2.8
30-34	4.3	4.3	3.3	4.0
35-39	6.5	6.8	5.2	5.7
40-44	8.0	6.5	6.8	6.6

thirty. If they become effective users of contraceptive methods, a substantial number of births may still be averted. This conclusion is even more applicable to those who have expressed only a favorable attitude toward fertility regulation.

Conclusions

The history and socioeconomic composition of Lapu Lapu Village offers affirmative evidence in support of the Turner hypothesis. This hypothesis seeks to find a place for the squatter community in a new definition of urban social organization for the developing world. It attributes to squatters the achievement motives and desire for improved socioeconomic status which have proven to be an essential part of self-managed social evolution throughout the world.

One of the consequences of this process, when successfully negotiated, is the transformation of traditional rural folk into effective urban residents. In Lapu Lapu Village, that goal appears to have been achieved. A corollary is the expectation that, as social status of the urban migrant improves, his interest and practise of fertility control will likewise increase. On this score the evidence from Lapu Lapu Village is inconclusive. Fertility regulation is a function of fertility — those having the largest number of children being the most likely to be acceptors of contraception. There is a reservoir of interest which if translated into acceptance could make a difference in the lives of the residents of Lapu Lapu.

References

Bonilla, Frank. "Rio's Favelas." *AUFS Reports, East Coast South America Series*, Vol. 7, No. 3, 7, 3, American Universities Field Staff, Inc., 1961.

Carino, Benjamin V. "Hope or Despair: A Comparative Study of Slum and Squatter Communities in Five Philippine Cities." *Philippine Planning Journal*, 3, 1 (1970): 8-14.

de Coulanges, Fustel. *The Ancient City*. Garden City, New York: Doubleday and Company, Inc., 1956.

Doughty, Paul L. "Behind the Back of the City: 'Provincial' Life in Lima, Peru", In William Mangin (ed.), *Peasants in Cities*. Boston: Houghton Mifflin Company, 1970.

Hackenberg, Robert A. and Beverly H. Hackenberg. "Suburban Growth in Southeast Asia: A Squatter Barrio in Davao City." *Journal of Human Ecology*, In press.

Hendershot, Gerry E. "Cityward Migration and Urban Fertility in the Philippines." Paper prepared for presentation, Population Association of America, Washington, D.C., 1971.

Laing, John E. "Family Planning in Greater Manila, 1970. Characteristics of Acceptors." Reprint of Family Planning Evaluation Office, University of Philippines Population Institute, 1970.

Macisco, John J. Jr., Leon F. Bouvier, and Robert H. Weller. "The Effect of Labor Force Participation on the Relation Between Migration Status and Fertility in San Juan, Puerto Rico." *Milbank Memorial Fund Quarterly* 48 (1970): 51-70.

Mangin, William. "Squatter Settlements." *Scientific American* 217 (October 1967): 21-29.

. *Peasants in Cities*. Boston: Houghton Mifflin Co., 1970.

Sjoberg, Gideon. *The Preindustrial City Past and Present*. Glencoe, Illinois: The Free Press, 1960.

Turner, John C. "Barriers and Channels for Housing Development in Modernizing Countries." *Journal of the American Institute of Planners* 33 (1967).

. Housing Priorities, Settlement Patterns, and Urban Development in Modernizing Countries." *Journal of the American Institute of Planners* 34 (1968a): 254-363.

. (with Rolf Goetze). "Developing Incentives to Guide Urban Autonomous Growth." *SEADAG Papers on Problems of Development in Southeast Asia*, No. 46, The Asia Society, New York, 1968b.

Weissmann, Ernest. Statement made at 403rd meeting, April 25, United Nations Economic and Social Council, Social Commission, U.N. Bulletin No. E/CN 5/L, 313, 1966.

Wood, Arthur Evans. *Hamtramck*. New Haven, Connecticut: College and University Press, 1955.

12

Adaptive Processes and Development
Policies in a Frontier Resettlement
Community

Carlos A. Fernandez II

The Problem

Resettlement is a vaguely defined concept which takes many forms and serves varied goals. For our purposes, resettlement or land settlement is the "large-scale internal transfer of population to vacant and frontier lands under the sponsorship and assistance of government and private agencies." Using a notable case from the Philippines, Narra, our problem is to determine whether the removal of settlers to frontier areas resulted in that sustained growth and development which the resettlement was meant to bring about.

The ideal of resettlement is to give the *landless* a chance to own land, to operate as independent landowners, encouraging greater productivity and a new and better life. From this point of view we may ask:

1. What are the social factors which serve as incentives or constraints to the success of resettlement?;
2. What criteria should one use for assessing the results of resettlement?; and
3. What are some of the policy implications from past resettlement experience?

Discontinuities in an Enduring Program

In the Philippines, over the last fifty years, resettlement has become well established, and to this day is an integral element of the comprehensive agrarian-development program. In the face of uneven man-to-land pressures and outmoded systems of tenure and production, yet with considerable vacant lands in the outlying frontier areas, land settlement has been an appealing measure and is accorded strong, continuing, if perhaps sometimes unquestioning, support.

The prewar government efforts (1913-1939) met with limited success, bringing a few thousand families to the agricultural colonies in Mindanao but hardly affecting populating pressures in the high density areas. The toll on the settlers was heavy, resulting in high rates of turnover and abandonment of farms. In extreme cases settlers lost their lives in land conflicts with the indigenous inhabitants.

217

The general social unrest of the postwar years, compounded by an armed insurgency of discontented peasants (Hukbalahap) provided the major impetus for the renewal and expansion of the resettlement program. "Land for the landless," the original fighting slogan of the Huks, soon became the pervasive theme of a combined ameliorative-pacificatory program. This counterinsurgency objective soon yielded to broader land development and tenure-reform goals, embodied in the charters of five successive resettlement schemes. Organized resettlement reached its highpoint during this period with the establishment of twenty-two frontier settlements accommodating close to 24,000 families.

It was during the first postwar decade (1945-1955) that optimistic expectations increasingly gave way to a sense of urgency, and not infrequently, disillusionment over the diminishing ability of the resettlement program to cope with persistent and increasing problems of land tenure, growing population pressure, and low agricultural productivity. Consequently, a program of leasehold conversion was adopted, aimed at the abolition of share-tenancy. The purchase and redistribution of large agricultural estates became a complement to land settlement and, more recently, replaced it as the major arm of an integrated agrarian-reform program.

The basic blueprint for resettlement—the goals and procedures—have endured changes in national administrations from the U.S. Civil Goverment (1913-1935), through the Philippine Commonwealth (1935-1946), to the Philippine Republic (1946-1970). However, government support and public interest have been sporadic from year to year, resulting alternately in severe cuts or generous increases in funds, in turn creating a wax-and-wane tempo of population movement to the new settlements. In retrospect, resettlement over the years has been a vaguely defined and little understood safety valve measure which is handily revived with every crisis situation—the Huk insurgency, the Taal volcano eruption, dislocation of squatters from Manila and Quezon City, displacement of agricultural tenants in the untested hope that population movement might be a solution. The time is ripe for a rethinking before the next revival.

Narra: The Frontier Setting

This chapter is based on research conducted in Narra, Central Palawan, first from January to August 1967, and again from June to November 1971. Narra is at once a resettlement project, a townsite *(poblacion)* and, more recently (in 1971), a municipality. This chapter is concerned largely with the first two phases of Narra's development.

The history of Narra's settlement began with the slow, long-sustained seasonal migration of *Kaingin* (swidden) agriculturists from the outlying island town of Cuyo. Initially these pioneer settlers stayed only for the duration of the rice-cropping season, but in the mid-1930s they came to settle permanently on the coastal flatlands which they claimed as homesteads. More families came after the war, and these homestead-clusters became the nucleus of pioneer settlements.

The decade following the Second World War saw the opening of Narra as a government resettlement project, accommodating hundreds of settler families from areas damaged and disrupted by the war. In response to this critical need, the government established resettlement projects (Narra among twenty-two others) where displaced peasants, surrendered dissidents, and landless Filipinios in general, might acquire agricultural lands.

Narra was officially established in 1949 as an agricultural colony of the Rice and Corn Production Administration (RCPA), and was converted in 1954 into a resettlement project administered by the Land Settlement and Development Corporation (Lasedeco). In 1956, the Lasedeco was abolished and the National Resettlement and Rehabilitation Administration (NARRA) took over its management functions. The NARRA gave way ten years later to a new agency, the Land Authority (LA) which shortly was revamped and reorganized in 1971 to become the National Land Reform Council (NLRC).

The Narra settlement sprawls over 23,300 hectares of gently rolling, richly forested land about 33 kilometers in length and varying from 8 to 15 kilometers in width. The whole settlement is divided into five agricultural sectors, which are in turn subdivided into six-hectare farmlots. Each sector can accommodate some 200 to 250 settler families.

As originally planned, the local agency was to administer the Narra project for twenty years, anticipating that after such time, the settlers would be economically self-sufficient and able to take over the administrative functions themselves.

Today Narra is stranded midway in its development, and the agency foresees the need to stay on for another twenty years. Settler families were still coming in 1970, and in 1972 new areas were prepared for another 200 families. Since 1954, 2,666 families have been admitted into Narra.

Settler Categories

There are basically four types of settlers according to the recruitment procedures of the agency:

1. settlers who were residents in the area before the opening of the Narra project—*pioneer settlers*;
2. settlers who came to Narra on their own and applied at the local agency for land allocation—*local settlers*;

3.   settlers who applied at the National Agency and came to Narra with full
     government assistance—*moved-in settlers*;
4.   settlers who applied at the National Agency, paid their transporation to
     Narra and were accorded partial subsidy and assistance upon arrival—
     self-propelled settlers.

The earliest comers to the Narra area are the *pioneer* homestead seekers
who came in the 1920s and 1930s without any government assistance. These
voluntary migrants claimed land parcels measuring 21 hectares as provided for
in the homestead law. When the resettlement project was opened in 1954,
those inside the Narra reserve were allowed to keep their lands well in excess
of the six hectares allocated to the settlers, so long as the pioneers were able
to show evidence of development. The pioneer settlers (seventeen of them),
are entirely Cuyonon, occupying adjacent farms in the Antipoloan sector, on
the outskirts of the townsite. Compared to the other settlers, the pioneers
have the decided advantage of a 5-15-year headstart and larger land parcels
(12-21 ha), having chosen prime agricultural lands, adjacent to each other.

The *local settlers*, like the pioneers, are voluntary migrants, unassisted by
the government. Coming after the settlement project opened, they claimed
only 6-hectare parcels. Although unable to take advantage of the National
Agency's recruitment services, they came and filed applications at the local
agency. Not waiting for official approval, these local applicants proceeded
to clear and settle on land parcels of their choice within the reservation.
Those who came in 1954 settled on lots along the highway, with kith and kin
claiming adjacent parcels. The latter-day local applicants are settlers' children
and dependents who, since their arrival have gotten married, established their
own families, and now desire their own farms. Other local settlers came to
Narra without the intent of engaging in agriculture and first worked in nearby
logging and mining companies. When these operations folded, they applied
for land and engaged in farming. Still others are settlers' relatives, who came
at the invitation of their kin, and by this time are established in the settlement. These local settlers, approximately 800 families, expected no government assistance other than land allocations.

The majority of Narra's settlers were accorded full government subsidy
and assistance. Coming with the barest resources, they are in dire need of
such aid as transporation, housing, subsistence, clothing, seeds, farm implements, medical services, and even the most basic items such as matches. The
amount of assistance given to these *moved-in settlers* has drawn criticisms, to
some degree invidious, from both the pioneers and local settlers who have
disparagingly called them "eat-lers" or "sick-lers." These are, however, the
settlers that planners had in mind when they drew up procedures for resettlement. Today these fully-subsidized migrants who arrived in batches of ten to
one-hundred families at a time make up 61 percent of the total settler
population.

More recently, in the mid-1960s, pressures for resettlement reached a new peak. The National Agency slowed down recruitment as resettlement was given a low priority in the overall agrarian-reform program. The backlog of applicants has increased fourfold as the Mindanao projects became the setting of prolonged socio-political disturbances. The applicants in order to beat this slack and to hasten the process of removal to Narra, offered to pay their transporation if the local agency would extend partial assistance to them as *self-propelled settlers*. In terms of social origins, they differ considerably from the other settlers in that they faced the urgency of removal. Some were victims of natural disasters, floods, typhoons or volcanic eruptions; others were victims of fire in cities or are displaced by urban renewal. Some 200 self-propelled settlers (7 percent of the total) have come to Narra since 1965. Since they came singly or in smaller groups, the local agency is able to extend more assistance, e.g., alloting cleared, abandoned farms rather than forested lots.

Beyond matters of recruitment, the agency treats settlers as if they were all alike. This is administratively convenient but it overlooks the significant fact that *settlers differ in terms of the initial resources at their command*.

The Resettlement Experience: Blueprint

The process of transferring to a frontier area may be viewed from two standpoints: the agency's and the settler's. The agency sees resettlement as a series of developmental stages that settlers go through in the process of achieving the formal resettlement goals. The agency's concern is to provide the settler with various services and material assistance at each stage. The summary chart below is a schematic representation of the resettlement experience, indicating the various development phases, the activities undertaken at each stage and the duration of each phase.

Summary of the Agency's Plan of Work
for Resettlement (Narra, 1966)

Phase	Activities	Duration
I	Recruitment and Screening: Processing and approval of applications	3 weeks
II	Removal from the old home to the new setting	5 days

III	Cushioning and Stabilizing the Settlers
	    a. temporary housing
	    b. subsistence aid
	    c. medical services
	    d. permanent housing
		first 6 months – 1 year

Phase	Activities	Duration

IV	Land Development
	  a. allocation of farm and homelots
	  b. land clearance and cultivation
	  c. allocation of work animals
	  d. provision of seeds, fertilizers, farm implements
	    and other agricultural extension services
		first 5
		years

V	Land Ownership
	  a. settling of accounts
	  b. tilling of land
		first 10
		years

It is interesting that the agency has no long-range development plans for the settlement as it does for the settlers. The resettlement charter specifically states that the agency expects to phase out its administrative functions and its assistance at some point when the settlement is self-sufficient economically and able to administer itself as becoming an autonomous municipality. To our knowledge there has been no provision for preparing the settlers for the eventual turn-over. In August 1971, through legislation, Narra became a municipality, but there was no turn-over of administrative functions, rather we find two administrative bodies in the community, the agency and the Municipal Council. Not a single municipal official—elected or appointed—is a settler.

The Resettlement Experience: Realities

Phase I. Recruitment and Screening

Application forms are obtained and filed at the Central (National) Agency. In theory, the agency treats applications singly, and draws contract terms with a single applicant. In practice, for convenience in processing and removal, settlers are recruited in batches of ten to one-hundred families. Chances are that applicants from the same community or region will be grouped in a single batch. Normally it takes three weeks from the time of filing for applications to be processed and approved.

In theory, all Filipinos have equal resettlement opportunities. Certain factors, however, have introduced preferential recruitment of settlers from some areas, e.g., favors will tend to flow in the direction of a new president's home region. Some applicants wait for years, sending three or more applications before getting the agency's approval; others proceed to Narra on their own, without bothering to file applications.

Phase II. The Removal

Transporting the settler and his family with their belongings from the old
home to Narra is one of the major services rendered by the agency. The agency
provides each batch of settlers with escorts—a doctor, finance officer, and team
leader— to ensure comfort and safety of travel. Transportation expenses are
charged to the settler's account except in cases where the government or other
agencies underwrite the expense.

The strategies for removal vary. Some come to Narra with little or no
knowledge of the place, while others make prior visits to the settlement before
applying. Still others come alone and later send for their families as soon as
land and housing are ready for them. Whereas in most cases the agency has to
extend loans to settlers for transportation, some settlers pay their way to minimize or entirely avoid indebtedness to the agency.

Finally, the actual removal of settlers is supposed to be timed so that they
arrive in Narra early enough to clear their lands and plant at the onset of the
rainy season. This ideal has not always been followed. As a result of the failure
to coordinate the movement of settlers with local planting schedules, some
settlers have had to wait for months before they could start land clearance,
meanwhile living on subsistence rations charged to their account.

Phase III. Cushioning the New Settlers

Two items which incoming settlers need immediately upon arrival are housing and subsistence, the latter until after the first harvest. The local agency
prepares bunkhouses, divided into one-room living quarters, which settlers
occupy from six months to one year. In the interim, they are expected to construct cottages on their home lots, using housing materials provided by the
agency. During this same period, and until they are producing their own food,
families are provided with rations and other basic household items, all charged
to their account.

Not all the settlers need housing assistance. Some stay with kin or friends
until they are able to construct their own homes. Others come well ahead of
their families, and send for them when they have the house ready. They may
spend from a few weeks to a few years in the bunkhouse. Delays in constructing homes is to a large extent a result of the agency's inability to provide
promised housing materials. And even when the materials are available, settlers
sometimes waive their right to such loans because of sharp increases in costs:
materials which cost ₱ 800 in 1967 cost ₱ 3000 in 1972.

Subsistence rations are given on credit to settlers, to sustain their families
while clearing the land and planting the first crop. The rationing periods vary,

three months for some families, eighteen months for others; where some families ask for an extension of this period of assistance, others decline the assistance. Settlers often complain about the lack of variety of the foodstuffs given to them and charged to their accounts. The administrator on the other hand deplores their selling or trading these items for other foodstuffs, but not too disapprovingly: "If they do not have taste for [Scandinavian] sardines, [Australian] butter, and [CARE] powdered milk, it is just as well. We do."

Medical assistance. The agency maintains a medical staff. The majority of the settlers, coming from nonmalarious regions, have their first bout with malaria in Narra. Palawan today is the primary malaria region of the country, reporting fully 25 percent of all the malaria cases in the nation. The disease is endemic to the area, and while knowledge of prevention measures are slowly being accepted, the medical facilities of the agency remain meager.

Phase IV. Land Development

The settler's life in Narra is centered on developing the land allocated to him, carving a farm from the forested landscape. Farm lots measuring 6 has. on the average, presurveyed and subdivided into rectangular parcels, are allocated to the settlers soon after arrival. Prime lands are those closest to the town and closest to the road. Ideally the system of allocation is by random draw and allows the settlers no choice in the selection of parcels. A random allocation of lands finds its rationale in the agency's attempt to "randomly intergrate" settlers of various ethnic origins. This, of course, is only the *ideal*, for settlers have worked out various means to obtain parcels more closely approaching their preferences with respect to topography, closeness to the road or to relatives, irrigation potential, thickness of forest growth.

The majority of the settlers, with the exception of the indigenous Tagbanua and the pioneer Cuyonon, come from parts of the country where slash-and-burn (*kaingin*) cultivation has long since disappeared from the cultural landscape. The settlers in Narra, are by experience, relatively sophisticated lowland-rice agriculturists, having worked in irrigated, perhaps even mechanized farms, employing modern scientific farming methods.

For men steeped in the tradition of lowland (irrigated) agriculture, *kaingin* agriculture is an entirely alien experience. This is true for both the settler and the agricultural extension workers in Narra, who turned to the Tagbanua and the Cuyonon to teach them how to gird and cut trees. This initial experience alone led many settler families to turn right around and leave the settlement. Serious injuries and deaths resulting from accidents were few and isolated, but widely known and publicized, and they did not help the sagging morale of the migrants.

The agency soon recognized the necessity of helping the settlers by extending loans for land clearance (₱60 per hectare) but this was, on the whole, little help since additional labor was scarce and loans were commonly used to augment the subsistence, as settlers fell further and further behind schedule in land development. Moreover, funds for land clearance were not enough for everyone, and this was an added reason for discontent.

Because of the lack of knowledge and skill in clearing forested lands, gross errors were made, and the effect on the physical environment was disastrous. Continguous parcels were cleared thoroughly thus exposing the top soil in vast areas to an acute laterizing process. This was further aggravated by the tendency of the Luzon settlers to plow the cleared areas, something any experienced kaingin farmer would not do, for it destroyed the thin layer of fertile topsoil. The areas thus cleared were cultivated for two years, and no sooner abandoned for fallow than invaded by *kugon* grass (*Imperata*), leaving large cleared areas as virtual *green deserts*, reclaimable only by irrigation. This almost wanton clearing of the forest cover led to the destruction of valuable watersheds, reducing the irrigation potential of Narra to a few topographically favorable pockets suitable for intensive rice cultivation. Valuable timber, direly needed for housing and construction, was carelessly cut, burned, or left to rot. What could have been an easy and cheap source of construction materials literally went up in smoke, and the irony of it is that today Narra imports lumber from Manila. One of the agency's agricultural extension workers estimated that no less than 60 percent of all farmlands allocated to settlers is *kugonal* (grass-infested wasteland), and can only be reclaimed by proper irrigation methods, 20 percent is still forested, and the last 20 percent may be classified as productive. Less than half of this productive land is irrigated.

The highpoint of development in Narra comes with irrigated rice cultivation, the goal of most settlers. Three out of every five settlers (N=500) are "rice-specialists," because they plant no other crop but wet/lowland rice. The stipulated advantages of large-scale irrigated agriculture tend to overshadow some real dangers that come as a result of inadequate ecological, socioeconomic, and public-health precautions.

The settlers' propensity to lowland rice culture places a high premium on work animals, the acquisition of which is at best, a tedious and complicated process. Since Narra has been in operation, 1,177 heads of carabao have been given out (on credit) to settlers. What the records do not show is that a number of these animals which are legally owned by the agency, have changed *holders*— the original allocatees having used them as pledges for loans and subsequently lost the animals by default in payment of the loans. According to the agency records one out of every two settlers should have a carabao, making allowance for the deaths and theft. The agency's policy is to give priority in allocation of carabaos to settlers whose farms have been cleared and are ready for plowing; however, this is not always the case. We know of settlers who have acquired work animals even before they cleared their lands, and they rent out the animals at ₱8.00 per animal working day. There are of course close to two thousand settlers who have been waiting for their work animals for the last several years. Some settlers are known to have as many as six heads of carabaos, obtained through allocations and direct purchase from private dealers, just as others have lost their animals through pests or theft. Those who have no animals are not entirely without alternatives: they may rent (in cash or by sharing the crop) or they may borrow.

Each settler is bound by contract to personally occupy and cultivate the land assigned to him, and not engage in occupations other than farming, if by so doing, he would neglect the development and cultivation of his land. The contract further states that his rights to the land are non-transferable except by inheritance. His absence from his farm for more than six months without the agency's permission is reason enough to discharge him from the settlement, in which case his outstanding accounts become due.

In August 1967, 815 settlers out of 2,666 were reported to have abandoned their farms, 500 of whom were still living in the settlement but temporarily engaged in occupations other than cultivation of their farms. The remaining 315 cases were reported either to have gone back to their old homes or to be non-contactable, thereby releasing their farms to new applicants. On inspection, the lands in question were found to be occupied by farmers who had squatted on them for the last few years without the agency's knowledge. Some of these squatters claim to have bought the original holders' rights to the land, others claim occupancy and right of use on the basis of rent, borrowing, or share-cropping arrangement with the original holders. The agency's decision concerning the 500 who abandoned cultivation but remained on their land in Narra came in the form of a strong admonition for them to return to cultivating the land or lose their land rights. The investigating officer admitted that the government can not really take a strong hand, considering that the agency, to some extent, has not fulfilled its part of the contract. The same official estimated that 80 percent of the total land allocated is either abandoned or idle, and only 20 percent may be considered as currently productive.

What are the alternatives open to settlers who leave their farms? Not counting those who left the settlement permanently, settlers leave their farms idle only temporarily. They may take on agricultural opportunities by borrowing lands from other settlers or homesteaders; they may join the town-based non-agricultural labor force, or they may revert to share tenancy on already productive agricultural lands. Leave-taking from their land will allow them to earn a living, and hopefully a little extra for developing their as yet unproductive lands.

An equally interesting counter development in Narra is the attempt by other settlers to consolidate their landholdings. The Narra charter defines the 6-hectare lands as family-sized farms. The settlers who have developed their original holdings to a point where they have irrigation systems and access to farm machinery find these farms uneconomically small. Various strategies have been employed in acquiring rights to land other than the original 6 hectares.

In one case a settler "purchased" the land rights to two parcels adjacent to his own, giving him a total of 18 hectares of prime riceland, fully irrigated and mechanized. In 1968 he got together with twenty-three other settlers in his area whom he *helped*—by providing loans and extension services—in planning and laying out rice paddies. These parcels, which previously were planted to upland rice and a few to rain-fed lowland rice, were gradually converted into irrigated rice paddies fed from his own reservoir. He assumed the management of these twenty-three parcels, which were organized into a corporate farm, the other members gradually paying him for the physical improvements. The local agency did not look too kindly on his activities, claiming that he is becoming a petty landlord, nonetheless admitting the economic success of the venture. In another case a settler finances and manages the cultivation of 16 hectares of irrigated rice land, worked by four share-tenants (settlers who have temporarily left their farms), while his own farm lot, located some 15 kilometers from the road, and 25 kilometers from the townsite remains forested.

It is interesting that the agency has not made any provisions for settlers to acquire more land, or to consolidate land when the situation calls for it. In the absence of such provisions, the settlers have devised the following:

1. Several members of a family apply for the usual 6-hectare parcels, but they arrange to have adjacent farms allocated to them. For instance, three settler applicants who are brothers, have 18 hectares of land together, which is being cultivated by one of them. This method is considered *legal*, but one needs *brothers* and foresight.

2. Borrowing lands that are not cultivated by the original holder allows the more enterprising settlers more space, if only on a short-term basis. Borrowing of lands is sanctioned by the agency, which encourages and even arranges for it, especially for the newly arrived settlers. Borrowing, as the term suggests, stipulates no rent or share of the crop. The original holder, especially if he is not cultivating the land himself, is only too glad to have someone work on his land, so the land inspectors will not declare it abandoned.

3. On occasion the settlers illegally surrender their land rights to another person because of dire financial needs. This extra-legal arrangement varies from case to case, as the settler may surrender only the management rights, or he may agree to leave the farm altogether. Under such arrangements, one may gain control or possession over as many land parcels as one wants. The agency clearly prohibits such turnovers, but on the whole remains ineffective in enforcing its policies.

4. Outright purchase of private lands or applying for homestead rights over public lands are the methods highly preferred by those who have the capital and desire to acquire larger land parcels.

Phase V. Land Ownership

Repayment of loans constitute the final stage in the settler's development. Except for farm and residential land allocations, all other material goods and services extended to the settler by the agency are considered farm loans. In our survey of 500 settlers who have accounts ranging from ₱300 to ₱12,000, 16 have started to pay back, 4 have paid more than half, and none has made plans to make regular payments or has any idea when he may be able to repay in full. No one expressed the need for acquiring his land title. Many express dissatisfaction with the record keeping and accounting system of the agency, citing numerous cases of unscrupulous officials padding the settlers' accounts. Only 4 of the 500 respondents claim they keep complete private accounting of the services and goods loaned to them, supported by receipts. Others are hopeful that by some legislation their accounts will be canceled, or would even enjoy seeing the agency records lost or burned.

In 1971 the agency awarded land titles to 117 out of a total 2,666 recipients. We have verified that 13 of them have since lost ownership through sales or loan default. Not one of the 2,207 residential lots that have been allocated is titled. If the final test of success is the formal ownership of land, settlers in Narra still have a long way to go.

Success in Narra

Our general observation of the resettlement experience leads to the impression that settlers have developed differentially from the common starting line. In a more systematic fashion, we find that:

1. There is a general consensus among Narra residents that settlers have developed divergently: *some are more successful than others*.

2. The distinction between those who succeeded and those who did not is expressed in terms of:

    a.   extent of land development;
    b.   general style of living;
    c.   ownership of agricultural production equipment;
    d.   ability to send children to college (and retroactively, the children's earnings augment the family income);
    e.   active participation in community affairs.

3. Success and failure are seen as two ends of a continuum, at some point along which people may be placed.

4. The distinction between success and non-success is real in the sense that people are able to place and rank individual settlers in terms of indicators which are meaningful to them. The respondents (40 raters) agree in general on who the most successful settlers are (picking 30 out of a possible 200 nominees). The raters were either reluctant or unable to give names for the less successful, explaining that most of the Narra settlers fall into this class anyway. With caution, this may be read to mean that the general distribution of the people in the stratification system is *pyramidal*, with a handful of success cases at the apex and the great mass of the less successful ones at the broad base. There are subtle variations in the conception of success among the various categories of raters:

a. Agency administrators tend to view settlers' success in terms of the formal goals of resettlement;
b. Teachers and the merchants stress indicators of successful social adaptation and active community participation;
c. Settlers view their success in terms of personal, small-scale, positive departures from their life in the old home, placing strong emphasis on economic security whether or not they follow the rules of resettlement.

The Strategy for Success

Assuming, for purposes of analysis, that settlers are dependent upon the agency for the scarce goods and services they need to get started in the frontier setting, assuming further that the agency (with the best of intentions) could not efficiently provide 12,000 settlers and their families with the needed assistance, it follows that success rests on:

1. skill in establishing social alignments with or bridges to the sources of the needed goods and services; and
2. business sense in converting whatever goods and services have been procured into efficient and productive ends, thereby, maximizing income and profit.

The settler's procurement skills and business acumen can be analyzed in relation to his:

1. allocation of resources initially controlled;
2. command over and access to additional resources;
3. awareness and response to market opportunities.

1. *Employment of resources initially controlled.* Our survey (*N*=300) shows that aside from their personal belongings and basic household items, settlers

come to Narra with cash savings ranging from ₱250 to ₱10,000. The average is
₱1,500 for the success cases and ₱500 for the non-success cases. A few isolated
cases brought farm machinery (tractor, rice mill, irrigation pumps). In the long
run, the strategy employed in allocating initial resources is as important as the
amount of these resources. For instance, one settler spent ₱800 for clearing his
forested land while another spent ₱350 for soil preparation and fencing a parcel
of land he rented, leaving his farm uncleared. The former had to abandon his
farm after two years; the latter earned a ₱2,000 net profit in two seasons from
the vegetable plots on rented land.

2. *Access to and control over additional resources.* If needed goods and
services are available locally, in theory, all settlers should know of the sources,
and on a priori grounds, none of the sources should be foreclosed to any settler.
This was not so in Narra. Credit and loans are virtually foreclosed to any settler,
excepting the successful cases who may easily find some *empleado* to vouch
for them.

For most settlers, during their first years in Narra, the agency is the sole
service-delivery source, and the agricultural extension worker their only link.
Through time the settlers get to know other sources, thus widening their options.

Insofar as social alignments and bridges with service networks are concerned,
the successful settlers tend to have more firm and efficient bridges. Unlike most
of the settlers, the successful settlers tend to socialize freely with the *empleados*
and the *maestros.* Their ties have very definite social class overtones. Often
these settlers are married to civil service employees or their college-educated
children join the bureaucratic ranks. Their bridges extend beyond the confines
of Narra to the top national-level officials in Manila, giving them extra
leverage.

3. *Awareness of business and market opportunities.* Another requisite of
success, and perhaps the most crucial one, is acumen in converting procured
goods and services into efficient investments, thereby increasing and maximizing income and profit. Successful settlers view farming as a business enterprise,
not merely as a way of life. The successful settlers distinguish themselves by
their ability to anticipate contingencies and plan for them, which we find to a
much lesser degree among the non-success cases. The former show a systematic,
if rudimentary, appraisal of their agricultural business ventures, keeping records
of gains and losses. These successful settlers are farm managers, recognizing
that they must mobilize human and nonhuman resources and coordinate them
into an efficient and persistently productive effort. They have tried minimizing
risks by diversifying economic activities, channeling increments from the farm
to a small retail store, or transporation (pedicab) business. They are entrepre-
neurs and a well-demarcated social group in matters of formal education,
exposure to media, travel, and employment experience.

The Emerging Community

Today, Narra is a burgeoning community, a blend of urban concentration and frontier shiftlessness and ingenuity. Where we expected to find a neat, grid-like pattern of settlement with settlers living and tilling their own land, we found a formless community spilled out of its confines onto the roads.

The three major elements that shaped Narra's growth are: (1) increased population; (2) bureaucratic expansion; and (3) market growth. The first has had its greatest impact in the farm sector, the center of the settlers' development efforts. Land development proceeded from the townsite outwards, and from the roads to the hinterlands. The farms closest to town and along the roads are the most developed. Narra's growth is increasingly focused on its urban elements: the bureaucratic sector, the market, and towards an integration of the two, with the farm sector lagging behind. Settlers have turned to nonfarm channels of income, away from dependence upon natural resources. The townsite is an important service center, the regional urban center for the south and central Palawan. Its early colony-like features with sharply drawn social boundaries have become increasingly blurred with the greater integration of the farm sector, the bureaucracy, and the market into a more or less natural community. In the past we observed a community with sharply-bounded social groups defined in terms of ethnic and social origins, the temporal order of arrival (pioneers, local, moved-in settlers), or the locus of settlement (farm, town, city). Today we note the emergence of across-the-board, vertically-integrated groups such as successful and non-successful settlers, the regulars and *casuals* among the bureaucrats, the large-scale merchants and small-scale shop keepers and peddlers.

Conclusions

Resettlement programs viewed in the abstract, hold bright promise for the *landless* and the poor. A dream shared by both planners and beneficiaries is that once land is acquired, prosperity will follow. Land holding has a special fascination, encouraging exaggerated expections, clouding realistic assessments of the chances for success. The backlog of applications from aspiring settlers bears this out.

The best that can be said for the Philippine program to date is that it gave the settlers opportunity to own land, "to exert themselves and use their labor and talents, and their meager resources to get a reasonable but modest income." Left on their own the majority of these settlers would not stand an even chance. Given their backgrounds as poor tenants, with low educational attainment, and limited technical or managerial skills, the settlers are in a very vulnerable position. It is not surprising to find them sliding back to their old tenant-dependent roles, given the spirit and the method with which the social and human problems in Narra have been handled. One is struck by the uncanny resemblance of the status-group relations—empleado-settler, successful settler-unsuccessful settler—in Narra with those in proto-typical hacienda. The settlers relate to the *empleado* who controls the goods and services they need in a manner not unlike their relations with the *amo* (landlord, employer) and his *encargado* (overseer). Viewing the *empleado* and the agency as "surrogate landlords" is not far-fetched. For that matter we can justifiably say that resettlement, for most, is a process of transplanting the old way of life to a new setting.

This sketchy account of settlers' life in Narra shows that land acquisition is not of itself a sufficient ingredient for enhanced agricultural productivity. Giving land to landless tenants does not make them owner-operators, much less self-sufficient and independent farmers. In the old setting—the hacienda—they participated minimally in the farm-production process. All management functions—marketing, accounting, planning—were all assumed by the *amo*. These are functions not learned over night.

In the Philippines one needs only to be *landless* to qualify for resettlement. But settlers vary in backgrounds and resources. Some are at the bottom rung of the economic ladder in their old homes and virtually have no choice but resettlement; others are independently secure and therefore can afford the risk of starting anew in the frontier. We might assume that the former are the least likely and the latter, the most likely to succeed. The agency's recruitment procedures give priority to the former, the most deserving but the least provisioned. Following this line of argument, the agency could either recruit the former with substantial subsidization, or recruit the latter with little or moderate assistance. What in fact happens is that the agency recruits *both* but provides *moderate* but generally inadequate assistance regardless of need.

Resettlement agencies should accept the almost inevitable high rates of turnover. Land holding procedures should be more flexible than the stringent policy of each—*tiller-to-his own-land*, which is *anti-developmental*. This will allow successful settlers to develop idle and abandoned farms and convert them into productive land even though this might be interpreted as contrary to the spirit of *equity*, the essence of the Land Reform Program—a philosophy which ardent ideologists would pursue at the cost of productivity. At the same time, means need to be found to deter the reversion to tenancy.

Successful settlers seem able to provide other settlers with goods and services the agency is unable to for lack of funds. Although the frontier situation presents a unique case insofar as land ownership has not figured prominently in the development pattern, this may not be true in the future. Through cooperative ventures the least successful settlers may be able to see *positive* results and at the same time learn the basic procedures of modern agriculture.

The agency must realize that resettlement is one step in a wider process of the settlers' quest for *a better life*. Whether successful or not, settlers find no motive compelling them to work their acquired land or to reside permanently in Narra and will leave when they perceive new opportunities. Thus we may say, resettlement is not a terminus, but a continuing process—a growth and developmental experience which takes place within or beyond the limits of an acquired piece of land, with or without the material and technical assistance of a resettlement agency.

13

Coping with Internal Migration in the Philippines: Problems and Solutions

Aprodicio A. Laquian

The problem with internal migration in the Philippines is that it is not usually regarded as a problem. As such, a search for solutions involves looking at policies and programs designed to cope with some other problem. When the city authorities in Manila tear down squatter areas and relocate the people to places outside the city, this is seen as a housing problem, a social welfare problem, or even a police problem. When Christian settlers fight pitched battles with Muslims in Mindanao, this is seen as a peace and order problem or a land grabbing problem. When agricultural extension workers in Central Luzon call a meeting and only old men and women and children attend, this is regarded as a problem of backwardness of the rural areas, of apathy, traditionalism or a part of the Huk problem.

And yet, in all these cases, we see problems related to internal migration. Internal migration, however, seems to be too abstract, too far removed from the immediate problems that concern public authorities. Hence, in the policies and programs of the Philippine government, there are very few measures for coping with internal migration directly. There are some which have an indirect influence on internal migration, but the links between these measures and internal migration are not spelled out. The real consequences of such measures are usually not anticipated and the benefits from them are rarely optimized.

The Problem Identified

Demographers usually identify two aspects of the Philippine population problem. First, the rate of growth of the population is too high: at 3.2 percent a year, the Philippine population doubles in approximately twenty-three years. Already, the Philippines ranks twentieth among the countries of the world, with its population of 36,684, 486 (1970 census). With a land area of 115,000 square

The author is grateful to Romeo B. Ocampo and Josefa Edralin, both of the College of Public Administration, University of the Philippines, for assistance in the preparation of this chapter.

miles, the Philippines has nearly twice the population of Canada, which has more than thirty-three times as much land area.[a]

Another aspect of the population problem in the Philippines is its maldistribution. Close to one-seventh of the total population is concentrated in the Greater Manila area, which makes up only .01 percent of the national territory. The provinces surrounding Manila are also densely populated and have, in fact, been growing at a most rapid rate. Thus, Rizal province, which had 2.8 million inhabitants in 1970, is 94.8 percent urban. Bulacan province, which also shares a boundary with Greater Manila, had 836,050 inhabitants, 47.8 percent of which are urban. The provinces of Laguna and Cavite are both more than 50 percent urban; the former had a population of 698,469 and the latter 519,040 in 1970. Among the country's sixty-one chartered cities, four are in the Metropolitan Manila area. The combined populations of the cities of Manila, Caloocan, Pasay, and Quezon make up 7.02 percent of the Philippine population.[1]

The second largest urban concentration in the Philippines is Cebu City, which had a population of 345,004 in 1970. While Cebu dominates the southern part of the Philippines, it only accounts for .94 percent of the country's total population. Cebu probince, which has benefitted a great deal from the city's growth, has become 40.3 percent urban in 1970.

The large population concentrations around the Metropolitan Manila and Metropolitan Cebu areas are, of course, the result of rapid rural to urban migration. Studies of internal migration in the periods covered by the three latest censuses in the Philippines (1939-48; 1948-60; 1960-70) reveal that the trend toward concentration continues. It is true that net migration into the core cities of Manila and Cebu has not been significant and has tended to be negative in the later censuses. However, a trend toward "suburbanization" has been observable in these places revealed by the high net in-migration into provinces that surround them. Since 1939, the province of Rizal has always showed a positive balance of migrants because of the tremendous growth in that section adjacent to Greater Manila. In the 1960-70 census periods, about 603,445 persons were added to the provincial population by net in-migration. The trend is the same with the provinces of Balacan, Cavite, and Laguna.

Aside from waves of rural to urban migration, another perceptible trend in the Philippines involves considerable movement to predominantly rural areas. In the early 1900s, the movement of people to agricultural settlements in the Cagayan Valley, Mindoro and Mindanao was a response to "land hunger" as well as conscious governmental policies to encourage growth in these areas. Migrants to the

---

[a]Authorities differ as to the actual growth rate of the Philippine population. The figure of 3.2 percent is from Mercedes Concepcion's estimates. The National Economic Council, on the other hand, sets a high of 3.7 percent per year.

Cagayan Valley were mostly Ilocanos from the northern part of Luzon. The Mindoro provinces were mostly settled by Tagalogs, though some Ilocanos found their way to these places too. In Mindanao, most of the settlers were Visayans, mostly from the Eastern (Samar and Lete), Central (Bohol, Cebu, and Negros) and Western regions (Panay, Negros, and Romblon). The southward migration to Mindanao is continuing to this day. In fact, new generations of Visayan migrants are now leaving the northern coasts of Mindanao (provinces of Misamis Occidental and Oriental and Surigao) and moving farther south.

Since 1939, the Southern Mindano provinces of Cotabato, Davao, and Zamboanga have consistently shown positive balances of net in-migration. The Visayan, Ilocano, and Tagalog migrants to these places were mainly looking for agricultural land. As a result, though urban concentrations have formed in this region, they have mainly been port cities, market towns or lumber boom towns. In the 1970 census, all provinces in Northern, Eastern, and Southern Mindanao, as well as the region of Sulu, had percentages of urban dwellers well below the national average. Between 1948 and 1960, more than two million people were added to the population of Mindanao as a result of in-migration.[2] Another 1.3 million were added during the period between 1960 and 1970. Certain significant changes in the economic and social conditions in Mindanao have occurred as a result of these changes. First, the opinion of Wernstedt and Simkins that "it is highly unlikely that the same strong emphasis upon agriculture which has characterized earlier periods of Mindanao settlement will continue"[3] is already being borne out by the migration patterns. Writing in the mid 60's, these authors assessed that by 1972, "all available farm land will be occupied" in Mindanao. Most migrants will be attracted to urban places such as Iligan and Cagayan de Oro in Northern Mindanao, and Davao in Southern Mindanao. Data from the 1970 census confirm these trends.

As Concepcion has written, internal migration in the Philippines may be seen as two main streams. The first stream is toward Metropolitan Manila, originating from all parts of Luzon and the northern Visayan provinces as far as Samar. The second stream goes toward Mindanao, originating mainly from the Visayan Islands as well as some parts of Luzon.[4] To this date, these two streams have relieved population pressures from each other. The open lands of Mindanao have provided an alternative to the cityward migration to Manila, and vice-versa. However, with the saturation of Mindanao with settlers and the attainment of maturity by many of its settlements, there is a grave danger that the rural-urban stream toward the Metropolitan Manila area may accelerate. Of course, the opening up of other urban places in Mindanao and other parts of the Philippines may serve to limit this movement somewhat. In the past cities of Mindanao have failed to attract large volumes of migration. Now, they must accommodate more people or the exodus to the Manila area and other Luzon urban centers may accelerate to critical proportions.

The Problems Created

As previously mentioned, the problems associated with internal migration in the Philippines are not generally traced to this demographic fact. However, sophisticated analysis is not required to trace the relationships between migration and urban-rural problems.

Urban problems are obvious enough. They are most severe in the service area since the influx of thousands of people into a city where services are already seriously over-extended often results in the breakdown of such services.[5]

In the rural areas of Mindanao, where the ethnic balance has been altered by the influx of migrants from the Visayas and Luzon the immediate perils arising from internal migration have been serious. It has been estimated that from 1903 to 1960, the proportion of Muslim Filipinos in the population of Mindanao has gone down from 31 percent to less than 20 percent.[6] The pressure of Christian settlers has resulted in open warfare. This is especially so in the province of Cotabato, where in 1960, Muslims made up about 35 percent of the population. In areas already dominated by Christians (Zamboanga del Norte, Bukidnon, Davao, and Zamboanga del Sur), there are few fights between ethnic groups. However, the problems from Christian incursion are already felt even in places where Muslims are still in a majority, such as in Lanao del Sur, where 96.6 percent of the people are Muslim.[7]

The problems of racial strife and open violence between migrants and indigeneous peoples are dramatic. In the long run, however, the more mundane and everyday problems of rural and especially city life arising from internal migration are more difficult to solve and require more concerted efforts. Problems of critical proportions arise in the sending areas, which lag behind the growing sectors as their populations move elsewhere. There have been convincing arguments that national development has to be achieved by a proper marshalling of the developmental forces arising from urbanization. If the Philippines is to develop in a sustained manner, internal migration's contribution to the urban problem must be recognized as such, and measures set up to cope with problems that it creates.

Solutions Offered

The effort to view governmental or non-governmental programs and policies as having an impact on internal migration and contributing to certain problems caused by it is relatively new. Policies and programs in the Philippines are usually in response to specific problems (peace and order, housing, agricultural productivity, road building, etc.). Planners of such policies and programs take a responsive, not an active view of population and demographic trends. If too many people have no housing in Manila, housing should be provided. If there is a need for employment in the manufacturing sector, investments in that area should be encouraged. The process is usually not carried to its logical conclusion which would, for example, recognize the fact that providing housing in Manila may accelerate the migration of people there and compound the housing problem or that sectoral investments in manufacturing may result in population concentrations in metropolitan areas where the investors may prefer to locate their industries. In other words, thinking in this area has usually been fragmented, uncoordinated, and sectorally oriented. Governmental programs, as observed by Ocampo, are usually seen as dependent variables, responding to population and demographic trends, not independent variables that may influence these trends themselves.[8]

For the sake of logical neatness, we may divide governmental and nongovernmental programs in the Philippines into four major groups: those that encourage people to move to certain areas; those that discourage them from moving to certain areas; those that encourage them to stay where they are; and those that try to cope with problems already at hand as the consequence of in- or out-migration. For every governmental program one analyzes, of course, it is highly possible that intended or unintended effects may involve any or all of these types of problems. In our analysis, which here is confined to a few government programs, we base our classification on the most important objective of the program as well as the "modal" results of the program. This linkage between goals and results is most important for some programs may have no success in achieving their goals and may, in fact, have the opposite results when implemented.

Encouraging Migration

Population pressures in rural and urban areas of Luzon and the Visayas would be worse today if considerable numbers of people from these areas had not elected to move to Mindanao, the Cagayan Valley, Mindoro, Palawan, and other "frontier" places in the Philippines. It is difficult to estimate how many of these movers were directly influenced by public schemes for resettlement. Wernstedt and Simkins estimated that less than 10 percent of the net migration to Mindanao can be accounted for by settlers in government sponsored projects.[9]

Government schemes encouraging people to move to Mindanao were initiated by American authorities who took over the Philippines at the turn of the century. The "homestead" idea, introduced in 1903 under the Public Land Act, granted public land to squatters who had cultivated it for several years. Holdings were limited to 40 acres for individuals and 2,530 acres to corporations. However, instead of attracting small farmers, which was the intention of the act, it was more successful in encouraging corporations to invest in Mindanao. Prominent among these were large Japanese abaca (Manila hemp) plantations in Davao, a pineapple plantation of Del Monte in Bukidnon, and several coconut plantations in Basilan and Zamboanga.[10]

The homestead scheme's failure to attract small farmers resulted in the introduction of "agricultural colonies," subsidized by the government. Such colonies were started in 1913, but by 1917 it was obvious that they were also doomed to failure. Only seven such colonies were founded. By 1918, the government was introducing a new scheme, this one aimed at people who already had some small capital and other resources. By 1939, the National Land Settlement Administration (NLSA) was established. Commonwealth Act 441, which created this agency, stated that its goal was "to afford opportunity for small farmers and tenants from congested areas to own farms and to encourage migration to sparsely populated regions."[11] However, because of the Second World War and other developments, the NLSA was able to open only two settlements — one in Cotabato and another in Isabela. In 1950, the organization was dissolved and replaced by the Land Settlement and Development Corporation (LASEDECO). This new agency survived four years, with a governmental investigation body recommending its abolition since its operations were characterized by "corruption, inefficiency, political favoritism and gross negligence." On June 18, 1954, the National Resettlement and Rehabilitation Administration (NARRA) was created, "to help speed up the free distribution of agricultural lands of the public domain to landless tenants and farm workers who are citizens of the Philippines, and to encourage migration to sparsely populated regions."[12]

Under the NARRA resettlement schemes, considerable amounts in subsidies were extended to settlers in frontier areas. First, the agency prepared resettlement sites. Then, prospective settlers were selected and carefully screened for economic, personality and other characteristics. The agency then provided free transportation to the settlement sites. Each settler family was provided with housing materials, a farm lot of six to ten hectares, a home lot of 600 to 1,200 square meters, a water buffalo, one set of farm implements, ten pieces of farm tools, a subsistence aid adequate until the time of the first harvest, technical assistance by an agriculturist, and other assistance from the government, channeled through local or community government structures (roads, schools, medical clinics, artesian wells, etc.).[13]

Free land was given to the settler; however, all other subsidies and advances had to be paid on an installment basis within ten years, with repayment (without any interest) beginning after the third year of settlement.

As the LASEDECO before it, the NARRA did not last long. By 1960, it was abolished and its functions taken over by the Land Authority. More recently, the Land Authority was also abolished and the function of resettlement lumped with activities of the Department of Agrarian Reform.

Measured against its goals or providing "land to the landless" and encouraging migration to certain regions of the country where population pressures on the land were less intense, land settlement schemes in the Philippines have a sorry record. However, they were successful in providing publicity to Mindanao as the "land of promise" and triggering off spontaneous migration. Net migration to Mindanao since the turn of the century has been significant, perhaps because people realized that the government fully intended to encourage people to move to Mindanao, that there were opportunities there, and that considerable governmental assistance could be counted on. Far more important was the increase in governmental services that followed these population movements. Roads and bridges were built, opening up large portions of Mindanao. Medical aid, especially effective against malaria, the main barrier to the settlement of many parts of Mindanao, was extended to the people. With more interpersonal contacts, the Christian Filipino's fear of the Muslims was lessened and new settlement communities in "Moroland" were founded. All these combined to achieve the net effect of settling much frontier land in Mindanao. To date, one out of every four Mindanao residents reports his birthplace as some area other than Mindanao. When one takes into consideration both inter-provincial as well as intra-regional movements, nearly one-third of the population was living in a place other than the place of birth.[14]

Have government policies and programs, which encourage migration to Mindanao, had an effect on cityward migration in the Philippines? Has the existence of the frontier eased migration to the metropolitan areas of Manila and Cebu? It may be argued that migrants to Mindanao and other frontier places were people looking for agricultural land and thus would not be the types to move to the cities.

This argument would be plausible, were it not for the possibility that the migrants may not be moving *to* but rather moving *away from* certain places. A study of conditions in so-called "sending areas" indicates that the latter situation may be the case. The Ilocos region in Northern Luzon, the Central Plains of Luzon, the whole of the Visayas, and the northern coastal regions of Mindanao are areas of above average population density. Soil and other agricultural conditions in these sending areas show evidence of over-use and abuse. About 60 percent of the land area of the Ilocos region is suffering from gravel wash and soil erosion. Conditions in the Central Visayas are worse, with 90 percent of the soil cover suffering from erosion and 60 percent of these being classified as "severely eroded."[15] The sending areas are also lashed by typhoons and suffer from too much rain (Leyte and Ilocos) or too little rain (Cebu and Misamis). Finally, land tenure systems in the sending areas are far from ideal. Tenancy in Central Luzon is high, with almost three-fourths of farmers not owning the land they are working on. Farm lots are small, especially in the Ilocos region where the amount of arable land is meager to begin with. In the provinces of Negros, large sugar haciendas have pushed smaller farmers from agriculture. All these factors have contributed to a "push" from the countryside. Studies of migrants who live as squatters and slum dwellers have shown that when conditions in the sending areas are unbearable, the people just move out, with no particular strategy or long-range plan. Thus, it may not matter too much whether the move is made to the city or a frontier area. Anything is better than the present situation.

Discouraging Migration

Governmental attempts to discourage migration to certain areas in the Philippines take two main forms. First, there are attempts to discourage people from moving to very large metropolitan areas such as Manila. Second, there are attempts to keep people from moving to slum and squatter communities within the metropolitan areas themselves. The first type of effort attempts to influence inter-regional or inter-provincial migration. The second type is mainly an effort to influence intra-city or local movements.

Keeping people from moving to metropolitan areas in the Philippines is an extremely difficult job. Freedom of movement is a dearly held right of every Filipino, embodied in the Constitution and long revered as a tradition. Still, the former mayor of Manila, Antonio Villegas, tried very hard to confine city services to bona fide city residents. Though he never went to the extent of Governor Ali Sadikin of Jakarta in trying to prevent non-Jakarta residents from staying in the city, Mayor Villegas tried most powers granted him under the law.

The city of Manila, because of its premier position in the country, usually collects enough tax income to provide ample urban services for its residents. When Mayor Villegas was elected in 1963, he embarked on his "Libre ang Filipino" ("Free to the Filipino") program which provided free education for Manila residents from grade school to the university. This was an excellent political program since most Filipinos consider education as a precious gift.[16]

Administering the "free education" program, however, was a difficult task. Many residents of surrounding cities and municipalities, not to mention people from the provinces, tried to enroll their children in Manila schools, resulting in an increase in the city's enrollment. By 1968, more than a third of the city's budget went to education.

To Manila residents who paid taxes and expected the benefits from their educational system to go to their families alone, the influx of many people to the city seemed unfair. However, it was almost impossible to weed out students whose families were not residents of Manila and to prevent other students from coming in. A legal procedure for school enrollment was devised which required presentation of an affidavit, subscribed and sworn to by the head of family, that the student being enrolled was really a child of a Manila resident and that the parents resided and paid taxes in the city. An investigative procedure was also installed, whereby a member of the Manila Police Department was sent to the address of the affiant in order to verify residency. However, there were so many loopholes in the rules and procedures that they did not deter enrollment of non-residents. Many lawyers would draw up the affidavit for a fee and some policemen were "influenced" to look the other way.

The liberal and democratic intent of Mayor Villegas also conflicted, some-what, with his desire to limit educational services to Manila residents. As a nationalist who took his Philippine history seriously, Mayor Villegas had a per-sonal dislike for the "Residence Certificate" system, which he saw as a survival of Spanish tyranny. One of the symbolic acts of the Philippine revolutionaries in 1896 was the tearing up of the *cedula personal* a forerunner of the present resi-dence certificate. Mayor Villegas took this symbolic act to heart and openly refused to collect fees from residence certificates (amounting to only fifty centavos, per Filipino adult, all of which went to the city treasury). He argued that the residence certificate had lost its usefulness since anyone with fifty centavos could purchase a residence certificate and state a fictitious address, nor did it serve as a good source of income for the fee was too small.

The dilemma of a liberal administrator in the Philippines is illustrated by the conflict between free education and the residence certificate. In order to offer adequate services at the local level, it is necessary to confine such services to those who are paying for them. At the same time, freedom of movement guaranteed as a citizen's right may not be hampered by such control measures as residence certificates or identification cards. This conflict seriously undermines attempts to discourage internal migration to certain areas in the Philippines.

In the Philippines, as elsewhere in the Third World, poor rural-to-urban migrants usually end up in slum and squatter communities. Intensive studies of such communities reveal that there is also a high rate of intra-city migration, with squatters and slum dwellers usually moving from one community to another. Public authorities have tried to control such movement within the city of Manila. Their efforts have ranged from fencing off certain areas threatened by squatter "invasions" to actual posting of army and police forces in certain areas to prevent squatters from coming in. Most efforts have been unsuccessful.

An interesting case study of attempts to prevent the movement of people to a certain squatter community may be seen in the story of Barrio Magsaysay. On April 2, 1971, fire destroyed Barrio Magsaysay and left nearly 40,000 persons homeless.[17] While relief measures were immediately undertaken by the govern-ment, planners and other officials saw the fire as an opportunity to plan what had been one of Manila's most controversial squatter areas. The National Housing Corporation and the Peoples Homesite and Housing Corporation were ordered by the president of the Philippines to draw up a complete housing program for the fire victims. Orders were given that squatters should not be allowed to build on the "cleared" areas until the plans and new houses were ready.

In three days, the National Housing Corporation announced plans to build four-story condominium units to accommodate some 600 families. At the same time, the Philippine National Red Cross started distributing galvanized iron sheets to squatter families who wanted to build their own homes. The Department of

Social Welfare extended financial assistance to homeless squatters who cared to return to their original provinces, but only sixty-seven families took advantage of these "one-way tickets." Many squatters stayed with relatives or friends in other parts of the metropolitan area while they awaited the result of the government's public housing program.

The association of squatters, suspicious of the true government intent, formally announced that they wanted the land they had been squatting on for years and were not interested in condominium housing. Interpreting the promise as a "government scheme to rob them of their legitimate lots," they warned the government that they would not be "bulldozed" from their lots and protested strongly against the presence of six truckloads of soldiers in the fire area.

Developments in this case followed a predictable path to violence and confusion. With the building materials from the Red Cross and others they could salvage, some families rebuilt their squatter shanties. The mayor of Manila, insisting that his planned condominium housing was better, threatened to bulldoze the shanties. The squatters, aided by student activists, formed a "human barricade" in order to prevent the machines from entering. In the ensuing skirmish, the police shot and killed one fifteen-year-old boy and hurt many others.

To date, attempts to prevent the squatters from returning to their community have been largely unsuccessful. Although the government has been able to prevent occupancy of most of the cleared land by providing temporary barracks built by the army public housing is being built at a slow rate and the dangers of invasion are always present. Doubts are expressed whether the squatters would be able to afford the housing being planned by the government. The lowest rent contemplated was Pesos 30 per month, close to a quarter of the average monthly family income of most squatter families. More than a year after the tragic fire in Barrio Magsaysay, things are still quite unsettled and it is not certain if attempts to keep the squatters away from the place will be successful.

The events in Barrio Magsaysay, while having all the drama of a crisis, are similar to other government attempts to deal with the squatter and slum situation in the Philippines. The clearing of squatters from the walled city of Intramuros in 1963 and their relocation to Sapang Palay shows the same pattern of confusion, lack of inter-agency coordination and political charges and counter-charges that marked the situation in Barrio Magsaysay. What these governmental efforts prove is the incapacity of the Philippine bureaucracy in dealing with relatively unfamiliar problems. They also reflect the great difficulties involved in trying to cope with social problems that arise from population movements.

Encouragements to Stay in Place

Many policymakers, worried about problems caused by rapid rural to urban migration, express the opinion that if people would only stay in their rural communities, many problems would be solved. Even those who accept the inevitability of rural-urban migration sometimes express the hope that people remain in intermediate cities instead of moving to the metropolitan areas. Much of the debate on the "optimum size" of cities, "growth poles," "poles of attraction," etc., reflects such thinking.

Although several programs are designed to discourage population movement in the Philippines, a closer look at the government's land reform program, the extension of credit to farmers and the efforts to achieve regional development, may suffice to illustrate this approach to the problem of population distribution.

Land reform has traditionally been an important program because of its association with social justice. When the Americans took over the country at the turn of the century, they tried to buy large landed estates owned by elite families and to break up the "friar lands" for resale to tenant farmers. These efforts, while symbolically important, did not accomplish much. It is estimated that of the country's more than one million farmers in 1970, only 37 percent owned the land they were tilling. Of the remaining non-owner cultivators, 63.6 percent were share tenants.[18]

There is no dearth of laws governing land reform in the Philippines. As early as the 1930's, the Rice Share Tenancy Contracts Act (Act No. 4113) was passed. After the Second World War, with agrarian unrest spawning a full-blown Communist rebellion, Republic Act No. 34 was passed, which regulated rice share tenancy according to the "70-30" formula. The 1950's witnessed the passage of laws on land purchase and resale programs, credit and marketing facilities for farmers, community development, cooperatives, agricultural extension, and other attempts to improve the lot of the peasant farmer. The Agricultural Tenancy Act (Republic Act 1199) was passed in 1954. This was followed closely by legislation fixing the minimum wage for agricultural workers, providing for tenancy mediation, and creating a Court of Agrarian Relations.

In August 1963, the Agricultural Land Reform Code was approved by the Philippine government. This legislation established the owner-cultivator and the family-sized farm as the basis of Philippine agriculture, and sought "to achieve a dignified existence for the small farmers free from pernicious institutional restraints and practices." The need to translate these lofty goals into reality resulted in a comprehensive and complex governmental machinery.

At present, the goal of the government's land reform program is to include 66 provinces and 1,506 local units (cities, municipalities, and municipal districts). The program intends to shift tenant farmers to a leasehold system, and then, eventually, turn them into owner-cultivators. The government purchases the private agricultural land worked by the tenant farmer turned lessee and when the farmer is able to, he can buy the land from the government. Farmers' cooperatives are encouraged with financial and technical support from the government; loans are made to farmers; agricultural extension and community development assistance is provided; and all sorts of aids are extended by the government to help the tenant farmer become an independent producer. It is hoped that with a happy, productive and properly motivated farmer cultivating the land he owns, there will be little risk that he will join squatter and slum colonies in the cities.

Perhaps it is too soon to judge the progress of the land reform program in the Philippines, but as of 1970, the Land Authority admitted that the program "has had only limited success with less than four percent of the share tenants in pro-claimed land reform areas converted to registered leasehold status, two percent having unregistered written leases, and nine percent said to have arrived at oral agreements."[19] Several defects were cited in the system, among them the lack of coordination among government agencies involved in land reform, inadequate financial and logistical support to field personnel, shortage of effective legal officers to assist in converting share tenants to leaseholders, and absence of an efficient mechanism for granting of land titles.

The government's response to the deficiencies in the land reform program has been another reorganization. The Department of Agrarian Reform was created; a special fund amounting to $1.2 million was set aside for land reform education; and an agrarian reform special account was created in the government's General Fund. From 1964 to 1971, a total of 1.5 billion pesos were appropri-ated for land reform agencies. However, the record shows that only 472 million pesos (about 32 percent) have actually been programmed for release, and that the actual financial outlay of the government for land reform has been much below its targets.

Since the main shortcoming of land reform programs in the past was lack of funds for purchase and resale of big landed estates as well as provision of support to farmer-owners, the Philippine government has set up a formal mechanism for credit extension to farmers. The Central Bank of the Philippines, through its rural banks, the Development Bank of the Philippines, and the Philippine National Bank set up a financing scheme for farmers in 1971. The Central Bank has floated bonds "to mop up the excess money and credit supply in the urban sector, flush out hidden resources and idle money, and disperse them into the rural sector."[20] It also plans to double the number of its rural banks setting up 100 banks per year in order to create a total of 1,000 rural banks all over the country.

The Development Bank of the Philippines will concentrate on extending credit to small-scale and export-oriented industries. It plans to do so through some thirty privately-owned development banks which are participating in the program. The Philippine National Bank plans to concentrate its lending opera-tions to cooperatives, especially to handicraft manufacturers and retailers. Short-term loans will be extended to cooperatives registered with the Cooperatives Ad-ministration Office and medium-term loans are given preferably to agricultural producers and industrial cooperatives.

If the sad experience with the Agricultural Credit Administration provides any indication, the future of these new credit schemes may not be bright. De-faulting on loans is scandalously high among farmers in the Philippines. One can only hope that conditions have changed and that the loans extended to farmers will help to improve their lot in life, making them less prone to be pushed out of the rural areas.

Another approach which encourages people to remain where they are and not move to very large cities is regional development. In the Philippines, this approach is relatively new. In the current Four Year Development Plan, "regional development will be undertaken in order to reduce the income gaps in the different regions of the country."[21] However, in the same plan, the ineffectiveness of present schemes for regional development is openly acknowledged. The document states that of the thirteen regional development authorities created by the Philippine Congress, "only five are operational . . . the others are merely paper organizations."[22]

An institution which is actively used by the Philippine government to foster regional development through the dispersal of industrial and other activities is the Board of Investments (BOI). The BOI prepares an annual investment priorities plan, determines preferred and pioneer areas of investment, and encourages the growth of selected industries in the different regions of the country. However, in the pursuance of its job, the BOI has to act within the limits of national policies and programs that directly or indirectly result in the concentration of development in the Metropolitan Manila area. As Sicat has written:

> The BOI has tried its best to incorporate within its industrial priorities formula a positive weight so that proposed industries which are located outside the Metropolitan Manila area could get favored treatment. The results, insofar as our acquaintance with their attempt is concerned, show that the ranking industrial priorities are not affected at all.[23]

The location of projects favored by the BOI between July 1968 and December 1969 reveals the truth of Sicat's statement. In this period, the BOI approved investments in 161 plants totalling 2.9 billion pesos. The bulk of these plants were located in Luzon, 49 in Southern Luzon, and 27 in Manila and suburbs. About 48 were in Mindanao, while a small number (12 plants) were in the Visayas. Of greater significance is that the plants in Manila and Southern Luzon were larger and involved more funds than the ones in Visayas and Mindanao. Thus, in spite of its goal of industrial dispersal, the BOI is still contributing to the concentration of development in the Metropolitan Manila area.

This concentration, however, is governed by forces beyond the capacity of the BOI to reverse. Sicat, in a recent paper, observed that continued concentration is due to "a particular bias of national policies" which include exchange rate controls tariffs, finance, etc.[24] When the exchange rate of the peso to the dollar was changed, for example, devaluation benefited exporters and investors concentrated in the Manila area.

The so-called "Green Revolution" has had a tremendous impact on the rural

Philippines. Land reform, agricultural credit, rural community development, and other schemes have been tried to improve the lot of the peasant farmer. However, there is still no evidence that improvement in the farmers' way of life will result in less migration to cities. The opposite effect may in fact happen. As farmers become progressive, they may adopt urban ways and eventually move to the city.

Attempts at regional development (especially those centered around intermediate cities) are too recent for valid generalizations. Certainly, if stated ways and means become fully operational, migrants may stay in these progressive areas instead of moving to metropolitan centers. The Philippines has to reconsider its national and regional planning concepts and practices, exploring the full spatial implications of sectoral economic and social development plans. Regional development plans must be integrated with national policies and programs, and a national urban strategy developed that would identify areas of urban growth as well as rural development.[25]

Coping with City Problems

Rapid rural to urban migration has swelled the population of metropolitan areas such as Manila and Cebu, with predictable results. The frustration faced by administrators and politicians in attempting to cope with service and other problems is typified by efforts to cope with squatting and slum dwelling.

The squatter situation in the Philippines is serious, if not critical. In a recent study, I found that the proportion of squatters and slum dwellers to the total population is 14.2 percent in Baguio, 25.0 percent in Cebu, 22.3 percent in Davao, 10.0 percent in Iligan, 32.0 percent in Iloilo, and 33.0 percent in Manila. The rate of growth of squatters is more than three times that of the average urban population growth rate. As squatter areas continue to grow, they spread the malaise of unemployment, crime, epidemics, fire, and other hazards to other parts of the city.

Faced with this urban challenge, public authorities have tried relocating squatters in other areas, distributing land to bona fide squatters (either on site or in resettlement areas), low income housing, and sites and service schemes. In Manila, Cebu, Baguio, and Davao, relocation sites outside the city limits have been opened up by national and local government authorities for former squatters. Such sites, however, have generally lacked facilities, taken squatters far from their place of work and made life so difficult that many of the people have left. An interesting exception has been the relocation sites in Baguio where people were provided with services and houses at low amortization rates. These communities have become viable and people have not only stayed but also improved the sites.

Anthropologists usually link squatters' demands to own the land they occupy to rural survival, while reformers and crusaders interpret it as a drive for social justice in a society where land and other benefits have always been the monopoly of the elite. However, obvious economic reasons explain such demands even though most land squatted upon is marginal (marshy, hilly, close to nuisances, and too expensive to develop). Responding to squatter demands for land is politically productive in getting the organized votes of squatters. Thus, in the short run, the needs of squatters and politicians coincide, and this may explain the many instance when high government officials have granted land titles or "rights of ccupancy."

The long-term effects of a policy of land redistribution are sure to be negative to the society as a whole. In the first place, when development plans are prepared for urban areas, policymakers and administrators will be faced with the fact that it will cost a lot of money and entail a lot of effort to plan alternative uses for slum lands that are privately owned. The suggestion has been made that instead of outright sale, limited leaseholds (say for fifty years or so) should be given to squatters. This time period would be sufficient to see families through a "transition" and to give the government enough resources to propose and implement realistic plans. However, the legal complexities of land tenures other than outright ownership are distrusted by many squatters, and the pressures for outright land sale are strong.

Equally as vociferous, although less intense, are peoples' demands for low income housing. Estimates of the housing need for the period 1960 to 1980 was for about 8.2 million units, a fifth of which would be needed in urban areas. The particular areas of need involve new units for replacement of *barong barongs* (shanties), provision for households currently doubling up, other units for losses, obsolescence, and disasters, and new household formations. In these projections, the first need for "unacceptable" housing is most pressing. In 1963, about 10 percent of the "unacceptable" and "substandard" housing units in the country was accounted for by Metropolitan Manila alone. Again, the impact of rapid rural to urban migration is revealed in these figures.

Housing presents a critical dilemma to developing countries such as the Philippines. Estimates of resources needed to house most Filipinos properly far exceed the country's productive capacity. Government institutions providing housing have to tread a thin line between operating at a loss and bankruptcy. It is obvious that replacing the 15 percent unacceptable or substandard houses found in the Philippine urban areas would require tremendous subsidies. Since the squatter's capacity to pay is meager, the government would have to shoulder most of the burden. However, the government's resources are limited, and they are needed for investments having a higher return to capital than housing.

Conclusions

Solutions which anticipate problems of internal migration and prevent them from happening would be more effective, in the long run, than curative solutions.

Too many authorities try to cope with bits and pieces of the problem, seeing only the obvious fragments. This may be due, in part, to the manner in which we have divided our academic disciplines and governmental functions. Whatever the reasons, our capacity to formulate preventive rather than curative programs is dependent on a fuller understanding of the internal migration process, and this is achievable only if we see the process as a whole.

The key issue exemplified by the Philippine experience of trying to deal with internal migration is the question of intervention. There are those who argue that policies and programs designed to influence or control migration are really based on a value judgment that prefers balanced to unbalanced growth. In the absence of conclusive proof that concentration of people in a primate city is anti-developmental, these people argue against intervention. The current state of the art is still characterized by debates on whether the costs and benefits of "natural" or "market processes" contributing to primacy outweigh those of "interventionist" processes that favor investments in rural areas or intermediate cities. Until some light is shed on even basic factors like costs, it is argued, any model of development may be acceptable.

In this debate, while I have more sympathy for those who "describe and understand" compared to those who "prescribe and do," I also see dangers in a stance that allows "copping-out" of the system by saying that internal migration is happening, it is a natural process and thus it must be good. As in most other social science problems, the policymaker and the analyst are caught in the classic dilemma of values and means. In the old days, if the policymakers and politicians decided that more investments were needed in rural areas and intermediate cities, administrators and technocrats simply figured out the most efficient and effective means of doing this. In this world of systemic analysis, however, we question not only the means of governmental action but the ends as well.

We can only escape the current dilemma through understanding the wishes and needs of people directly involved in the process: the migrants, the people they leave behind, and those they join. Governmental action should provide maximum opportunities for realizing these wishes and wants. In the past it was believed that this was possible through the absence of constraints on movement. However, evidence from most developing countries who are feeling the problems arising from internal migration demonstrates that the seeming lack of constraints eventually breeds greater constraints by the accumulation of ills. The slums and squatters in most cities of the Third World are not only symbols of freedom of movement, they are also signs of neglect and apathy on the part of those who could have done something about them. The answer to the question of how to cope with internal migration, therefore, is not intervention and control *versus* freedom and neglect: it is finding ways and means of increasing options so that the individual freedom of the migrant might be enhanced and the benefits from his actions accrue not only to him but to the whole society.

Notes

1. For more on maldistribution, see Leandro A. Viloria, "Manila," in A. Laquian (ed.), *Rural Urban Migrants and Metropolitan Development* (Toronto: Intermet, 1971).
2. Frederick L. Wernstedt and Paul D. Simkins, "Migrations and the Settlement of Mindanao," *The Journal of Asian Studies* 25, 1 (November 1965): 102.
3. Ibid.
4. See Elvira M. Pascual, *Population Redistribution in the Philippines* (Manila: Population Institute, 1966).
5. A. Laquian, *Slums and Squatters in Six Philippine Cities*, a project undertaken with the support of SEADAG (Typescript).
6. Wernstedt and Simkins, "Migrations and the Settlement of Mindanao," p. 101.
7. Ibid.
8. Romeo B. Ocampo, "Governmental and Non-Governmental Programs Influencing Migration in the Philippines," Report A-3, UP-Intermet Project (Typescript).
9. Wernstedt and Simkins, "Migrations and the Settlement of Mindanao," p. 92.
10. Ibid., p. 87.
11. Josefa Edralin, "Programs that Directly Affect Migration in the Philippines," Report A-3, UP-Intermet Project, 1972, (Typescript).
12. Republic Act No. 1160, June 18, 1954.
13. For more on NARRA resettlement schemes, see Carlos A. Fernandez II, "Adaptive Processes and Development Policies in a Frontier Resettlement Community," Chapter in the present volume.
14. Wernstedt and Simkins, "Migrations and the Settlement of Mindanao," p. 95.
15. For more on this, see A. Laquian, *The City in Nation-Building*, (Manila: School of Public Administration, 1966).
16. Ibid.
17. The account of the Barrio Magsaysay fire and its aftermath is drawn mainly from the appendix of a master's thesis of A. Bruce Etherington, Department of Political Science, University of Hawaii, 1972.
18. Republic of the Philippines, *A Review of Land Reform* (Quezon City: Land Authority, 1970).
19. Ibid.
20. *(Manila) Sunday Times*, September 26, 1971.
21. *Four Year Development Plan* (FY 1971-74), (Manila: National Economic Council, 1970), p. 5.
22. Ibid., p. 115.
23. Gerardo P. Sicat, "Economics of Regional Development: Interaction of National and Regional Policies," paper delivered at the Seminar on Planning for Economic Development of the Iligan City-Lake Lanao Area, February 20, 1970 (Mimeographed).

24. Gerardo P. Sicat, "Regional Economic Growth in the Philippines, 1946–1966," (Mimeographed).
25. For a fuller elaboration of this view, see A. Laquian, "The Need for a National Urban Strategy in the Philippines," *SEADAG Papers*, No. 72-8.

14

The Effect of Infant and Child Mortality and Preference for Sons Upon Fertility and Family Planning Behavior and Attitudes in Taiwan

David M. Heer and *Hsin-ying Wu*

Hypotheses and Questions Posed

For several years a major debate has raged concerning the factors determining the success of family planning programs in less developed nations. One school of thought believes that success is largely dependent on the availability of appropriate contraceptives. A second school of thought is of the opinion that while the availability of appropriate contraceptives will prove highly valuable, this factor by itself will not be sufficient to reduce birthrates to desired levels. The latter group contends that persons in the less developed nations are still rationally motivated to have large families and will continue to have them until institutional changes occur which will change that motivation. Evidence for this viewpoint comes from recent findings concerning desired family size in many of the less developed nations. For example, in Taiwan, a nation generally considered to have a highly successful family-planning program, the average number of children desired according to recent information was about four. (Finnigan and Sun 1972).

Several social changes have been proposed as contributing to reduced motivation for high fertility. The current study focused on two such changes: (1) a reduction in the level of infant and child mortality, and (2) a reduction in the high preference for sons.

Hypotheses Concerning the Relation of Infant and Child Mortality to Fertility and Family Planning Behavior and Attitudes

The possible effect of infant and child mortality on fertility and family planning behavior and attitudes can be subdivided into two components: (1) the effect of the community level of infant and child mortality, and (2) the effect of the individual experience of child loss. Differences in the community

Funds for this research were provided by contracts between the Office of Population of AID and Harvard University: AID/csd 2153 and AID/csd 2478. Supplementary funds were provided by a grant from the Population Council to the University of Southern California.

253

level of infant and child mortality can plausibly affect the behavior and attitudes both of those married couples who lose a child and those married couples who do not. When the level of infant and child mortality is high, all couples who never suffer the loss of a child may, nevertheless, fear such loss and may decide to have additional children as insurance against the possibility that one or more of them may die in the future. The individual experience of child loss may also have important consequences for fertility behavior and attitudes. Comparing couples who have lost a child with couples who have not, the couples suffering child loss may logically, (1) exactly compensate for the loss of their children, i.e., end up with the same number of living children as those who have never lost a child, (2) undercompensate for their loss, i.e., end up with fewer living children than those couples who have not lost a child, or (3) overcompensate, i.e., end up with more living children than those couples never experiencing the loss of a child.

In short, when considering the impact of infant and child mortality upon fertility behavior and attitudes we must consider four different categories of respondents: (1) respondents living in a high-mortality community who have not experienced the loss of a child, (2) respondents living in a high mortality community who have experienced the loss of one or more children, (3) respondents living in a low-mortality community who have not experienced the loss of a child, and (4) respondents living in a low-mortality community who have lost one child or more.

Our study was purposefully designed so as to be able to secure respondents in each of these categories. Accordingly, we were able to test two separate hypotheses for our study population. The first of these is that a high rather than a low level of infant and child mortality in the community would foster high fertility both among couples who lose a child and among those who do not. Our second hypothesis was that at any given level of infant and child mortality in the community, those couples suffering the loss of a child would have at each parity level higher subsequent fertility, lower use of contraception, a larger number of additional children desired, and a higher ideal family size.

In preparing for the current study we made plans to select a locale where family planning methods were available and where birth control was being practiced. We also made plans to choose two sites differing as much as possible in their level of infant and child mortality (given the constraint that both sites had to be fairly close to Taipei). We also planned for a large sample so that the number of cases of women who had experienced the loss of one or more children would be sufficient to make statistically precise statements. Finally, we were aware that we would need to have a statistical control for many other variables which might plausibly account for any observed relationship between the two variables.

In designing the study so that interviewing would take place in two sites differing maximally in their level of infant and child mortality we gave ourselves the opportunity to separate out an areal effect from the effects of differences on the individual level. For example, we made it possible to discover that after adjusting for individual differences in educational attainment, in economic status, and in the experience of child loss, respondents in the high-mortality area had higher fertility than respondents in the low-mortality area. Unfortunately, if this were the whole of our procedure we would not be able to state that the remaining difference in fertility behavior by area was caused by the difference in the community level of infant and child mortality. A plausible alternative would be, for example, that the remaining fertility difference by area might be due to the lower average literacy level of the high-mortality area and higher average literacy level of the low-mortality area. To discover the specific effect of living in a high-mortality area versus a low-mortality area we would have to interview substantial numbers of respondents in each of many different areas so that we would have, for example, substantial numbers of respondents in high mortality, high literacy areas and in low mortality, high literacy areas as well as the more prevalent high mortality, low literacy areas and low-mortality, high literacy areas. Such a survey was obviously impossible given our budgetary constraints.

On the other hand, we could seek to measure the specific effect of the community level of infant and child mortality through another means. This was to measure on an individual level the perception of the probability of child survival. If the community level of infant and child survival was to have an influence upon fertility, it would do so through affecting the individual couple's perception of the chances of child survival in that community. Hence if we could show that the perception of child survival was related to actual child survival and that differences in perceptions of child survival were associated with differences in fertility behavior and attitudes, we could show that the community level of child survival did have an effect on fertility behavior and attitudes.

However, no one had as yet attempted to measure individual perceptions of the probabilities of child survival. Therefore, we could not be sure that we would be able to measure these perceptions reliably. Thus several outcomes of our work were possible each with its own consequences for the validity of our hypothesis. These were as follows:

1. There would be no areal differences in fertility behavior or attitudes after holding constant individual differences in educational attainment, socio-economic status, individual experience of child loss, and other variables on the individual level other than perception of child survival. In this case we would be able to reject the hypothesis that the community level of child survival was an important force affecting fertility behavior and attitudes.

2. There would be no areal differences in fertility behavior or attitudes after holding constant differences in all of the individual variables; moreover, individual perception of child survival would be an important source of influence

on fertility behavior and attitudes, and, furthermore, the individual perception would be closely related to the community level of infant and child mortality. In this case we would have confirmed the hypothesis that the community level of child survival affected fertility.

3. There would be substantial areal differences in fertility behavior or attitudes after holding constant differences in all of the individual variables including the perception of child survival; however, individual perception of child survival could be measured only with a low degree of reliability and would not be substantially associated with fertility differences. In this case we would not have compelling evidence that the community mortality level affected fertility; nevertheless, we would have grounds for belief that the community level of infant and child mortality might be an important factor in explaining differences in fertility.

Our procedure for testing whether the individual experience of child loss had an effect on fertility behavior and attitudes was much simpler than our procedure for testing whether the community level of child survival had such an effect. To test this hypothesis we needed a large enough number of cases to obtain some statistical precision and we needed to hold constant those variables which might be associated with the experience of child loss and had been shown from previous studies to be importantly related to fertility behavior and attitudes. The length of lactation was one such factor that previous work had shown to be important. If a child dies, a mother who has been breastfeeding soon ceases her lactation and the period of postpartum amenorrhea associated with that lactation comes to an end. For this strictly biological reason, in a population in which prolonged breastfeeding is common, women experiencing the early loss of their baby will have a shorter interval to the next birth, other things being equal, than women who do not experience the loss of a child. The other variables which we needed to hold constant were the variables that had been shown in one or more previous studies to have associations with fertility behavior and attitudes. These included age, parity, educational attainment, birth-control knowledge, the wife's labor forces status, and husband's income.

Questions Concerning the Impact of Son
Preference on Fertility and Family Planning
Behavior and Attitudes

A pronounced desire for a minimum number of children of a particular sex may have an important effect upon fertility provided there is no feasible and inexpensive means of choosing the sex of each child born. However, a review of the published literature indicates that the process whereby son preference affects fertility may be more complicated than many persons have assumed (Freedman and Takeshita 1969; Poffenberger 1967; Repetto 1972).

In the present study we decided to include attitudinal items in our questionnaire designed to measure the preference for having sons rather than daughters. We also decided to look at the impact of the sex of surviving children upon subsequent fertility. However, as Repetto's (1972) study suggests, preference for sons may exist despite the fact that couples having mostly daughters have the same subsequent fertility as couples having mostly sons. In this case, it would have to be assumed that the disutility of having an additional daughter was as great as the utility of having an additional son.

Setting for the Survey, Details of the Data Collection, and Characteristics of the Respondents

Setting for the Survey

A crucial element in the study design was the plan to examine the association between the community level of infant and child mortality on the one hand and fertility, desired family size, and the acceptance of family planning on the other. It was therefore proposed that the interviews be gathered in two separate communities and that within the constraints of feasible data collection these two communities would differ maximally in level of infant and child mortality.

Interviews in the low-mortality community were conducted in Hsinchuang township and in the high-mortality community in Kungliao township. Both of these townships were located in Taipei county. It had been originally contemplated that both interviewing sites would be rural townships. However, in the original rural township chosen to represent a low-mortality community it turned out that we could not find a sufficient number of good interviewers and therefore an adjacent township, Hsinchuang, was substituted. Because Hsinchuang had a considerably larger population than the original choice for the low-mortality community and because it was officially classed as an urban township, it was decided that interviews in Hsinchuang would be conducted only in areas outside of the central town.

It is evident from table 14-1 that not only did Hsinchuang township have more people than Kungliao but its rate of population growth had been very much greater. From 1964 to 1969 the population rose 47.1 percent in Hsinchuang and only 7.1 percent in Kungliao. It is also evident from table 14-1 that Kungliao and Hsinchuang townships differed as much in almost every aspect of modernity as they did in infant and child mortality. The proportion of males engaged in manufacturing in Kungliao was negligible, the proportion so engaged

Table 14-1

Characteristics of the Population of Taiwan and of Hsinchuang and Kungliao Townships, 1969

	Taiwan	Hsinchuang	Kungliao
Total population (in thousands)	14,096	42.936	19.256
Percentage change in population 1964–1969	+14.8	+47.1	+07.1
Crude birthrate per 1,000	27.7	34.5	34.1
Crude deathrate per 1,000	5.0	5.2	7.4
Crude rate of natural increase per 1,000	22.7	29.3	26.7
Percentage of females 15 years and over illiterate	36.1	27.6	55.5
Percentage of employed males 15 years and over in manufacturing	14.8	33.1	03.9
Percentage of employed males 15 years and over in agriculture and fishing	40.4	25.3	68.9
Percentage of females 15 years and over employed in non-agricultural activity	12.4	13.7	6.5
Death rate per 1,000 for children 0–4 years	06.2	05.0	09.1
Percentage of females 20–24 years old currently married	51.8	52.8	65.8
Total fertility rate per 1,000 females	4,120	4,400	6,130
Total fertility rate per 1,000 currently married women 25 years old and over	2,995	3,180	4,625
New IUD acceptors as percentage of married women 15 to 49 years	6.5	7.7	9.4
New pill acceptors as percentage of married women 15 to 49 years	2.7	1.2	2.1

in Hsinchuang was considerably higher than the average for all of Taiwan. There are many new factories along the highway leading from Hsinchuang into Taipei. The establishment of these factories was a basic cause of the high population growth rate in Hsinchuange and the very high rate of net in-migration.

The contrast in mortality between Hsinchuang and Kungliao is evident. This is reflected both in the crude deathrate and in the death rate for persons under five years of age. Although random fluctuations from year to year exist in each township due to the small size of the base population, the death rate for infants and young children during the five years preceding the interviews was on the average at least twice as high in Kungliao as in Hsinchuang.

Finally, consider the variable related to fertility. In 1969 the crude brith-rate was actually higher in Hsinchuang than in Kungliao. However, this was not because fertility was higher in Hsinchuang than in Kungliao but because of differences in age composition. The total fertility rate per 1,000 females, which is a pure measure unaffected by age composition, reveals the substantially high fertility of Kungliao. Part of the reason for the lower fertility rate in Hsinchuang township was the higher age at first marriage. This is indicated indirectly in table 14-1 by proportions of females married at ages twenty to twenty-four. However, marital fertility at older ages (the principal target of family planning programs) was also considerably lower in Hsinchuang than in Kungliao. This is operational-ized here as the total fertility rate for currently married women twenty-five to forty-nine years of age. Despite the difference between the two townships in fertility of older married women, successful family-planning porgrams in terms of IUD and pill acceptance rates existed in 1969 in both Kungliao and Hsinchuang townships.

It is also necessary to recognize that in the five-year period preceding 1969 considerable change took place in the variables shown in table 14-1. A marked decline in infant and child mortality occurred, particularly in Kungliao. Illiteracy for both males and females declined substantially in both townships. In Hsinchuang the proportion of employed males engaged in agriculture and fishing dropped very substantially while the proportion in manufacturing rose. Declines in the total fertility rate occurred in both Hsinchuang and Kungliao. Taiwan's family planning program was initiated on an island-wide basis in 1964. In Hsinchuang input into the family planning program began at a high level and continued without very much increase throughout the period. Achievement from the program (in terms of new acceptors) was high from the beginning and did not show much pattern of change. In contrast, in Kungliao formal input into the program was not initiated until 1966 and the achievement of the pro-gram was accordingly very much greater at the end of the period than at the beginning. The possible effect of the family planning program is indicated by the substantial decline in the fertility of currently married women twenty-five years old and over which could be observed both for Hsinchuang and for Kungliao. Moreover, a rise in the age at marriage in Kungliao (but not in Hsinchuang) also contributed to the reduction of the total fertility rate in that township.

In summary, the data shown in table 14-1 illustrate very clearly the very great contrasts between the two communities selected for the study. The two communities had been selected because they differed so much in their level of infant and child mortality. However, it was impossible to approximate a maximi-zation of this difference without also creating very large differences in all other aspects of modernization.

Details of the Data Collection

The household registration system in each township was to be used to transcribe all households in which there was an ever married female. In all such households all ever married women were to be interviewed. In one-fifth of the households currently married males, if present, were to be interviewed. The households in which males were to be interviewed were the third, eighth, thirteenth, eighteenth, etc., household in each lin (small subunit of a township).

The plan of interviewing was for the whole team of interviewers to contact all respondents in a particular village during a given time interval, usually around a week or more. The team traveled jointly to the village in the morning (by motorcycle in Kungliao and by bicycle in Hsinchuang). In all cases they returned from the village before dusk. Return travel in daylight hours was made necessary by the very poor, often extremely muddy, unpaved roads, particularly in Kungliao township. Thus interviewing during the evening was precluded. At least partly because of this interviewing strategy, there was a rather low rate of completed interviews for males. As a result of the difficulty in interviewing males who were not a home during the day, Dr. Wu eventually decided that a revision was necessary in the original plan whereby male interviews were confined to households where the right-hand digit of the household number was three or eight. In the event that an interview with a male in the originally designated household could not be obtained, the interviewer was asked to find a currently married male either in the household with the next lower or next higher household number.

Interviewing of females was completed in September 1970 and that of males by the end of November 1970.

The number of completed interviews by township and by sex was a follows:

	Female	Male	Total
Kungliao	2,677	501	3,178
Hsinchuang	4,137	863	5,000
Total	6,814	1,364	8,178

The percentage of eligibles who were successfully interviewed can be computed only for females. For Kungliao females, the percentage was 77.4 and for Hsinchuang females 78.8 percent.

General Characteristics of the Respondents

Table 14-2 presents a summary of the characteristics of the respondents of each sex interviewed in each township. As one would expect given the substantial differences by township shown in table 14-1, we find that the respondents

Table 14-2

Basic Characteristics of the Respondents by Township and by Sex (Means and Proportions are in all Cases Calculated on a Base that Excludes N.A. responses)

	Hsinchuang		Kungliao	
	Females	*Males*	*Females*	*Males*
A. Basic Demographic Data				
Mean age at interview	37.10	38.40	41.40	45.10
Mean age at first marriage	20.10	24.80	18.30	23.50
Proportion currently married	89.20	100.00	83.80	100.00
Proportion definitely past menopause	20.20	–	31.40	–
Mean number of reported induced abortions	0.26	–	0.12	–
Mean number of live births	3.95	–	5.20	–
Proportion living and eating with relatives outside the nuclear family	45.50	30.60	61.10	57.10
Proportion with Chinese-mainland origin	3.80	17.50	1.40	5.00
B. Basic Data on Socioeconomic Status				
Mean number of school-years completed	4.16	7.35	1.52	3.64
Proportion never reading a newspaper	60.40	21.80	91.90	58.30
Proportion of females currently employed outside the home	10.50	–	1.30	–
Mean annual income of husband (or male respondent) in National Taiwan dollars	28,637	37,259	13,687	14,845
Proportion of husbands (or male respondents) who were farmers	26.40	17.00	39.70	41.50
Proportion of husbands (or male respondents) who were fishermen	0.00	0.00	33.40	13.40
Proportion of husbands (or male respondents) who were production workers	42.00	45.50	14.10	13.40

Table 14-2 (cont.)

	Hsinchuang		Kungliao	
	Females	*Males*	*Females*	*Males*
C. Variables Concerned With Desired Fertility				
Mean additional number of children desired	0.66	0.61	0.68	0.56
Mean number of children advised for daughter (or for son)	3.75	3.62	4.54	4.42
Mean number of girls advised for daughter (or for son)	1.60	1.54	2.04	2.03
Mean number of boys advised for daughter (or for son)	2.16	2.09	2.50	2.43
Mean ideal number of children if life could be lived over	3.82	3.62	4.61	4.41
Mean ideal number of girls if life could be lived over	1.62	1.57	2.07	2.01
Mean ideal number of boys if life could be lived over	2.20	2.05	2.53	2.44
D. Variables Concerned With Child Survival				
Proportion of births taking place 5 or more years prior to the interview surviving to age five	94.10	—	91.00	—
Proportion stating chances for child survival are much better than formerly	49.00	71.70	53.20	79.60
Mean proportion perceived as surviving to age 15 from 20 births	95.90	94.60	92.00	90.90
Mean proportion perceived as surviving to age 15 from 100 births	95.20	94.30	90.80	89.20
Mean proportion perceived as surviving to age 15 from mean number of births to women in the area	98.90	97.90	96.60	97.20
E. Variables Concerned With Preference For Sons and Reasons For Preferring Sons				
Proportion wanting two or more sons among next three children if they already had one boy and one girl	95.10	93.50	97.40	90.80
Proportion stating that couple with four girls should have another child	59.10	56.20	76.20	73.40

Proportion stating that couple with four boys should have another child	26.60	21.60	47.60	37.20
Proportion stating that couple with two girls and one boy should have another child	34.20	25.40	53.30	48.30
Proportion stating that couple with two boys and one girl should have another child	11.10	8.60	25.90	19.20
Proportion citing sons as most important source of old-age support	57.40	42.30	85.50	71.60
Proportion citing savings as most important source of old-age support	35.00	42.60	9.10	21.80
Proportion citing government pension as most important source of old-age support	1.30	9.30	0.90	2.90
Proportion citing non-government pension as most important source of old-age support	0.30	2.50	0.00	0.00
Mean number of sons necessary for old-age support	1.77	1.49	2.32	2.38
F. Variables Related to Family Planning				
Proportion entirely in favor of birth control	60.20	74.4	65.00	63.60
Proportion currently using:[1]				
IUD	7.60	13.10	5.70	5.80
Ota ring	5.20	5.90	4.10	2.40
Oral contraceptive	2.20	5.20	0.90	0.40
Female sterilization	4.60	5.50	2.60	3.80
Male sterilization	0.10	0.60	0.00	0.00
Condom	0.60	3.10	0.10	0.60
Jelly or cream	0.40	0.80	0.10	0.20
Rhythm	2.30	5.60	0.10	0.80
Diaphragm	0.10	0.70	0.00	0.00
Withdrawal	0.10	0.70	0.00	0.00
Proportion ever using abortion[1]	14.20	3.50	7.30	0.40

1. Proportion is based on all respondents; and women born in 1924 or earlier, men with wives born in 1924 or earlier, and women not currently married are automatically assumed not to have used a contraceptive method.

in Kungliao often differ markedly from those in Hsinchuang. In Kungliao, average socioeconomic status is lower, desired family size is higher, actual fertility is higher, child survival is less assured and is perceived as being less assured, and the reliance on sons as the chief support in one's old age is more pronounced.

However, the differences between the two townships should not obscure certain similarities. In both townships the desired number of children is sufficiently high to guarantee a substantial rate of natural increase, and the preference for sons is quite pronounced. Although substantial proportions of respondents in both townships manifest their entire approval of birth control nevertheless the proportions actually practicing contraception are rather low.

Results of the Survey

Dependent and Independent Variables

We shall examine the results of several Multiple Classification Analyses (Andrews et al. 1967) in which the dependent variables are respectively: (1) the number of subsequent births among currently married women of third parity or higher and with the third birth at least one year prior to the interview, (2) the number of subsequent births among currently married women of second parity or higher and with the second birth at least one year prior to the interview, (3) current use of contraception among currently married females born in 1925 or later, (4) current or previous use of contraception among currently married females born in 1925 or later, (5) additional number of children desired, (6) number of children advised for daughter, (7) number of children desired if life could be lived over, and (8) attitude toward birth control.

The main object of these analyses is to examine the apparent influence of: (1) the number and sex of the respondent's first three live births one year following the third live birth, (2) the number of survivors of the respondent's first three live births one year following the third live birth, (3) the sex of the first two live births and their survival status one year following the second live birth, (4) the number of sons born and whether or not they all survived, (5) the number of daughters born and whether or not they all survived, (6) the percentage of births who died before age fifteen, (7) the perception of child survival, (8) township — which serves as an imperfect proxy of the community level of child mortality, and (9) an index of the preference for sons.

It is obvious that the apparent effect of these variables upon the dependent variables cannot be examined without statistical control for other relevant variables. Among the most important of these other relevant variables are elapsed reproductive interval since the pertinent birth, age, the number of living sons, and the number of living daughters. The other variables which are held constant include the respondent's educational attainment (and newspaper reader-ship), labor-force status, educational aspirations for a nephew and for a niece, knowledge of birth control, mean length of breast feeding (lactation), husbands occupation, and husband's income.

Of the nine principal independent variables, the first six and the eighth need no further explanation. It remains necessary to explain in some detail the index of perception of child survival and our index to measure the preference for sons.

The index of perception of child survival was constructed from three separate items giving equal weight to each item. The first item concerned the proportion among twenty births surviving to age fifteen and was derived from answers to the question, "If twenty children were born in the ts'un (village), how many would you say would live to age fifteen and how many would be lost?" The second item concerned the proportion among one-hundred births surviving to age fifteen and was derived from a question analogous to the preced-ing. The third item concerned the proportion surviving to age fifteen among the number of babies born to the average woman in the area and was derived from two questions, the first relating to the average number of babies born per woman and the second relating to the number of these which would survive to age fifteen.

The index to measure preference for sons was constructed out of eight items. The wording of each of these is presented in Appendix A of Heer (1972). Seven of the eight items in the scale were constructed out of questionnaire items asking the respondent whether hypothetical families should go on to have another child. To illustrate, for the first item of the scale the respondent was asked to look at a picture of a family with one boy and four girls and another picture of a family with one girl and four boys. The respondent was assigned a score of zero if he recommended that the family go on for another child when there was one boy and four girls but did not recommend the family with one girl and four boys to go on; the respondent was assigned a score of two if he recommended that the family with one boy and four girls not go on but that the family with one girl and four boys go on for another child. Respondents who stated that both fami-lies pictured should go on or who stated that neither family pictured should go on were given a score of one. Persons scoring zero clearly show son preference and persons scoring two clearly show daughter preference. The final score was constructed by averaging the eight items together and then categorizing those with an average score of one or more as having no son preference, and those with average scores less than one into two categories of moderate and high son pref-erence. An unfortunate drawback to the index of son preference is that respon-dents who had a very high ideal number of children did not reveal any son preference to some of the situations portrayed. Therefore, unfortunately, per-sons with high ideal family size tended to concentrate in the category of moderate son preference. It has not proved possible to obviate this difficulty with the son-preference index.

It is also necessary to make clear the meaning of the elapsed reproductive interval since the pertinent birth. For women under age forty-five, the elapsed reproductive interval since the pertinent birth was defined as the interval between the month and year of that birth and the month and year of the interview. For women forty-five and over, the elapsed reproductive interval since the pertinent birth was defined as the interval between the month and year of that birth and the month and year the woman reached age forty-five.

Number of Subsequent Births Among
Women of Third or Higher Parity

Table 14-3 contains the results of two Multiple Classification Analysis (MCA) runs in which the dependent variable is the number of subsequent births among currently married women of third parity or higher and with the third birth at least one year prior to the interview. In Run A we used as a principal independent variable the number of survivors of the first three live births one year following the third live birth; in run B we used the number and sex of survivors of the first three live births one year following the third live birth. In both runs we also use township, perception of child survival, and preference for sons as principal independent variables.

From table 14-3 we see that the average number of subsequent children is 2.73 (among women for whom the median elapsed reproductive interval was 11.9 years). Run A, which shows the effect of child loss without regard to sex, reveals this variable to be of fair importance with a Beta of .06. If there are three survivors, the adjusted number of subsequent children is .052 less than average whereas when there are only two survivors, it is .233 greater than average. Thus after adjustment for the effect of other variables, respondents with only two survivors went on to have .285 more children than respondents for whom all of the first three live births survived. In other words, respondents losing one of their first three children had made up 28.5 percent of their loss by the time of interview. This result is rather precise since the 95 percent confidence limits are only plus or minus 11.8 percent. Results for women losing more than one child are much less reliable. Respondents in the sample losing two of their first three children made up only 6.4 percent of their loss (with confidence limits of plus or minus 14.0 percent), and respondents losing all of their first three made up only 3.2 percent of their loss (with the very wide confidence limits of 31.7 percent).

In Run B we show the effect of the number and sex of survivors from the first three live births. When there have been no child deaths, there are, after adjustment, fewer subsequent births the larger the number of the first three births which were male. Adjusted subsequent fertility after three surviving sons is significantly smaller than after three surviving daughters. Furthermore,

Table 14-3

Number of Subsequent Births Among Currently Married Women of Third Parity or Higher and with Third Birth at Least One Year Prior to the Interview

Mean is 2.729	Value of multiple R^2 for run:	
Number of cases is 3,898	A	0.632
Standard deviation is 2.261	B	0.633

Rank of each predictor in terms of size of Beta:

	Run	
	A	B
Elapsed reproductive internal since third birth	0.820	0.820
Mean length of lactation of all live births beginning with the third	0.156	0.154
Age	0.141	0.139
Township	.078	0.077
Educational attainment	0.076	0.076
Number and sex of survivors of the first three live births at one year following the mother's third live birth	—	0.062
Number of survivors of the first three live births at one year following the mother's third live birth	0.046	—
Preference for sons	0.040	0.039
Husband's income	0.032	0.032
Educational aspirations for nephew	0.031	0.030
Perception of child survival	0.028	0.029
Labor force status	0.027	0.028
Husband's occupation	0.027	0.027
Birth control knowledge	0.006	0.005

adjusted subsequent fertility after two surviving sons and one surviving daughter is significantly smaller than after one surviving son and two surviving daughters. Unfortunately, the sample, large as it is, does not contain enough cases to examine the effect of sex of surviving children on subsequent fertility if there have been one or more child deaths.

In both Run A and in Run B of table 14-3 respondents with a low perception of child survival go on to have about .24 more additional children after adjustment for other variables than those with a higher perception (the differences both in Run A and in Run B are statistically significant). However, the fact that most respondents are in the category perceiving 95 percent survival or greater means that the predictor as a whole has only a small value of Beta (.03). Preference for sons also exerts a significant effect in the predicted direction. However, the variation in the adjusted coefficients between the categories of this predictor is relatively small.

Township is also shown to have a significant effect on subsequent births. After adjustment for other variables, Kungliao respondents go on to have about .35 more births than those in Hsinchuang. If our measure of perception of child survival were completely reliable, one could state that the difference by township was due to some factor other than the community difference in child survival. However, in a reinterview conducted approximately 12 months after the first interview the measure of perception of child survival proved to be of very poor reliability.

Of the control variables for Runs A and B in table 14-3 only one deserves special mention—the mean length of lactation of all live births beginning with the third. In both runs this was the second most important predictor. Respondents with a very long mean length of lactation had substantially fewer subsequent births than other respondents. However, the largest number of subsequent births came from women with six to eleven months of lactation. Apparently, the women who did not breastfeed at all or whose mean duration of lactation was less than six months utilized contraceptive methods with greater frequency than other groups of the respondents.

Number of Subsequent Births Among
Women of Second or High Parity

Table 14-4 has as its dependent variable the number of subsequent births among currently-married women of second parity or higher and with the second birth at least one year prior to the interview. The mean number of subsequent children is 3.07 (among women of whom the median elapsed reproductive interval was 12.0 years). In table 14-4 the focus of interest is on the impact of the sex and survival status of the first two live births. Given the sex composition of the first two births, we can examine the effect of child survival. When the first two live births were sons, subsequent fertility, adjusted for the effect of other variables, was significantly greater after the loss of one son than without child loss. Similarly, when the first two live births consisted of one son and one daughter, adjusted subsequent fertility was significantly greater if the son had died than if both children had survived. On the other hand, when two daughters had been born adjusted subsequent fertility was not significantly higher after the loss of one daughter than without such loss. Nor, when the first two live births consisted of one son and one daughter was subsequent fertility significantly higher if the daughter died as compared with the situation where

Table 14-4

The Number of Subsequent Births Among Currently Married Women of Second Parity or Higher and with Second Birth at Least One Year Prior to the Interview

Mean is 3.065

Number of cases is 4,491   Multiple R^2 is   0.612

Standard deviation is 2.393

Rank of each predictor in terms of size of Beta:

Elapsed reproductive interval since second birth	0.862
Age	0.195
Mean length of lactation of all live births beginning with the second	0.149
Educational attainment	0.068
Sex and survival status of the first two live births at one year following the second birth	0.061
Township	0.054
Labor force status	0.046
Educational aspirations for nephew	0.036
Husband's occupation	0.034
Perception of child survival	0.033
Preference for sons	0.033
Husband's income	0.032
Birth control knowledge	0.014

both children survived. The number of cases in the several categories where there were no survivors from the first two live births is so small that the average adjusted number of subsequent births shown for these categories are not meaningful.

Now let us consider to what extent adjusted subsequent fertility compensated for various types of child loss. Where two sons had been born and one of them had died, 46.1 percent of the loss was made up with 95 percent confidence limits of 26.6 percent. Similarly, where one son and one daughter had been born and the son died, 49.9 percent of the loss was made up with confidence limits of 27.1 percent. On the other hand, where two daughters had been born and one had died, subsequent fertility compensated for only 4.1 percent of the loss with confidence limits of 28.6 percent. Furthermore, where one son and one daughter had been born and the daughter had died, subsequent fertility made up for only 29.6 percent of the loss with confidence limits of 31.1 percent.

We may also examine the effect on subsequent fertility of the sex of the first two live births when there have been no child deaths. In accordance with our hypothesis, the number of subsequent births is significantly larger if two daughters were born and both survived than if two sons were born and both survived.

The remaining principal independent variables of table 14-4 act much as they did in the runs shown in table 14-3. After control for other variables, Kungliao respondents have significantly more subsequent children than Hsinchuang respondents; also those who perceive that less than 85 percent of babies born will survive have significantly more subsequent children, and those with no son preference have significantly less. Of the control variables, elapsed reproductive interval since second birth, age, and mean length of lactation show an important influence.

Ever Use of Contraception

Contrary to hypothesis, a high perception of child survival is negatively related to current or previous contraceptive use, although the differences between categories are very small and are not significant. Preference for sons is associated negatively, as expected, with current or previous contraceptive practice. Although the difference in the adjusted coefficients is not large, the proportion ever using contraception is significantly greater in the no-preference category than in the high-preference category. The difference by township in previous or current contraceptive practice holding constant other variables is substantial and highly significant. The adjusted coefficient for Hsinchuang is almost 8 percentage points higher than for Kungliao.

Current Use of Contraception

The three runs with respect to this dependent variable are not presented in tabular form but will be briefly described. The independent variables are identical to those used for the runs shown in table 14-5. Overall, the attempt to predict current contraceptive use among women born in 1925 or later was not very successful. On each run the value of multiple R^2 was only .125. Notwithstanding, in general, the patterns of association between the various predictors and the dependent variable are quite similar for current use and ever use. As before, when one, two, or three sons had been born, respondents who did not have a son were more likely to be practicing contraception after adjustment for other variables, but the difference was only significant in the case where two sons had been born.

Additional Children Desired

Table 14-5 presents the results with respect to the additional number of children desired by currently married respondents with wife born in 1925 or later. The values of multiple R^2 found in each of the three runs in this table—approximately .52 in each case—are higher than those observed for any of the other dependent variables examined.

Table 14-5
Additional Number of Children Desired Among Currently Married Respondents with Wife Born in 1925 or Later

Mean is 0.660	Value of Multiple R^2 for run	
Number of cases is 5,543	A	0.518
Standard deviation is 1.079	B	0.519
	C	0.523

Rank of each predictor in terms of size of Beta:

	Run		
	A	*B*	*C*
Number of wife's sons and their survival	0.48	–	–
Number of living sons of wife	–	0.48	0.45
Number of living daughters of wife	0.32	–	0.30
Number of wife's daughters and their survival	–	0.33	–
Wife's age	0.19	0.19	0.19
Township	0.09	0.09	0.09
Percentage of wife's births dying before age 15	–	–	0.08
Wife's labor-force status	0.08	0.08	0.08
Birth-control knowledge	0.07	0.08	0.07
Sex	0.07	0.07	0.07
Preference for sons	0.05	0.05	0.05
Husband's occupation	0.04	0.05	0.05
Educational attainment	0.04	0.03	0.03
Educational aspirations for nephew	0.02	–	0.02
Husband's income	0.02	0.02	0.02
Perception of child survival	0.02	0.02	0.02
Educational aspirations for niece	–	0.01	–

The number of sons and their survival, with a Beta of .48, proves to be the most important variable of Run A. At each number of sons born, the adjusted coefficient is lower if all of the sons have survived than if some have died. When one, two, or three sons have been born, the results are particularly strong, and are all statistically significant. For example, when two sons have been born, those who have lost one or more of them wish to have .60 more children on the average after adjusting for the impact of other variables than those who have not suffered the loss of a son.

The number of daughters born and their survival, featured in Run B, does not have an equal impact on the additional children desired. The value of Beta is only .33 in contrast to the value of .48 for the number of sons and their survival. For each number of daughters born, women who have lost one or more daughters desire more additional births, holding other variables constant, than women who have not lost a daughter. However, the difference is significant only when one daughter has been born.

Run C tests the effect of the percentage of births who died before age fifteen holding constant the number of living sons and the number of living daughters. The difference in each category are small and for the most part not statistically significant. However, if 25 to 49 percent of the births died, the adjusted coefficient for mean number of additional children desired, (-.16) is less than zero at a statistically significant level.

The differences by township are quite considerable and highly significant. In all three runs township is the fourth most important variable in terms of the size of Beta (.09 in all three runs). In all three runs the mean additional number of children desired in Kungliao after adjustment for the impact of the other variables was .14 greater than average and in Hsinchuang .07 less than average.

The adjusted coefficients for each category of perception of child survival were all small and were not significantly different from zero.

Respondents with no preference for sons wanted fewer additional children and those with a moderate or high preference for sons wanted a greater number of additional children. The differences in the adjusted coefficients for three categories of this predictor were small but statistically significant.

Number Desired If Life Could Be Lived
Over Again

In the analysis of this variable (not shown here in tabular form), the runs include all respondents of both sexes, thus adding a new variable—sex. As we suspected, the number of children desired if life could be lived over is in part merely a rationalization for the existing number of living children, and therefore, not the optimal measure of desired number of children. For this reason and for reasons of space we are not presenting a full analysis of this variable.

Contrary to our hypothesis, respondents who perceive that less than 85 percent of children survive to age fifteen want fewer children than average; in all three runs the adjusted coefficients are significantly less than zero. The adjusted coefficients for the other two categories of this predictor are not significantly different from zero.

After adjustment for other variables residents of Kungliao would have about .39 more children, if they could live their life over, than residents of Hsinchuang. The difference is very highly significant.

Attitude Toward Birth Control

In three different runs with this variable (not shown here), the values of multiple R^2 are extremely low—about .14. When two sons have been born the mean attitude toward birth control, holding constant the effect of certain other variables, is more favorable if none of the sons have died than if one or more have died. The difference is statistically significant. However, the identical comparisons for the situations when one, three, or four or more sons have been born do not yield statistically significant differences.

Surprisingly, holding constant the impact of other variables, respondents in Kungliao are more favorable to family planning than those in Hsinchuang. The difference is substantial and highly significant. The difference by township in the adjusted coefficients reverses the difference in the deviations from the grand mean. When other variables are not held constant, respondents in Kungliao are slightly less favorable to family planning than respondents from Hsinchuang.

Neither the perception of child survival nor the preference for sons contributes much to explaining attitude toward birth control although moderate son-preference is associated significantly with an unfavorable attitude to birth control. In all three runs the most important variable, with Beta equal to .20, is birth-control knowledge. Holding the other variables constant, birth-control knowledge is related in a very strong positive manner to attitude to birth control.

Summary of Findings For Each Principal Independent Variable

In what follows we shall summarize the statistically significant findings by a separate examination of the adjusted coefficients for each of the principal independent variables in all of the tabulations in which it appeared.

1. *The number of survivors from the first three live births one year following the third live birth.* This variable was related significantly to the number of subsequent children after the third live birth. After adjustment for the effect of other variables, respondents with only two survivors went on to have .285

more children (with 95 percent confidence limits of plus or minus .118) than respondents for whom all of the first three live births survived.

2. *The number and sex of survivors from the first three live births one year following the third live birth.* Adjusted subsequent fertility after three surviving sons was significantly smaller than after three surviving daughters. Furthermore, adjusted subsequent fertility after two surviving sons and surviving daughter was significantly smaller than after one surviving son and two surviving daughters.

3. *The sex and survival status of the first two live births one year following the second live birth.* In the situations where either two sons had been born or one son and one daughter, adjusted subsequent fertility was significantly greater after the loss of a son than without child loss. Furthermore, the adjusted number of subsequent births was significantly larger if two daughers were born and both survived than if two sons were born and both survived.

4. *The number of sons born and their survival.* Among those respondents who had borne exactly two sons, both current contraceptive use and current or past use were significantly greater (after adjustment for the effect of other variables) if both had survived than if one or both had died. Furthermore, when either one, two, or three sons had been born, respondents losing one or more sons desired significantly more additional children after adjustment than respondents who had lost no sons. Additionally, when either one or two sons had been born, respondents losing one or more of them would advise their daughter to have significantly more children after adjustment for the effect of other variables than respondents suffering no loss of sons. When one son had been born, respondents who had lost that son wanted significantly more children if they could live their life over than respondents who had not lost that son. Finally, when two sons had been born, respondents were significantly more favorable to birth control, after adjustment, if neither son died than if one or more of them had died.

5. *The number of daughters born and their survival.* This variable provided only one statistically significant result. If one daughter had been born, respondents who lost that daughter wanted significantly more additional children after adjustment for the effects of other variables than respondents whose one daughter survived.

6. *The percentage of births dying before age fifteen.* If 25 to 49 percent of the babies had died, current or previous use of contraception was greater than average after adjustment for the effect of other variables (including the number of living sons and the number of living daughters). Furthermore, respondents with 25 to 49 percent of their births dying wanted, after adjustment, significantly fewer additional children than average. These results are congruent with the finding that respondents having an initial loss of children do not compensate fully for all of the births which they have lost. Thus holding constant the number of living sons and the number of living daughters, we should expect greater use of contraception and fewer additional children desired if there have been previous child deaths. On the other hand, after adjustment, respondents

experiencing no deaths advised significantly fewer children for their daughter than average and those experiencing the loss of either 25 to 49 percent or 50 percent or more of their births advised significantly more children to their daughter than average.

7. *Township*. After adjustment for the effect of other variables, respondents from Kungliao, the high-mortality township, had significantly more subsequent children both after the second and after the third birth and reported a significantly lower proportion ever using contraception. Furthermore, after adjustment, residents of Kungliao wanted significantly more additional children, would advise their daughter to have significantly more children, and would want significantly more children if they could live their life over. Surprisingly, however, residents of Kungliao were more favorable to birth control after adjustment for the effect of other variables than residents of Hsinchuang.

8. *Perception of Child Survival*. After adjustment, respondents who perceived that less than 85 percent of children survive to age fifteen had a significantly larger number of subsequent children after the second and after the third live birth, than those who perceived a higher proportion of children to survive. Unexpectedly, respondents perceiving less than 85 percent survival, would, after adjustment, advise their daughter to have fewer children and have fewer children if they could live their life over.

9. *Preference for sons*. After adjustment, respondents with no preference for sons had significantly fewer subsequent births after the second and after the third birth and reported a significantly higher proportion ever using contraception than did respondents with a high preference for sons. Furthermore, both the adjusted additional number of children desired and the adjusted number of children advised to one's daughter were significantly higher than average when there was high or moderate son preference and significantly lower than average when there was no son preference. Additionally, the adjusted number of children desired if life could be lived over was significantly lower than average for respondents with no son preference. Finally, attitude toward birth control was less favorable than average, after adjustment, among respondents with a moderate son preference.

The Net Effect of Mortality Change Upon
Natural Increase

If the level of infant and child mortality had no direct effect upon fertility, it is obvious that a decline in mortality would serve to accelerate the rate of natural increase. Conversely, it is possible that the net effect of mortality change upon natural increase might be to reduce the rate of natural increase. For this to be true, the fall in natality induced by mortality decline would have to be of greater magnitude than the decline in mortality itself.

We have hypothesized that a reduction in infant and child mortality would have two effects, a community effect and an individual effect. Let us consider first the degree to which our results confirm the effect of the community level of infant and child mortality upon subsequent fertility independent of the effect of individual child loss. We had hypothesized that differences in the community level of infant and child mortality caused individual differences in perceptions of child survival and that these individual differences in perception caused differences in subsequent fertility. According to our hypothesis there should be no direct relation between the community level of infant mortality and subsequent fertility but only an indirect relationship mediated through variation in perceptions of child survival at the individual level. Nevertheless, our results indicate that township is a more important variable than perception of child survival in explaining subsequent fertility after either the second or the third birth. A major reason why the direct relation between township and subsequent fertility still exists after control for individual perceptions of child survival is the failure to achieve reliable measurement of the latter variable.

However, it would be incorrect to assert that the true effect of the community level of infant and child mortality upon subsequent fertility is the sum of the township and the perception-of-child-survival effects. This is because the two townships differ on almost every other aspect of modernization in addition to differing in mortality level. For example, in 1969 the proportion of females twelve years old and over who were illiterate was 26.0 percent in Kungliao and only 10.5 percent in Hsinchuang. It is very plausible to assume that this difference in literacy between the two townships also had an effect upon subsequent fertility.

We cannot yet answer the very important question as to the effect of reduction of infant and child mortality upon natural increase. If the community level of infant and child mortality had no effect upon subsequent fertility, it is probable that a reduction in infant and child mortality would lead to an acceleration of natural increase because on the individual level couples apparently do not fully compensate for child loss (Our tabulations indicate that up to the time of the interview compensation was far from complete; it is likely however, that if we were to follow all couples up to the end of their reproductive period we would find that compensation was more nearly complete). Conversely, it is possible that a reduction in infant and child mortality could lead to a reduction in the rate of natural increase. The conditions under which this is likely are (1) that the observed adjusted township effect on fertility measured nothing more than the effect of the community level of infant and child mortality and (2) that age at marriage and the perception of child survival were both substantially influenced by the community level of infant and child mortality.

The Effect of Son Preference Upon Fertility
and Policy Implications Therefrom

Our data show very clearly that subsequent fertility is very much affected by the sex of the existing children. The greater the number of males, the lower is subsequent fertility. Our result is in contrast to the results of Repetto, who analyzed this relation among respondents in India, Bangladesh, and Morocco.

In addition, we have shown that an attitudinal measure of preference for sons is also correlated with fertility and family planning behavior and attitudes. The relative weakness of the attitudinal measure is probably related to the fact that there is in fact very little variation in son preference in our study population; practically all respondents have high son preference.

Two policy options are possible if high son preference tends to elevate fertility and if fertility reduction is desired.

One possibility is governmental encouragement of research efforts to find a feasible and inexpensive means of allowing couples to choose the sex of their children. Considerable progress toward this goal has already been made (Rorvik 1970; Etzioni 1968). Our findings indicate that in our study population such a technological innovation, if utilized, might have a substantial effect in reducing fertility. Naturally, there would be many additional consequences if parents could freely choose the sex of their children. Free choice by parents in determining the sex of their children has been advocated by Postgate (1973) and attacked by Etzioni (1968).

A second possibility is to introduce social policies which will reduce the preference for sons. Our study revealed a heavy reliance on sons for support in old age. A reduction in this dependence on sons through the introduction of a governmentally-sponsored old-age security system should help to reduce the high preference for sons and accordingly reduce fertility (Ridker 1971; Ridker and Muscat 1973).

References

Andrews, Frank, James Morgan, and John Sonquist. Multiple Classification Analysis. Ann Arbor: Institute for Social Research, University of Michigan, 1967.

Blacker, C.P. "Stages in Population Growth." *Eugenics Review*. 39 (1947): 88-102.

Davis, Kingsley. *Human Society*. New York: MacMillan, 1949.

Etzioni, Amitai. "Sex Control, Science and Society." *Science* 161 (1968): 1107-1111.

Finnigan, Oliver and T.H. Sun. "Planning, Starting and Operating an Educational Incentives Project." *Studies in Family Planning* 3 (1972): 1-7.

Freedman, Ronald and John Takeshita. *Family Planning in Taiwan: An Experiment in Social Change*. Princeton: Princeton University Press, 1969.

Fredericksen, Harald. "Determinants and Consequences of Mortality and Fertility Trends." *Public Health Reports* 81 (1966): 715-727.

Harrington, Judith. "The Effect of High Infant and Childhood Mortality on Fertility: The West African Case." *Concerned Demography* 3 (1971): 22-35.

Hassan, Shafick. "Influence of Child Mortality on Fertility." Paper presented at the 1966 meeting of the Population Association of America, New York City, 1966.

Heer, David M. "Economic Development and Fertility." *Demography* 3 (1966): 423-444.

Heer, David M. "Determinants of Family Planning Attitudes and Practices." Final report for Contract Number AID/csd 2478 concluded with the Office of Population of the U.S. Agency for International Development, 1972.

Heer, David M. and John Boynton. "A Multivariate Regression Analysis of Differences in Fertility of United States Counties." *Social Biology* 17 (1970): 180-194.

Heer, David M. and Dean Smith. "Mortality Level, Desired Family Size, and Population Increase." *Demography* 5 (1970): 104-121.

Heer, David M. and Dean Smith. "Mortality Level, Desired Family Size, and Population Increase: Further Variations on a Basic Model." *Demography* 6 (1969): 141-149.

Knodel, John. "Infant Mortality and Fertility in Three Bavarian Villages: An Analysis of Family Histories from the 19th Century." *Population Studies* 22 (1968): 297-318.

May, David A. and David Heer. "Son Survivorship Motivation and Family Size in India: A Computer Simulation." *Population Studies* 22 (1968): 199-210.

Notestein, Frank W. "The Economics of Population and Food Supplies." *In Proceedings of the Eighth International Conference of Agricultural Economists.* London: Oxford University Press, 1953. Pp. 15-31.

Poffenberger, Thomas. "Age of Wives and Number of Living Children of a Sample of Men Who Had the Vasectomy in Meerut District, U.P." *Journal of Family Welfare* 13 (1967): 48-51.

Postgate, John. "Bat's Chance in Hell." *New Scientist* 58, 480 (1973): 12-16.

Prabhu, Pandarinath. *Hindue Social Organization.* Bombay: Popular Book Depot, 1963.

Repetto, Robert. "Son Preference and Fertility Behavior in Developing Countries." *Studies in Family Planning* 3 (1972): 70-76.

Ridker, Ronald. "Savings Accounts for Family Planning, an Illustration from the Tea Estates of India." *Studies in Family Planning* 2 (1971): 150-152.

Ridker, Ronald and Robert Muscat. "Incentives for Family Welfare and Fertility Reduction: An Illustration for Malaysia." *Studies in Family Planning* 4 (1973): 1-11.

Rorvik, David M. "You Can Choose Your Baby's Sex." *Look* 34 (1970): 88-98.

Rutstein, Shea. "The Relation of Child Mortality to Fertility in Taiwan." In *1970 Social Statistics Section Proceedings of the American Statistical Association,* 1970. Pp. 348-353.

Thompson, Warren S. *Population and Peace in the Pacific*. Chicago: University of Chicago Press, 1946.

Weintraub, Robert. "The Birth Rate and Economic Development: An Empirical Study." *Econometrica* 40 (1962): 812-817.

Wyon, John B. and John Gordon. *The Khanna Study: Population Problems in the Rural Punjab*. Cambridge: Harvard University Press, 1971.

Part V

Directions for Research

Introduction to Part V

Having examined various aspects of the relationship of population to development, what now? What do we need to know to proceed more effectively, to plan more wisely? And how might we go about it? These are the questions to which this concluding part is addressed.

There are, as we have seen, many ways by which knowledge in this area is obtained, varying from anthropological observation to sample surveys to mathematical modeling. Without question the sample survey in its KAP[a] incarnation, has been a leading method of investigation. The field problems associated with these surveys are well recognized and there is by now a formidable literature having to do with the scientific selection of cases and the construction of questionnaires. There are also a number of convenient programs for the tabulation of data from these surveys — along conventional lines — and for the estimation of selected parameters. Still the KAP survey is often spoken of slightingly as a device that at fairly high cost in both time and money yields rather superficial and sometimes invalid data several years after they might be needed. Some go so far as to suggest that the findings from KAP surveys can generally be guessed with reasonable accuracy by experienced workers and thus the whole exercise is largely, as Newton said of experimentation, to "convince the vulgar." To add to the indictment, the data obtained from KAP surveys, especially that relating to attitudes, have not proven to be highly reliable on the level of the consistency of individual responses, although aggregate distributions have displayed reasonable stability. Finally response rates, at least in the United States, appear to be falling, leading one to wonder if this affliction might not in time also spread to KAP surveys in developing countries where up till now respondent cooperation generally has been satisfactory.

All of this has led to growing disenchantment with the sample survey as an instrument of inquiry in the population field.[b] Not the least part of this stems

---

[a]This familiar acronym refers to sample surveys of individuals for the purpose of obtaining information about their knowledge (K), attitudes (A), and practice (P) relative to the use of contraception. Such surveys frequently obtain supplementary information on pregnancy, fertility, and various individual characteristics.

[b]This disenchantment has not however deterred the launching of the World Fertility Survey a massive undertaking under the aegis of the United Nations and various cooperating agencies and with technical supervision by the International Statistical Institute.

from the poor analytic yields of these surveys. This is the problem of the chapter by Sirageldin, who points out that the fault does not lie solely in the quality of the data but in lack of ingenuity (or theory if you prefer) in the way data are analyzed. The scheme of analysis which he proposes is still being perfected but even in its present form suggests how greater meaning can be wrung from sample survey data. Others, notably Professor Goodman of the University of Chicago have, in recent years, concerned themselves with this same general problem — how to extract greater meaning and understanding from survey data. There are of course inherent limitations to the depths one can go in probing individual behavior with such information, but as Sirageldin's piece makes plain, we can go much farther toward understanding the underlying structure of behavior than conventional modes of analysis have in the past taken us.

As to what problems we should turn our attention, regardless of how we obtain or analyse the information, the concluding chapter by Irene Taeuber presents an agenda which reflects years of travel, study, sympathetic observation — and much thought. There was a time not many years ago when the conventional wisdom proclaimed around foundations and other funding agencies held that the critical factor in short supply was the idea — the research problem or the program innovation. It was said the wherewithal and institutional arrangements required for research were not the problem. Let us hope that is still the case and that the excellent and challenging ideas proposed by Taeuber will be pursued by the most skilled scientists that can be mobilized and moreover that the results will inspire and inform the doers of this world to do their jobs with more telling effect.

15 The Survey Method in Family Planning Research and Evaluation
Ismail Sirageldin

Introduction

A well known review of knowledge, attitude, and practice (KAP) surveys and evaluation of family planning programs (Mauldin, Watson, and Noé 1970: 5-12, lists ten uses and consequences of KAP surveys:

1. Description
2. Generating support for a family planning program
3. Assisting program administration
4. Measuring private sector activity
5. Providing denominators for acceptance rates
6. Validating service statistics
7. Evaluating a program by measuring change
8. Measuring fertility and fertility change
9. Advancing social science, and
10. Institution building

This is a relatively optimistic view of the expected utility of surveys in general and particularly KAP surveys. It is in contrast to the often cited difficulties of doing technically solid studies "with few qualified nationals, in a foreign language, with largely illiterate people, in an alien culture, on a personally delicate matter that is difficult of measurement, . . ." (Berelson 1964: 3).

Furthermore, Philip Hauser (1967) argues that ". . . KAP surveys, along with many other sample surveys, have exhibited two major deficiencies. First, they have in general failed to include adequate efforts to study the reliability of their data; and, second, they have failed to make adequate efforts to obtain measurements of the 'intensity' of the opinions or attitudes reported . . . it is a moot question whether surveys do not mislead as much as they inform . . ." Mauldin (1970) concludes that ". . . KAP surveys score poorly in terms of reliability of individual responses, but rate highly in terms of the consistency of aggregate distributions over time," and ". . . there appears to be a marked tendency to underreport both knowledge and practice in some cultures and this obviously limits the usefulness of KAP surveys in detecting trends and in drawing conclusions about the level of practice in a population." A few studies have attempted to examine validity and reliability and indicated a tendency toward underreporting

of knowledge and practice (Stoeckel and Chaudhury 1969; Green 1969). In
general, however, there is a consensus on the usefulness of family planning surveys but at the same time a recognition of the "need for further methodological
research in this relatively new area of study" (Kirk 1969; Ryder and Westoff
1971; Mauldin 1969; Sirageldin and Hardee 1970).

In this chapter, we argue that there are conflicts among the implied objectives or the expected uses of KAP surveys; that some of those uses are beyond
what a scientific survey can or ought to do; that there are two main users of
survey findings who could have different objectives, namely the "local" family
planning program and the "foreign" aid-giving agencies; that a large part of
response validity and reliability could be traced to the quality of interviewing,
to the wording and sequence of the questions asked, and to the lack of adequate
probing; and that the apparent universal goal of comparative international fertility studies, although needed and useful, might be premature given our lack of
methodological experience in various regions and cultures, and might discourage
independent methodological developments in certain countries.[a] Finally, we
propose a survey design for family planning research and evaluation.

Our discussion will be limited to knowledge, attitude, and practice (KAP)
surveys and will refer mainly to Pakistan and Bangladesh. However, many of our
conclusions can be generalized to most of Southeast Asia.

Objectives of Family Planning Surveys

Survey research is a new science. Only in "the last twenty-five years has it
become a scientific tool, able to produce qualified, reproducible information
that can be used to test hypotheses or to provide unbiased measurement of quantities or relationships" (Lansing and Morgan 1971). Much of survey research's
early development came from sociology and, more recently, from economics.
Even though the use of sample surveys as a research and evaluation tool in family
planning is recent, at least 130 major KAP studies have been conducted since
1949 and, more recently, hundreds of minor KAP surveys and other types of
population surveys have been done (Population Council 1970; Reynolds 1972).
It seems that new tools tempt us into what is called by Abraham Kaplan (1964)
the law of the instrument, a law illustrated by the child who, given a hammer,
discovers that a great many things need pounding. It seems that we need
continued restraint, using surveys only where they are appropriate.

---

[a]However, many variables and questionnaire wordings recommended for international
comparative surveys are often adaptable to studies in countries differing widely in culture.
"Even if an investigator decides to part from the lists of variables recommended, his work
will probably be enhanced by the stimulus of comparison with what has been thought essential and desirable by others." United Nations, "Variables and Questionnaire for Comparative Fertility Survey," *Population Studies No. 45*, Department of Economic and Social
Affairs (New York: United Nations, 1970), p. 4.

It is not a simple task, however, to determine the appropriate uses of surveys in general and of family planning surveys in particular. While the ultimate purpose of survey research is usually explanation, prediction, or evaluation, descriptive data are useful in estimating various population characteristics, e.g., the extent of unemployment, patterns of migration, the extent of contraceptive practice, the quality of housing, the incidence of child morbidity, or the extent of poverty. Such data are useful not only to *estimate* the various distributions for the aggregate or for parts or subgroups of the population, but also to analyze the impact of some government policies such as changes in tax rates or abortion laws on different groups in society, and, if repeated, can provide data on changes over time that serve as social indicators.

Most descriptive survey research is the responsibility of governments. The census bureaus in many countries collect data on items such as employment, family expenditures, and fertility through special surveys. In Pakistan and India a large number of KAP surveys have been done directly by or under the control of the Family Planning Program. This might explain why the "uses" of KAP surveys included "the generation of support for a family planning program." Positive findings of such surveys are indeed supportive and useful in the initial stages of a program. However, KAP surveys are sometimes viewed by administrators as policy tools whose utility stems only from their supportive elements while critical findings are suppressed. Costs may also include the large number of low-quality KAP-type surveys that have been conducted in various countries, probably for the main purpose of providing supportive (and usually immediate) data. The negative externalities of such low-quality surveys on the development of, and utilization of the findings of well-designed, high-quality surveys cannot be underestimated. However, we must not confuse the utilization of supportive findings from well-designed scientific surveys with those of low quality.

Freedman mentioned the following five conditions which make family planning surveys helpful in developing countries:

1. In the context of a desire for massive social change there is little information about how much change has already occurred.
2. There is likely to be a gap of understanding between the leadership and the masses which is much greater than in developed countries. The mass media all communicate in one direction, to the masses, and feedback is poor.
3. Traditional ideology exists about family planning. The ideology may not fit the facts.
4. There may be many people in favor of a program who do not realize that others are too.
5. There is need for surveys, to check on the effectiveness of the programs. (Freedman 1964)

The first two conditions have the potential conflict discussed in the text. (See also, Lansing and Morgan [1971] on the inappropriate uses of surveys.)

The Problem of Response Validity and
Reliability

As mentioned earlier, validity and reliability of responses to questions concerning knowledge and practice of family planning have been subjected to intensive
criticism and discussion. Two recent studies of response validity in Bangladesh
may help to illustrate some apparent misinterpretation. In a study by Green (1969)
a panel of 519 couples (residing in Dacca in one of four government employee
housing colonies, from the bottom two government grades and ranging in occupation from low-level clerks to sweepers) was interviewed in February 1963 and
again in August 1964. During the interim, an action program in family planning
was instituted in the area. Individual records were kept about family planning
educational and motivational activities and purchases of supplies. In the 1964
reinterview (the year after the action program survey) respondents' responses
were compared with their expected knowledge and practice and were given a
validity score accordingly. Green concludes that there is substantial underreporting of both knowledge (16-29 percent) and use (13-35 percent) of contraceptives depending on the intensity of the score and the sex of the respondent.
Stoeckel and Chaudhury (1969) report similar results for a study of 183 women
in Kotwala Thana, East Pakistan (Bangladesh). They find that ". . . over one-
third of the known users of contraceptives indicated they had never used, while
less than 10 percent indicated they had no knowledge of family planning."

In his conclusions, Green (1969) recommends that in the absence of more
certain information "survey data on knowledge and use of contraceptives in
developing areas might justifiably be adjusted upward by as much as 20 to 30
percent." This conclusion is open to serious question because of the non-
representative nature of the sample and more generally because we know little
about either the magnitude or the structure of the total response error.

There are two approaches, although not mutually exclusive, to examining
problems of response error. The first approach focuses on the interviewer,
including problems of questionnaire content and design. The second approach
focuses on the respondent. Some studies indicate that interviewers tend to
record material which conforms with their own attitudes on controversial issues.
Also, interviewers may vary in their probing habits without this variation being
randomly distributed (Hyman 1956). A major problem, however, in the analysis
of interviewers' bias is the lack of satisfactory criterion variables for measuring
their performance. Studies by Axelrod and Cannel (1959) and Sudman (1966)
have developed a systematic scheme for such evaluation. Especially in developing countries, it is the motivation of the interviewer, her/his understanding of
and belief in the importance of the study, the quality and frequency of supervision, and the appropriateness of the instrument that matter most. It is useful
to look at the interviewing situation as a stimulus-response process where it is
essential that the stimulus be standardized (e.g., controlled) through adequate
training of interviewers.

The second approach focuses on the respondent who must be motivated to participate in a survey and become involved in the interviewing process. Establishing and sustaining rapport is usually a challenge for the interviewer. On the other hand, many respondents enjoy being interviewed since they can say what they feel without being criticized or disapproved (Axelrod and Cannel 1959). There is an implicit assumption that people will tell the truth unless there is a valid reason to conceal the truth, e.g., illegal or immoral activity, and respondents' errors are accordingly explained only in terms of ambiguity, irrelevance, misunderstanding, sensitivity, or inappropriateness of the questions, not in terms of respondents' willingness to lie. This assumption however, may not be true at all times and/or in all cultures and societies (Gastil 1958). After reviewing various validity studies, Lansing and Morgan conclude that

> when one considers that the other sources of information, even ignoring the conceptual and matching difficulties, may themselves be subject to error, and the final fact, that there is not much use merely measuring error if one does not know why it arose or what to do about it, it may seem more profitable to invest the time and energy in better pretesting, re-interviews, investigation of consistency of people's reports, etc., rather than experimental validity studies (Lansing and Morgan 1971).

Recent findings from a study in Pakistan and Bangladesh confirm these conclusions.

In 1968/69 a national KAP-Fertility (IMPACT) survey was conducted in Pakistan and Bangladesh.[b] Three sets of questions, varying from general to

---

[b]The Pakistan National Impact Survey was conducted by the Pakistan Family Planning Council in 1968/69. The survey was carried out by interviewing approximately 6,000 ever married women and about 3,000 husbands. Information on pregnancy history, knowledge and practice, basic socioeconomic characteristics were asked of the respondent. The questionnaires were written in five languages. Basic data on about 400 Secondary Sampling Units were collected during enumeration. Also, a sample of community leaders was interviewed. The analysis was completed in 1970 and a report submitted to the government in early 1971. For details about the design of, and people and organizations involved in the Survey, see *1968 IMPACT Survey Publications,* No. 1 and No. 2 (Karachi, Pakistan: Family Planning Council, January 1969), and (Hardee and Sirageldin 1970: 637-39). Our discussion in the text borrows heavily from work and analysis done as a group endeavor. Full acknowledgment will appear in the forthcoming report mentioned above. But to the extent that the author has been deeply involved for almost three years in almost all the survey operation from its planning, operation, to its analysis and report writing some "personal" acknowledgment to others involved must be made. First, Dr. Nafis Sadik, then the Deputy Director General (Technical) of the Family Planning Program in Pakistan who was the prime mover and the problem solver behind this complex study. Dr. Gilbert Hardee, then Population Council Advisor (Social Research), Karachi, was along with the author the main consultant to the study in all its phases. The senior and junior staff of the West Pakistan Research and Evaluation Center in Lahore and of the Center Evaluation Units in Dacca and Lahore have done an impressive job given the circumstances. Above all, we must acknowledge the dedicated work of an able men and women field staff and their supervisors who worked together in a delicate area of research in a traditional society and difficult terrain. This is only a partial personal acknowledgment.

more specific, were asked in the same interview to elicit knowledge about family planning and family planning methods. The distribution of responses are given in table 15-1 and all tables refer to interviews of wives. The proportion indicating knowledge increase from 50 percent in response to the first question to 78 percent to the last question. Stopping after the first question would have resulted in 30 percent underreporting of knowledge, attributed mainly to validity problems. It is now evident that a large part of underreporting is a result of questionnaire design and/or interviewer's quality and supervision.

Another interesting finding is the response to the question on abortion. First, respondents were asked to mention all methods of family planning (modern and traditional) which they know. Less than 1 percent of the wives mentioned abortion as a method. However, the interviewer was then instructed to read a complete list of all methods, including abortion, and ask whether the respondent recognized each particular method as family planning. The number of respondents

Table 15-1
Percentage of Wives Knowing About Family Planning and Family Planning Methods

| | Percentage Who Know About Family Planning | | | | |
| | | Bangladesh | | Pakistan | |
Type of Question Asked	All	Rural	Urban	Rural	Urban
1. General Question About Family Planning	50%	48%	78%	37%	83%
2. Specific Question About Family Planning Knowledge	62	51	71	75	84
3. More Specific Question About Family Planning Methods: Knowledge About					
Any Method	78	64	82	97	98
Any Modern Method*	73	63	81	83	92
Any Traditional Method**	59	44	51	96	96

Source: National Impact Survey. Tables are based on interviews with approximately 2,910 wives in Pakistan and 3,088 wives in Bangladesh, all currently married.

*Modern methods include condom, diaphragm, foam, jelly or cream, tampon or sponge, IUD (loop), pill, male and female sterilization, and abortion.
**Traditional methods include abstinence, rhythm, douche, withdrawal, breast feeding.

who recognized abortion after the list was read increased from less than 1 percent to 38 percent. This may suggest that the respondent attributes little importance to abortion as a method and/or that the Family Planning Program message does not suggest abortion. However, when the concept of family planning is clarified to include abortion, establishing it as a permissible topic within the interviewing situation, the respondents admit knowledge.

We must argue, however, that validity studies may not improve the credibility of research if it is perceived by program administrators as a political tool. Under a new administration, and after its completion, the IMPACT Survey came under severe criticism. For example, it was argued that the reported incidence of female sterilization is suspiciously high. Most of the women, it was claimed, confuse IUD insertion and an operation and accordingly most of the reported sterilizations (if not all of them) must have been IUD cases – thus, explaining the low reported incidence of IUD use, a major Program input. To test this hypothesis all reported sterilization cases in the survey in the Panjab were identified. Two senior lady doctors were sent to reinterview and medically examine these respondents. Out of forty-three women designated to be reinterviewed in the Panjab Region, thirty-eight were located and all were sterile, either as a result of a tubectomy or other operation. No confusion existed between the IUD and sterilization.

To summarize, we examined one objective of Family Planning Surveys, namely, description, investigating the potential danger of conflicting objectives that convert surveys into political tools. We also examined briefly some of the problems associated with response validity and reliability. Our main thesis is that many of the problems faced in family planning surveys are not unique. A large part of the problem could be minimized by having fewer and better surveys – better in the sense of quality control. In the next section we examine the predictive and evaluative use of family planning surveys, proposing a methodology for planning and analysis.

Research and Evaluation Needs in Family Planning: A Brief Outline

In general, a "family planning program" attempts to influence, in a given period of time and for a given society, the number of births the average family will have during its reproductive life. This is partly done by attempting to reduce the number of unwanted births a family would have had in the absence of the "program," and partly by reducing the family's goal of surviving children to a number that is compatible with the society's desired rate of population growth. Freedman and Takeshita (1969: 37) indicate that effective availability "requires that couples who want to limit family size must know what to do and where to get supplies and services. Most importantly, if they are to be led to act in a new way not specifically sanctioned by tradition, they must feel that this action is sufficiently safe and respectable."

The establishment of such a program creates the need for answers to three sets of questions. The *first* is related to setting a target reduction in the rate of population growth in a given period and to establishing how much society should spend on a family planning program as opposed to other alternative investments. Attempts to answer these questions are commonly based on macro-economic models that attempt to estimate the returns to population control.[1] However, current models seem to lack both adequate specification and reliable data inputs and their conclusions are generally subject to serious scientific criticisms.[2]

The *second* set of questions are more substantive and relate to program designs and operations, i.e., finding the most efficient way(s) to achieve program objectives given budget, personnel, and time constraints. These include two major areas of concern. The first attempts to specify the conditions necessary for effective fertility regulation, to identify the target families most likely to adopt contraceptive practice, to identify the effective information, education, and motivation media required to reach and influence the target families, and to identify the combination of methods that are most likely to be accepted and used and the best way(s) od delivering them. (These are complex questions, however, that cross boundaries of many sciences and we do not have adequate answers to many of them. Our current theoretical understanding of the various factors related to attitudes and choices influencing fertility behavior seems to be in its formative stages.[3] And some of the reported findings are suspected of circular reasoning. For example the following general hypothesis is usually presented, ". . . any values which are favourable to trying out family size control . . . lead to the practice of birth control" (R. Hill 1968; 249). The question is whether a society exists whose values are favorable to family size control but not to the practice of birth control. The second area of concern focuses on management research problems. National family planning programs are usually large-scale operations that need not only medical and educational skills but also a high level of managerial skills. Operation research that attempts to find means to minimize waste and detect bottlenecks is needed for developing a successful program (Reinke 1970).

The *third* set of questions is related to the evaluation of program activities and achievements. The evaluation process is built by defining a set of program objectives and appropriate judgmental criteria, after allowing appropriate time lags for the diffusion process. Given the number and complexity of variables involved in program evaluation, increasing reliance should be given to techniques involving multivariate analysis. These techniques permit an analysis of the combined and separate effects of a set of variables upon a behavioral variable, a situation which closely parallels the multi-determinate nature of the practice of contraception or the factors leading to a fertility decline. The solution to these complex problems requires a broad data source. The survey method, despite its limitations, is one means of providing basic data in order to answer many research and evaluation questions.[4] We shall examine critically the design and findings of a recent national KAP survey in Pakistan and Bangladesh (the IMPACT Survey), which is representative of the current state of the art and suggest a methodology for planning and analysis.

The Anatomy of an Evaluation Survey:
The Case of the National IMPACT Survey

Family planning activities in what was then Pakistan started on a voluntary basis as early as 1952 and the first National Governmental Program was initiated in 1960. The vastly expanded National Program during the Third Five Year Plan (1965-70) marked the first full recognition of population control as an important element in Pakistan development planning. The objectives of the 1975-70 Family Planning Scheme were the reduction of the birth rate from 50 to 40 per 1,000, protecting 25 percent of the nation's estimated 20 million fertile couples by 1970 in all geographic areas of the country except the tribal.[5] Progress toward these goals were reported monthly by the Pakistan Central Family Planning Council and were based on the flow of routine service statistics. The IMPACT Survey was conceived as an evaluation of the (1965-70) Pakistan Family Planning Program during the first three to four years of its operation, providing the first national baseline data on socioeconomic, demographic, and family planning variables.

The design of the IMPACT Survey closely followed the conventional designs of the extended-type KAP surveys, but with some important innovations. It included a detailed pregnancy history of every woman interviewed, eliciting information from both wives, husbands and a sample of local leaders in all the secondary sampling points; it placed more emphasis on measuring program inputs as conceived and utilized by the population, and included independent assessment (during the enumeration process) of the availability of family planning, health, and other social facilities in the sample points. The universe consisted of all households in Pakistan and Bangladesh (except those in the tribal areas). Within the national sample, subsamples were drawn from which statistically reliable estimates can be made for: (a) Pakistan and Bangladesh and (b) rural vs. urban. Both the rural and urban strata were further sub-divided into five subuniverses based on size in the case of urban areas and on a crude index of modernity in the case of rural areas. The sample was internally self-weighted within urban and rural strata by Pakistan and Bangladesh. In early 1971, a report based on the survey findings was submitted to the government of Pakistan and is scheduled for publication in the near future, however, the full analytical potential of the data is yet to be realized.[c]

For purposes of this discussion, a brief summary of the findings is presented within a simple analytical framework, depicting the input-output relations of the program, given the population characteristics and the social setting.

The *first* step required an assessment of the relative fecundibility of the wives interviewed. This was done by classifying respondents by age, age of youngest child, and pregnancy status, as illustrated in table 15-2. It is evident from table 15-2 that married women, 20-29 years old who were not pregnant and whose youngest child was less than five, were responsible for almost half of the total reported live births although they comprise only 24 percent of wives under

Table 15-2
Percentage Distribution and Live Births During the Last Twelve Months for Various Target Population Groups in Bangladesh and Pakistan

	Bangladesh			Pakistan		
	% Distri-bution	Live Birth/ 100 in last 12 months	Births as % of all births	% Distri-bution	Live Birth/ 100 in last 12 months	Births as % of all births
Age < 20 and no child	8	6	2	5	4	1
Age < 20, child, not pregnant	8	58	18	5	61	11
20-29, youngest < 5, not pregnant	24	48	46	26	49	49
30-39, youngest < 5, not pregnant	17	34	23	19	37	27
Pregnant, < 40	16	9	6	14	7	5
20-39, no child or age of young-est 5+	13	4	2	16	6	3
Age 40-49	14	4	3	15	7	4
	100%		100%	100%		100%

---

[c]A doctoral student is working with the author on differentials of fertility and another on the determinants and implications of spouse communication using the data set of the IMPACT survey. Also, the author is currently involved with others at Johns Hopkins University in developing an analysis methodology for family planning evaluation using the IMPACT Survey as a basic data source.

fifty years old (28 percent under forty) in Bangladesh and 26 percent (31 percent under forty) in Pakistan.

The *second* step examines the extent of wives' desires for additional children compared to the actual number of living children (reality) and to some expression of ideal family size (table 15-3). For both Pakistan and Bangladesh about 39 percent of all wives interviewed reported no desire for additional children. Interestingly enough, 11 percent expressed no desire for additional children although their number of living children was smaller than the indication of their ideal family size. If these intentions or desires for no more children are taken at face value, we may conclude that a strong potential demand for family planning already exists and accordingly acceptance rates should be relatively high. However, other factors influence such decisions. For example, aside from the inherent problems of response validity, wives, although expressing no desire for additional children, may not practice family planning because of sterility, lack of motivation or lack of knowledge about the "effective" availability of family planning services.[d] In table 15-4 we attempt to evaluate the demographic

Table 15-3

Desire for More Children by Number of Living Children and the Ideal Number in Bangladesh and Pakistan

	Percentage of Women Who		
	Desire no more Children	*Desire more Children*	*All*
Number of living children more than ideal	16	1	17
Number of living children equal to ideal	12	1	13
Number of living children less than ideal	11	35	46
No numerical response	–	–	24
	39	37	100

[d]We recognize that there will always be a gap between the measured variables and their intended theoretical construct (Blalock 1964: 3-26). It is the analyst's contribution to acknowledge this gap, indicate its implications, and reduce it to a minimum. A preliminary analysis of these variables indicates that there is a tendency towards internal consistency. For example, among the wives whose number of living children was equal to or greater than their stated ideal, a small proportion indicated that they have a desire for additional children. The proportion of women who desired additional children was more than eight times greater for women without sons, than for women with sons. Also, a larger proportion of the first group were pregnant at the time of the interview which may indicate that their expressed desire for additional children could be a rationalization of their situation.

Table 15-4
Percentage Distribution of Various Target Populations by Relationship of Living to Ideal Number of Children and by Desire for Additional Children

| | In Bangladesh | | | | | |
| | Living children, equal or exceed ideal | | Living less than ideal | | | |
	Desire no More	Desire More	Desire no More	Desire More	No Numerical Response	Total
1. Age less than 20, no child	0	0	1	70	29	100%
2. Age less than 20, have child*	2	1	2	60	35	100%
3. Age 20-29, youngest less than 5*	22	2	8	35	33	100%
4. Age 30-39, youngest less than 5*	50	2	8	8	32	100%
5. Pregnant, age less than 40	12	5	5	43	35	100%
6. Age 20-39, no child or youngest 5 or older*	22	2	21	33	22	100%
7. Age 40 or more	53	1	23	3	20	100%
ALL	26	2	10	32	30	100%

| | In Pakistan | | | | | |
| | Living children, equal or exceed ideal | | Living less than ideal | | | |
	Desire no More	Desire More	Desire no More	Desire More	No Numerical Response	Total
1. Age less than 20, no child	0	0	3	81	16	100%
2. Age less than 20, have child*	1	4	4	70	21	100%
3. Age 20-29, youngest less than 5*	21	3	9	51	15	100%
4. Age 30-39, youngest less than 5*	56	0	8	16	20	100%
5. Pregnant, age less than 40	12	4	9	57	18	100%
6. Age 20-39, no child or youngest 5 or older*	21	2	12	56	9	100%
7. Age 40 or more	55	3	22	9	11	100%
ALL	30	4	11	42	13	100%

*Also not pregnant at the time of interview.

relevance of these stated intentions and desires. Among women 30-39 years old, with youngest child age four or less, and non-pregnant, who were responsible for 23 percent of all births in Bangladesh (27 percent in Pakistan), about 58 percent indicated no desire for more children (64 percent in Pakistan). This percentage was only 30 percent among the similar but younger group of wives (age 20-29) who were responsible for 46 percent of all births in Bangladesh (49 percent in Pakistan).

The *third* step, accordingly, is to examine the "effective availability" of contraceptives to various groups of target couples. By "effective availability" we mean that couples know about family planning methods, feel that practicing family planning is both sufficiently safe and respectible, and know what to do, where to get supplies and services, and whom to contact for advice. The survey findings indicate that most of the wives who admitted knowledge about family planning *as a concept* first heard about it during the 1965-69 period, i.e., during the Program Plan period. The percentage of wives who reported such knowledge were 80 and 88, 70, and 87 percent for rural and urban Bangladesh, rural and urban Pakistan respectively. These findings illustrate the success of the program in spreading the concept of family planning among the target population. Spreading the concept, however, does not indicate that it has a positive meaning to the respondents. In this survey, about 27 percent of all wives interviewed mentioned negative statements about family planning, e.g., "Family Planning is killing life," or "Family Planning is interfering with God's will." We cannot indicate whether these expressed negative attitudes have any implications for actual behavior, given the respondent's demographic characteristics, without further analysis.

In terms of knowledge about methods, the IUD seems to be the method most frequently mentioned by wives (42-82 percent) followed by male sterilization (31-65 percent), female sterilization (38-64 percent), oral pills (30-58 percent), and the condom (20-61 percent) with rural Bangladesh exhibiting the least knowledge of available methods and urban Pakistan the most.

Knowledge about family planning as a concept and/or general knowledge about family planning methods are not, by themselves, sufficient for "effective knowledge"—defined as a subset of "effective availability." According to the structure of the Pakistan Family Planning Program, people also need to know about personnel and places where they may seek basic services. The "program" provided such facilities in all program areas at the time of the survey. In table 15-5 we present a continuum of combined knowledge about methods, personnel, and places,[e] with cross-classifications by rural-urban residence and other

---

[e]This is essentially a partially ordered scale where the members of one class bear some relationship to the members of another class and a complete ordering is not possible. For example, persons who are informed about both personnel and places could be identified as better informed than those who only know about one or none. However, we cannot say that A is better informed than B if one knows only about personnel and the other about places. Only a system of equivalence between knowledge about places and personnel will produce a complete ordering. See for example Coombs (1953: 471-535).

Table 15-5
Wives' Knowledge of any Family Planning Method, Personnel, or Places and Whether They have Ever Gone to Family Planning Places by Various Characteristics

	Know Any Method			Know Personnel			Know Places			Know Personnel and Places			Ever Gone to Places		
	Total	Bang	Pak	Total	Bang	Pak	Total	Bang	Pak	Total	Bang	Pak	Total	Bang	Pak
All Pakistan	77	72	88	27	23	36	21	15	29	14	8	22	4	3	5
Urban/Rural															
Rural	75	70	85	26	22	37	18	13	29	12	8	21	4	3	5
Urban	91	85	94	31	25	33	26	19	30	19	10	24	6	4	7
Age of Wife															
Less Than 20	69	64	81	18	16	24	13	11	19	7	5	11	1	–	1
20-29	77	71	86	28	23	34	21	14	31	14	9	21	2	2	3
30-39	82	76	91	32	24	42	25	16	36	17	11	26	6	4	8
40+	77	69	88	30	24	40	21	11	37	14	6	25	3	2	4
Age of Youngest Child															
No Children	69	62	80	21	16	28	17	11	25	9	4	15	1	1	2
Less than 5	79	72	89	29	23	37	22	14	32	15	9	23	3	2	5
5 or More	78	71	89	29	23	38	22	13	35	14	8	25	3	2	4
Number of Children															
0-2	73	67	83	23	18	30	17	11	26	10	6	17	1	1	2
3-4	77	68	89	30	24	40	23	16	32	16	10	24	4	4	4
5 or more	84	79	93	33	27	42	24	16	41	17	11	28	8	6	12
Wife's Schooling															
No School	75	66	86	27	20	35	20	12	29	13	7	21	4	3	5
Some School	88	86	96	31	28	43	27	21	50	16	12	33	5	3	11

Percentage of Wives

– Percentage less than 0.5

responsible characteristics. Although 72 percent in Bangladesh and 88 percent in Pakistan reported knowledge of at least one method, less than one-third reported knowledge of any person who gives advice on family planning in the locality, less than one-fourth reported knowledge about any place from where they could seek help or advice about family planning in their locality, less than one-sixth reported knowledge of *both* personnel and places, and only 4 percent indicated that they had ever gone, for any purpose, to any such places (although about 22 percent indicated they had met a person who gives such advice). The difference in extent of "effective knowledge" is greater between Bangladesh and Pakistan than between urban and rural within each region. The implications of these findings will be discussed later in the chapter when we examine a proposed evaluation methodology. The rest of table 15-5 indicates that the probability of wives indicating knowledge of personnel, places, or both increases by the age of the wife (but not after forty), by whether they have a child, by the number of children, and by whether the wife had any schooling. For example, the probability of knowing both personnel and places varied from 5 percent or less for young Bangladesh wives (less than twenty) to 11 percent for women 30-39.

In table 15-6 we evaluate the demographic relevance of "effective knowledge" using the same classification of relative fertility. (We may stress that our use of the term effective knowledge is purely definitional and has no implication to the "quality" dimension of such knowledge.) We rearranged the population into three general groups: the "hi-fertility target-population" that includes three age groups (less than 20, 20-29, 30-39) non-pregnant and with one child under five years of age; the "future target population" that includes all pregnant wives less than forty and all young, childless, non-pregnant wives (less than twenty); and finally the "less fertile groups" that include older wives in their forties and non-pregnant wives, age 20-39, and with a youngest child at least five years old. This classification serves a useful purpose in focusing our attention on the demographic relevance of various evaluative statements. Table 15-6 illustrates some interesting conclusions. With the hi-fertility groups, effective knowledge increases with age and is highest among women over thirty regardless of their relative fertility (i.e., regardless of the age of their youngest child and/or whether women were forty or older). The currently pregnant wives ranked high in terms of effective knowledge. Whether their knowledge about personnel and places was a result of being pregnant (e.g., some of their pregnancies were unwanted) or whether pregnancy was in spite of their knowledge (e.g., because of contraceptive failure) seems to be an important program implication—the former implying a program which is "catching-up" with clients' needs as opposed to indicating problems in providing services. We cannot speak about "effective knowledge" without examining its relation to past and current practice and, in a newly introduced program, the wives' future considerations of such practice.

Table 15-6
Wives' Knowledge of any Family Planning Method, Personnel, or Places and Whether They Have Ever Gone to Family Planning Places by Various Characteristics

	Percentage of Wives														
	Know Any Method			Know Personnel			Know Places			Know Personnel and Places			Ever Gone to Places		
	Total	Bang	Pak	Total	Bang	Pak	Total	Bang	Pak	Total	Bang	Pak	Total	Bang	Pak
Target Population:															
1. Age Less than 20 and no child	63	57	78	16	14	23	11	9	17	6	5	9	–	1	–
2. Age Less than 20 and have a child and not pregnant	70	69	84	20	18	23	13	11	19	7	5	11	1	1	1
3. Age 20–29 and Youngest less than 5 and not pregnant	77	70	86	26	22	33	20	14	30	13	8	20	4	3	5
4. Age 30–39 and Youngest less than 5 and not pregnant	82	76	92	33	25	42	25	16	35	18	12	25	8	6	10
5. Pregnant & Age less than 40	80	76	88	29	24	38	21	14	33	14	9	23	3	2	4
Less Fertile Group															
6. Age 10–39, no child or Youngest 5 or more and not pregnant	21	28	14	28	22	36	25	18	34	16	9	24	5	3	6
7. Age 40 or more	77	70	88	30	24	40	22	11	37	14	6	25	3	2	5

– Less than 0.5

The *fourth* step in our analysis is to examine the extent of use in the sample of wives, its relation to effective knowledge, and its demographic relevance. Wives are classified into seven groups in terms of their past, current, and future practice. It is evident from table 15-7 that although current and past use is relatively low, it is higher among the older subgroup (30-39) of the high-fertility groups, i.e., (with child less than five years of age) especially in urban areas. In this same group the majority of past users, in urban areas as opposed to rural, indicated willingness to consider some method of family planning in the future. Furthermore, some knowledge about family planning is better than none in terms of considering future use (although at this point we are not examining which is the cause and which is the effect). Respondents' statements about considering future use may have no relevance to actual practice although they were somewhat specific about methods and many who did not want to consider a method in the future provided specific reasons.

The fact that a sizable number of wives are willing to consider future practice and that this number is relatively larger among those who know about a family planning method is in itself a logical indication of possible program success. In table 15-8 we examine the relationship between family planning practice and effective knowledge. Knowledge about personnel or places, and especially about both, is highly related to past, current, and expected future use. Limited diffusion of effective knowledge may partly *explain* the apparent low level of current use. Another possible explanation is that the program has expanded too fast and too thin resulting in lower quality of services (table 15-9). The population is divided into three major groups in terms of whether they will (or will not) consider using each of the following methods of family planning, namely, the pill, IUD, male and female sterilization. (The residual are the current users, don't know, inapplicable.) The IUD and male sterilization were among the main methods introduced by the program while the pill was not an official method at the time of the survey. It is interesting, however, to note that a larger proportion of the wives indicated willingness to try the pill as compared to the IUD or sterilization. Since "side effects" was the main reason for rejecting the latter two, it is possible that experience with the program services resulted in dissatisfaction. Table 15-9 illustrates that there is a limit on how many wives would accept contraceptive practice without changing their perceived quality of services and their basic motivational barriers. These are speculative assertions that cannot be inferred from our present analysis with any degree of confidence. An examination of future intentions could reveal future dynamics of family planning practice.

For the purpose of evaluating a family planning program we would, ideally, seek answers to the following questions:

1. What are the existing patterns of fertility and family planning among the target population?

Table 15-7
Practice Among Target Population Groups

In Urban and Rural Bangladesh

Rural (N = 2,516)

Target Population	Don't know any method Won't Consider	Will Consider	Know but never practiced Won't Consider	Will Consider	Past Users Won't Consider	Will Consider	Current Users	All*
Target Population								
1. Less than 20; no child	51	3	37	9	–	–	0	100%
2. Less than 20; child; not pregnant	43	1	43	12	1	–	–	100%
3. 20–29; youngest < 5; not pregnant	37	2	42	13	2	1	4	100%
4. 30–39; youngest < 5; not pregnant	32	2	45	11	1	1	8	100%
5. Less than 40; pregnant	32	3	48	15	–	2	2	100%
Less Fertile Group								
6. 20–39; no child or youngest < 5	37	1	52	6	0	0	3	100%
7. 40 or over	38	1	55	4	1	0	2	100%
ALL	37	2	46	10	1	1	3	100%

Urban (N = 568)

Target Population	Don't know any method Won't Consider	Will Consider	Know but never practiced Won't Consider	Will Consider	Past Users Won't Consider	Will Consider	Current Users	All*
Target Population								
1. Less than 20; no child	44	2	49	5	0	0	0	100%
2. Less than 20; child; not pregnant	26	2	31	29	5	2	5	100%
3. 20–29; youngest < 5; not pregnant	14	0	54	16	3	8	6	100%
4. 30–39; youngest < 5; not pregnant	13	1	51	11	3	7	14	100%
5. Less than 40; pregnant	19	0	53	22	1	6	0	100%
Less Fertile Group								
6. 20–39; no child or youngest < 5	19	1	65	5	4	0	5	100%
7. 40 or over	18	0	69	1	3	3	5	100%
ALL	19	1	55	13	3	5	6	100%

In Urban and Rural Pakistan

Rural (N = 1,735)

Target Population	Don't know any method Won't Consider	Will Consider	Know but never practiced Won't Consider	Will Consider	Past Users Won't Consider	Will Consider	Current Users	All*
Target Population								
1. Less than 20; no child	19	7	50	25	0	0	0	100%
2. Less than 20; child; not pregnant	20	1	45	31	0	1	2	100%
3. 20–29; youngest < 5; not pregnant	19	4	43	29	1	2	3	100%
4. 30–39; youngest < 5; not pregnant	12	2	47	27	4	3	5	100%
5. Less than 40; pregnant	17	5	42	31	–	4	0	100%
Less Fertile Group								
6. 20–39; no child or youngest < 5	19	2	58	15	1	2	3	100%
7. 40 or over	17	1	60	15	2	2	3	100%
ALL	17	3	49	25	2	2	3	100%

Urban (N = 1,175)

Target Population	Don't know any method Won't Consider	Will Consider	Know but never practiced Won't Consider	Will Consider	Past Users Won't Consider	Will Consider	Current Users	All*
Target Population								
1. Less than 20; no child	16	5	49	30	0	0	0	100%
2. Less than 20; child; not pregnant	5	0	39	54	0	0	2	100%
3. 20–29; youngest < 5; not pregnant	7	1	41	40	–	5	6	100%
4. 30–39; youngest < 5; not pregnant	6	0	41	30	3	7	14	100%
5. Less than 40; pregnant	7	3	33	42	3	11	1	100%
Less Fertile Group								
6. 20–39; no child or youngest < 5	8	3	53	24	1	3	8	100%
7. 40 or over	11	0	66	11	4	3	6	100%
ALL	8	1	46	31	2	5	7	100%

– Less than 0.5.

*Percentages may not add to 100 because of rounding errors.

Table 15-8
Family Planning Practice by Knowledge and Effective Knowledge in Bangladesh, Pakistan, and Both Countries Combined

Practice of Modern Methods[a]	Don't Know Personnel or Places	Know Personnel Only	Know Place Only	Know Personnel and Places	Total[b]
Never Used and Will Not Consider in Future					
Bangladesh	78	12	5	5	100%
Pakistan	61	15	8	16	100%
Total	72	13	6	9	100%
Never Used–Will Consider in Future					
Bangladesh	57	22	6	13	100%
Pakistan	51	13	12	24	100%
Total	53	17	10	20	100%
Ever Used					
Bangladesh	27	18	14	41	100%
Pakistan	14	13	18	55	100%
Total	21	15	16	48	100%
Current Users					
Bangladesh	23	22	13	42	100%
Pakistan	14	14	17	55	100%
Total	19	18	15	48	100%

[a]Modern methods include IUD, sterilization, condoms, pills, foam, diaphragm, tampon, or abortion.
[b]Percentages may not add to 100 because of rounding.

Table 15-9
Percentage of Wives Considering Future Use of Contraception by Method and by Reasons Would not Consider, Bangladesh plus Pakistan

Method	Percentage Considering	Side Effects	Husband/ Wife Dislikes Method	Opposed to Family Planning	Other	Desires Pregnancy	Meno- pausal	Current User/or Don't Know	Total*
				Percentage Not Considering Because of:					
Pill	31	3	5	17	12	20	7	5	100
IUD	8	25	6	17	13	18	7	6	100
Sterilization									
Female	6	18	9	18	14	21	7	6	100
Male	4	13	13	17	16	19	7	12	100

*Percentages may not add to 100 due to rounding.

2. To what extent do program activities reach target couples?
3. What are the present and expected intermediate and final effects of program activities on target couples?
4. What are the reasons for differential program effects?

To summarize, we presented limited analysis of survey data in order to make some evaluative statements concerning the relationship between program inputs and intermediate output. In the next section, we will examine a refined methodology, making some dynamic inferences concerning family planning programs and their operations. Current research at The Johns Hopkins University aims at developing this methodology and testing it on existing data.

A Proposed Methodology

Data requirements and research assumptions impose important limitations upon our analysis since reliable data on births and on infant and child mortality, available on a regional basis and which combined with data on program inputs and "environmental" variables, are either non-existant for most of the developing countries or of a very low quality. Also, we would like to relate not only final output (e.g., the birthrate) but also intermediate outputs (e.g., knowledge and contraceptive practice) to program inputs and the environmental factors, since this type of information might be of great relevance to program design and planning.

In general the sample universe may be divided into two or more sub-universes that are lagging and leading in terms of their "social setting factors." Subsamples of the target population that are large enough for independent analysis as discussed below may be drawn from each sub-universe. As a first approximation these may be the familiar rural-urban divisions. Our concern, however, is with the level of various social inputs in each sub-universe. For example, at the one extreme, areas with the fewest and smallest schools and hospitals, with high illiteracy rates, without adequate roads, without factories, with primitive agriculture, with the least locally monetized trade, and possibly with a high rate of morbidity and mortality are grouped together. At the other extreme are areas with more schools (and better quality schools), high literacy (male and female), better roads and communications, more industrialization, less morbidity and lower mortality. The middle group(s) could be further classified if data permits. Emphasis must be placed on the availability of social inputs (e.g., schools, teachers, hospitals, beds, doctors, roads and their quality, type of agriculture as well as level of industrialization) that are changing over time according to overall social planning or because of a self-dynamic process. Thus if we divide our universe into four sub-universes, say A, B, C, and D, we expect to find $A_t < B_t < C_t < D_t$ in period t in terms of some social setting criteria (i.e., development) as approximated by our variables mentioned above. After n years (e.g., three years) in period $t + n$ we expect A_t to approach B_t and C_t to approach D_t in terms of the level of those factors.

Careful attention must be given to the secondary sampling units (SSUs). Villages (parts or combinations) in rural areas and electoral units of 200-300 households serve this purpose. Independent measures (probably made during enumeration of the environmental factors), as well as the family planning program inputs, may be assembled for each such unit in order to provide estimates of within class variability. The units of analysis are wives and preferably should include husbands. The following set of data might be collected:

1. Families and individual (e.g., wives and husbands') background and situational information (e.g., socioeconomic and demographic characteristics, communication, and mobility behavior),
2. Individual knowledge and utilization of program inputs (as planned by program operations),
3. Intermediate program outputs: individual knowledge and practice,
4. Fertility behavior or final program output.

To a large extent, these types of data are collected in KAP surveys without the needed focus on scope or an appropriate sample design.

A separate analysis for each sub-universe and for the population as a whole should be systematically organized in terms of a set of dependent variables that reflect what is being evaluated, explained and described. Three sets of variables are involved: fertility, contraceptive practice, and knowledge. In evaluating current fertility behavior, for example, we will account for differential practice and knowledge, and in analyzing current practice, we will account for differential knowledge, all within the individual constraints and social settings. These are limited dependent variables and raise special difficulties in handling them in multivariate analysis (Lansing 1971: 296-300; Tobin 1958). Our concern at this stage, however, is to present a general conceptual frame of analysis.

Explanatory variables may be classified into various sets according to their assumed logical sequence in the decision process, for example:

1. Background factors: age, rural/urban background, education, past mobility . . .
2. Situational factors: general economic situations, current place of residence (SSUs) . . .
3. General value systems: attitudes towards hard work, ambitions, planning ahead . . .
4. Program inputs and facilities.

These general relationships may be summarized in mathematical notation as follows:

$$B_i = f(X)\,g(S) \,\vdots\, l(P) \,\vdots\, m(M)$$

where

B_i =   birth rate or some measure of individual fertility, where i refers to the ith universe

$f(X)$ =   the set of background variables and constraints

$g(S)$ =   the set of situational variables

$h(V)$ =   the set of value system variables

$l(P)$ =   the set of program inputs

$m(M)$ =   the set of intermediate output variables (i.e., knowledge and practice).

We cannot assume that there are no one-way causal relations among the explanatory variables. For example, education and "effective knowledge" about family planning cannot be treated at the same level of the causal process since the level of formal education will affect effective knowledge but not vice-versa. However, if we use both to predict use in a multiple regression, we may find that effective knowledge explains everything, i.e., formal education had nothing to do with practice. However, a causal model may look as follows:

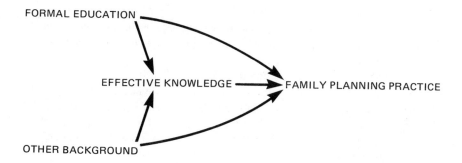

FORMAL EDUCATION

EFFECTIVE KNOWLEDGE ⟶ FAMILY PLANNING PRACTICE

OTHER BACKGROUND

The assumption of a causal sequence is implicit in many discussions concerning the net benefit of family planning programs, e.g., that environmental factors will influence program operations and not vice-versa. However, multivariate sequential analysis has not been attempted systematically for purpose of evaluation.[f] In a sequential model, the dependent variable is first analyzed against the

---

[f] Path analysis has been used with interesting results in a general model to examine the relative contributions of various factors in explaining total fertility in Taiwan. The variables were ordered in a chronological pattern with minor departures (Freedman and Takeshita 1969: 331-339). The technique, however has some problems. For example, it is based on calculating a set of coefficients without much flexibility. For a critical discussion of path analysis see Heise (1969).

set of explanatory variables that are clearly prior in the logical sequence, i.e., affecting the rest of the explanatory variables, but not affected by them. We then analyze the set of pooled residuals, i.e., the unexplained variance against the second "more immediate" set of explanatory variables (Morgan, Sirageldin, Baerwaldt 1966). To the extent that the model is not sequential, the use of residuals from the first stage of analysis in a second stage will produce a downward bias in the second stage-estimates. The degree of bias will be related to the degree of correlation between the first set and the second set of the explanatory variables (Goldberg 1961). The question becomes how one selects the variables for the first stage and for the subsequent stages of analyses. One procedure, which we recommend, is to select those variables which are prior in time and in the logical (decision) sequence (Lansing 1971).

Interaction effects also influence our methodology.[g] It seems unrealistic to assume that various factors affecting human behavior are additive in nature. Indeed, if both intercorrelation and interaction effects are present, multiple correlation will measure neither of them properly and only with the more flexible search procedures will one find the two effects (Lansing and Morgan 1971: 333). It is possible to build a priori interaction terms but in an area in which we do not know much and with the very large number of possible combinations, intuitions may fail. A systematic search process for interaction effects has been developed and formalized in computer program by Sonquist and Morgan (1964) and has been utilized in many areas of social research.[6] Indeed, most family planning programs' design and planned operation assume the presence of interaction effects, e.g., the effect of knowledge on practice is not the same for all age groups.

We are now ready to specify our analysis design.[h] Within each sub-universe (i.e., the A, B, C, D mentioned earlier, see p. 305) we attempt the *first stage* of the multivariate analysis (i.e., the Automatic Detection of Interaction Effect program) by using the first set of the explanatory variables that are identified as prior in the logical sequence (e.g., background and situational variables) to explain birthrates or some other measure of fertility.

---

[g]The concept of interaction may be defined technically as follows: consider the function of the variables $f(x,z)$. $f(x,z)$ will be defined as a function with no interaction if and only if there exist functions $g(x)$ and $h(z)$ such that $f(x,z) = g(x) + h(z)$. Interaction effect will exist whenever the value of $f(x)$ is dependent on that of z (Graybill 1961: 265-66).

[h]Indeed, if one knows exactly what the power specification of the model is, there are sophisticated methods of estimating a complex model that could be employed, including simultaneously estimating the error variance of some variables, and the sizes of some unobservable variables. Our proposed methodology, however, assumes no adequate a priori knowledge about the basic structure. This note was suggested to the author by James N. Morgan.

Various subgroups of the population, differing in their fertility characteristics according to the combination of explanatory variables used in the analysis, will be identified within each sub-universe. These combinations define a basic structure for each sub-universe. Comparing these structures gives valuable insight into the relationship of fertility differentials to different levels of "modernization," i.e., differences between sub-universes A and D. It is also possible to examine for each group (within each sub-universe) the availability of program inputs and the extent of effective knowledge and practice. Comparison of these findings between the sub-universes that vary in their modernity (A vs. D) is equally interesting. To the extent that there is some truth in the A-D classification, i.e., A will be moving towards D, over time in terms of social inputs, differences in program input-output mixes could have predictive value. The following diagram illustrates the possibility:

Level of social inputs	$A \longrightarrow$	$B \longrightarrow$	$C \longrightarrow$	D
First State: Basic Background Variables	A_1	B_1	C_1	D_1
RESIDUAL ANALYSIS				
Second Stage: Policy and Behavioral	A_2	B_2	C_2	D_2

The arrows between A and B indicate that the level of social inputs (used to define A and B) is increasing over time towards the level of B. A_1 indicates the structure of A in terms of some independent variable, fertility in this instance, as classified by the first set of explanatory variables. A_2 indicates the effect of the second set of explanatory variables on the dependent variable after allowing for the effect of the first set (i.e., residual analysis). Two types of inferences can be made: the *first* is to compare A_1, A_2 on the one hand with D_1, D_2 on the other and the differences are then related to differences in the levels of the social inputs. The *second* is to superimpose the A_1 structure over D, call it D_1' and examine for D_2'. The purpose is to examine for the effects of the second set of explanatory variables by controlling structural differences related to basic levels of the social inputs.

This analytical framework allows flexibility in identifying interaction and making dynamic inferences about the population. After three or four years the survey may be repeated, retaining its basic design. During this period the level of social inputs is expected to increase, i.e., A_{12} approaches B_1 (where the subscripts refer to A_1 in year 2). If these dynamic changes in the social inputs are related to fertility independently of program inputs, then we would expect to find A_{12} (in the second survey) to have changed and approached B_1 (of the first survey). The same analysis discussed in the previous paragraph could be repeated. As mentioned earlier, an attempt is currently being made to develop this methodology and test it on the Pakistan IMPACT data.

Summary

In presenting a brief review of the survey method's role in family planning research and evaluation, we concluded that the utility of KAP-type surveys would be enhanced if more attention were given to design, planning and analysis. A brief discussion of some of the recent studies relating to response validity indicates that this problem is not unique to family planning surverys and can be minimized through quality control and built-in probing.

We utilized the findings of a recent national family planning survey (IMPACT-1969) to present a systematic analysis, attempting to answer a sequence of evaluative questions. The findings illustrate that although the majority of the women reported knowledge about family planning methods, a much smaller proportion (about 15 percent) indicated effective knowledge (i.e., the availability of personnel and facilities) and the small proportion of ever users (about 8 percent) were concentrated in the latter group. In terms of future use, women are reluctant to use existing methods because of side effects or dissatisfaction with either the methods or the services given. The systematic link between program inputs and intermediate outputs results in meaningful evaluative statements and conclusions although we were not able to make causal interpretations.

Finally, we proposed a survey design and analysis methodology that aims to answer some of these problems. The methodology is a variant of experimental design, and the analysis is based on a sequential model. The development of this methodology is currently in progress, using data from Pakistan and Bangladesh.

Notes

1. For a recent review of the field see Robinson and Horlacher (1971). For recent contributions see Barlow (1967), Newman and Allen (1967), Simmons (1971), Tempo (1971) and Zaidan (1971), also World Bank (1972).
2. For critical discussions of the cost-benefit analysis of population control, see Clark (1970), Leibenstein (1969), Myrdal (1967) especially Appendix 3 and 7, and Ohlin (1967).
3. See for example Easterlin (1969).
4. See for example Mauldin, Watson and Noé (1970), Mauldin and Bean (1969: 542–51), Kirk (1969), and Reynolds (1972).

5. For a detailed discussion of the Pakistan Family Planning Program (1965-70) see Envir Adil (1969: 15-30).

6. See for example, Morgan, Sirageldin, Baerwaldt (1966) and John Ross (1966). The following is a brief description of the computer program's algorithm:

> "There is a dependent variable and a set of explanatory variables (each a set of categories or sub-classifications). For each explanatory classification, the computer examines the explanatory power achievable by using it to divide the data into two subgroups. Power means reduction in unexplained variance, indicated by the "between sum of squares" of a simple analysis of variance with one degree of freedom (the weighted sum of squares of the subgroup means minus the usual correction factor, $N (\overline{X}^2)$."

> "For a predictor with K classes, maintained in some logical or ordinal order, there are K-1 possible ways to use it to dichotomize the sample, and the one with the greatest explanatory power is retained, while the computer goes on to repeat the process with each of the other predictors. The best overall division is then the best of the best (best split on the best predictor). That split is actually carried out, and the process repeated separately on each of the two subgroups thus formed . . . . The process can be stopped when there are a stated number of final groups, or when no group contains more than some small percentage of the original total sum of squares, or, best, when no further split could reduce the unexplained variance by as much as some small fraction of the original sum of squares, say .005" (Lansing and Morgan 1971: 335-36).

References

Adelman, Irma. "An Econometric Analysis of Population Growth." *American Economic Review* 53, 3 (1963): 314-339.

Adil, Envir. "Pakistan's Family Planning Program." In N. Sadik et al. (eds.), *Population Control: Implications, Trends and Prospects.* Proceedings of the Pakistan International Family Planning Conference at Dacca. Islamabad: Pakistan Family Planning Council, 1969. Pp 15-30.

Axelrod, Morris and Charles F. Cannell. "A Research Note on an Attempt to Predict Interviewer Effectiveness." *Public Opinion Quarterly* 23 (Winter 1959): 571-575.

Barlow, Robin. *The Economic Effects of Malaria Eradication*. Bureau of Public Health Economics, Research Series No. 15. Ann Arbor: School of Public Health, University of Michigan, 1968.

Berelson, Bernard. "Sample Surveys and Population Control: Introduction." *Public Opinion Quarterly* 28, 3 (1964): 361-366.

. "KAP studies in fertility." In B.B. Berelson et al. (eds.), *Family Planning and Population Programs*. Chicago, Ill.: University of Chicago Press, 1966. Pp. 655-69.

Blalock, Hubert M., Jr. *Causal Inference in Nonexperimental Research*. Chapel Hill: The University of North Carolina Press, 1964. Pp. 3-26.

Blake, Judith. "Are Babies Consumer Durables?" *Population Studies* 21, 3 (1968): 185-206.

Bogue, Donald J. "Family Planning Research: An Outline of the Field. In B.B. Berelson et al. (eds.), *Family Planning and Population Programs*. Chicago, Ill.: University of Chicago Press, 1966.

Chow, L.P. "Evaluation of the Family Planning Program in Taiwan, Republic of China." *Journal of the Formosan Medical Association* 67, 7 (1968).

Clark, Colin. "The Economics of Population Growth and Control: A Comment." *Review of Social Economy* 28, 1 (1970): 106-109.

Coale, Ansley J. and Edgar M. Hoover. *Population Growth and Economic Development in Low-Income Countries*. Princeton: Princeton Univ. Press, 1958.

Coombs, Clyde H. "Theory and Methods of Social Measurement." In Leon Festinger and Daniel Kats (eds.), *Research Methods in the Behavioral Sciences*. New York: The Dryden Press, 1953. Pp. 471-535.

Drakatos, C.G. "The Determinants of Birth Rates in Developing Countries: An Econometric Study of Greece." *Economic Development and Cultural Change* 17, 4 (1969): 596-603.

Easterlin, Richard. "Toward a Socio-Economic Theory of Fertility: A Survey of Recent Research on Economic Factors on American Fertility." In S.J. Behrman, L. Corsa, and R. Freedman (eds.), *Fertility and Family Planning: A World View*. Ann Arbor: University of Michigan Press, 1969.

Enke, Stephen. "The Economics of Population Growth and Control: Correcting More Confusions." *Review of Social Economy* 28, 1 (1970a): 96-100.

. "Leibenstein on the Benefits and Costs of Birth Control Programs." *Population Studies* 24, 1 (1970b): 115-116.

Freedman, Deborah S. "The Relation of Economic Status to Fertility." *American Economic Review* 53, 3 (1963): 414-426.

Freedman, Ronald. "Sample Surveys for Family Planning Research in Taiwan." *Public Opinion Quarterly* 28 (Summer 1966): 91.

Freedman, Ronald and John Y. Takeshita. *Family Planning in Taiwan: An Experiment in Social Change*. Princeton: Princeton University Press, 1969.

Goldberger, Arthur. "Stepwise Least Squares: Residual Analysis and Specification Effort." *Journal of the American Statistical Association* 56 (December 1961): 998-1000.

Graybill, F.A. *An Introduction to Linear Statistical Models, Volume I*. New York: McGraw-Hill, 1961.

Green, Lawrence W. "East Pakistan: Knowledge and Use of Contraceptives." *Studies in Family Planning* No. 39 (1969): 9-13.

Hardee, Gilbert and Ismail Sirageldin. "A Summary Statement on Pakistan's National IMPACT Survey." In N. Sadik et al. (eds.), *Population Controls: Implications, Trends and Prospects.* Proceedings of the Pakistan International Family Planning Conference at Dacca. Islamabad: Pakistan Family Planning Council, 1969. Pp. 637-639.

Hauser, Phillip. "Review of B.B. Berelson et al. (eds.). Family Planning and Population Programs." *Demography* (Summer 1967).

Heise, David R. "Problems in Path Analysis and Causal Inference". In Edgar F. Borgatta (ed.), *Sociological Methodology*. San Francisco: Jossey-Bass, 1969. Pp. 38-73.

Hill, Reubin. "Research on Human Fertility." *International Social Science Journal* 20, 2 (1968): 226-262.

Hyman, Herbert N. *Interviewing in Social Research*. Chicago: University of Chicago Press, 1954. P. 197.

Kamerschen, David R. "The Determinant of Birth Rates in Developing Countries: Comment." *Economic Development and Cultural Change* 20, 2 (1972): 310-317.

Kaplan, Abraham. *The Conduct of Inquiry: Methodology for Behavioral Science*. San Francisco: Chandler Publishing Company, 1964.

Kirk, Dudley. "Methods and Results of Surveys for Evaluation of Family Planning." Paper prepared for the meeting of the *International Union for the Scientific Study of Population*, London, (September 1969).

Lansing, John B. and James N. Morgan. *Economic Survey Methods*. Ann Arbor: Survey Research Center, The University of Michigan, 1971.

Leibenstein, Harvey. "Pitfalls in Benefit-Cost Analysis of Birth Prevention." *Population Studies* 23, 2 (1969): 161-170.

"More on Pitfalls." *Population Studies* 24, 1 (1970): 117-119.

Mauldin, Parker and Lee Bean. "Current Status of Family Planning Research and Evaluation." In N. Sadik et al. (eds.), *Population Control: Implications, Trends and Prospects.* Proceeding of the Pakistan International Family Planning Conference at Dacca. Islamabad: Pakistan Family Planning Council, 1969. Pp. 542-550.

Mauldin, Parker, W.B. Watson and L.F. Noé. "KAP Surveys and Evaluation of Family Planning Programs." Unpublished Paper, The Population Council, April 1970.

Morgan, James. "Analysis and Interpretation of Cross-National Surveys."
    Interdisciplinary Topics in Gerontology 2 (1968): 106-110.
Morgan, James, Ismail Sirageldin and Nancy Baerwaldt. *Productive Americans:
    A Study of How Individuals Contribute to Economic Progress.* Ann Arbor:
    Survery Research Center, University of Michigan, 1966.
Mydral, Gunnar. *Asian Drama: An Inquiry into the Poverty of Nations.* New
    York: Random House, 1968. Pp. 1941-1075.
Newman, Peter and R.H. Allen. *Population Growth and Economic Development
    in Nicaragua.* Prepared for the Government of Nicaragua and U.S. Agency
    for International Development/Nicaragua. Washington, D.C.: Robert R.
    Nathan Assocs, 1967.
Ohlin, Goran. *Population Control and Economic Development.* Paris: Organi-
    zation for Economic Co-operation and Development, 1967.
Population Council. *A Manual for Surveys of Fertility and Family Planning
    Knowledge, Attitudes and Practices.* New York: The Population Council
    (Demographic Division), 1970.
Reinke, William A. "The Role of Operation Research in Population Planning."
    Operation Research 18, 6 (1970): 1099-1111.
Reynolds, Jack. "Evaluation of Family Planning Program Performances: A
    Critical Review." *Demography* 9, 1 (1972): 69-86.
Ridker, Ronald G. "Desired Family Size and the Efficacy of Current Family
    Planning Programmes." *Population Studies* 23, 2 (1969): 279-284.
Robinson, Warren and David E. Horlacher. "Evaluating the Economic Benefits
    of Family Planning." *Studies in Family Planning* 39 (1969): 4-8.
    "Population Growth and Economic Welfare." *Reports on Population/
    Family Planning* 6 (February 1971).
Ross, John. "Predicting the Adoption of Family Planning. *Studies in Family
    Planning* 9 (January 1966): 8-12
Ryder, Norman and Norman Westoff; *Reproduction in the United States, 1965.*
    Princeton: Princeton University Press, 1971.
Salter, Leonard. *A Critical Review of Research in Land Economics.* Madison,
    Wisconsin: University of Wisconsin Press, 1957.
Schultz, T. Paul. *Effectiveness of Family Planning in Taiwan: A Methodology
    for Program Evaluation.* Report, P. 4253. Santa Monica: RAND Corpora-
    tion, 1969.
Simmons, George B. *The Indian Investment in Family Planning.* An Occasional
    Paper. New York: The Population Council, 1971.
Sirageldin, Ismail and Gilbert Hardee. "A Flexible Interaction Model for
    Analyzing Sample Survey Data for Planning and Evaluation of Fertility
    Control in Pakistan." In *CENTO Symposium on Demographic Statistics.*
    Turkey: Office of U.S. Economic Coordinator for CENTO Affairs, 1970.
Sirageldin, Ismail and Samuel Hopkins. "Family Planning Programs: An Economic
    Approach." *Studies in Family Planning* 3, 2 (1972): 17-24.

Sonquist, John and James Morgan. *The Detection of Interaction Effects.* Ann Arbor: Survey Research Center, The University of Michigan, 1964.

Stoeckel, John and Moqbul Choudhury. "Pakistan: Response Validity in a KAP Survey." *Studies in Family Planning* 47 (1969): 5-9.

Sudman, Seymour. "Quantifying Interviewer Quality." *Public Opinion Quarterly* 30 (Winter 1966): 664-667.

TEMPO. *Population Growth and Economic Development: Background and Guide.* (Revised Edition). Prepared for the Agency for International Development by TEMPO. Report, 71 TMP-45. Santa Barbara: General Electric Company, Center for Advanced Studies, 1971.

Tobin, James. "Estimation of Relationship for Limited Dependent Variables." *Econometrica* 26 (January 1958): 24-36.

United Nations. *Variables and Questionnaire for Comparative Fertility Surveys.* Population Studies No. 45. New York: Department of Economic and Social Affairs, United Nations, 1970.

World Bank. *Population Planning.* Sector Working Paper (March) Washington, D.C.: World Bank, 1972.

Zaidan, George. *The Costs and Benefits of Family Planning Program.* World Bank Staff Occasional Paper No. 12. Baltimore: John Hopkins University Press, 1971.

16 Ancient and Emerging Questions
Irene Taeuber

The phenomenon of rapid growth is relatively recent. The cohorts that include those whose lives were saved in the reductions in infant and childhood mortality in the late 1940s and the early 1950s are only now reaching the ages of migration, employment, marriage, and childbearing. The impact of growth on economy, society, and people is accelerating. Many of the questions that are asked and much of the research that is undertaken are products of the relations of a decade or so ago rather than the emerging problems and tensions of the 1970s and beyond. Some of the current questions can be noted here though space limitations preclude sufficient discussion.

It may be indicative of academic lethargies that the one paper on marriage and the family that was presented at the three SEADAG seminars was that of William Liu of Notre Dame University on *The Myth of Nuclearization of the Family System in Cebu.* The traditional family and networks of relations that have preserved the high fertility are significant areas of research but they provide few clues as to the dynamics of the family in a milieu of change, one of whose aspects is declining fertility.

The interrelations of social institutions and the social structure with demographic stability and mobility are among the deepest and the most difficult in contemporary societies. Specifically, what are the relations between rigidities in class or caste structure, barriers to anticipations and mobility, and the persistence of traditional family values and reproductive levels? To phrase the concern in a highly relevant form, are the prevalent coincidences between communist type social and political organizations and declining fertility also causally linked?

The relations of population processes to political stability and social order are multidirectional. The design of research is difficult and the barriers to implementation are formidable. The approach may lie less in general argument and cross-sectional concurrence at national levels than in intensive study of specific problem areas and specific instances of instability, civil disorder, or rebellious activity. The phenomenon of disorder pervades rural areas as well as the marginal populations of cities. There may be interrelations here. Political factors in rural areas may propel migrants to the cities. If the additions to the marginal populations of the cities continue, the disintegration of urban facilities and amenities may propel flights from the cities. It is obvious that present dynamics cannot continue into the indefinite future, whether in rural areas or in cities. The introduction of the political dimension in population research will not solve problems but it could contribute to solutions.

317

New approaches and new thinking are permeating population fields with the current orientations to environmental concerns and the present discussions of the limits to growth. A recurrent theme of the three seminars was that the type of development that can be achieved in the densely settled and rapidly increasing populations of the contemporary world cannot be that characteristic of today's industrialized and urbanized populations. The strategies of reconciling the aspirations of the people of the great cities and the rural areas of Southeast Asia to a new type of development without ostentatious consumption have not been perfected.

The questions of the limits of growth are not remote and academic in the setting of regions such as Southeast Asia. These limits may be basically economic but the concomitants of insecure and insufficient incomes, basic necessities, and amenities may be closer dangers than the ultimate limits in economic or demographic terms. The possibilities of conflict and cataclysm are far more serious when the recuperative capability of the society is muted and when passive acceptance of deprivation is no longer tolerable.

There are demographic questions the neglect of which is one of the most curious aspects of the contemporary scene. These questions concern the levels and the course of mortality. The process that generated present growth was declining mortality. Projections into the future usually assume continuity in the decline in mortality while focusing on the stability or decline in fertility. Nutrition, health, and vitality are interrelated, and all are related to the level of mortality. In the long run, the levels of mortality and fertility are interrelated. Over a time that cannot be specified, further declines in mortality or even the preservation of achieved levels require declines in fertility.

The thrust of the argument is that we are approaching a time for new decisions and new action orientations. But decisions by whom? And actions in what fields? Specifically, what are the needs for demographic and related knowledge.

Queries in Population Fields

There have been major analytical advances in the concepts, the methods, and the techniques of demographic study. Four are of special note: (1) the formal demography of human reproduction; (2) the micro-analysis of detailed reproductive histories; (3) cohort projection techniques; and (4) models and estimation techniques using limited data. There have also been major advances in the techniques for the measurement and analysis of migration and distribution. There are cohort approaches and retrospective lifetime residence histories. Mobility is treated in terms of probabilities or migration propensities; there are equilibrium approaches to distribution and redistribution. The advances in the spatial sciences and human ecology have further extended the analysis of population movements. The field of population studies, however, has not expanded

its research agenda in a way that matches either the increased level of methodological sophistication or the needs in developmental fields.

What, then, are the major questions for demography in the context of the
countries of Southeast Asia? A reasonably comprehensive list would include:

1. *Growth and migration.* What are the independent variables influencing
age at marriage, the fertility of the married, mortality, and growth; mobility
and migration; rurality or ruralization, urbanization or metropolitan formation?

What are the impacts and interrelations of education, occupation, the labor
force participation of women, social security benefits, monetary or real income,
schools for children, the status of girls and women, and nuclear versus other
patterns of family living? What are the interrelations, cross-sectional and temporal, and what are the time lags among demographic variables, such as:

a.   Advancing age at marriage and the childbearing of the married;
b.   Fertility, family size, and mobility in local areas, migration to other areas,
     family change, and the locus and reproductive history of the next generation;
c.   Mobility, marriage, fertility, and mortality within rural areas or village com-
     munities, within urban areas, and within metropolitan regions;
d.   Migration, and mobility, distinguishing as major patterns: rural to rural,
     rural to urban, or to metropolitan; urban to urban, to metropolitan or to
     rural;
e.   Types and durations of mobility and migration and their demographic
     correlates, distinguishing movements by temporal durations and consider-
     ing the joint and separate movements of the sexes.

2. *Diversity and differentiation.* The demography of regional, ethnic, and
subcultural groups: distinctive aspects, symbiotic relations, assimilative or inte-
grative processes, and persistence in conflict or accommodation.

3. *Demographic responses to pressure.* The definition of pressure, the
changing types and interrelations of pressure, and the ongoing impacts of modern
developments, such as the relation of the newer techniques and procedures in
agriculture currently referred to as "the Green Revolution."

4. *Demographic interrelations with social structure, social stability, and
social change.*

5. *Demographic, economic, and social interrelations with the persistence
of order in local levels and political stability at national levels.*

6. *The effective stimulants to fertility decline and the diffusion and speed
of decline, once initiated.*

This outline lists many questions for demography, whereas the concern of
the seminars was research that would be relevant to policy and action. What, then,
are the major population questions for policy and action? The core issue is the

decline in fertility. Is decline a long and slow process, essentially a by-product of development and economic and social transformation? What are the possibilities for immediate and swift declines in fertility? Are present statements and actions concerning goals and programs, direct or indirect, sufficient? Can plans and actions proceed on a basis of voluntary consensus, or is it time to consider sensitive problems of movement beyond voluntarism? What are the possibilities of more intensive persuasions through education and indoctrination?

Priorities in Research

Two questions have basic implications for plans and strategies, whether for research or for participation in developmental activities. First: to what extent should priority in research be accorded the immediately relevant as contrasted with basic research? Second: What is the role of the foreign expert? How can there be effective use of such experts?

The problems of priorities for basic research are serious whether from Southeast Asia or elsewhere. External sources of support and funds from governments are both available mainly for directly action-oriented research, particularly in family planning fields. Organizations within governments and university institutions that are specially funded are subject to external assessments of the needs for research and its contributions to developmental needs. The possibilities for basic research are limited largely to autonomous and privately financed institutions. The strategy for research involves the integration of basic and applied designs that contribute to fundamental knowledge and at the same time provide hypotheses for the evaluation or guidance of action. It is the innovative experimental project in development strategy that may provide the locus for research that is both basic and applied.

The questions of the roles of foreign experts broaden into those of influences of foreign institutions and their faculties. Cooperation as colleagues is the ideal but the problems of moving toward this ideal outside a limited area of basic research must be recognized. The difficulties of the expert and the problems of using experts are not restricted to western experts in non-western countries or even to experts from developed countries in developing countries. The same nexus of difficulties surrounds the expert from one developed country in another or from one less developed country in another. While the abolition of the word "expert" is perhaps desirable, evasive terminologies do not solve more basic difficulties.

Postlogue

Southeast Asia is a distinctive region where demographic knowledge is limited and existing demographic theory simplistic. Perhaps the most distinctive of all the characteristics of countries and cultures, peoples and resources, is variation.

The diversities are so major that almost any generalization is valid somewhere but no generalization is valid everywhere. There are major resources for future development with the advanced technologies anticipated for the late twentieth and the early twenty-first centuries. There are great river valleys that could support populations equal to those of the Ganges or the Yangtze. But there are also rural populations so densely settled that the problems of absorbing the 60 percent increase in men in labor force ages projected for the years from 1970 to 1985 seem insoluble. There are pressures of population on resources that threaten order in local areas and political stability over wide regions.

The seriousness of the population problems and the vanishing time for resolution are demonstrated by studies of the structures, dynamics, and distributions of the populations in the several Southeast Asian countries. In the years prior to 1968, age at marriage was advancing in the Philippines but marital fertility was increasing rather than remaining constant at traditional levels or declining. Fertility has remained at high levels in Thailand and in Indonesia. What has happened – and is happening – is quite simple and understandable. At some traditional, pre-, or early colonial period, expectations of life at birth were twenty to twenty-five years, crude death rates forty or more. The family institutions, the traditions, the values sustained birthrates at forty to forty-five or more. Today the expectations of life at birth have increased to fifty, sixty, or even more years, while birthrates have remained at the ancient levels.

This widening of the gap between persisting traditional rates of reproduction and declining mortality has characterized some but not all of the countries of Southeast Asia up to the present time. There has been a swift transition in Singapore, and there is declining fertility in Malaysia. There are also the tragic devastations and deaths in the population of the Indochinese peninsula.

Projections of the demographic past provide perspective on the future population but tell nothing about economic and social interrelations or the changing dynamics of births, deaths, and migrations in future years. Economic transformations in agriculture and village life are associated with the complex of practices and technology we call the "Green Revolution." Economic transformations in non-agricultural and urban sectors are associated with continuing immigration from rural areas, rapid natural increase in city populations, and generally increasing gross national products. There are also social changes that are related to various demographic variables and to demographic transition. There is increasing education and there are ever more widespread demands for education at higher and higher levels. There are social changes and vaulting aspirations that may threaten ancient stability and presage future instability. There is an altered status of children and the aged; there are altered roles and aspirations for women. There are new and diffusing means of communication, particularly in the transistor radio. Urban growth and rural change are linked in the movements to cities and the countermovements that bring knowledge of the folkways and the values of the city to the countryside.

The listing of research areas or projects is valuable but it should not be done casually. Incisive and definitive research is being done within the countries of Southeast Asia. In these countries, however staff, facilities, and support are limited. The decision for one area or type of research is thus a decision against another. There is urgency in having knowledge that contributes to the resolution of population problems. Hence there are two lines of development that are essential in the present and the future. The first is a renewed emphasis on the training of research and technical people within and outside the countries, together with their appropriate placement. The second is a selection of research areas of maximum contribution for the use of the limited scientific personnel and facilities available at present.

What, then, are the basic problems? What is essential in research? The critical problem is the rate of growth; the critical component in growth is fertility. The critical questions concern the conditions under which, and the rates at which, fertility declines. In European countries there were long transitions of a century and a half or so. There was a transition of more than a century in Japan. Neither type of transition is assured automatically in the countries of Southeast Asia, nor would either type be adequate if it occurred.

There is recognition of the problems of population growth in the adoption of "policies" by governments and "family planning programs," generally in or associated with health services. As yet, there is limited knowledge of the impacts of the programs on current or cohort fertility and on national rates of population growth.

These comments may seem unduly negative if the time orientation is a short one. But in the context of decades and quarter-centuries the alternative "solution" may come through increases in death rates rather than declines in birthrates. The economic, social, and political outlook for the future is jeopardized seriously by the continuation of high rates of population growth. It is difficult to specify a limit to the time that is available for the reduction of rates of growth through declining fertility. It is possible to state that the prolongation of the time intensifies the difficulties of the transitions in future years if it does not place smooth transitions at hazard. The social and economic programs most often mentioned that might contribute to changes in marriage and fertility are land reform; income equalization; labor intensive employment in development schemes; change in the character of education, in the social roles of women, and in the traditions of the family; social and legal actions to raise the age at marriage and to supplant children as sources of income and security. But little is known about how to accomplish these things and what effect they might have.

Against this background, there are five immediate questions for research:

1. Are the economic developments that are the usual bases for declining fertility sufficient to counteract the depressant impacts associated with the rapidly increasing numbers of people?

2.   What are the social relations affecting marriage, family, and fertility? Are there social approaches to transformations in traditional structures and historic values that would facilitate declining fertility prior to comprehensive economic development and increasing distributed real income?

3.   What are the relations among the demographic variables? These include mortality and declining fertility; rural retention and the out-migrations of rural youth; urbanization, of what types and over what time periods; declining mortality, family ideals, attitudes to life, and fertility.

4.   Are the present concepts of family planning programs antiquated? These programs are generally associated with voluntarism, a high respect for the information on the numbers of children that women say they desire, and status as peripheral activities apart from major developmental thrusts.

5.   Are there feasible alternatives to present approaches? What would be the policy approaches, the strategies, the personnel, and the resources if a nation operated on the premise that economic and social development, the survival of the people, and the destiny of the nation were related directly and rather immediately to the achievement of that lowered fertility which alone is compatible with the maintenance of the lowered mortality?

List of Contributors

James N. Anderson, University of California, Berkeley.

Ramesh Chander, Department of Statistics, Government of Malaysia.

Carlos A. Fernandez, II, Institute of Philippine Culture.

Dorothy Z. Fernandez, Department of Statistics, Government of Malaysia.

Beverly Heckart Hackenberg, University of Colorado.

David M. Heer, University of Southern California.

Gerry E. Hendershot, Brown University.

Gavin W. Jones, Population Council.

Aprodicio A. Laquian, International Development Research Centre Ottawa, Canada.

H. Leedom Lefferts, Jr., University of Colorado.

Lee McCaffrey, Johns Hopkins University
School of Hygiene and Public Health.

James A. Palmore, Jr., East-West Population Institute.

Masri Singarimbun, University of Gajah Mada.

Ismail Sirageldin, Johns Hopkins University.
School of Hygiene and Public Health

Peter C. Smith, Population Institute, University of Philippines.

Hsin-ying Wu, National Taiwan University.

About the Editors

John F. Kantner is Professor of Demography in the Department of Population Dynamics at the Johns Hopkins School of Hygiene and Public Health. An officer on the boards of the Alan Guttmacher Institute and the Foundation's Population Fund, he is also a consultant to the Population Division of the United Nations and a member of the International Union for the Scientific Study of Population. Professor Kantner's professional interest in Southeast Asia dates back to 1957, when he spent a year at the University of Indonesia. He later maintained contact with international demographic developments when he served as an employee of the U.S. Bureau of the Census and as an associate of the Population Council in New York. He has lived in Pakistan, where he was involved with Johns Hopkins research activities and associated with Punjab University. Professor Kantner received the Ph.D. from the University of Michigan in 1953.

Lee McCaffrey received the M.A. in demography in 1969 from the University of Pennsylvania. She has been employed as a research specialist in that university's City Planning Department and as a medical researcher by the State of Pennsylvania's Office of Mental Retardation. Since 1972, she has been a research associate on the faculty of Johns Hopkins University.